Strange Country

#B 1st o.p.

TED   25 —

This is a Strange Country

*Letters of a
Westering Family,
1880–1906*

This is a Strange Country

Letters of a Westering Family, 1880–1906

EDITED AND ANNOTATED BY BYRD GIBBENS

University of New Mexico Press
Albuquerque

To the people I treasure

in their

own

journeys

Library of Congress Cataloging-in-Publication Data

This is a strange country: letters of a westering family, 1880–1906 /
edited and annotated by Byrd Gibbens. —1st ed.
    p.   cm.
  Bibliography: p.
  Includes index.
  ISBN 0-8263-1107-5
  1. Pioneers—New Mexico—Correspondence. 2. Brown
family—Correspondence. 3. Pioneers—Colorado—
Correspondence. 4. Frontier and pioneer life—New Mexico.
  5. Frontier and pioneer life—Colorado. 6. New Mexico—
Biography. 7. Colorado—Biography.
I. Gibbens, Byrd, 1936–
F801.T48 1988
978.9′04′0922—dc 19
[B]   88-28274

Design by John Cole.

Contents

Acknowledgments

*T*he bridging of distance (inner and outer) may be the task par excellence of human beings. Essentially, that is what these letters are all about. They are not merely news notes to keep faraway family informed. They are poignant attempts at integration, at centering. They are conversations—negotiations, salvaging that of the old essential for dealing with the new. They are dialogues through which Charles and particularly Maggie Brown re-centered and integrated what it meant to be a Virginian with what it meant to be a New Mexican. In addition to having historical significance, the letters offer a paradigm that makes visible the relatively unconscious processes operative on any frontier, in any change—the pulling of invisible threads through time and space to extend the past into the future.

When Lillian Schlissel came to the University of New Mexico in the summer of 1981 to conduct a seminar, "Pioneer Women's Experience," one of her first efforts was to locate a body of correspondence from a nineteenth-century New Mexican family. She wanted to offer her students the opportunity of analyzing raw data; she also wanted to further her commitment to bringing to the public domain personal documents that provide stepping stones to the past. It was on this quest that she discovered, boxed and gathering dust, in the archives of the University of New Mexico Special Collections Library some four hundred weathered letters labeled "Charles A. Brown Collecton, #277."

The letters had been donated in July 1965 by Mrs. Lolita Cox Smith of Virginia. Her friend Mary Augusta Brown Gose (daughter of Charles and Maggie Brown) had salvaged from trunks and desk drawers all the correspondence she could find remaining from her parents' years

vii

on the Colorado and New Mexico mining and farming frontiers in the late 1800s. Mary's aim had been to put the letters in chronological order, edit them, and supply connecting information. But she died having just begun the massive task. A keen sense of history made Lolita Smith suspect the value of Mary's work. Hoping scholars could use the documents to study conditions in southwestern New Mexico in the late 1800s, she offered the collection to the University of New Mexico.

Sensing the value of the letters, Dr. Schlissel proposed I, one of her students, study closely what they could yield in terms of insight into the frontier's effect on family configuration, male/female relations, child rearing practices, and strategies of cultural change—a proposal I leapt to. The process from initial transcription of the fading penmanships to analysis and setting of the corpus in historical perspective stretched long and challenging. As the endeavor draws to completion, I feel deep gratitude for having been able to give my energies to bridging the nineteenth-century experience of Maggie and Charles Brown into the twentieth century. My first thanks is to them for their determination to span the distances between themselves and their family and friends with this volume of correspondence. My second thanks is to Mary Augusta Brown Gose and Lolita Cox Smith for the initial energies of collecting and preserving the documents. To Mrs. Lillian Keller Peters of Staunton, Virginia, a contemporary relative of Maggie Keller Brown I give thanks for her enthusiastic sharing of Keller family materials she has documented in her own extensive geneological studies.

My final thanks stretch to a range of scholars, archivists, editors, and friends. Lillian Schlissel, director of American Studies at Brooklyn College and Marta Weigle, chair of American Studies at the University of New Mexico, scrutinized this manuscript through countless drafts. Whatever is not finely honed is my lapse, not theirs. Ferenc Szasz and Anne Boylan at the University of New Mexico sharpened the historical context and family demographics. From the University of North Dakota, Elizabeth Hampsten shared her seminal theories on literary analysis of immigrant letters and diaries. JoAnne Liebman, at the University of Arkansas at Little Rock, proofread the entire final draft of the manuscript. Librarians in the Special Collections of the University of New Mexico, the University of California at Santa Barbara, James Madison University, the Huntington, and the Arkansas History Commission Archives greatly facilitated my research.

A support community across the country responded to various drafts of the manuscript, shored me up, and replenished my inner vision during years of researching and revising. In Albuquerque, New Mexico: Rowena Rivera, Arthur and Henrietta Loy, Jan Cummings, Marilyn and Dwayne Sheppard, Charles Biebel, the Hammars; in Seattle, Washington: Patricia Alley; in Santa Barbara, California: Carol Bond, Prudence Myer and JoAnne, Zelda Bronstein; in New Orleans: Vivien and Ed Michals, Ben Wren, Ken and Barb Ackron, John Watson, William Barnwell, David Shroyer, Gillian and Burlie Brown; in Wichita, Kansas: Suzanne Reed; in Madison, Wisconsin: the Abbotts; in New Iberia, Louisiana: Alice Marie Macmurdo; in Little Rock, Arkansas: my exceptionally supportive colleagues and students at the University of Arkansas at Little Rock, especially the indefatigable secretary of the English Department Veneta Hines and my Quaker friends; in Waveland, Mississippi: Louise Gibbens (my mother, a pioneer in her own right) and still a moving force Noyes Gibbens (my father), the Wests (including the animals); in Dallas: the Heinens; and very present in the memory of all his friends: Charles Preston.

The editors at the University of New Mexico Press, particularly Dana Asbury and Barbara Guth, I thank for their keen editing skill and their enthusiastic support. And for her generous assistance in many final tasks, I thank Stella de sa Rego, photoarchivist in the University of New Mexico Special Collections Library.

1

Introduction:

The First Strange Country

*T*he formula western has romanticized the image of the strong, silent man knowing and "doing what he has to do" to save his helpless woman from the savage wilderness. The letters of Maggie and Charles Brown, however, penned in the crunch of the actual moment, expose the often tragic reality of the frontier: for both men and women there was an emotional and intellectual imperative to sort out values, to rechart inner and outer roadmaps. The often bleak confusion of this challenge is generally lost in histories, memoirs, and formula westerns where the yesteryear, viewed from a secure present, glows golden.

The Browns' experience, while similar to that of other families speculating and pioneering in the late 1800s on the mining/ranching frontiers of Colorado and New Mexico, will surprise quite a few readers, for the stark, *real* western experience bears scant resemblance to the romanticized fictions popularized by the likes of John Wayne and Louis L'Amour.

When in 1880, thirty-two-year-old, gentleman physician Charles Albert Brown of Virginia convinced his young wife, Maggie, to let him try his luck for a time in southern Colorado mining camps, he dragged them both into the upheaval of the age and initiated a life of dislocation. Their letters bring to historical consciousness a microcosm of the times—the response of a man and a woman to the West, the West which became for the man a "fey," a mirage of wealth whose lure he followed, uprooting his family some twenty-four times in thirty years.[1] At each move he repeated the all-too-common refrain: "I came West to strike it rich and I mean to do so."

Charles Brown, like numbers of his peers, fled a depressed Virginia economy and a cloying family network to prove his manhood and find fortune in the mines of southern Colorado, leaving (for what turned out to be a year and a half) his wife Maggie and his baby daughter, Mattie, to board around with relatives until he should either return with pockets loaded or call them to join him. In the heady excitement of the mining bonanzas, this phenomenon of the "waiting woman" was common, as was the phenomenon of the naive man who in 1880 still believed that he could mine gold with a pick-axe and shovel.

The frontier correspondence of Maggie and Charles Brown of Virginia comprises some four hundred letters exchanged between the Browns in Colorado and New Mexico [1880–1906] and their families in Virginia. The original documents are now housed in the archives of the University of New Mexico Zimmerman Library; they were donated by Mrs. Lolita Cox Smith of Virginia, close friend of Mary Augusta Brown Gose, the only one of the Browns' seven children to survive to adulthood. Considering the correspondence a monument of her parents' intense yet unsettled lives, Mary Gose started compiling an account of the trek west. She died, though, with the work barely begun. Through friendship and a sense of history, Lolita Cox Smith offered the over four hundred letters and Mary Gose's typescript to the University of New Mexico.

I have as part of a legacy from Mary Augusta Brown, born in Rincon, New Mexico, June 1, 1894, a quantity of family papers that you might like to have for the University library. It seems to me that the material gives a rather sharply delineated picture of conditions in southwestern New Mexico in the late 1880s and has some value as a research source. [Mrs. Lolita Cox Smith, Cumberland, Virginia, to University of New Mexico Library, July 1, 1966]

The collection affords a unique account of frontier experience, a step inside larger history, with the voice not only of an individual but of a family. What we learn of the macrocosm, the political/historical world, emerges in the context of the microcosm, the personal world, as those larger events impinge on the world of the family. The often conflicting points of view dramatize frontier crises that precipitated new behavior or intensified the grip on traditional codes. The different voices bring to relief the contrasting fictions out of which frontier men and women lived and the poignant, often unfinished quality of their stories.

In the decades following the Civil War, Reconstruction policies battered the southern economy as Yankee militia had earlier devastated southern fields and farms. Old families buckled under in the depression of 1872 and advertised plantations for sale at $6,000 to $10,000, which before the War would have sold for $100,000 to $150,000. The wounds of war and the pride of a humiliated aristocracy steeled Virginia (saddled with the largest postwar debt of all the southern states), despite its need, against immigration of any but the exceptional newcomer. Protective, even in defeat, of its southern honor, the old South, particularly Virginia, was determined that their way of life, which lost the war, should still survive. To work its acres left fallow by emancipation of blacks, war deaths, and emigration, Virginia faced the humiliating necessity of having to promote itself outside the Old Dominion. Still, a stolid caution prefaced the Virginia Bureau of Immigration's advertisement for prospective buyers: "Sluggards and careless, wasteful men living in the illusion that fortunes can be made in a year should go elsewhere."[2] Newcomers, then, were needed but not welcome.

Across the continent, however, everyone was welcome. Promoters for Colorado and New Mexico advertised in their pamphlet "Where to Go to Become Rich," "millions of acres waiting to be turned to agricultural use." New Mexico's governor Lew Wallace claimed that gold, silver, and copper were in such abundance in New Mexico that "the armies of the world might be turned into these districts without exhausting them in a hundred years."[3]

Railroads, opening fresh tracks, staged mighty campaigns to populate the new lands. One of their advertisements, of the kind likely seen by Charles Brown, read:

FREE INFORMATION
ABOUT THE SOUTHWEST

Kansas, Colorado, Utah, New Mexico, Arizona, California and Old Mexico OFFER THE BEST FIELD for Farmers, Fruit-Growers, Stock-Raisers, Capitalists, Merchants, Miners and Mechanics of all trades. Maps, papers and pamphlets giving detailed information, MAILED FREE on application to
H.L. Cargill,
Special Agent, Dept. of Immigration
Topeka, Kansas

C.B. Schmidt
Com'r of Immigration AT&SF RR
Topeka, Kansas

In the West, wild-eyed speculators (be they "careless, wasteful men" or not) were welcome. A number of southern gentlemen succumbed to the temptation and joined the surge west to restore their fortunes.[4] Twentieth-century scholars like Duane Smith identify what the nineteenth-century starry-eyed speculator failed to see: "Mining loomed larger than life with its possibilities of instant wealth, its lure of new opportunities."[5] Ironically, the romance of "striking it rich" grew stronger as its reality diminished. Despite the fact that as early as the 1850s the day of the lone miner who bagged a fortune in a few days was over, men from the depleted South were particularly vulnerable to the mythic claims of the West.

Nineteenth-century America viewed western speculation not as flight but as patriotic enterprise. A respected Virginia physician under whom Charles Brown had interned counseled him:

> Your determination to go west is the best conclusion you ever arrived at; Virginia is no place now for a young man. The advice given to young men to stick to the old state is all fudge. You have ere this found out that—in our profession at least—neither the amount of labor you do, nor your degree of success; nor the fidelity with which you stick to your business will guarantee you a livelihood.
>
> In the West it is different; there the chance to get into business is better, and you are sure to get what you earn. There is a code in existence amongst those people to pay what they owe—they are the most reliable and responsible set of people that I have ever met with. . . . I stick to it that a majority of the people in this country [Virginia] are totally unmindful of their obligations; and that a Virginia thief is the worst thief in the earth. When you go west, I would advise you to go far west. [1876, Virginia, I.A. Lockridge]

Charles's own father-in-law, Washington James Keller, had worked for six months for a cousin in Larned, Kansas. His reports gave first-hand encouragement to Charles:

> You have no idea of how this country impresses itself on one who has never seen a treeless fenceless & in many instances houseless country not a shade tree to be seen I thought I could not stay a week I could see no prospect & there seemed a want of everything & in fact there is a lack of everything except land

there is plenty of fine land & if any person will get a lot of this land & then go to work & put all the labor that is necessary to make a home for a human being on it in the course of 8 or 10 years he will have one of the finest most productive farms in America.

In the final analysis, a complex of forces pushed and pulled the young southern doctor to the western mining camps. While Maggie's father supported Charles with unflagging confidence, Charles's mother and sisters eyed his proposal to wester with almost militant skepticism. Sharp businesswomen themselves, they perhaps caught the personal inadequacy and fear underpinning Charles's proposal. Perhaps their pressure, too, drove him to misrepresent his failures as he moved his checkered way across the Southwest.

The families back in Virginia were significant forces throughout Charles's and Maggie's western wanderings. Alternately offering comfort and challenge, they, almost as much as the mines and deserts, often precipitated the crises of Maggie and Charles's new frontier. The letters chronicle the world of Virginia as well as the frontiers of Colorado and New Mexico. Trouble in one arena reverberated in the other. Washington Keller's lawsuit against his "lunatic wife," Millie Brown Gillespie's challenge of disparity in pay scales of male and female faculty, Amelia Jane Keller's near scandal with her first cousin—these and many other Virginia conflicts unsettled Maggie and Charles at Colorado mining camps and on New Mexico ranches. Yet the distant families sent support, too. In the stillbirths and in the sudden deaths of one child after the other, in the fires, the crop disasters, the job losses—Maggie and Charles felt the support of the Virginia community.

In the rich southern tradition of hospitality and care for one's own, both Maggie's and Charles's families viewed themselves as refuges offering love and protection. In the lived reality, however, only the Kellers met the lofty standard. Charles evidenced latent hostility toward his mother and sisters all his life, and Maggie gave direct vent to the strain she felt the Browns put on the marriage.

Although few letters sent to or received from Charles's mother and sisters remain, they influenced more of Charles's and Maggie's western behavior than did those of the Kellers. It is clear that escape from the doting manipulation of the women in his family was a key reason that Charles left for the West. The southern family of the nineteenth century, with its combination of tradition, high expectations, and protectiveness, often drove sons to radical breaks as the only means of escaping such binding frustration.[6]

Charles was rooted in the southern code of gentility, and while he seemed all his adult life to be the improvident husband, in reality he was more nearly the southern gentleman. He was more spectator than he was participant in his western activities. Teaching Sunday school in Colorado mining camps, overseeing irrigation ditches in Rincon, New Mexico, riding as mail clerk on the Great Needles Run between Albuquerque and the Mojave—he lived out of his southern tradition and was ever the gentlemanly observer.

The Brown line in the United States began with an ancestor seeking, like Charles, a way out of a depressed economy. Johannes Braun (the name was later Anglicized to Brown), Charles's paternal grandfather (who died in 1850 when Charles was only two), was a man of drive and intelligence. Born in the ship-building town of Vegesack, Germany, July 2, 1771, he left for the United States in 1797 when the dissolution of the Hanseatic trade agreements brought the region's prosperity to a standstill. For Johannes Braun, Pennsylvania and Virgina were the frontier that Colorado and New Mexico became for Charles.

After studying theology in the German Reformed Church in Chambersburg, Pennsylvania, Johannes began his pastoral duties in the widespread parishes of Virginia's Rockingham and Augusta counties. In the early 1880s he married Elizabeth Falls. They located in a small parsonage near Bridgewater, Virginia, and there raised eight children to adulthood. Home duties fell almost exclusively to Elizabeth because Johannes serviced a congregation that covered over two hundred miles. With vigor he fought the proselytizing efforts of the surrounding Methodists and United Brethren. His energies focused also on social concerns. He established the first pauper (public) schools in his territory, composed texts for the students, and even supervised the teachers. For his bilingual parishioners, he translated scholarly treatises, and he authored an antislavery treatise, "Slavery and Property in Human Beings." Something of a legend in the German Reformed community in Virginia, his circuit of churches still held memorial services for him a full fifty years after his death.

While Charles's paternal grandparents had only indirect influence on him, his maternal grandmother, Millie Rice, controlled and spoiled him directly. After his father's death, her home in Bridgewater, Virginia, and especially her personal library, became Charles's escape from the strict home regimen of his mother and sisters. With doting solicitude Millie Rice left money to finance Charles's studies at the university, creating a bondage of gratitude that gave him little option other than to become a physician.

Charles's parents, John George Brown and Mary Rice, exerted different kinds of pressures on his life. Charles Albert, born March 27, 1848, was their sixth child. Charles's father, John George, died in 1857, leaving the eight-year-old Charles to the domination of a matriarchal system that hovered and demanded. During his life, John Brown was a respected physician and also the Rockingham County representative to the Virginia legislature, where he served long and well enough to be mentioned in a Bridgewater newspaper some fifty-seven years after his death as an "able leader." Though Charles could have had little memory of this father figure, his vocation of physician and avocation of public servant echo this early role model.

The matriarchy that ruled Charles's life was empowered by his mother, Mary Rice. Her few extant letters, along with the attitudes of Charles and Maggie to her, suggest she was rigid, stern, and prone to self-pity. The searing losses she lived through, in measure, explain her bitter old age. Between the years 1857 and 1868 she lost her husband and four of her eight children. In addition, she was thrown into humiliating poverty after her husband's death.

When her husband died in 1857, Mary assumed responsibility for family finances. After the Civil War she was forced to sell their impressive Greek-columned home in Bridgewater. In true southern fashion, Mary trusted, without written agreement, a family friend to invest the eight thousand dollars accruing from the sale. The gentleman died soon after receiving the money, and because there was no legal record of the business, his family (in a breach of southern honor) refused to stand by the transaction.

In the years after the Civil War, Charles's older brother, Will (who was considered a war casualty), sponged off the family rather than contributed to it. Drinking heavily, he became an increasing burden, living into his seventies an aimless, unproductive life. Thus, in their reversal of fortune, the female Browns were forced to support themselves. Charles's two sisters asserted leadership. Charles's sister Millie (six years his senior), a widow by 1879, was a shrewd businesswoman as well as an intellectual. She eventually assumed presidency of a female college in Corinth, Mississippi, where she brought the "family" to live until her mother's death in 1885. Her letters to Charles scold and counsel. Charles probably viewed her competence as a reproach to his general improvidence. Distance relieved him from having to measure up to her.

A less-spirited personality, Charles's other sister Mary Ella (four years his senior) remained single; and with Millie she supported their mother and Will, variously teaching school and running a small boardinghouse.

This proud Virginia family, diminished by death and financial reverses, foisted onto Charles its hopes for a restoration of respect and fortune. When he enrolled at the Medical School of Virginia in Richmond to study surgery and practical medicine under two outstanding doctors, he carried the pressure of family honor with him.

After his graduation, Charles interned for two years in West Virginia under Dr. I. E. Lockridge. Then, in 1874, he set up practice in West View, Virginia, where he boarded with his second cousin Washington James Keller, father of his future wife, Martha Magdelene (Maggie) Brown.

Whether Charles's infatuation with his beautiful third cousin Maggie began before or after his residence at the Kellers is not clear. But once he was there, she clearly charmed him. "A Virginia beauty, with vivid blue eyes and flowing black hair (fifty four inches long)," Maggie was spirited and popular. Well-educated for a woman of her time, Maggie had finished studies at the highly thought of Methodist Female Institute in Staunton, Virginia, where she was considered a fine scholar. Reflecting the tenor of her Virginia community, she was class and race conscious. She wrote in her early years west: "If I can't go with my equals, I will not go with my inferiors." Her egalitarian posture of later years contrasts with her early sense of elitism. A popular coquette, she was spoiled by her mother and had not even learned how to cook before she married. Mary Gose later reminisced about her mother: "Everything was beautiful, everybody petted her and she was the beautiful Maggie Keller." Obviously reluctant to give up her rounds of play and parties, Maggie dallied two years before consenting to Charles's pressure to marry. When the engagement was finally announced, it was applauded by Washington Keller and his wife, Amelia Jane.

Washington James Keller, who received most of the long string of Maggie's and Charles's warm, trusting letters from the frontier, was the youngest of seventeen children. His mother was a sister of Charles's paternal grandmother, Elizabeth Falls. Years later Maggie, in a letter from New Mexico, reflected on the two sisters as studies in contrast: Elizabeth Falls, wife of the dynamic Johannes Braun, had black eyes and dark hair, and ironically was "one of the dependent little women," while her sister, Maggie's grandmother (whom Maggie felt she herself resembled), had blue eyes and light hair and was "just as independent & energetic as could be."

A small, wirey man (around 5′6″, 130 lbs.), Washington Keller supported his family into his eighties by hard manual labor. Born near Wytheville, Virginia, September 24, 1823, he ran an iron foundry there until the middle of the Civil War, when his Union sympathies ironically made him suspect and attacked by both sides. Having lost everything by the end of the war, he moved his family to West View, some two hundred miles northeast, where he became a jack of all trades, growing broom corn, making brooms, doing construction work, farming, and casting patterns for foundries.

His letters reveal an unpretentious man, sensitive, good humored, and resilient. His faithfulness in writing Maggie during her years west gave her perhaps the one stable force in her life. The fact that he was almost always nonjudgmental probably encouraged her to the openness she showed in sharing highly painful moments of her frontier struggles.

Part of Washington Keller's spriteliness was a sexual vitality. In the course of his almost ninety years he had three wives, the third a winsome teenager whom he married when he was seventy-five. However, it was only by his first wife, Maggie's mother, Amelia Jane Jordan, that he had children.

Amelia Jane probably shaped Maggie's life as much by her death as by her life. Her tragic death occurred December 23, 1876, two days before Maggie's and Charles's scheduled wedding date. Her dying wish (which the young couple honored) was that Maggie and Charles be married beside her coffin. The Staunton newspaper gave the following account of the bizarre funeral/wedding service:

FUNERAL OF MOTHER AND MARRIAGE OF DAUGHTER

It becomes our painful duty to record the death by burning of Mrs. W. J. Keller, of West View in this county, whose maiden name was Amelia Jane Jordan, of Salem, Roanoke county, which occurred under the following circumstances: Her husband, on Thursday last, wishing to take the oil can to Staunton for the purpose of having it replenished, she filled the lamps, and poured the remainder of the oil in the can into a glass jar which she placed upon the mantel over the cooking stove in which she was baking preparatory to the marriage of her daughter which was appointed to take place on Xmas day.

Observing at dinner that there was a flavor of kerosene oil in the coffee, she suspected that the glass jar into which she had put the oil upon the mantel over the cook stove was leaking and went to examine it, and when she picked up the jar the bottom fell out, the oil fell upon the hot stove beneath, which put it in flame, which ignited the clothing of Mrs. Keller, and burned her breast, face and arms so badly that she died the next morning in spite of all the medical aid which could be rendered by Drs. Wm. L. Walters and Charles Brown.

. . . In trying to extinguish the flames her daughter Maggie, aged 21 years, was burned on her right arm and hand but fortunately not very seriously. The wedding apparel of the daughter, with some bed clothing, was burned.

At 11 o'clock on Saturday morning the remains of Mrs. Keller were taken to the Church where the funeral was preached by Mr. Wilson of the Methodist Church South. Then the remains were taken back to the house of the deceased, where the wedding of the daughter Maggie, to Dr. Charles Brown of that neighborhood, formerly of Bridgewater, took place, in compliance with the expressed wish of the mother on Saturday afternoon instead of on Monday as originally intended.

The deceased leaves 4 children all small except the daughter just married.

The bereaved husband is one of our best citizens, and has the sincere sympathy of the whole community. [Unidentified clipping, Staunton, Virginia, 1876]

Maggie left no record of her feelings, standing there beside the open coffin. The state of shock may have numbed her to both her dead mother and her new husband. Only later references give fleeting hints: a Virginia minister turned circuit rider in El Paso reminding Maggie years later of her "dear mother's" dying words: "I'm so glad I have a Jesus"; Maggie's own flush of pleasure at Charles's praise: "You are like your mother." The inner resilience that later steeled Maggie in the twenty-four uprootings in thirty years, the deaths of six of seven children, may have forged itself then beside the coffin and the bridal wreath. Thus began what would be her life pattern: an absorbing of shock and a moving on.

The sudden death of Amelia Keller confronted Maggie with dramatic responsibility for the family that survived. Even intact southern families burdened the older children with supervision of the young; so the tragic loss only intensified a normal bonding for the motherless Kellers.

It was consoling for Maggie to fret over the three young children: Daniel Albert (Dannie), age ten; Amelia Jane, seven; and Washington James (W. J.), three. Maggie's latter letters suggest she froze them (at least in her mind) at those early ages. Ever after (even when they had reached their twenties) she referred to them as "the children."

Though she and Charles set up housekeeping right next door to Washington and the little family, it wasn't Maggie but Amelia's older unmarried sister, Bettie Jordan, age sixty, who moved in with her brother-in-law and cooked for and supervised the children. Such surrogate parenting was an expected role for an unmarried sister. Maggie's responsibility for "the children" had to do mostly with giving emotional support. They were all one family. Maggie treated her own young daughter, Martha Amelia (Mattie), born to her and Charles a year after their marriage, as a sister to the aunt and uncles next door.

Within the next two years, Washington Keller married a widow, Mattie Spangler, whom he wrongly believed had substantial wealth and whom he wrongly expected would provide good mothering for his children. By 1881, three years later, he was in the throes of a bitter divorce proceeding against her.

But in 1879, he was merely finding her a disagreeable presence. Her carping may have been his chief motive for leaving her and the children for several months to follow a cousin to Larned, Kansas, a newly opened railroad town. The loading and weighing business they started, though, failed, and by 1880, Washington was back with his children and nagging new wife in Virginia with little to show for his venture. That brief stint made him part of the western spirit, however, and solidified him as the strongest ally Charles had in his later moves through Colorado and New Mexico.

The Virginia economy of 1879 was still flagging from the aftermath of the financial depression of 1873 and the unproductive policies of Reconstruction—all of which made a physician's role in 1879 difficult. People needed treatment but they had little money to pay doctors. In addition to the bind of the economy, Charles felt other frustrations: his mother and sisters pressed him for support; Maggie and little Mattie needed financial security. The cry that was in the wind, "Go West, young man," offered him escape.

The cry was not all illusion because Charles was receiving enthusiastic reports from personal friends who already were reaping profits from Colorado mines. Joseph Dinkle (part of an old Virginia family) wrote Charles from his mining camp in Colorado where he and several other hometown men were seeking quick wealth:

I would not stay here one day if I did not like the country that
you may be assurred of if you come you will find that I have not
told you the half to use the language of the queen of Sheba, as to
myself and what I am doing. Jim and I are mining. We have the
half interest in a Silver mine, our prospects are very faltering at
present but mining is a very risky business. When you write to
me you direct Alma Park County, Colorado Try. Our mine is
there and we will be there at the time this summer we are going
to move up to the mountain Wednesday and procede to open the
mine hoping to here from you in due course of time.

> I will close for the
> present
> Your most cinsere friend
> Jos H. Dinkle

Remember me to all inquiring friends.

In the early 1880s when Charles approached Maggie with a serious
proposal to wester, he played to her sympathies. Though there was,
neither then nor later, no evidence that he was ill, he argued that his
health necessitated the move. Wild claims by railroad promotors advertised the West as a panacea for all physical ills: "rheumatism, gout,
stiff joints, Brights disease, St. Vitus' dance, sterility, syphilis, alco-
holism."[7] The flux of health seekers to the West, Charles emphasized,
would create rich openings for doctors. Miners, too, in their unsanitary
camps, required physicians; and because in such camps physicians were
a sought-after breed, they could charge exorbitant rates: five to ten
dollars a visit. Somewhat confused that mining land and farming land
were one and the same, he pointed out to Maggie that there was fine
farm land, cheap and available since the Homestead Act of 1862. Probably his most cogent argument, though, was the evidence of the depressed Virginia economy. Maggie could not gainsay that.

Charles's talk of going west found scant support from Maggie. For
her, "home" was the place where family lived together. Her role was
to center family. West was divisive. But her voice counted little against
the frontier fever burning at that time in Virginia.

In the end, Charles won. With many misgivings, Maggie agreed to
let him try Colorado mining camps for a limited time. Charles was
elated. *If* fortune looked good, he would either collect quick money
and return "with his tail up" to Maggie, Mattie, and Virginia, or he
would send for them to homestead there in Colorado. Neither expected
that the separation would last for more than a few weeks. During the

wait Maggie would "board around" with relatives and friends, an insecure and frequently embarrassing arrangement, though not unusual for the times. Other women Charles and Maggie knew were awaiting husbands in the West in similar fashion, earning their keep by working for the families with whom they stayed.[8]

When he left Maggie and eighteen-month-old Mattie for Hayden Creek, Colorado, Charles made no long-range provisions for them. He expected that family and friends would provide "hospitality" while he was gone. To Maggie's credit, she bore her own expenses, refusing to be beholden to a host family for even a postage stamp. Already she was a far cry from the spoiled southern belle who had married Charles.

In dealing with Charles's decision to speculate in the West, Maggie was trapped by contradictory cultural dictates. The "cult of domesticity" demanded that she at once and the same time center her family in a stable home *and* be obedient to her husband.[9] In this case, she had to forego the home in order to be obedient. And while Maggie was a supportive wife genuinely in love with her husband, she was not a mindless woman. She sensed, far better than Charles, the risk in mining. She sensed, also, that her Charles was an inveterate dreamer.

Charles left for Colorado in April 1880. Contemporary attitudes toward men on the frontier glorified their endeavor. But men like Charles call into question Frederick Jackson Turner's thesis and its now legendary image of the strong, silent, single-minded individual challenging the wilderness, to tame and to civilize it.[10] In particular, Charles's complex family situation suggests a tangled web of motives. Chance reversals, conscious and unconscious decisions—all generated that national phenomenon—the westward movement. Charles Brown, setting out for Colorado, sought gold, adventure, distance from the hovering presence of mother and sisters, and a foothold into the real world of real men. Suspicion of these motives caused conflicting emotions in his young wife Maggie.

2

Colorado/Virginia:

April 19, 1880–July 19, 1881

*B*en Myers writes very different from what you do   there is
very little money out there and a great many going around with
their "knap sacks and frying pans" not having a shelter. . . . My
dear write me the true state of things and for Mercy's sake do
not deceive me. [Maggie, Staunton, Virginia, to Charles, Hayden
Creek, Colorado, June 6, 1880]

When Charles Brown moved to Hayden Creek, Colorado, in April 1880,
he became part of a "tidal wave" that was sweeping into the Rocky
Mountain mining territory. That was actually the last great wave of
emigration from east to west, and it had a character different from
the earlier agricultural frontier patterns. While the goal of Overland
Trail and Great Plains pioneers was settlement, the goal of the miners
was quick wealth. Homesteading, if it featured at all, came as an
afterthought.

The letters in this chapter document patterns of behavior so typical
of both mining men and their waiting women that they seem almost
fictive. But closely studied, the correspondence also documents a unique
struggle of two individuals attempting to bridge gaps in distance and
goals in an effort to survive as a family.

The Colorado that the southern gentleman Charles stepped into
streamed with other dreamers who thought their picks and shovels
could unearth what in reality only the heavy machinery of big businesses could dislodge. The myth that had lured the Spaniard Francisco
Vasquez de Coronado in 1540 to seek Seven Cities of Gold remained

deep in the heart of the Southwest in 1880. Gold, in fact, was the motive that populated the West. The almost hysterical cry in 1849 from New Helvetia, California, of "Gold! Gold on the American River!" just confirmed the ancient expectation.

Eastern newspapers bannerlined the news: men were hauling out of the ground as much as eight hundred dollars a day.[1] By the end of 1849 more than seven hundred ships had arrived in San Francisco Bay carrying a total of forty-five thousand gold seekers. Some forty thousand emigrants had poured overland into California by wagon.[2] The gold placer deposits on the western slopes of the Sierra Nevada were so rich that those very first miners dug out their gold with knife, horn spoon, or shovel and "washed it."[3]

But such easy success did not last long. Simple instruments were quickly shoved out by the complex efficiency of the rocker or the cradle. And by the early 1850s, as the loose gold became exhausted, technology took over western mining. Gold discoveries in the Nevada, Montana, Dakota, and Colorado lodes necessitated heavy machines that could sink shafts, break loose ore, hoist it to the surface, crush and extract precious metal.

Colorado's gold and silver—discoveries of the late 1850s—were locked into deep veins that could be penetrated only by powerful and sometimes sophisticated machines and then refined only by precise chemical processes requiring capital and knowledge. Whitney, Hearst, Tabor, Comstock—the big financeers—were the ones who made millions from the Colorado mines. They bought into claims, financed construction of heavy smelting mills and stamper machines, backed road and railroad construction, and employed scientifically trained engineers.

Despite this reality, after John Gregory's gold discovery along the South Platte in May 1859, wild-eyed men swarmed from one booming gulch to another with pick, shovel, and frying pan, persisting in the belief, as historian Joseph King writes, "that mining involved nothing more than digging gold or silver out of the earth in much the same manner as a farmer harvests his potato patch."[4] Thousands organized and schemed. J. P. Whitney observed that mines fascinated men as nothing else did and often resulted in "a credulity and easy confidence not allowed in the consideration of other business subjects."[5] Even otherwise conservative, experienced businessmen succumbed to the glamor of mining.[6] Such dreamers, though, formed the bulk of the 60 percent of the Colorado population that came and left during the 1860s and 1870s. When they left, they were usually more destitute than when they had come.[7]

The eastern business slack spurred additional enthusiasm for the West. In the 1870s overbuilding of the railroads had precipitated falling prices and contributed to a long and fairly severe depression.[8] The eyes of the nation focused on the West, and it was that gaze Charles Brown followed. And it was that distant West that Maggie Brown eyed with uncertainty and skepticism.

During what stretched into a year and a half of waiting, Maggie saved at least fifty-two of Charles's letters to her; and Charles in his single battered trunk of belongings, amid the slosh and grime of ramshackled mining shelters, still preserved fifteen of Maggie's letters to him. Filled with news, stress, desire, suspicion, and sparks of humor, the letters traveled at least one a week between the tacky mining camps of Colorado and the genteel towns of Virginia. Even when the contents stung, the salutations of the letters were tender: "My own love," "My darling & beloved wife"; "My own precious husband," "My dearest and best of husbands." Unsettled, boarding around, fearful about little Mattie's fragile health, anxious about the Colorado camps with their unkempt men, boisterous saloons, and loose women, Maggie wrote letters that churned with emotion. Charles's letters, on the other hand, generally bubbled with excitement. He saw opportunities to make money everywhere: medicine, farming, hunting, stock investment, real estate and, of course, mining—the future looked dazzling. From her Virginia vantage point, though, Maggie saw only frenetic activity.

Understandably, Maggie feared the truth behind the rumors that made their way east. Unfamiliar with the western geography, she responded with fear for Charles to news of danger anywhere in the West. Stories of Indian massacres were part of the documented history of the Overland Trail emigrants. After Custer's invasion of the Dakota Black Hills, stories of Sioux fury spread. And the attacks by the Ute Indians on the small mining camps that were placed illegally on the Colorado Ute's reservation in the Gunnison area to the west of Charles were reported in eastern newspapers with emphasis on the savage resistance of the Indian to the "blessings" of civilization. Maggie was terrified that Charles might be massacred by angry Indians.

The real presence in the mining camps of vigilante groups, saloons, and prostitutes disturbed many in the East. Even Horace Greeley, whose "Go West, young man!" had become a clarion cry, warned of the West's temptations: drinking, gambling, sex. Maggie begged Charles for assurance that he was not being corrupted by saloons and prostitutes. And with each of his assurances, she begged for more. But it was not only moral uncertainties that were disconcerting.

A pronounced "if" quality in Charles's letters disquieted her: *if* some intangible materialized, *then* a bonanza would come. Indefatigable optimism pulsed through his letters—he bolstered each blunt reality (a failed mine, a lost deal) with a shining dream. Maggie, in Virginia, saw the reality of Charles's depleted finances. He seldom sent her money. And since Maggie refused to accept hospitality gratis, she took on increasing amounts of domestic work for the families she stayed with.

Worry about Charles's financial acumen spilled over into her letters, in a free kind of emotion that, along with the concern, illustrates Maggie's openness with Charles:

Don't go in debt! don't go in debt! I beg you . . . My dear write me the true state of things and for mercy's sake do not deceive me. [June 6, 1880]

now Dear please dont spend any money if you have any I would rather keep it and add to it by degrees than run such a risk now I say no more expect I have incurred your displeasure, but cant help it. I bought me a pair of shoes out of that money you sent me and I will kept 50 cts for postage the rest I will hand over to Uncle Will for board as my month was out the fifth of this month. [November 7, 1880]

Hardly a passive wife, Maggie waited and planned.

If Charles had imagined the West would lessen his family's cloying presence, he was mistaken. His glowing descriptions of the West had the unexpected effect of making them want to join him. Even before Maggie could leave Virginia, Charles's mother was writing to say she would follow him to Colorado. Charles's behavior suggests he welcomed his family's financial assistance but disliked the possibility of them being there in Colorado as his neighbors.

His vascillation emphasized his ambivalence. In June 1880, Charles wrote his family that he had found a suitable place on which all of them could settle, *if* they raised $2,500. His find was the Hayden Ranch, about 320 acres of fine land, some 70 acres planted in wheat and oats, fenced and supplied with water. He envisioned himself planting fruit and raising cows and horses, while his sisters opened a school.

Having piqued his family's interest, Charles then dallied in the bargaining, making an inch of progress to a mile of error. Maggie was hostile to having Charles's family with her in the West. Playing, perhaps, to Maggie's distaste for moving the Browns west, Charles fumbled his negotiations with the ranch owner and finally piled together enough excuses to blame the scheme's failure on circumstances beyond his control. Angry because they had put effort into raising the needed money, Charles's mother and sisters accused him of snarling the deal and claimed they were sorry they had ever mentioned anything about coming out to Colorado.

At the same time (October 1880) the ranch venture fell through, the mining camp at Hayden Creek folded. Charles wrote Maggie begging her to agree to let him throw in his luck with a friend, following the mining boom down to southern Arizona, where silver discoveries in the late 1870s had launched the territory into a heady boom region.[9] Disenchanted, Maggie balked. But Charles, dreading a return to Virginia as destitute as he had left, offered a compromise. Rather than go to Arizona (which to Maggie had seemed a true foreign country) he proposed that he go to nearby Kerber Creek, Colorado, where four mining camps were experiencing what the "boys" thought would be a boom rivaling that of Leadville.

Darling just please let me have a chance at Kerber. If there is no chance there I will . . . get help to come back. But I have great cause to believe that we can do well there. Write to me soon and tell me to stay awhile longer. But If you insist upon it I will come [back]. [October 21, 1880]

Maggie acquiesced. And by October 25, 1880, Charles had moved to Bonanza City, the most promising of the Kerber Creek camps. Charles was not misrepresenting the popular feeling about the region. A twentieth-century history records: "So promising was the outlook that by January, 1881, Bonanza was spoken of as the 'New Leadville.'"[10]

Settled in Bonanza, Charles made little pretense of establishing his medical practice, although he advertised himself as a physician; he focused on mining and particularly on a small claim he staked some fifty yards behind their cabin. He named it the *Maggie Brown*. Together he and his young partner worked the required ten feet into the rocky ground. Charles bragged to Maggie that each day he toughened and could dig longer. Assaying the first quartz from his hole himself, he found four ounces of silver. The proximity of some high-yield mines boded well for Charles's vein.

Almost immediately upon his move to Bonanza, Charles invested in lots—a sure-money thing whose price, in a boom, might quadruple overnight. Charles singled out one to build his permanent cabin on— the one, he told Maggie, that they would live in. He bargained to buy lumber and to hire carpenters. The lumber arrangement, for some reason, took months to complete. And the carpenter deal fell through so that in the end Charles built most of the cabin alone.

An ironic twist to the negotiations (which Charles surely thought would calm Maggie for a time) was that the prospect of the house fired Maggie's desire to move soon to Colorado. Charles resisted, arguing the fierce cold and the scarcely begun cabin. Unconvinced and deter- mined, Maggie wrote their aunt, Mrs. Elizabeth Coyner, who was living some forty miles north of Charles in Colorado Springs, asking her opinion whether, indeed, the weather should prohibit her from joining Charles in December. Allying with Charles, Aunt Betsy urged Maggie to await the spring. As if to emphasize the danger of cold, she enumerated deaths of children from diptheria there and told how dis- tressing it was for her "to see the Hears [sic] so often all most evry day we see it sometimes twise a day" [December 6, 1880]. With such a pronouncement, what could Maggie do but give in and ready herself for a bleak Virginia winter.

Charles, initially relieved of Maggie's pressure, soon felt his own bleak winter—snowed in, womanless. Mining camps, unsightly in good weather, in bad weather became piles of filth and disorder. Inside their smelly tents or log cabins, the men were trapped in a mess of loose hay, rough blankets, and the stench of unwashed bodies and unwashed clothes. Outside they sloshed through muddy passages where garbage rotted and cesspools stank—a dismal setting, especially for a Virginia gentleman.

Charles wrote melancholy, lonesome letters, laced with sexual desire for Maggie.

Nothing has happened of any interest since I last wrote except that I showed your picture to two or three men the other night and one of the men remarked, that that was enough to keep any man stripped. [December 8, 1880]

Longing ran undercurrent to every letter:

Write to me soon and write me all the love in your soul for I do so long to hear it poured out, there is nothing in the world that I apreciate more than I do it, I feel as if it was all that I had in this world. . . . Oh! how I wish I had you in my arms at this time. Ahh wont it be bliss to be together once more? Then nothing but death will part us. I feel that I could kiss that little "tater hole" if I would do any good, to have it back with me. And I think I will kiss the other when I get to it for its so sweet. [February 16, 1881]

Repeatedly Charles assured Maggie he was faithful. And once, probably to show her he was not seeking prostitutes to satisfy his sexual cravings, he spelled out his substitution for her in un-Victorian frankness:

My virtue is all right and I think that it will remain so for I do not care to meddle with any of the women that I see here but I look forward to something nice soon. I know that it will be the best in the world, so I am satisfied to think of how nice it will be and go and jack off. Now don't blame me for I do get awful hard up some times. [April 16, 1881]

Charles showed sensitivity to Maggie's wish to avoid pregnancy during that time of uprootings. Several letters show him helping her calculate her arrival in the West to synchronize with her ovulation cycle, what that age erroneously thought to be a "safe period." When Charles thought he could bring Maggie out west in the fall, he had written her:

Darling when you go to come out set the time so that you will have seven days to come on, so that there will be no danger when you come, of course you know what I mean. I suffer so for it I don't think I could wait with it right by me & I would not like to be of any trouble to my darling—for I know how she suffers in that way. [September 20, 1880]

Maggie, too, wanted Charles sexually. She wrote him as the time finally approached for her to join him in Colorado that she wanted him "so so much" that she was almost willing to have a boy for him.

I want to see you so so much I do think if you wanted to see me as badly as I do you would I wont say it for I know you do nearly I am almost willing to have a boy for you but if I start Monday I will be clear of it all & I don't want to get in "that way" at once. [June 26, 1881]

Such mutual sexual desire runs counter to most popular and some scholarly conceptions of the stoic Victorian. In his study of letters of California miners separated from wives and sweethearts, for example, Andrew J. Rotter found sex generally missing from those letters home.[11] Likewise John Faragher, in his analysis of Overland Trail diaries, held that sex was seldom mentioned. Of course, travel diaries were usually seen as public records; thus the absence of sexual allusion would not predicate behavior.[12]

Carl N. Degler, in his research on nineteenth-century sexual behavior, concludes that the twentieth century has misjudged Victorian sexuality, confusing the counsels of advice books and religious leaders with actual practices of individuals. Where many writers of the mid-eighteen hundreds, Degler argues, seemed to describe antisexual behavior as a norm, in fact they were only warning against excessive or perverted sexual activity. Degler cautions against characterizing an entire age by descriptions and proscriptions found in marital advice books: "The attitudes of ordinary people are quite capable of resisting efforts to reshape or alter them."[13] There is, indeed, a growing body of evidence showing that the very force of proscriptions against sexual indulgence, like its tandem temperance movement, testifies to the presence of vigorous sexual activity.[14] The letters of Maggie and Charles during their separation probably represent a common attitude to sex in companionate marriages.

With Maggie and Charles, though, separation fed suspicion as well as desire. From the beginning, recriminations and reassurances flew back and forth: "Have you kissed any one since you did me? *I tell you you had better not*" [June 6, 1880]. That was in June of 1880; still in February 1881, Charles was protesting his fidelity:

I hardly think it is worth while telling you again that no woman can ever come between you and I. . . . darling, if you love me, trust me and I'll call God to witness my fidelity. You are all that I love in this world and I can't bear for you to doubt me. [February 9, 1881]

Yet, while Charles insisted that Maggie's doubt pained him, he in his turn pressed her to assure him her love for him remained strong:

Bab, do you love me as much as ever? I do hope so if I ever found out that you did not love me or was untrue in the least, I think it would kill me. You are all that I work for all that I care

for, and I never intend whilst I live to give you up so blindly
again. [March 14, 1881]

It is clear that Maggie did not cloister herself during her separation
from Charles. Escorted by relatives and friends, or even by an occasional male who found her attractive, she socialized. And she flashed
her partying before Charles as if to remind him of what a desirable
woman he was missing. One comment she made suggests small slips
from propriety: "I know at times I am a *little* wayward, but you are
so good and dear you forgive me so nicely. . . . I will go with you
hereafter through thick and thin, then let come what will" [March 19,
1881].

Rumors fed natural suspicions. The couple's separation sparked gos-
sip in both the Colorado and Virginia communities. Charles received
a letter from a perfect stranger, a professor at the University of Virginia:

I did hear that you were a drunkard, and a gambler but, of
course I got it from a quarter that everything must not be
believed, and I doubted the story when I heard it. I heard
something about your dear wife from the same quarater. I did not
believe [it] when I heard it, let alone after I met her. I dont
believe everything I hear, but of course I did not know you or
Mrs. B. I just took the stories for what I thought they were
worth. When you hear a tale it all depends upon who tells it. [J.
Woremouth, February 22, 1881]

With the spring thaw the young couple's suspicions abated, but Charles's money and house troubles continued. Unable to raise money for
completion of his cabin or for Maggie's and Mattie's tickets west, he
placated Maggie with promises. On her part, once spring arrived,
Maggie dreamed up a range of plans by which she herself could bring
money into the family: taking in boarders, selling confections and breads,
making gloves, setting up (with Charles) a home for invalids. Above
all, she wanted to be where Charles was.

Finally, in July 1881, Charles alerted Maggie to be ready to travel
(he *almost* had enough money for tickets), only to have an ironic fate
countervene with a near fatal illness for Mattie. What had seemed but
a passing sickness escalated into a bout with death. Nineteenth-century
women, raising small children, lived close to such sudden disaster.
Panicked, Maggie wrote Charles twice in a single day: she feared soon

they would be sole comforts to each other and that Mattie, their only child, would be dead. It was inconceivable to Maggie that the pinched, thin figure, discharging pus and blood on the sickbed, was the same frolicking child who only days before had been helping to pack trunks to go to "Colonadie."

Although the attending physician had prognosed the worst, Mattie's fever did finally break. The bout with death quickened Maggie's determination to bring the family together, and overriding Charles, she managed to secure for herself better than half the money for the Colorado tickets. Maggie's behavior is a noteworthy blend of spirit and geniality. Faced with a similarly improvident husband, Mary Hallock Foote, whose life in many ways paralleled Maggie's, drew on her own savings to buy a ticket to meet her husband in New Almaden, California, in 1876. But her action was filled with resentment, and she charged her husband with negligence.[15]

The letters that follow document a time of separation not remarkable in the ferment of the mining frontier of the 1880s. Charles's ambitions, his abortive projects to make quick wealth, his winter gloom, his elaborate hopes characterized other Colorado speculators. Maggie's fears, her suspicions, her assertiveness, her enforced dependence on husband and friends marked other "waiting" women.[16] Unique, though, with Maggie and Charles are the words that passed between them—words, tumbling with spontaneity and hardly the thing of stereotypes.

Letter Texts April 1880–July 1881

Charles to Maggie

Haydens Creek Col.
April 19th 1880

My darling Babe

I rece'd your dear letter when it was too late to answer it, but will try to answer it now. You asked me to tell you how I like things generally, well I must say that I dont like things generally, but I think I can make something after a while as soon as I get settled, am now, making an attempt to plant some vegetables.[17] James D. has promised that he would furnish every thing seeds and all, and board me and give me half I made on the ground, expect to plant about three or four acres of cabbage potatoes tomatoes turnips mellons beets &c, which will require very little

time and labor & they all sell very high $20.00 per Lb for
Potatoes, Fruit $20.00 per Barrel and so on am afraid it will be
very lonesome here, but Jim says he will cut off a piece of land
for me to build on and I think I will take it, if Haydens C don't
soon improve. Miss Goodwin is a nice girl & will give you plenty
of company, (that is if I stay) but things must improve by Fall or
I am coming back.   As soon as I can get my garden planted I am
going to start out and see more of this country, I find that some
people observe the Sabbeth and some dont. If I can succeed in
my garden I will have enough to bring me home and some thing
left, & then I can make some thing practicing, have only made
one dollar yet, but hope to make more soon, by-the-way D.
Walters has several of my Journals and there was one of the
same that I wanted today. None of the boys that came with me
are doing any thing yet. I had a call yesterday, but the man was
in a hurry and left before I got to the place, they all seem glad
that I have come, and I may like it better after awhile. Its right
hard to tell what will turn up in this roling country

The Rocky mountains have got the right name they all seem to
be rocks as you pass by them, but after you get on top they put
on a better dress. There is large tracks of roling grass land and if
there was more rain it would be very productive in other things,
the grass is short, but said to be very nutritious. There is no
snakes here there is a few up near what is called timber line, but
not so many as there is in Va. The water is just splendid, The
other page is for you alone. You may read this to our friends if
you wish.

My darling I never knew how much I loved you untill since I
left you, and my heart yearns for your society now, yes I know
my baby misses me and I am sorry that I have left you but I
hope my love that we will be with each other soon. How I long to
see your dear face once more. Does my little baby call for Papa
much? Bless its heart papa loves his baby I feel some thing like
Bruce D. says: but I can't help but think, do you ever think?

There does not seem to be any thing but virtuous women in
this country the boys have been looking around—

My cold is getting much better, have not suffered with cold
since I have been here until yesterday, my hands got cold. There
is plenty of fishes in the brooks, plenty of deer & we have been
eating some deer meat since I came.

Give my love to all my friends I cant call names for lack of
space. Miss Mattie & love to yourself—Affect C.A.B.

Maggie to Charles

West View

May 24th/80

My dear husband

I sent a card to you yesterday telling you to send my mail
hereafter to Staunton in care of Charles W. Shuff but am afraid
you did not get it so will send another this morn. Mattie is better
much love
Your aff wife
M. M. Brown

Charles to Maggie

Hayden Creek Col
June 6, 1880

My darling Wife

I should have written to you sooner, but have been so busy
that I could not, work hard all day and am two tired to write at
night but most of our hard work is done now, and I shall be able
to write often and will pay up for lost time and you will not have
to scold me for not writing oftener. It is right hard to write when
there is a lot of boys around talking and laughing, but I have
them all asleep now and will not be troubled by them. I sit and
think and think of how much I would love to have you with me, I
don't have any doubt about us getting along here, altho I have
not done as much this month by a great deal as I did last, it is
because there has not been much sickness in this vicinity and I
am [not] known out of it yet, but there is a strong probability of
Haydens Creek being in a short time a good sized mining camp
and then I am ahead of any one else and rapidly gaining the
confidence of the people. Will not be able to send you any money
untill the last of this month; but I will send it then, have been
obliged to get me a pair of boots and some clothing everything
has worn out except my new suit and I keep that when I go out
practicing, had to get overalls to wear here on the road, building
fence clearing up new ground &c and very hard on clothes, but I
am almost done with it now. No I have no source of my own yet,
but Jim says that I can have all I want to cultivate on his. I am
trying to get one but don't know how soon I will be able to do so.
I ask no man for credit and credit none except those who have
nothing and you know that I am obliged to do some of that kind

of practice, but they do not expect it all the time, and I can say pay me what you owe and my visit in advance, and I will go. They never make a fuss about it here.[18] I want you to collect any and all gardin seeds that you like when you come for we had some trouble to get them this year. Think you had better go to home families first and stay there around and then go to Salem you would feel better whilst you are there and enjoy yourself more, I would not advise any one to go to the plains to live. I cannot imagine a more desolate place and there you seldom ever see rain true we have had two rains & one good snow since I have been here but the streams never get too low to irrigate will write again this week and you will hear from me twice a week from this on. Oh! how I wish that I had you with me this eve never to leave me, will never leave you behind me again. I get so lonesome that I dont no what to do—

Give love to all friends and write to me often was so sorry to hear that our little darling was sick but she is well long ago. Kiss the little love for me and tell her that her papa loves her so much can she talk yet? You dont tell me—Write to your devoted and your loving

C. A. Brown

Maggie to Charles

June 6th/80
Bridgewater, Virginia

My dear husband

I sent off your letter the other day; but will write or commence one now. Uncle Henry was in today, and says Ben Myers writes very different from what you do   there is very little money out there and a great many going around with their "knap sacks and frying pans" not having a shelter.[19] And Tom Keller saw Will Wynant in West Crowfard and he said that the young men that went from there wrote very discouragingly   how is this?   be care full or you will have to retract some you have said   write me what you clear very month—be sure now for I am afraid you are so sanguine; just think how hard the winters there. Don't go in debt! don't go in debt!! I beg you. Please write me about your business you said you were going to buy a team did you? have you a riding horse of your own? have you bought any cloaths yet? have you taken up a claim? Ben M writes he is "running Jim

Dinkle's ranch" be ware of the name. Is Joe Myers there? have
you kissed any one since you did me? I tell you you had better
not Now answer all my questions

                                    Sunday June 7
   My darling [Sunday] is the day there enlived by the sweet
sound of church bells   I do think it is the sweetest sound   I have
not been to church since I came to town—Mattie has been so
sick—she is getting better, and I never saw a little thing eat like
she does. I was realy disappointed that I did not get a letter last
night. Do you read your bible?[20] I feel so sad today   I am afraid
you don't give the true state of things   is your health good yet? I
think after harvest on the last of this month I will go to Uncle
H's   they will let me work for my board there. You say you can
"see the money" but no one else can; I tell you this thing of
seeing the money and not in your own hand is not what it is
"cracked up to be"   I will not go to Lone Fountain for Mattie
seems to be getting better and more hardy   it will cost too much
any way. Wrote a letter to New Hope but it has been treated
with silent contempt   it was an affectionate letter too to Millie
[Charles's oldest sister]. I think if things go on this way I will be
lost to the family for I am not going to trouble them.[21] My dear
write me the true state of things and for mercy's sake do not
deceive me. Next week I expect to die most and I don't care
much if I do
Charlie [Shuff] had a bet with me the other day that I would
never go to Col'   I bet I would but had not much idea of leaving
Va either. If I do go and the people I come in contact with are
wicked and regardless of their maker it will kill me outright   in
your first Dear letters you allways said "God bless" you or
something of that kind. but now you do not. Oh! where is my
darling good husband! I am going to read the XXIV Psalm.[22]
Done. My own darling will I ever behold that dear dear face
again why is it I am so sorriful

(June 9th) I have received no letter since the one dated the 23 of
May which will soon be three weeks and it was almost three
weeks after mine was written. Well suppose you have not time to
drop a card even: so I will try to support my self

June 11th   It is with very sad heart I carry this letter to the office been looking for a letter for 2 weeks and have not gotten any but the one written the 23rd of May. I am quite well and fatter than I have been since I married.[23] Mattie is looking well too.

Charles to Maggie

Hayden Creek Col
June 8th 1880

My darling Babe

Have just rec'ed your card & letter of 24th May and was very glad to get, your letters are like August rains, always welcome and all come at once. I generally get two at a time altho they are written a week apart. Yes I wrote to Mary Ella [Charles's sister] that she could get a school here if she would come out with you in the fall, but I think she had better stay in Va untill I can do some thing definate, I think it all the better that I did come out here. I might have stayed in Va and been poor all my life. There is some chance of me making some thing here, but I cant make much untill I have you with me, If I can raise money enough & am able to build my house, I intend to send you the money to come out, before Jim goes in, for I don't think he will come back before Jan. I will have to take the big deer hunt before then, for I will have to be gone about a week and could not have you by your self. & I must lay up some venison for winter, and we wanted to kill enough to sell about two hundred dollars worth, besides what we want for ourselves. I conditionally bought a horse of Jim day before yesterday, and we traded his off for another one yesterday. The one that I got of him I was to pay eighty dollars for her and the colt but she had some tricks that we did not like, the one I have now I think would suit you as soon as I can make her ride easier. She is very gentle, as much so as any horse I ever saw, she will have a colt in a few days and when that grows up I shall ride it and give you Flora. She is eight years old and a splendid bridle mare I expect to have a colt in her belly all the time—and all that I dont want for my own use will be yours. I have not paid for her yet, but I am to pay for her as I get the money and when she is paid for she is mine, but if I conclude not to take her at any time, it is no trade, but I am to have the use of her as much as I wish. Expect you had better leave the socks. I can get them here for forty cents but you get you what goods you need. Have quit chewing and only smoke now and do not care for the chew. Better give our little darling Bismuth & Ipecac, and bathe her in cool water right often. I wish that you could see some of the pretty cactus flowers here, they are grand. I enclose a red one. Of course I appreciate your flowers. It is time for me to go to the mail. Write soon to your affectionate & devoted husband C. A. B. Kiss my little babe & my big one too CAB

Charles to Maggie

Hayden Creek Col
June 13th 1880

My darling Babe

I have just been thinking how much I want you am getting so tired of this kind of a life, have not been well this week, and I think it is because bad fare have been cooking myself and have to cook by fire, and burn all my bread in fact I don't think I can cook by a fire place;[24] am getting nearly well again, have been bilious & felt weak and dizzy, but took a pill and feel much better. I can't decide where to put our house, think I have found a location at least where I will have a place for a good garden with a nice cool spring in twenty feet of the door, but am not certain that the spring runs all the year, but the creek runs within forty yards and it is cool and nice all the year round, what do you think? Do not wish to build until I think the place will suit you. The practice is small here but there is a good chance of its getting good it is good now as for as pay in comparison with West View is concerned but I mean a big practice. I think by fall I will be able to pay Amie K's passage if she will promise to stay with us a year, we have thirteen chickens with one hen that has three little ones nearly large enough to eat and I have two hens setting and have had plenty of eggs, The wind blows here all the time but I never feel it like the winds in Va. but when there is a rain coming (which is not often) I feel it in my legs. If there was much rain here I think the whole country would wash away for it is all sand from the foot to the tops of the mountains, except on some level parts that are what they call "Doby" that they build adobe houses with and that is as washy as the sand, and that is just what makes the bottom land so rich. There is some of the longest trout here that I ever saw, have seen them two feet long, but

those large ones are in the river about two miles off. You had better sell the feather bed and try to bring all the bed clothes you can for these that I have will not be fit to use except those that can be washed, next summer we wish to start a boarding house for invalids, and will need all the covers that we can get[25] and we can get a spring mattress for our own use and I am afraid that the tick will cost too much to send it or if you cant get what you think it is worth give it to ma. Did Emma Rife refund the money for the $^2/_2$ gold piece? I think if my darlings were with me that I could be happy but I cant be so untill they are, You dont know how I long for your dear faces and I hope and trust that the time is not far distant when we shall meet again, and then, we will not part untill death, if it is left to me. Tell Aunt Mary that she ought to see the variety of wild flowers that are here, they are not thick, but there are cactus Annums of seven or eight different varietys, and colors, of the most gorgeous hews. Will send her some seed in the fall & if they will not grow I will send some of the plants next spring there is one that looks like the Rock Lilley with plant-like bunch of grass & each blade has its spear or spike for defence   hope our little darling is well by this time—tell me all about how she is getting along. Kiss her for me, and a thousand for your self darling   Love to all of Aunt Mary's family
                    Affectly CAB.
Dont think it would pay to bring any thing in the eating line for you will be loaded any way would not be surprised if you don't have to come by your self—for if Jim dont come to time I will not wait on him[26]
Love affectionately CAB

Charles to Maggie

Hayden Creek, Col.
June 18th, 1880

My darling Babe
   I have just rec'd your letter of numerous dates but mailed on the 11th. You said that you had sent one on the fourth. I have not rec'd it, in fact I have not gotten a letter from you for two weeks before this one, and I have written six or seven. It seems that they miscarry and you must not blame me for not writing for I do write to my babe. I think my lamb was right blue when she wrote this letter, but you must not be blue, darling, for God will

bring us out all right. Ben Myers did not tell the truth in his letter, he is working for Jim at twenty five ($25) dollars per month and board. He is making money, but I think he expected to make a fortune in a few days, and as to the haver sack and frying pan men, there is thousands of men passing through this country on their way to the Gunnison Country and they are going on as cheap a scale as possible. Some of them have money and some in all probability have none.[27] There is plenty to do here and every one has money—unless they have been sick above and have come down to recruit, and get work but they do not stay long untill they have money. And then it takes all they can make to get a start. I have bought me a suit of over alls to do work on the place in, but do not wear them off of it, four pairs of socks, 1 pr. boots, handkerchiefs, did not do much practice last month because there was not much sickness, but I got more money than I ever did in Va.—and when I get you here and my vegetables all in it will not cost so much to live. Have every thing to buy and canned stuff costs right high but I can't live on bread and meat. It makes one sick and I will not let the others buy all.

The man that went from Bridgewater was one Simpson, that is a taylor by trade, and is after a big thing or nothing. He was offered four dollars a day at his trade in Denver but would not take it, in fear he could get more some where else. No wonder he writes discouragingly.

I lost my account book last month and can't tell exactly what I make but I think about $25 dollars. Have got a new one, and can keep it strate now. Jos. M. is in Ohio some where, do not expect him here. Don't intend to go in debt. Jim went into the tin business by him self. I don't think we will make another team just now.

I have seen nothing that I would like to kiss since I have been here. [There is no church] the population is too small to build one, and there is part of it that don't want any. I find them all honorable and, but few Christians. Their worst wickedness is swearing, all seem to be addicted to it.[28] But you will not be exposed to it. You will be up here in your own little home. I wish you could get Anna K. to come with you. Maybe you could get Dilly to come with you, there is a very nice fellow here that wants a Va. wife, and he is very well off too. Anna can make her washing pay her hire, there is plenty of it and she can get good prices. You can board her for helping you. am so glad that both of

my babes are getting along so well in regards to health. It is one
of God's blessings that we should be extremely thankful for.
Write me often, darling. Now may God bless you and bring you
to me soon. Goodbye, lamb.

Affect.& Lovingly, C. A. B.

Charles to Maggie

Hayden Creek Col
June 24th/80

My darling & beloved Wife
    I have just rec'd a letter & card from you one dated on the
16th & the other on the 17th telling me that all is well, and I
thank God for it for I have been very uneasy about you and so
glad that your health is getting good, now don't scold me, if your
back has not gotten well yet don't you think that you had better
put a blister on it? I have so much faith in them, and our little
darling how glad papa is to hear that she is well, do you teach
her to say papa's baby yet? I know my lamb says it sweetly. If
Engleman is not in S[taunton] go to any one that can take a good
picture, but don't go to the same man any more for I don't look at
the picture once a week, it spoils your dear face so much that it
hurts me to look at it. The babes picture is good. This is the first
letter that I have written this week, because the boys have been
at home and they interfer so much that I can't write, and then I
have been working right hard and always feel too tired to write
at night, suppose that you got more than you wanted last week &
week before I had leasure then to write and wrote. Suppose that
you try to make this kind of an arrangement with Anna K. that
she will come out with you, and live with you and that we will
board her for what she does for us, and I will ensure her all the
washing that she can do, at fifteen cents per piece and if she
washes an hundred pieces per week it is equal to five dollars per
week and when we get our boarding house started why then we
can afford to pay her, regular wages, there is very little white
goods here to wash, the men all wear colored shirts—and
drawers she can wash twice as many of them as she could of
white shirts.[29] I have written to those at home if they were so
anxious to come out here, they should raise twentyfive hundred
dollars, and I would buy the Hayden ranch which has about three
hundred & twenty acres in it with good improvements and is

considered one of the best ranches in this country & I think it is
cheap at the price, and if they make the raise there is some first
rate places for us to put a house there away from the road, am
rather afraid that living up here puts me two far from the road,
and I lose a great deal that I would get if I was closer. I do so
long for you that I feel some times if I dont soon get able to send
for you that I will have to come back myself, it makes me sick to
think of the seperation. I'll never leave you behind me again. Oh!
My darling if God will only give the time when I shall meet you
again how thankfull I shall be. There seems to be so little
sickness just now it discourages me the weather is very warm
and the snow has all left the mountains except in some small
patches; Just be patient my love. I cant get ready for you soon
enough for you to come on the excursion. Am going to build my
house of logs & cover it with paper untill I am able to get
shingles   what do you think of that for a roof?

Charles to Maggie

Hayden Creek Col
June 28th 1880

My darling Babe

As I have come in during the heat of the day to rest from my
labors I have concluded to write you a letter, have not heard
from the mail today, but expect to get it in the course of the day
and then finish this but will write some now. Have just ordered
the logs for my house they will be made within the next two
weeks but will not be fit to put up before the middle of August
and by that time I will be able to go right ahead with it. Am not
making any thing worth talking about this month for it is one of
the healthy months here, I hear of very little sickness anywhere.
The weather is very warm and is consequently very healthy as
there is no maleria or any thing of the kind, of course you know
that I am well or I would not be doing any thing. There is very
little rain here get some little sprinkles & we are obliged to
irrigate, but they tell me that in July there is plenty of showers
that make things grow right along. Just recd a letter from you,
don't pay any attention to any of Ben Myers tales there is no
truth in it   there is not an indian within an hundred and fifty
miles and no one is thinking of going to fight them.[30] There is no
truth in it. He denys that he wrote what you heard he did. Think

Ben is right much of a liar, but dont tell any one that I said so. Enclosed you will find one of the most pungent oders that I have seen since I have been here; it smells something like sweet shrub. If you can you had better bring some of the marsh roses that you can find. The wild rose seems to do so well the whole place is full of it and it is very troublesome think I will have to have a hand to help me get my camp straight it is pushing over too much. When do you think of going to Uncle Harries? Would like to hear from you on that point   would like to know how they are all getting along. How long does Aunt Bet expect to stay down the Valley? Am going to have a nice horse out of my colt. He paces already and I think that he will make a real nice small horse if the mountain lyons don't kill it for me, they kill colts some times they seem to like their meat better than any other. They were never known to bother a man, are very shy of a man, Tell my babe that papa wants to see her ever so much. It is getting very late and I wish to go to the office tonight. Kiss both of my darlings for me an hundred times. Tell Geo. Tate that I found the piece of ore and the assayer don't seem to think much of it thinks its iron. Write soon to your Affect husband, C. A. Brown

Charles to Maggie

Hayden Creek Col
July 18th 1880

My darling Wife
  Have rec'd yours with the enclosure of "Western Bill" who is no other than Bill Dinkel and I must say that it is full of lies & misrepresentations from beginning to end. The "North Park" Country is about an hundred and fifty miles from here and no one has heard of any Indians being any where near there. The prospectors or mine hunters had some trouble in the Gunnison with them, but that was because the prospectors were over mining the Indian reservation. The U.S. soldiers tryed to keep the prospectors out but were unable to do so.
  The Hayden place is one of the best in this country and I consider it a bargain at the price. There is about seventy acres of wheat and oats on it now which will bring the old man a thousand dollars for his share and he has not struck a lick he rents it for half and furnishes the horses & feed. It makes near about a thousand dollars worth of hay. There is no fruit here because no

one has planted any. There are plenty of wild currents, raspberries &c Any kind of fruit can be raised if planted. The H[ayden] ranch is under pretty good fence and has plenty of water. we can keep forty cows on it, and sell many pounds of butter at from thirty five to forty cents per pound, and can fix up a churn to run by water power that will relieve us of all the labor of churning and cost but little. Millie [Charles's sister] can get music scholars, and make some money that way. In short there is plenty of ways for all of us to make money here if we have a home of our own. I can put up extra rooms and get just as many boarders as we want at from twenty to twenty five dollars per month. There is bound to be a town some where about the place and we can sell off all the land that we dont want in town lots, in short if I dont see the money in the thing I would not advise them to come. Rece'd a card from Aunt Betsie [Elizabeth Coyner in Colorado Springs] a short time ago and wrote her a long letter, but have not rece'd an answer yet expect it every day. She seems to be glad that I have come to Col. and was really blessed to receive a card from me, which I wrote to find out if she was in Colorado Springs yet. Asked me to write her a long letter which I did. Have not much to write about, and must close. Did you get the money in Reg[istered] letter? Sent it on the eighth to S[taunton] care C[harles] W S[huff]. Kiss my babe and yourself and love to all the family. Write soon and often if you write but little

> Affect & Devotedly
> C. A. B.

Charles to Maggie

> Hayden Creek Col
> July 26th 1888

My darling Wife

I have not written you for about a week and have been intending to write every day but every day some thing would turn up to prevent and now I am determined that I will write, Have been trying to make some arrangements to move down to Hayden C. I think I am losing money staying on Cotton Wood, and it costs me very nearly as much to board myself as it does to get board.

28th   Have just returned from working the road. Have worked

two days thought it would be easyer than to pay $3. for road
taxes, and am done for this year.[31] Rec'd a letter from home
telling me to make some arraingements about buying the Hayden
Ranch they say that they can raise the money within two months.
The old man is not at home but the old lady wrote to him last
night. And I think he will be at home soon, and the sooner the
better. If I am not very much mistaken they can raise about four
thousand dollars, and that will give us a nice start. The floods on
Cotton Wood destroyed my cabbage and one of my potatoe
patches, but I will have enough potatoes for all of us. I have so
little news to write that I can't write a long letter. Am so nervous
from work that I can hardly write. Kiss my little babe and tell
her papa expects to see her soon and wants to love her so much.
I know that my darling wife wishes to see me but not any more
than I do her, some times I get so blue thinking about my loved
ones, that I feel just like getting & going back to old Va. Am
truly glad that you have gotten your money. I always direct in
CWS's care my letters must get lost on the road—Write soon to
your affect Husband—God bless both of my loved ones.
Affect C. A. Brown

Charles to Maggie

Hayden Creek Col
Aug 4, 1880

My beloved wife
  I started to write you a letter this evening and the pen was so
bad that I gave it up so will write now with a pencil, and the
next with a pen. Rece'd a letter from you tonight that was
written just before you left Staunton, hope by this time that you
are having a nice time at Uncle H's am sure that you will have it
there. If you can get the corn to dry I think it would be nice, for
you can only get <u>can</u> corn here and at twenty five cts per can tho,
it is very nice I don't like as much as I do dryed corn. Have not
been able to hear from Hayden yet, and if I do get the ranch we
will not live with the rest of the family for we could not get along
and I will not have any thing to do with it if I cant hold the purse
strings. Old Mrs. H[ayden] says she does not want the old man to
sell because she is tired of running around. I have written to the
old man, but have not heard from him. Before I left Cotton Wood
I ate some raddishes and they gave me a bad case of dysenterry,

which had lasted me two weeks untill I came down here and now my bowels are in <u>first rate</u> order, better than they have been since I came out here. If I don't see a better chance to make money by fall I shall come back to Va. Am not making more than expenses now, but am doing better than I did before I came down here. If the times turn out well here, as they must do from indications and a good population comes, I will get a big practice, for I am getting a very good reputation. Have been having some big rains here this month, one of them produced a considderable flood. Was up to see my potatoes today and they are doing nicely gathered about half bushel of beans and brought them down for dinner tomorrow. You can tell Will & Jake that if they want hard work at from $1.50 to 2.50 per day & board they can get plenty of it here but they will have to work for thirty dollars per month until they learn something about mining. There is about two or three hundred mines in these mountains & some of them must turn out well. One was 60% silver to [writing illegible] gold which will make about $175.00 per ton—Yesterday the tops of the mountains were covered with snow but this was not cold. Am told October is the hotest month here. Rece'd a letter from Aunt B[etsy Coyner]. She says she is in better health than she has had for a long time think I shall enclose it—

Give my love to all of the family. And kiss my lambs ever so often. Hoping that God will bless my babys & bring us together. I will close. Kiss.

Affect & Lovingly
C. A. B.

Maggie to Charles

White Hall [Virginia] Aug [1880]

My precious Husband

I have just received your <u>dear</u> letter. Am so glad to hear that you have the least idea of sending for or coming to me.

Well now, I will write you some news. Willie W. & Jennie Irwin have gone over the mountain to farm or rather put out a wheat crop on the land Uncle H[arry Wynant] got over there this winter. Jake is here of course going for the widow strong. Says he can't get her to marry until her health gets better. About 4 weeks ago cousin A. was sick[32] (like I was before you left)[33] and it was reported that she had twins and Mrs. Irwin said she had out her horse to go to see her. <u>I wish I could hear you laugh</u> Mrs. Irwin was up yesterday to see me and as soon as Fannie[34] introduced me she said, "Let me kiss you for Charlie's sake." So I did.

I did not go to Harrisonburg as I thought Monday, but will go tomorrow if nothing happens. I was so, so sick last night with sick headache but did not throw up. This morning I took a dose of salts.

I have been feeling jolly all evening. I told Cousin Jake I expected to get something sweet in the mail and I did. God bless my darling. How I love you. Write often.

I have been fixing Fanny up to go to Shenendoah to attend a Synod. I think she has broken with her Valley fellow. She has an idea of coming with me to get a nice fellow. They are all disappointed you did not come down before you left. Mattie has gotten so she can say anything she wants to. I wish you could see her. I will send you a lock of her hair. I won't cut it off if you don't wish it. Cousin Jake says it is ruby red. I said it is <u>his</u> baby's hair anyhow. I think he would like to have one like it. well my love, write often. Am going to bed now and dream of thee. I have been so blue for the last few days but feel better now. Have to be very skimpie of money but will try to make shift. A sweet Goodnight loved one, the best and dearest of husbands. Be sure I will keep just as good for <u>you</u> and <u>you only</u>.

Your aff. wife,
Maggie Brown

Charles to Maggie

Hayden Creek Col
Aug 12th 1880

My darling Wife

I am real sorry that I have no money to send you at this time, but hope to be able to send you some soon, I think that before long I will be able to make some arraingement that I will have my loved ones with me. I will not tell you just now what it is for fear that you will be disappointed, but if I take it I will be sure of a living as something to lay up but I will have to move my location. I shall not move except for the better, and if I don't see some thing more in sight than I do now, by the first of Oct. I shall come back to Va. but I have been assured that I will. Rece'd

another letter from Millie [Charles's oldest sister] and she seems
to think that they are all anxious to come out here, but I have
not been able to hear from Old Mr. Hayden. If I can get his place
I shall be contented, for I can see how we can make it and if I
get the place that I hinted at I know I can make it. The man
came to me this time. Simpson has been over in Gunnison ever
since he came, where they have to pack things for fifty miles on
Jacks and I have heard that flour was at one time one dollar per
pound—flour is four dollars & twenty five cents per sack here,
bacon from 11 to 13½ cents per lb.   the place I think of going,
you can make bread, and sell all that you want, there is a
comfortable house that I am to have. I don't want any pay for
what I do for you. All I ask is your company—that is more to me
than any thing else in the world, and if I can just get you with
me I shall be happy. You could come by Col[orado] Springs
[where Aunt Betsy Coyner was living] and I don't think it would
be out of the way—and I would meet you there. What is Millie
W[ynant] doing now? Please tell me some thing about the family.
You have not said any thing about them. Take good care of that
little thing of mine. Tell Mattie that papa loves her and wants to
see his little girl ever so much. God bless you both and send you
to me soon. I love you so much. Cousin A is not thinking of
having a babe yet is she? Give my love to all the family, and kiss
your self and Mattie for me and write soon—to your Affectionate
and Loving
Husband————C. A. Brown

Charles to Maggie

>Hayden Creek Col
>Aug 22nd 1880

My darling Wife
    Would have written last week but the card that I rec'ed from
you hurt my feelings, so that I didn't like to write until I rec'd a
letter from you. Please don't write any thing of that kind on a
postal. I know that you are impetuous but please have some
respect for my feelings, but my feelings were hurt but to receive
your last letter repaid it all. Darling your old man has a hard
time, don't do or say any thing that will add any thing to his
trouble. My health is better than it has been for years, have
gained five pounds since I recovered from dysentery weigh (154½)

and am increasing in weight. Am sitting on the floor and writing on my trunk, and you know there is not much good writing to be done. Was afraid that I would not be able to pay my board this month, but practice has commenced again, and I think after a little I will be able to send you some more money. I wrote to Mr. Harry Wright to send you five dollars that Sam owed me and you will get it shortly if you have not gotten it already. Am going to write to Ma this eve that I could not buy the H[ayden] place. He will not sell it now, and I am not sorry—for the man has lost nearly all his crops by hail and water, something they say that does not often occur here—but there are signs here of big floods. Tell Jake that I never expect to live in Va. any more untill I am able to do so, am tired of being a pauper. In all probability I will go to Canyon City after a while to live, the county seat. The country around here is somewhat on the decline and there will be a large number of people that will leave this fall for Southern Arizona, not wishing to winter in this country. The mines are not putting up much yet, it costs too much to open them up fast & I don't think there will be any pay ore gotten out this fall some of them have enough to ship a car load, but it has cost them more than it is worth to get it. They will have to go at least two hundred feet through the hardest kind of rock to pay ore and there are very few that are able to do so and these that are able seem to be afraid to do so. Nearly all of the talk here is mines and mining—I hope and trust in God that we may soon meet and when we do meet we will never part until death doth us part. I have never known how much I loved you, untill we have been separated Oh how I long to see you, I think some times if I could just see you for two hours & hug and kiss you that long that I could feel contented for a while, but never mind love we will meet after a while and be happy. Now when you write to me write a long letter & tell me of my babe & my wife—Kiss M[attie] for me and give my regards to all of the family. Will write again in a few days again. God bless my darling and protect her is always my prayer—

Affect Your husband
C.A.B.

Maggie to Charles

Bridgewater Sept 19th/80

My dear husband
   To say I have been disappointed in the last week at not getting

a letter from my <u>dear</u> would not half express my feelings. Last night my heart <u>just</u> sank within me. I just thought my darling must be dead or he would not treat his loving wife as he has. Never fail to write often, for if you do <u>so often</u> disappoint me you will cause me to loose all the flesh I have <u>gained</u> since I came down here: I was saying to Fannie I felt like leaping for joy my health is <u>so</u> good, but I will not be well long at this rate   see how nervous <u>I</u> am now from loosing so much sleep last night thinking of what might have happened to my loved one. Dear I feel now that you are the one love of my heart and if we could be together once more our happiness would be implicit. I wrote to C[harles] W. S[huff] yesterday to know if you had sent any letters but he said not. Wrote that old capt. Holms had droped dead Friday from old [word smudged] poor old man so wicked too. I am getting too nervous to write more now. My dear I will finish this letter and send by cousin Jake. Mattie is looking very well and is just what you always wished her to be very affectionate.[35] They all say she looks so much like "Charlie," Now do plese write to me <u>soon</u> when to come for I would realy like to come there if you go to Canon City, but if not I think if you make any thing atall suppose you come back and buy a few acres over at Bealton [a new railroad junction in north central Virginia] it is settling up there right fast.

Cousin Jake was over there last week and bought more land for Uncle H[arry]. I would not be supprized if they sell out here and go over there   Aunt Becky says you ought to come back and go there too. Well all do.

I must close. Now for <u>mercy sake</u> do not make it so long before you write again.

Your <u>ever</u> loving wife
Maggie Brown

Charles to Maggie

Hayden Creek, Col
Sept 20th, 1880

My darling Wife

Yours of the eighth just received. Don't abuse me, love, I am troubled enough now. The plan I had of going to Canyon City, I am afraid, will fall through as I understand the man is fixing to sell the mines.

I have been receiving letters from home about buying a ranch and they expect the money soon and as soon as they get it, I want to try to give you the money to come out. I will proceed to build a home for them. There is a house on the place that is large enough for us and a very nice one too, and an out house that will make a very good kitchen with a good cellar under it and I think it will make us a nice home. We can live on the money I pay for board. I like the neighborhood better than Hayden Creek. Oh, how happy I shall be when I get my loved ones with me. If you only knew how much I miss the association with my beloved family and how I long for their society you would not scold me. I get so dull sitting around here waiting for someone to send for me that I hardly know what to do.

I went fishing the other day and caught fifteen trout that weighed two pounds. Was right tired when I came back, but it helped the blues.

Jim Dinkle came to me today and told me what he was mad about. Some one had told him a lie. I told him it was and that I would tell the fellow so but the fellow says that he did not tell him any thing, so they may fix it up among themselves. I am done with them.

Will let White hear from me by tomorrow's mail. Practice is getting a little better. Am almost up with my board. I got behind when I had so little. Did about fifteen dollars ($15.00) worth of practice in the last two weeks but did not get it all. One of the men sent me word he would see me in a few days. Have lost about seventy-five dollars ($75.00) by men going off and not paying me. they have got to make me secure in some way. Am getting a good name now and if there was enough practice, I would get it all. There has been another man here for three weeks and the people laugh at him. He has not had a call from any one but Jim Dinkel and Ben Myers. That was because Jim was mad at me. Jim has been working for Ben at half wages. Jim has lost friends by the way he has troubled me. I have four times as many friends as he has. There are very few that have any thing to do with him. I never feel influenced by the plotting of any one else.

I love my wife and baby. It would be right hard for me to do any thing else. I don't even enjoy the society of other women.

The little babe I spoke of to you is gone. I liked it so much because it looked like our little darling. It is true, it was younger, but it was as large and it seemed to take a fancy to me, and you know it is hard to resist the little things, you wont know how I wish, wish, and long long & keep on longing to see my loved ones, darling write me a long long letter for I do so enjoy them, dont write me any more scolding letters they hurt me, but I know that you regret them as soon as you send them off. Did not know that Simpson had gone home have not heard from him since he left here last spring, was uneasy about him—am really glad to hear that he is safe for the Utes were right bad up in the country that he went to and a great many were killed that no one knew any thing about. Tho there is no trouble now and the probability is that they will not bother any one in this state any more. Darling when you go to come out set the time so that you will have seven days to come on, so that there will be no danger when you come, of course you know what I mean. I suffer so for it I don't think I could wait with it right by me & I would not like to be of any trouble to my darling—for I know how she suffers in that way.[36] Give my love to all of Uncle H[arry's] family & the Shuffs when you see them   And write to me at once

Affectionately and lovingly

Your Husband

C. A. B.

Kiss little M[attie] & my M[aggie]
and God bless you both
P.S. Rece'd the flowers, but they had nearly all fallen to pieces, but I appreciated them just as much as if they were fresh for I knew the loving hands that fixed them up. God bless you love for your thoughtfullness, reced them last night, the box had caught all the perfume—Would like to have some of the apples that you have, they are worth eight cents per lb here.   C. A. B.

Charles to Maggie

Hayden Creek Col

Oct 3d 1880

My darling Wife

   I have been intending to write to you for several days, but have been hunting for my horse, and was in hopes that I could tell you something different about her, but can only say that I have not found her, though these old ranchmen assure me that she is not lost for good, that she will come down as soon as the snow stays long enough to freeze her out, but if I could get her now I could get an hundred and twenty dollars for her. You seem to think that I neglect you if I do I dont do it intentionally   You

dont know what difficulties I labor under, Now this morning I am
away from home writing. I call the old shed home—I have to do
so because there is such a racket that I can't write—You should
not be afraid to go on the ranch, for there are as many neighbors
there as here, and better ones, they have been very kind to me—
and then [it] is off the road from tramps, and at an easy distance
for my practice, and then I will know how to appreciate home and
family more than I used to—I feel that I never want you out of
my sight, any more, and I am certain that I shall never leave you
any more, dont be uneasy about the Dinkels they cant harm one
for they have very few friends, and there is no one but Jim that
are enemies of mine   Bill [Myers] is a good friend, old Black
Bill[37] has lost a child by their treatment of me, he employed the
old Irish Dr[38] untill his child was nearly dead and then some of
my friends went to him and told him if he didnt send for me it
would die, and he came in a very humble way, but when I saw
the child I told him that it could not live that it was too late for
me to save it and I think I could have saved it if I had had a
chance. Jim is off on a hunt. The man from Canon City is an
Englishman by the name of Corson. The way it came that I lost
my horse was this   I had her in pasture and the fence got
knocked down, and the mare got out, and strayed into the
mountain. My health is as good as it has ever been, better than it
has been for five years. I have been writing to Wight and W.W.
about money for you, but have none my self   expect to get some
soon and will send you some. You had better get all the early
varieties of seeds that you can, especially some of that corn that
your pa had, late corn will do no good here, but that will—snaps
and peas pay well—We are just having some of the equinoctial
storms. Have had two snows one the mountains and one in the
vallie but did not last any time there is snow on the mountain,
that fell last night, but it is bright and warm in the vallie   there
is no freezing here yet to amt to any thing. The P[ost] M[aster]
handed me a card that you sent him, saying that he didn't think it
was worth while for him to write, for you would certainly get
some of my letters. I write but you fail to get the letters but I
cant see how. Would like to write more but I would like to get
this in the mail this morning. Kiss my little babe and tell her how
papa loves her, and kiss your self a thousand times for me and
God bless you both for we must trust in him for all our future.—
give [final section of letter torn]

Charles to Maggie

Hayden Creek Col
Oct 10th 1880

My darling Wife

I am so sorry to write you bad news. I would have answered
your letter sooner but was waiting to write you some good news
but I rece'd a letter from Ma last night telling me that they were
not able to buy the ranch, and that they were sorry that they had
mentioned any thing about coming out here. Well I am satisfied
that the practice here will not pay enough to pay me to stay and
I will have to leave. there is a friend of mine that wishes me to
go up to southern Arizona[39] with him, and offers to pay my way if
I will go with him. He is one of the smart men of this community,
and has an invalid wife and a family of small children. His name
is Rogers is from N[orth] C[arolina]. He will have some money
and I think he wants me to clerk in some sort of business for him.
I will go with him, and if [I] see that I can't make it then I shall
come back to Va. From the reports of various men that have been
there the country is a good one far better than this. If I could
have had the money to start on I could have made money but I
cant start on nothing. I am going there and if I can't see a better
out look I shall start back as soon as I can get money enough to
get back on will not start before two weeks or the first of Dec.
The country is warmer than this but we have had very little cold
yet have had two snows, that layed on the ground about 3 hours
and we are having some today but tomorrow will be bright and
nice. It hurts me more than you can think that we are
disappointed in meeting soon but my love bear the burden that is
placed upon us and the meeting will be sweeter when it comes. I
shall raise some money and send you in about ten days. You need
not fear any Indians. Where I am going there is no danger of
them. It will not be so healthy there as it is here but it will be
the better for us. Keep up a good heart and pray God that we
may meet again soon   Oh! it hurts me so much to write this
letter for I know that it gives my darling pain, well if I don't do
some thing there I shall come home—there are a great many
people leaving here and going there. I am afraid the mines will
not turn out well in this place and [letter torn]

You shall have enough money to buy your board. the horse will
not cost me any thing as Jim D[inkle] is anxious to get her back,

and run the risk of getting her so when I leave here I will leave out of debt. Kiss my little lamb and tell her her papa is just crazy to have her and Mama with him. Write to me soon lamb for I am awfully discouraged and want to see you both so much.

Give my regards to all of Aunt Mary's family and all friends that may inquire for me. Sadly but as ever

Affectionately Your Husband
C. A. B.

Charles to Maggie

Hayden Creek, Col
Oct 21st 1880

My darling wife

Since I wrote to you last one of my friends, a Mr. Love from Philadelphia, insists upon my going to Kerber Creek about forty miles from this place. There are some very rich mines discovered there and men are flocking there and a city is being built. By next summer there will be ten thousand people there. He says that he will board me and help me all he can otherwise. He bought a mine there that cost him sixty thousand dollars and he expects to put up the smelters. All the men are anxious that I should come.

Would have written you several days but have been waiting to get some money to send you and think I will be able to send you some more soon. Love says that he will see that I have a lot to build on and if I am able as I think I shall be to save all the money that I make I will be able to build on it soon. Then I will send for my loved ones. Be brave, my love, and bear this disappointment for you know I was not to blame. You had better direct your next to Bonanza City, Saquasche County, Col.[40]

It is getting late and I must lay over tonight.

Good night.

My mare does not cost me anything. Jim D[inkel] takes her back and runs the risk of finding her. the mail goes out early this morning and now I will have to close early. I am weighing more than I ever did in my life, 157½. Will enclose ten dollars ($10.00) today, hoping to be able to send you some more soon. Have myself warmly clad. Will send my little babe a silk scarf. Oh, but I'm anxious to see you all, my loved ones, but God will help us in due time. Be patient, love, and don't give way under this blow. It is hard but we have no other chance but to bear it. If there is any letters come to me after I leave the Post Master will send them to me and I will write as I get fixed. Write to me soon, love, for I need comfort from my dear wife. I am pretty sure that my going over there will shorten our separation. Give my love to the family and cheer up. God bless both of my loved ones and protect them is my prayer. Write soon.

Your husband, C. A. Brown

Charles to Maggie

Hayden Creek Col
Oct 21st 1880

My darling Wife

    I rece'd your letter tonight. I wrote two this morning one to you and one to our lamb. Darling just please let me have a chance at Kerber. If there is no chance there I will write to old Mr. Baylor and get him to help me to come back. But I have great cause to believe that we can do well there. I have given up all idea of going to Arizona   If I can get a town lot then we can build there and make some thing   there is as much excitement about that place as there ever was about Leadville and better mines. All the miners want me to go there. Come my darling cheer up if I hesitate about coming back it is because I dread to come back untill I know that I cant do any better here than I can there. Write to me soon and tell me to stay awhile longer. But if you insist upon it I will come. God bless you and my babe

Affectionately
Yours
C. A. Brown

Oh! How I wish to see you   I have sent Reg[istered] letter with ten dollars and another with handkerchief for Mattie.

Affect—Your Husband
C. A. B.

Darling if I did not love you so I could stand our trouble better—

Charles to Maggie

Bonanza Saguache Co
Col
Oct. 28th 1880

My darling wife

    I have been here for two or three days—and would have

written sooner but have been fixing up to keep the cold off. They all seem anxious for me to stay and if they can make it pay me enough I will but if not why then I will work hard and get enough to come home on and leave for home—There is an old man here says that I must stay, & he will build me an office and give me a town lab, and that he has plenty to eat and that I shall stay with him. He is an <u>old batch</u>, and can do well for us, and I think he will, but I am so anxious to see you that if things dont look well soon I shall come back. You don't feel our separation any more than I do, but oh! how much I dread poverty all my life but I love my wife better. And if I dont make some thing soon—I shall come back to my loved ones. This place is destined to go ahead of Leadville, but money will not compensate me for the seperation. Everything seems to be alive here. I can hardly write now because there are two or three carpenters at work in the house and they shake me so. Take comfort dear wife, don't give way, for you will see me soon either here or in Va

Write me here via Villa Grove—and if you say come home I will work hard and get money to come home on. Try and see old Mr. B[aylor] and see what he will do [about money].

Will write soon again—did you get the reg[istered] letter?

Affectionately
Your Husband
C. A. Brown

Charles to Maggie

Bonanza City, Col
Nov 5th, 1880

My own Darling

I received two letters last night and will try to answer all your questions. You had better keep the nice clothes that you made for me as I will have plenty and those will keep for another season.

I have just gotten me a lot that will cost me no money at all. The town company wants some one who will take care of their books and have given me a nice lot that I can get water on very easily to take care of the books. When the lot is paid for they will pay me for keeping them. The lot will be worth from three to five hundred dollars next summer. Will not rest until I can get one or two more. My board is costing me nothing and I am making some money but I have not received any yet.

Jim Dinkle never helped me that I know any thing of but he has cost me the loss of a whole summer. I worked for my board, and more too, and got no thanks and I left him when he did not want me to leave. As for Ben Myers, he knew that he was writing a lie. When he came out here J[im] D[inkle] hired him to work for an old negro partner of his at twenty-five dollars a month when others were paying thirty-five to fifty dollars. That looks like J[im] D[inkle] would help any one. After Ben wrote such a thing about me, he has had the impudence to ask me to get him a good job here. There is no one that has any respect either for Jim or Ben at Hayden Creek.

Of course I want the pictures. It will be too cold for you to come to this place this winter. Night before last the temperature was 15° below. Oh, but I must say that I did not suffer as much from the cold as I have in Virginia at freezing. It may have been that my heavy flannels protected me but the wind here is very dry.

I expect that I had better save all the money that I get and build a house. I expect that it will cost me about two hundred dollars. I wrote to C[harlie] S[huff] about that gold machine and he will work up the thing at that end and I will get the thing here so that we can both make some money by it and cost us nothing. And the parties that take hold of it will make some too.

Carpenters get four dollars per day here and have all that they can do. Houses are going up fast. the town is twice as large as it was when I came.

I will try and send you all the money that you need. Tell Mat[tie] that Papa came very near sending her a pair of kid shoes for winter but they were too high. It is high time that you had a good pair. Please go on and see J. B. Evans and ask him what he will charge me for a box of the tobacco per lb. such as I used to get from Dave when I was out at West V[iew]   there are several men that wish to send with me and by clubbing in we can get a box. it is not often that I smoke cigars but I don't know how you found out that I did.

Give my love to all, and if I could see you I think I could give you a big hug now. I long so much to see you. Kiss Mat and your self and write soon to your

Affect. Husband,
C. A. B.

Maggie to Charles

Staunton [Virginia] Nov 7th 1880

My dear

I will not be [letter torn]
have been so glad to have gotten a letter from you to answer
today. Have written three letters to Bonanza, but have received
a reply to none. Hope to get them soon though. I was dreaming
about you all night last night   do so often, but am so [letter torn]
as last night. We have been having very nice weather so far two
little freezes. Yesterday & day before were like summer days but
raining. The Ohio river is running now so the boat can run. If I
hear from the parties I have written to about the money to come
on I would like to come with Mrs. Eskridge[41] who is going some
time between now and Christmas. So if you find it will pay you to
stay and can make us comfortable I would like to come for I do
wish to see you so much. Dear send me a lock of your hair and
whiskers in the reply to this soon don't forget it. I have on the
dress Fannie Wynant gave me. Can I use calico in winter there?
is there any danger of Indians there? Aunt Mary has taken
Mattie and gone to a neighbors an all is very quiet   she is the
light and life of any house I go to. Sometimes I think if you could
just see her. When I came here the middle of May she measured
28 in. now she is 31 in. tall,

Nov 9   This morning my dear Charlie and I received your letter
of the first last eve C[harlie] said he will write to you and see
what he can do but he can't see any money in it [a gold machine
proposed by Charles Brown for Charles Shuff to go into
partnership on] Now dear of course that man will tell you there is
money in it he wants to sell. But look at pa, A. M. Jordan and
James Calhoun if you wish to see pattern right buyers then look
at Wm Shuff James Margins of Staunton both started out on
nothing   now Dear I don't object to you seeing about it but
please dont spend any money if you have any I would rather keep
it and add to it by degrees than run such a risk now I say no
more   expect I have incurred your displeasure, but cant help it.
Pa came to see me yesterday will tell you particulars in my next.

I am sorry you cannot find a country to suit your health you
know if your health was so good there it was good for anyone you
said "Just let me go I would not ask it but for my health's sake"

and that you knew you could make it after you got there   you
have been there 7 months the 5th of this month and what have
you to show for it if you have any thing keep it   do you think
that man is a better friend to you than I am or than he is to
himself? no! he is not   no one is that. I bought me a pair of shoes
out of that money you sent me and I will keep 50cts for postage
the rest I will hand over to Uncle Will for board as my month
was out the 5th of this month   you do not say whether you have
gotten any of my letters yet or not. If [it] suits you do as you
please   we will never be any better off until you settle some
place but when oh when will that be. do not spend the last
hundred dollars in that machine, if you do no one will help you.
V[irginia] gold is at the point of the plow share. This is not
Colo[rado] I don't know when Charlie [Shuff] will write   he is not
so easily duped or taken in by every excitement. Do not get mad
for I love you and don't want you to go blind   write soon.

Charles to Maggie

Bonanza City Col
Nov 10th 1880

My Darling
    Your letter of the 3d came to hand last night and was truly
glad to get it. I am always so glad to get your dear, kind letters.
I will try and write to you often. God bless you, you are a good
and loving wife and I am anxious to do something for you. Yes, I
think I had better remain here this winter and by spring I will be
able to have me a comfortable house for which I already have
twenty dollars and the lot. The house that I am staying in is a log
house with an earth floor and roof something like that house that
Jim B. lives in. I am living with Love and he is just as kind as he
can be and tries to help me with all his power. If I need money
he will lend it but I can get along without that kind of help. He
told me that I could have it and I told him that I didn't need it
for I know that he has places for all that he has. I like this place
more than I did Hayden Creek. The men seem to be more
generous and all anxious to see me do well, and anxious for me to
stay. Love was one of my friends from Hayden Creek. I treated
him there for rheumatism and he thinks I am a first class doctor.
    I lost my first case here, a little girl about five years old with
Typhoid Fever, the first death in the place. I worked with all my

might to save her but I could not. I was talking to her mother about you coming out but she thinks it will be too cold for you to come this winter, that it would be better for you to come in the spring and then you would become acclimated before fall. If I am not very much fooled I will have us a comfortable, if not a fine, house by next spring. We do not want any thing fine in this country.

Do not forget the tobacco for the tobacco that we get here is so sweet it makes me sick. Suppose you get a small piece and send me by mail so that I can tell if it is the same that I used to get. There are several that wish to go in with me and I would like for them to see what kind it is.

I have kept the bed clothes very well considering the life I have been leading. Had two blankets and a quilt washed twice. The comforts need it but otherwise they are all right. Just saw your inquiry about Indians. No there is none. I never hear as much about them as you do there.[42] Silver Cliff is about ninety miles one way and sixty miles another from here. I know some of the people there   The money that I sent you I got from a young man of that place.

Expect that I will see B[rook] E[skridge] in the spring.

You would not be more delighted with a sweet kiss than I would. You don't know how I do long for one. Kiss my little Matt for me and don't forget the pictures. Give my respects to all my friends and thank Mr. B[aylor] for me   Would you like for me to send you some small samples of ore from some of the mines? I wrote to Uncle Harry. Write soon to

Your affect Husband   C. A. B.

Charles to Maggie

Bonanza City Col
Nov 18th 1880

My own Darling

Your letter of the 7th received last night and was truly glad to hear from you—but you seem to misunderstand me about the placer machine. I dont propose that Charlie and myself put any money in the thing at all. the plan is this. The right to work the state is an hundred thousand dollars, now the way that all stock companys manage is to make stock of the whole [writing blurred] and add enough for working capital, make the stock large enough to sell considerably below par. Now I propose that we put the stock at two-hundred-thousand dollars, and put it on the market at fifty cents below par—rather, fifty per cent below par. Then that will give us an hundred-and-fifty thousand dollars. Take of that an hundred thousand for rights and twenty-five for working stock and we will have twenty-five left which we can make into stock or shares. Now if the gold diggings in Colorado are worth any thing at all, it will make a big profit for I know that the machine is a success here and stock sells at twenty-five per cent above par. All we have to do is to work the thing up. As far as I am concerned I can make stock here. I have but little money yet but I think that by Christmas I shall have a comfortable home on my lot. I had to pay five dollars to put a fence around it. It will be worth from two to four thousand dollars next summer. The land to build on is so scarce here among these mountains that the lots will be high and every one seems to think so for lots are getting very scarce now. Some are already selling for an hundred dollars. By next fall the town will be three miles longer, and from that to five. It is growing very fast now, and must grow faster next summer.

There is not a particle of danger from Indians here. There is a wide range of mountains between us and them, something like two hundred miles and the Indians were never known to bother a mining camp as long as this. They are afraid of the prospectors when there are so many. There are thirteen families here. They expect to remain and next spring there are plenty of these men who will bring their families. From what I can see I am gaining in favour with the miners and if I get their favour I will keep it for it is not easily lost.

Love's mine is, or will be, when developed, the largest silver mine in the United States. It is twenty two feet across the lead— and the average value of oar is $45 per ton now and when he gets in deeper it will be worth double that.

My own and best of wives I do so long to see you. I do think that you are the best wife I ever saw, but darling you will get your reward. God will bless any one that is so true and good, when we get together I will compensate you for your goodness You asked me to send you a lock of my hair and beard   enclosed you will find it. Some of the under part of my beard & I hardly knew where to cut the hair from over my ear tho as that is about the only place, that I can spare it. Darling the trip will be awfull

cold out here this winter. There is forty miles by stage to travel
and so cold. It has been snow every morning except one for a
week here but I do not suffer from cold as I did in Va. But if you
are willing to stand it I think that I can have the house ready.
Who do you expect to get money from? Would like to see little
Mat so much. How much does she weigh now? Does she seem to
think much of the Handkerchief that papa sent her? Kiss her for
me. Wages are all very high here. Carpenters from four to five
dollars per day other work from two and a half to three dollars.
Bread at a good sale for ten cents per pound loaf—restaurant
meals at fifty cents.

There is an old Virginian here from Lynchburg that wants me
to go out for two days to hunt oar, or what they call prospecting.
I will go for there is a good chance of us finding some thing and
then I wish to kill a bear to make little Mattie some furs. There
are some snow white rabbits here with feet as big as your hands
that they walk on the snow with—they are all up above timber
line where the snow is.

Write to me soon all tell me all the news—and would it not be a
good idea to send me a county paper now and then? it will only
cost a cent to send it and if it is old it would be new to me. Give
my regards to all my friends—and kiss yourself and the babe an
hundred times for me.

Affectionately   Your Husband

I write often it is strange that you dont get the letters. Have
written 6 or 7 letters since I have been here.   CAB

Charles to Maggie

Bonanza, Col.
Nov. 21st, 1880

My own Darling

I have not received a letter from you since I wrote last but I
will write to you by this mail because I am longing to see you and
when I write I feel as though I were talking to you. And then I
feel more content.

My lot is all secure and I have some money ahead to build with
but some of the men tell me that it will cost me about two
hundred dollars to build. I think that I can do most of the work
myself and save most of the two hundred. It has been very cold
here since I wrote last. It began growing colder the day that I

wrote, and it has been getting colder than I ever saw it—from twenty-eight to thirty-three below zero, but I didn't suffer from the cold. I get right cold in bed about daylight.

They have been striking some very rich ore here lately, some of it running as high as forty-three-hundred-and-fifty-six ounces per ton (4,356) A man would get rich on that if he got enough of it but everyone seems to think there is not much of it. An ounce of silver is just one dollar after cuts.[43]

I long so much to see you all that I shall make everything count until I do see you, but I'm afraid for you to come until next spring. Think Brook Eskridge would do better here than at Silver Cliff as this place is in the ascendancy and that declining, or at least, at its climax. There are no mines there to keep up such a boom as she has had and the mines here are good. And if he will come here, you and Mrs. E. could come out together.[41] We will not have any better house than we had in West View but I wish to make it comfortable. Don't forget the tobacco. If I could have you in my arms for a short time I could feel more contented. Tell little Matt that Papa wants a nice little picture. I think you had better have them taken separately because she makes you spoil yours and I am cheated out of the part I love best. Write to me soon and tell me all the news. don't you think I could enjoy a county paper sometimes. God bless my babies and protect them. Present my regards to all the family. My love and kisses to you and Matt.

As ever, your loving and affectionate Husband,
C. A. B.

Charles to Maggie

Bonanza, Col.
Dec. 3d, 1880

My own Darling

Yours of Nov. 23d to hand and was truly glad to hear from you but sorry to hear that you were sick. Expect that it is some ole tooth that is the trouble. Was glad to get the hair for I felt just like I was holding part of you in my hand. Almost felt that I could talk to you. But you know that I don't like for you to cut any of your long tresses: they are very dear to me.

Will enclose a prescription for Aunt Bet. Where is she?

The young man who is staying in the cabin with me went about

fifty yards from the back of the cabin and dug a hole and found
some nice quartz which I assayed and found four ounces of silver
in it.[44]

The weather is very cool here but not as cold as it has been.
There are a great many that are working their mines that are
deep enough to keep out of snow and wind. There is a smelter
being built about three hundred yards below me.[45] Went out this
morning to prospect the mineral but there is too much snow. It
will not be down until next spring. Then there will be a good
chance. Almost anything of that kind will sell well then. And my
partner and myself wish to get all we can by that time. He seems
to be very clever Dutch boy about twenty-two. Love has gone to
drinking so that I seldom see him any more. I never saw him do
this way before. I have done my best to get him off of it but have
given it up as a bad job.

We are boarding ourselves and keep what we find. Have you
heard from Uncle Harry's folks? We have no need of a cat at our
house. There is a white weasel that stays in the house and keeps
the mice and rats away. Weasels are better than cats; they can go
where a mouse can. It is getting very tame. Will run all around
our feet. After a while it will get so that it will not mind us at all.
It certainly is pretty. there are plenty of white rabbits here that
have snow shoes as big as your hand that walk on the snow with
in the winter. Wish that I could be with you today. I do so wish
that I could sit down with you and have a real good time. I think
I could take about forty good kisses just now without stopping to
take a breath. Kiss my little babe and my big babe and all the
pretty girls, but no boys. Write soon. Tell Charlie [Shuff] no
tobacco [has come] yet. God bless you all and protect you.

Affect. and lovingly   C. A. Brown

Elizabeth Coyner [Aunt Betsy] to Maggie

Colorado Springs Colo
Dec 6 1880

Dear Maggie

I was very much surprised to get a letter from you: you wont
to no if it would be prudent for you to come out hear in winter
with a little child: I will tell you just what I think I will not
advise any one to come out hear in winter; we have had the

coldest wether hear that I ever felt   I dont remember that I
ever saw so much ice in all my long life in November

I have not heard from Charlie Brown since he left Hayden
Creek   I thought he was there yet I sopoes he is froze up: if I
were you I would wait until spring   it is not only could to travel
but it is more neight than day: and if you are like me you will
wont to see all you can: when I ride in the cars I look out the
window all the time I see all that is to be seen: and this time of
the year it is not pleasent to be out for such a long trip: but your
husband will tell you what he thinks about it

And you wont to no if it would be out your way to come to our
City; as near as I can tell you it would be at least forty miles out
the way and that over rough and dangers road in icy times   I
think if you have a warm house and kind friends to stay with this
winter you had better stay until spring: perhaps you and Charlie
can come together and see us:

we have had such a dry summer that the stock men are
discouraged they cant get enough to eat for their cattle and
sheep: We have a great many deaths hear now among children:
Just while I am writing they are caring a little child by our house
to the Semetery the corages are going in front of our house
Diphthearie is very fatal hear: tis true this is a City but is
nevertheless distressing to see the Hears so often all most evry
day   we see it sometimes twise a day;[46] We have a great many
Doctors hear and some good ones too but they cant keep people
from dieing when ther time comes:

I hope I shall see you and your husband some day: I am glad
you had such a good visit at H. H. Wynants   I have had a good
many good visits there before now   Your Grama was a very old
lady   my friends tell me that I may live to be as old as she was:

I wish to tell you about traveling   you are too young to have
traveld much: I have traveld a great deal   it takes money: and I
put a pocket in some of my under cloths near the waist and I put
all the money in that I dont need for the present and when you
pass through a crowd and someone will cry pickpockets you must
never let on that you hear them: At Kansas Citty you will see a
great crowd: I hope I shall see you face to face; your Aunt and
friend

                    Elizabeth Coyner

Charles to Maggie

Bonanza, Col.
Dec 8th, 1880

My own Darling

Have not received a letter from you since I wrote last, but thought that I would write tonight so that it would go off in the next mail. Nothing has happened of any interest since I last wrote except that I showed your picture to two or three men the other night and one of the men remarked, that that was enough to keep any man stripped. It is a common thing for men to drink here and they think it is strange that I don't.

Was digging in our prospect hold today and got out some very pretty looking rock and I think that we will make something out of it. The first one that I find myself, I'm going to name it Maggie Brown. All mines have to be named something and every man calls his mine after something he fancies and the one name I fancy is M. B. Our claim is named *The Little Giant* and we want it to be one too.

Will send you a card that I got from Burnett and you may show it to Charlie [Shuff] and when spring comes we can see better what to do. Two of the machines are at work on the Sam Magil River and by spring we will know what they can do for I will get a full statement of the work. All that we will have to do is to write to the men that hold the placer claims and get them to dig a hole and sample the dirt from top to bottom and see what it will run to the pan—if it runs over an eighth of a cube per pan it will pay to work if there is not over two feet of earth to strip off of the gold sand and if the sample is found good then we will sample it ourselves—of course this ought to be looked into before there is any company raised—Why have I not gotten any picture of my loved ones? The snow is about eight inches deep here and will remain all winter. We are not far from timber line, that is as high as timber will grow on the mountains   the bald tops of the mountins can be seen from my cabin door. There is very little game, the cold has driven them all out. You may tell Charlie that am not in for spending any money on any thing but I think we can make this with out spending any.

Now my love write to me soon and tell me all the news that you can think of & send me a county paper some times. . . . — Kiss my little babe and my big one too. Love to the family

Affect—Your Husband
C. A. B.

Charles to Maggie

> Bonanza Col.
> Dec 13th 1880

My own Darling

Your letter of 4th rece'd last night—But have not rec'd papers, tobacco, or but one letter from Charlie [Shuff]—cant understand it. Dont think it would do any good to put my card in the paper, as every one that is in my reach knows me, and if there was fifty Dr's here and any other took it into his head to come he would do so but the boys all say that I'll get all the practice that there is to do. for they all seem to like me . . . Love and myself are very good friends yet, but I cant stand it to stay with a drunkard. I did my best to stop him and failed. Am very sorry to hear that B[rook] E[skridge] is so sensitive for there is very few men here that call any man Mr. and his name will either be Brook or Estridge with out the Mr. unless he can get up some title to his name   they are great people here for titles such as Maj. or Col. or Capt. General or something of the kind. When he comes I shall invite him to stop with me   I have an extra bunk and plenty of room. And in a week or ten days shall have a log cabin on my lot 12×12 but just to hold it untill I can build one that will be larger and cleaner for you. This will suit for an office but if I am not able to build another we can live in that for a while   there are plenty of people living in just such. Have not written home for some time but wrote to Millie in Miss[issippi].[47] Do not be discouraged will send you some money before long. Expressage is too high to send by unless it is worth more than seven or eight dollars per hundred. If the thing will not weigh more than four pounds and is not Liquid you can send it by mail at one cent per ounce   will do my best not to freeze but had the misfortune to have my ears frozen badly—forgot to wrap them up. They are entirely well now, and I take better care of them now. Who would you sell confections to? There is hardly any thing but men here now. Only six children that are old enough to go to school. Keep all the feathers you have for we will need them here. Would just like to see how they feel. Better to keep our babe at home until she is safe. The flowers are very sweet and nice and I appreciate them. Kiss my little lamb for them and tell her papa never forgets her. Regards to all the family and a thousand kisses for

you and Mat & God bless you both and protect you   Write soon
to your

Affect Husband
C. A. B.

Charles to Maggie

Bonanza City, Col.
Dec 22nd, 1880

My own Darling
   Would have written to you before this week but did not like to
write until I got some money for you. Enclosed you will find
twenty dollars ($20.00) but do not think it will be enough and will
send you some more by the time you leave. Money seems to be
scarce here and is apt to be until work begins in the spring, then
it will be plentiful. You see, all the men here spent their money
last summer prospecting and cant get it back before spring when
the capitalists will come in and buy most of the mines and hire
men to work for them. Then the men will scatter the money right
and left. Have been getting more practice in the last week than I
have had here, but no money. will get some of it in the spring
and will be more able to make more by giving the boys time.
   Will pull some of the noses of those fools who fret you if I ever
get to see them. Darling, I am sorry that I could not send the
money in time to get it for Christmas but probably you will save
more than you could save if you had it. Get my babe something
for Christmas—if it is [not] too late. All that I can send you is the
love that one human can give another. You have been a good,
patient wife and you deserve all the love that man can give but
some of these days, with God's permission, I can show you all the
love I feel this moment. I do so long to be with you and look into
those dear eyes. I know there is plenty of love there for me and I
so long to see you once more under our own roof. Would you be
content under an old log cabin for a while? You shall have a
better one if I can build it by spring but I can't wait longer than
then. The life that I am leading is a very rough one and I do not
enjoy it at all. But money is what I want, and must have,[48] and
as soon as I can get enough, I am going back to old Virginia, and
buy me a good home, and remain there as long as I live. Give my
love to all my friends and special regards to Aunt Mary's family.
Take good care of our little one and try to love its dad as much as

you can for he loves nothing else but you in this world. God bless
you, loved one, and give you a happy Christmas. Write soon to
me and tell me all the news.

Affect. and lovingly, your Husband

C. A. B.

Charles to Maggie

Bonanza, Col.

Dec. 30th, 1880

My own Darling

Your letter of the 18th came night before last and as I had sent
off a letter the night before I thought I would not answer right
away as I was out of stamps. But I forgot that I had some money
coming to me at the post office. My loved one, I begin to see
where I will make some money in the spring and I don't think I'd
be fooled. I have a place for the Maggie Brown now not far from
my cabin. I intend to dig it ten feet deep, that is, my partner and
myself. Then there are two men who will dig it forty feet more
for half of it. That will leave me one-fourth. From the indications
I think we will strike mineral in fifteen feet and it is in close
proximity to four or five of the best mines in the camp. Some of
them stand at from eighty (80) to an hundred (100) thousand
dollars. That, you see, will make our mine sell well and if I can
get enough to start on in Virginia I will come back. But not until
I do, for I see it here. Have you forgotten how to use a weak
solution of sugar of lead for our darling's eyes? You should use
something to act on her bowels, such as magnesia. I think, love,
that we will be as well fixed as M. and J. by this time next year.
You need not be uneasy about me not being true to you, would
rather die than be false to my darling but I think I trust you
more fully than you do me.

The gloves suit me exactly. If you have the time to spare I
would like for you to hook a pair for my partner. He has been like
a brother to me and he admires them very much. I'll send you a
dollar to pay for them. Will send you some money before long
anyway. But don't look for it until you see it. Make his gloves a
good deal larger than mine; about the size of Will Wynant's.

Have not commenced the house yet, can't get lumber. Will as
soon as I get it. It costs money to live here this winter: flour six
dollars per hundred pounds, potatoes from six to seven cents per

lb., cabbage seven cents per lb., and everything in proportion except beef which is ten and fifteen cents. Onions are ten cents per lb. The snow is deep and it costs money to get them here. Besides, all the vegetables freeze on the road. And those who have them have put up the prices. There is about a foot of snow on the ground. It fell within the last two days. Tell Charlie there is money in the grazing business here. More than I ever saw anywhere else. Give my love to all the family and kiss my babies for me. And remember that I love my babies better than anything else in the world. And that I neither drink or run after other women. God bless you both and protect you, Write soon.

Affect. C. A. B.

Charles to Maggie

Bonanza, Col.
Jan. 1st, 1881

My own Darling

I mailed a letter to you last night but today is the first day of the year and I thought I would write. I have been hard at work on the *Maggie B.*—with very good show of getting something but can't say what it will be or what it will be worth. It is sure to bring something. It is not more than fifty yards from our cabin and I can work all the spare time that I have. Some good miners think that we will get a good lead. I really have no news to write you a long letter. I really think that I have a good boy for a partner. He is nineteen years old, has no vices except some times when he forgets himself, he curses an oath. He never asks me to do anything that he can do for himself, is never glum like Jim Dinkel, never blames me for things that I don't do. He and I have been together for two months and have never had an unkind word or hard thought between us. When we go out to work he always wants to do the hardest part. I am beginning to think it would be best to build our house up here because there will be more business done here than below. It is about a mile from Bonanza and near the best mines. If I can sell the lot down there I will for I like this place better. Thus far I have seen no prostitutes in Bonanza but I understand there will be some soon as they are looking for them every day.[49] Wish they would not come for they are the curse of the camps. They are so many of them diseased that they set the men afire and many young man

that come to this country with good health go back perfect
wrecks to remain so for life. You need never fear me having
anything to do with them for if I were single even, I should avoid
them.

Please have the pictures of my babes taken and send them to
me. Get them separate for M[attie] spoils yours. Wish I could see
you both today, then I would be happy. God bless you both and
protect you, If I can get enough to start on in Virginia by spring,
you will never see this place but I am afraid that I will not. I
always hope for the best. I must see you. I can't stand it. Does
little M. talk about me often? Is her hair red yet? You say so
little about her. Where is Cornelius Jordan teaching this winter?
And write me an affectionate letter. And a hundred kisses to you
and Mattie.

Affectionately and lovingly
C. A. B.

Maggie to Charles

West View [Virginia]
Jan 4th/1881

My beloved husband
    I received two letters this en' from Staunton forwarded by
Charlie, I was truly glad to get them told Charlie of a
Reg[istered] letter came for me to give Uncle Will $10.00 which I
suppose he did as he kept all the money which I am glad he did.
Well I was over talking to Mrs Baylor about selling my things
and a bout going to you when Nellie E[skridge] & her aunt Mrs
Churmside who has lived at Rosita or near them for the last 9
years. She says it is better to go in Feb. than in early spring.
Now my own I would like so much to come then so if you can
raise me $40.00 I will come, and it may be I can bring some help
then Dear what you make you can lay up, and I could support the
family well if I could only get 4 boarders.[50] Yes any kind of house
with my good husband with me will be happy home. If I should
come could you meet me at the place the stage takes on
passengers. I am afraid I will have to sell my furnature at a great
sacrafice if I sell it now & if I [am] not able I would just let it
stay here so if we ever came back we would have some thing but
I had thought if I could sell it for enough to get me some trunks.
but I will see what I can do. . . . the measels is at Liz Russels. I

am uneasy about Mattie but hope she will get through all right if she takes them. I am so glad you got your gloves in good time. I will write to Charlie to send you a pound of tobacco as you wished. My husband I do so love [to] read these good letters of praize   I think they come from a kind loving heart. The reason I am so anxious to get with you is because I think I can make your life easier. Everyone says I don't cook like the same girl you left. I do hope I will stand the trip well; and come to you in health. I have rosy cheeks all the time and almost a double chin if I have the money to spare I will have a picture take[n] to send you before I come for fear I might fall off. and if I don't so you will know me when we meet if God will be so good to let us meet in this world. Mrs. Seaford says lay in a good quantity of bread & meat or Mattie will eat you out. She has gotten so plump and fat. I can get along with those miners or any of them and act so as to command respect too: I always have thought I could get along out there. I can't write more now but will write again soon.

Many kisses and a rocky mountain of love. Write soon and often to your devoted wife

Maggie Brown

Charles to Maggie

Bonanza, Col
Jan. 5th, 1881

My own Love

Have received two letters since I wrote before but I have been too tired to write when I came in at night. I have been working on the *M.B.* pretty hard for several days. Began on Saturday and worked half a day and layed by on Sunday. I have been working hard every day since. Have gone in about ten feet and I think we have only to work hard and go in far enough to make it a good mine. We have already got plenty of lead matter and we have only to work hard until we get the land. Will not send the samples yet. May be able to send you some nice ore from it. My partner says if we can make a raise by spring that we'll build a good house and bring you out. He has several prospect holes and proposes to sell all of them and put the money into the *M.B.* He will board with us. I wish to take up several lots here and I think they will bring in some money next summer. I think this will be the best part of the town. I have been talking to several of the

old settlers since I received your last letter and they tell me that
the last of February and all of March is very severe here. This
place is about two thousand feet higher than Rosetta and, of
course, much colder. And then in April I will probably be better
fixed for you. This is a hard country at best and it would be
better for you to wait until the weather is not so cold but I intend
that you shall come then if I'm not able to come back and start
well there. I don't mind the cold here as I did there. Probably I
am used to it, having been exposed to it here more than there. If
I can raise the money to pay her expenses I would like for you to
persuade Anna K. to come with you. You could afford to pay her
five dollars a week and take in boarders. You can get as many as
you want from six to seven dollars per week without lodging. It
is getting so dark that I can hardly write so I must give you a
good hug and a hundred kisses, and some for M. Give my love to
all our friends and take good care of yourself and write to me
soon and tell me all the news. Am writing by guess.

Affect. and Lovingly, your Husband
C. A. B.

Will write tomorrow night.

Charles to Maggie

Bonanza, Col
Jan 8th, 1881

My own Darling

I have not much to write about, but I know that you are
looking for a letter and I'll write if only to tell you of the *Maggie
Brown*. Of course we are not far enough in to tell you of what it
will be but we know that we have five or six feet and we have
every reason to believe that we will have one of the biggest leads
in camp; that is, if the ore turns out to be good, and indicataions
are some of the best in the camp. We have worked very hard and
are in about fifteen feet, nearly all rock. I told Bill Hainins, my
partner that we came under the old saying, "A fool for luck and a
poor man for children." He was the fool and I had the children.
He turned the joke on me and said that I must be the fool for he
had been digging all summer and had not struck anything but
that he had no children (he is only nineteen years old). I have
been after him to dig on the spot that we are on for a month. He
seemed willing but wanted to dig somewhere else all the time.

You see, I really am the discoverer of the lead but I could not do
anything by myself. I am getting so I don't mind hard work
anymore and have just been at it for a week. We did more work
today than any day yet. If I make a good strike before spring you
will never see Colorado as I will come flying home with my tail
up. Then I repay my darling for all her suffering and waiting by a
life of home-staying and affection. You do not know how much I
long for the time when I can take my loved ones in my arms once
more. God be praised, the time seems to be approaching rapidly
and when I think of it I only work the harder. My prayer tonight
is that God will protect my loved ones and show me where and
how to prepare them a home. I have felt that my prayers were
answered often and I feel that it will be now. And I intend to
work hard to improve the opportunity. Oh, I do wish and pray
that I may bring home enough to get us a good home and lay it in
your dear lap, then would I be happy and thank God from my
heart. I do thank him for protecting my loved ones and giving me
health that I can work for them. Write to me soon, Love. . . .
No, I don't get much cold. I'm getting used to it. I don't suffer as
much as I did in Virginia. Of course, you can give Mr. McCorkle[51]
the ore and give him my best regards. Has my little lamb gotten
well yet; you did not say in your last letter.

Affect.

C. A. B.

Charles to Maggie

Bonanza, Col.

Jan 10th, 1881

My own Darling

Just thought I would write to you about the *Maggie Brown*.
The quartz is beginning to have the color of mineral and that is a
very good sign. And if we are not able to sink it deep enough to
get pay ore, why then we will sell a small interest to get money
to run on. There is no telling what it will do. The probability is
that it may be worth thousands, and then it may not be worth
anything. But if we don't work in it whilst we are idle, we will
lose the time and I am getting every day so that I can stand hard
labor better. When I commenced, I could only strike a few licks
and then stop to take a breath but now I can strike a great many
hard licks before I stop. We have gone in twenty feet, and

probably a little more. If I can sell an interest, will send you part of the money to come out on when the weather gets so you can come. But I would have rather come back to you if I can sell for enough it will be that way too, but I can't come back without a good start and I am sure to get it here, in the spring every prospect hole will bring more than it cost to dig them, the excitement over the camp is running high and when that is the case everything sells high, some here in Leadville[52] sold for from fifty to an hundred thousand and they are striking more good leads here than they did there, all of the old miners say that for the amt of development that this is the best camp in Col and some go so far as to say in the world.

You are always asking if I drink. No, I do not, but if I want a glass of beer I go and take it. But that is very seldom. Nothing more. We have a miners committee here to protect each other from what is called "the gang." In other words, bar keepers, swindlers, pickpockets. they all clog together to rob any and everyone. We will not have a drunkard or anyone that hangs around a saloon or anyone that is intimate with saloon keepers. So you see, that if I was drinking, they would not have anything to do with me.

The weather is very cool but our cabin is warm and we do not suffer from cold. we work hard all day and sit up and talk until ten or eleven, or go out to see some of the other boys. We have plenty of covering and enough to eat and if I had my loved ones I would be happy. But sometimes I lay awake from two to three oclock thinking of you   Write soon love Kiss M & your self Affect C. A. B.

Charles to Maggie

Bonanza, Col.
Jan 17th, 1881

My own Darling

Your letter of the 8th came night before last but have not had time since to answer it until now. the tobacco ought to have been here the night before. Did you register it? It would be more sure to come that way. Have just been working on the *Maggie Brown* this ten days and we have struck mineral today. We will have to go some twenty feet deeper to get pay mineral. If it turns out to be good we will have eight feet of lead and that will make it sell

well. And as soon as we get to a place where it looks nice I will
send my box of specimens and I think they will please you. But
some that look the nicest are the poorest. But you know persons
that are not acquainted with the ores will not know the
difference. When we get down about fifteen feet more on the
Maggie Brown I'll help my partner on one of his claims for an
interest in it. I don't think we have far to go until we get to it. I
think the prospect for a home is brightening. I've hired men to
cut the logs for a house. It is impossible to get lumber for any
price. They will begin in the morning at three dollars per day,
which is cheaper than I can afford to stop for. You see Lou Taylor
could make money here. The wages are from two-fifty to three
dollars per day. Grub costs about fifty cents per day. Because of
the snow of which there is about two feet on the ground and from
four to seven feet up in the mountains. I think it would be better
for you to wait until Eskridge comes out for that would be the
time for you to come. They all tell me that they look for a big
snow in March.

They have two drug stores here and I will have to buy very
few drugs so that much will be saved. You ought to see me
sewing up my clothes when they rip. I expect I feel as awkward
as I look. You don't know how much I long to see my loved ones
or how anxiously I look forward to the time when I can go home
or have them brought out to me, but I prefer the former for then
we will have a good home to ourselves. But, darling, we must
leave it all to God. I think my prayers and my faith in His help is
the main cause of my good prospects and I think He will help me
on to the end. If I make a raise here I shall not do as the rest do,
stay here and spend it trying to make more. I shall go to Virginia
and lay it out in a home for my loved ones. And then for two or
three more babies. don't you think so? Give my love to all the
family and a thousand kisses for you and Mattie.

Affect. and Lovingly
C. A. B.

Charles to Maggie

Bonanza, Col.
Jan 25th 1881

Dearly Beloved
    Your letter of the nineteenth to hand. There is no need of your

being uneasy about me going into dangerous places for I am as much a coward about going under the ground as you are. We have stopped work on the *M.B.* and I will sell it as soon as anyone can get in here to buy. I don't think as much of it as I did. Am working on another claim now that promises better than it ever did. there is considerable excitement about it in camp. We have found some very pretty rock that is just like one of the best mines in the camp, but we have not got it in place yet. That is, we have not found the lead and we will have to work hard to find it. But work may develop it and if we do get it, it will be a big thing.

You need not be uneasy about the gang for they will not bother any one if they think he does not carry money on him, and then they will only ask for the money. As soon as the miners find out certainly that that is the kind of men they are, they give them just so long to get out of town. There has been no stages robbed or anything of the kind but we were afraid there might be. We are determined that that shall not be. Don't be uneasy. You need not be uneasy about me hurting myself, or getting hurt. I intend to work hard and get something by spring so that I can come back. Then if we get anything, it will be yours and our children's for don't you know, I might lose it. You are the best wife in the world. I know you better than you know yourself and those that abuse you now can never be friends of mine again. What did your Uncle Henry say? Was it about you, or me? If he said anything to injure you, I'll break his back when I come back. They may say what they please about me, but not about you. I hope to repay you for all this suffering you have had on my account, and them too. Write to me soon for I am always looking for a letter. Give M. plenty of kisses for me and take a thousand for your self. I am, as ever, your devoted husband,

C. A. B.

Charles to Maggie

Bonanza, Col.
Feb. 5th 1881

My darling Wife

You seem to think that I'm spending money here that I should send to you. But you are mistaken. I've delayed writing for a week because I have not had any stamps, nor money to buy them

with. There is a man promised to pay me some this eve and I
depend upon him for stamps. We have put the *Maggie Brown* out
to contract for sinking thirty-five feet. We give the man two-
thirds. The place that we are working on we are offering for six
hundred dollars. The man says he thinks he can sell it this week.
It will not be long anyway until he sells it. If he sells it I'll get
one hundred and thirty five dollars. It may be that he can get
more. If he does, why then we will get more. We have gone in
about twelve feet and worked two weeks on it and got six ounces
assay in silver and a trace in gold. And if we were not wanting
money we could go in deeper and get more for it. I brought suit
on two of my claims and the rest I'll get in a short time for the
mine buyers are coming in and the boys are all beginning to get
some money. Then there will be more practice. I have a good lot
and have the promise of a set of logs and after I get them on the
ground, then I can soon get up the house. And I think I can send
you some money shortly. Send your gloves and I can sell them.
You need not bother yourself about a servant for they are plenty
of them here easy enough. Some of these days those that are
treating you badly will surely regret it for I intend to make some
money here. Yes, if I am not able to bring you out in May, I shall
come back to Virginia. There was a friend of mine here last week
and he told me that he would sell inside of two weeks, that he
intended to give me a good lift for I have been trusting him all
the time because he had no money. He thinks he will get twenty-
five thousand and I have about a hundred and fifty dollars coming
to me at this time. Practice has been very slim. You see, if a man
has anything in this country a doctor can make his bill, something
he could not do in Virginia.

You seem to think that I don't love you. Why, I can't tell.
When you come and see how poverty has compelled me to live
you will then know how much I have loved my darling, for
nothing in the world would I live like this but for my dear wife.
And the prayer of my soul is that I might soon have her with me.
I know that I could make a good living if I had you with me. My
poor little babe, I'll send a prescription for her. If your pa was
here he could make four dollars a day building houses and plenty
of it to do. Write to me soon.

Your loving Husband
C. A. B.

Charles to Maggie

Bonanza, Col.
Feb. 9th, 1881

My own Love

Received two letters from you, one night before last and another tonight. Please don't let that report bother you for it all came from Ben Myers and Jim Dinkel but they are no friends of mine. I would not let them run over me. If they say I'm drinking or gambling, they tell lies for I do neither. I stay home and work unless I have a professional call. All miners are opposed to having any gamblers or drunkards as officers and we yesterday defeated all but two of the barroom set and I think now Bonanza will turn out to be a quiet town.

We have surveyed a new town that adjoins Bonanza and will call it Rolla. It will be the larger town and the boys want me to run for Mayor. I hardly think I will as it will not pay much and will interrupt my other work.[53] The last claim we have been working on looks considerably better than the *M.B.* but there are some miners that think that the *M.B.* looks very well for the depth and I think that when the men work out the thirty-five feet it will look good. You will be able to come out anyway by the first of May for I have a lot and the man is paid for getting out the logs. And I have considerable money coming to me and they all think that in six weeks there will be plenty of buyers in camp. Then I will be able to collect some money and sell what claims I have. I hardly think it is worth while telling you again that no woman can ever come between you and I. Now, I have perfect confidence in you but I don't like to have you go anywhere with strangers for with the report that Mrs. K. started they might think that you were down on me as well as she and say something that I would not like for any man to say to my wife. Though the man you went with treated you all right, the next might not. As he was so kind to you, I will send him some samples. For anyone who is kind to my darling is my friend and I will treat him so. You need not fear that I am making any foolish speculations for if I make a raise, the money goes into a home, for my loved ones. And I will save all I can make. I told you in one of my letters to send all the gloves you can make and I could sell them.

It has been snowing all day but it is not deep. That is what keeps all the mine speculators out. They say that this is the hardest winter they have ever known but I am not suffering from the cold. You are all that I love in this world and I can't bear for you to doubt me, write to me soon and write me a loving letter too, for I do so love to get them. Affect & Lovingly

C. A. B.

Kiss Mattie and receive all the kisses and love the paper can carry for your-self   Regards to the family

Affect   C. A. B.

Charles to Maggie

Bonanza Col
Sunday 13th 1881

My darling wife

Today is Sunday, but do not remember the date and I am alone. There is no news that I could write you except that it is cold and drizzling snow, but the snow is not deep, we have just passed through a thaw that has taken most of it off but it is too cold to work out of doors. There is a man here that wishes me to write your friend at the Univ. and ask him if he would like to have some fossels, he says that he knows where there are plenty of them of all kinds and descriptions. Fossels are some thing that all men that are trying to start a museum want, and all want some thing that others do not have. Of course I do not expect to have any thing to do with it myself, but I may get some thing out of it. There is only one thing that bothers me now and that is that I am so far from those that I love and darling I'll not rest untill I get you with me. I get so blue thinking of our seperation that I think some times, that I'll give up and take a running start and go home, and then I think of how little the chance of starting is in Va that I work harder and with a better will if we can get our town started here all right which I think we will, then I'll have a better chance than ever before. They wish to run me for mayor but I would rather have the police justice place and if I manage right I think that I can get it, there is more money in it, and that is what I came here for and intend to have it. Am getting very popular with all of the miners and there will be no trouble about getting it all that we are here now will work hard for me to get it. And if I get it I also can get the city practice. You need not fear that you will have a drunken husband or one that runs after

other women, for I love my wife too dearly for that, and am too
hard up to gamble if I wished. I never spend money except for
something to eat and for postage and a very little for tobacco.
Tell Charlie to tell me what a box of tobacco that he sent me will
cost there are some parties that wish to send for a box, and how
much there is in the box. If you come out with McCorkle find out
whether he will bring a trunk if not then you can bring two—one
of them on his ticket, it would not be well for him to bring any
thing more than a valice for traveling around in this country with
a trunk is rather expensive. He ought also to have two pairs of
blankets, no matter how he dresses. Over alls are best for his
business, for if he comes to a miner with fine clothes on they will
be shy of him. They are always on the look out for sharpers. I'll
be ready for you when he comes and will try and raise the money
for you to come on, don't want you to [writing blurred] if you can
help it. Kiss my little babe and a thousand for you love and God
bless you both   Write soon

Affectionately & Lovingly   C. A. B.

Charles to Maggie

Bonanza, Col.

Feb. 16th, 1881

My own Darling

I would have written last night but had to go out and now that
I have time, I'll write. Darling, I'm beginning to think that I'll
have a big practice here pretty soon. It is beginning to come in
now. I have been up two nights with women in the family way to
relieve their suffering, and when the time comes, I'll get the
cases. I have three cases on the list for next month. And
probably will have more of the same kind. And, of course, some
of every kind, am getting nearly all of the practice in the place,
altho there is another druggest Dr. in town. There are two drug
stores and the druggests do all they can for me, and when I have
them on my side, you know that they think that I am bound to
get the practice. One of them has just promised me an office in
his store, so you see I can have two offices one up where we will
live and one here, so will not cost me any thing, I have the
cutting and the hauling of the logs for the house paid for, and
then as soon as I can get money enough to get a thousand feet of
lumber I'll put the floor and roof to it, think I'll be able to send

you some money very soon, don't be discouraged there is a man that I think I can sell one of our claims to, and he promised me to come to look at it today, but I am not there and probably he will look at it this evening. All I ask is that my wife have confidence in me, and write me affectionate letters and I can work with more courage, the money must come out of this place, and if I cant get it here whey then I'll come home. You can come by the first of May, for then I'll have a house and some thing to look forward to. If this camp amounts to any thing I am sure to make some money and if it fails then of course I will. Write to me soon and write me all the love in your soul for I do so long to hear it poured out, there is nothing in the world that I appreciate more than I do it. I feel as if it was all that I had in this world, altho, I love my babe, yet my love for her is nothing in comparison to my love for the mother of it. oh! How I wish that I had her in my arms at this time and I think that I'll soon have her there. Ahh wont it be bliss to be together once more? Then nothing but death will part us. I feel that I could kiss that little "tater hole" if it would do any good, to have it back with me. And I think I will kiss the other when I get to it for its so sweet. How is our little babe? Has her eyes gotten well? Does she ever talk about papa? Don't cut her hair off and remember that I will never forgive you if you cut yours off for you know how I love every hair. It does not hurt me for them to talk about me if you don't believe it for there is no truth in any of it, and I don't care who thinks it is so, just so you trust me. Have you heard from Uncle Harry yet? Tell me all the news that you can think of and don't forget me. God bless you both. Regards to the family—

Your Affect & Loving
C. A. B.

J. Woremouth, University of Virginia, to Charles

University of Va
Albemarle Co
Va
Feb 22nd 1881

Mr Brown

My Dear Sir

Yours of the 13th received today. It gave me great pleasure indeed to hear from you.

We would be glad to get specimens of oars or any thing else from a distant State, You speak about paying freight. You had better send them by mail, small ones, unless they were examined by our Prof of Mineralogy a good many might not be worth paying freight on them. We want good specimens of everything we get. All I can say is if you wish to send any thing is to send in small quantities by mail. Large quantities come sometimes but the senders pay all expenses however do as you please, but pay all expenses if you send any.

I met your wife & child a short time ago. We often talked about you. I regard her a very nice lady, and little Mattie is as sweet as she can be, and as old fashioned as any body else.

I did hear that you were a drunkard, and a gambler but, of course I got it from a quarter that everything must not be believed, and I doubted the story when I heard it. I heard some thing about your dear wife from the same quarter. I did not believe when I heard it, let alone after I met her. I dont believe every thing I hear, but of course I did not know you or Mrs. B. I just took the stories for what I thought they were worth. When you hear a tale it all depends upon who tells it. You are a long way from home—I say home I dont think you will make Col[orado] your home there is not much money in Va, but it is as good as any other state to live in. No doubt you look forward to return to your native state, I expect you will say of Virginia what I say of my native Country—"Virginia with all thy faults I love thou still." Give my kind regards to Mrs. Brown when you write I should be glad to meet her again, and if you return soon—or when ever you do return, I should be glad to meet you, hoping you may be successful in the far West, and make money enough to buy a nice house, then return, take your dear wife & child in your barrow to part no more—

Yours truly
J. Woremouth

Charles to Maggie

Bonanza Col
Feb 24th 1881

My own Darling

I mailed you a letter night before last and told you that I would be able (I thought) to send you some money this week, well I just got it tonight, and I will send you twenty dollars in this letter

and hope that I will be able to do better than I have in the past
for things look better than they did   can't tell you much about
the house, but I think that I have every thing fixed, nearly all of
the lumber is paid for if the man will stick to the trade, and I
think he will, and the boys all say that they will help me to build
it. The lumber is ordered, for a house 16 × 20 feet and a seven
foot sealing. Now my love I am in the post office writing and it is
late, so you must not think hard of me for not writing a long
letter but remember that my heart is a great deal larger than the
20.00 bill that I send. Pay your debts, and don't be afraid to tell
me if you need any more money for all I work for is the comfort
of my loved ones, write me a loving letter, and please don't scold
me, you seem to fill your letters with it. Regards to all friends
and love many kisses for you & Mattie; would thank you for some
more tobacco, if you have the money to spare—Write soon to
your Affectionate Husband

C. A. Brown

Charles to Maggie

Bonanza Col
March 1st 1881

My own Darling

Your two letters of the 21st just received and it grieved me not
a little to hear that my little babes eye was so bad, but if Dr. S.
can reduce the inflamation, she is very young, and I think that
the eye will gradually recover.[54] Kiss the little love for me and
tell her how sorry papa is for his babe, and I am truly glad to
hear that my own darling is in such good health, and I think that
the time will not be long before we can be together. I have part
of the lumber on the ground to build the house, but it comes
slowly for it is hard to get hauling done.

Am beginning to get a good reputation, and I think will get a
great big practice. I intend to have a good house if it is small so
that my darling will be comfortable. The women got after me
today and made me get a new hat, some of them told me that
they "did not like to see their Dr. wearing a ragged hat and that
they would recommend a new one." You see I had been wearing
the old one to save expense. I got it at a reduced price $2.00.
They all seem to take a great interest in me, and are anxious to
see the day that I can get my family out. Nearly every one in the

two places are my friends. The children all like me. Wrote to Mr. W[oremoth] & will enclose his answer, seems to be a gentleman.

It has been thawing considerably in the last few days, but this will be the worst month of the winter so the old miners say   they expect some deep snow this month. The building is going on very rapidly, and by next fall there will be a considerable city here there is about three hundred houses now and nearly all of the lots are taken some of them sold at four and five hundred dollars a piece. A store room with twenty feet front and forty feet deep rents at from fifty to an hundred & fifty dollars per <u>month</u>. You see it is important for us to have our own house. The first thing is to get a house and then a bed, and then a stove, and then chairs, we can sit on boxes until we can get chairs   others do it. There are plenty of women that sit on boxes and eat out of tin plates and no one thinks any less of them for it. You will see from Mr. W.'s letter that he thinks very little of Mrs K as to his praises of you, they were unnecessary to me for there is none that know you like I do, but still it pleased me to think that others could appreciate my dear wife but it could not make me think more of her than I do. And those that try to injure you and me only belittle themselves. Now my love always write me just such letters as the last one and think the same way and I'll be satisfied for it does me good . . . Kiss yourself & our babe and write soon to Your Affect H.

                                             C. A. B.

Charles to Maggie

                                             Bonanza Col
                                             March 8th 1881

My own Beloved

I think by this time you have gotten the money, and hope that you have gotten some clothes. For you know that your comfort and hapyness is all that [I] work for and if that is accomplished I am hapy. Well the house is not built yet, the lumber is so hard to get, it is all paid for, and there is about 6 or 7 hundred feet to come yet, the rest is on the ground and the most of the work paid for and the rest I will do myself. The people are beginning to roll in, and I think that the money will begin to improve, too. The houses are going up fast and everything seems to be taking new life. There are more houses here now than there are in

Bridgewater, and you can hear the hammers going all the time and in every direction houses spring up like mushrooms. The carpenters are the men at this time that make the money. Their wages are five dollars per day and all that they can do. The mines are improving and indicate that the camp will not only be a good one but that it will be permanent and the only thing that is in the way of my happiness is my wife and child being so far away from me and when I get them here I'll be fixed. For I long and long all the time for them. Oh my darling you have no idea how much I want you, but I don't think it will be long. When the work on the mines begin, then there will be more money in circulation, and then things will be all in a hustle. No man claims to have come here for his health, but all for money and say that they mean to have it but the only money that is made just now is speculation in lots, and you can not understand that untill you come out and then you will see how it is done, By-the-way I get all the cigars that I want to smoke now and they dont cost me any thing, but I want some of that old Va tobacco badly, it is all sweet here and I cant chew it. I hope by the time that you get this that you will be in B[ridgewater] or rather at Uncle H's   he is one of the truest friends that I ever had and I'll never forget him for it if I ever make a good raise here he will not lose by it. You can tell him if he has any money to invest it would do well here, but he may think that it is too far from home, I bought a lot for ten dollars, and sold it for thirty next day and now it is worth fifty. If I had had a thousand dollars when I came here I could have made five of it by this time, but the fact is I have lost all the lots that I had because I had nothing to build with, but I have one that I mean to hold for I have my lumber on the ground. Kiss my babe and my wife all that they can stand. Love to all of the family. Write to me soon. Your affect. Husband

C. A. B.

Charles to Maggie

Bonanza Col
March 14th 1881

My own Darling
    am so sorry that I can't write something more encouraging about the house but I have not got all the lumber yet, it is so hard to get, unless I have a team on the ground when it is sawed,

some one else gets it, and I cant afford to keep a team there all of the time, but the man promised me today that he would saw most of it tomorrow, and pile it to its self, and when it was done, that he would drop me a card so that I could get it as soon as it was sawed, and that he would mark the pile sold. It seems very hard to get any real nice oar for Mr. Woremouth but I have three nice pieces for him as soon as I get one or two more will send them to him. What did you think of his affection for the old lady? Pretty good don't you think?

The weather has been very rough for the past two weeks, regular old Va March except much colder and the snow is gradually going away altho there was about three inches fell last night, it will be gone by the middle of April and then it will get warm gradually, that is what they call warm in this (8350 feet) altitude, but it would seem dreadful cold to you and I don't know my love that you could stand it before the first of May, but oh I am so anxious for you to come then and I pray God that we will meet by that time. Darling I am beginning to think that I have nothing like the passion that I used to have altho every night I have that old pain, but in the morning there is none of it left, it seems strange to me, the fact that it is there at night, and not satisfied, and gone in the morning.[55] By the way I sent this morning the first edition of the Bonanza Enterprise, printed on job press. What do you think of it? Will send one every week, hoping that you will enjoy them. Do think is strange that I cant hear from you, have not gotten a letter for a week and have written two, the roads must be blocked between us, with snow. Have not heard from the Reg[istered] letter of course you have gotten that by this time. I sent you twenty ($20.00) dollars when you get it don't forget the "Tobac" Dont like the twist as much as the flat hard plug. Oh how I long to kiss those dear sweet lips, "Bab," do you love me as much as ever? I do hope so if I ever found out that you did not love me or was untrue in the least, I think it would kill me. You are all that I work for all that I care for, and I never intend whilst I live to give you up so blindly again. Write to me soon loving kind and affect. writing. Love to all of the family. Kiss Mat and yourself and remember your

Affect & Loving H.

C. A. B.

Maggie to Charles

Bridgewater [Virginia]
[1881]

My Precious Darling

I have put off writing to you, my love, to acknowledge the receipt of the registered letter but I am doomed to disappointment. I got your letter of the first on the twelfth and on the envelope Charlie [Shuff] wrote that he would send the registered letter "tomorrow." It was a week Friday and none has come yet. I was so disappointed when Cousin Jake told me that he had no one that I could not eat a bite of supper although I had made some nice biscuit and fried chicken. I will be so glad when this is all over. I have written to Charlie and will send it directly to him by Mr. Page who is going up in the morning. They are all just as kind to Mattie and me as they can be. I feel real badly about not writing to you more often but I have to get my stamps from Uncle Henry and you see I feel a delicacy about it.

Cousin Jake went with us to town to a conference and got a bottle filled with that prescription for Mattie. It cost twenty-five cents (25 c). Today he got it filled again. He took some of the other himself.

I wore Cousin Mary's cashmere that she gave to Fannie. It fit me real nicely. I met brother Wilson. Tears came in his eyes when he saw me and I could not keep from crying either. The old gentleman has broken so very much.

We girls are in the school room, Cousin Jake has a girl in the kitchen, and Mr. Page has Lee in the parlour. I just feel like crying out, My darling, my darling, if I could only see you. I know at times I am a little wayward, but you are so good and dear you forgive me so nicely. How are you getting along with the house? When you send the money to come out on had you better not send it by post office money order? They all think this is a safer plan. My love, when will that be? I will go with you hereafter through thick and thin, then let come what will. I will have to close and go work out some rolls I have for breakfast. Oh, I wish I had the privelege of doing the same for you.

I wrote to Pa before I came here but have not heard a word from him. That was before I came here. Do write very soon & often for if I wait it means I can write cheerfully to my far away love.

Mattie often starts to "Colonadie" [Colorado], gets Fannie's shoes on and off she goes. Your ever loving wife

M. M. Brown

Maggie to Charles

Bridgewater [Virginia] Mar 23d, 1881

My <u>ever</u> dear husband

I got your ton of letters this eve I was so relieved to get it but am very sorry to tell you I have not gotten the reg[istered] letter yet but as soon as I get it I will drop you if only a card to let you know it is safe. But I was delighted to get your loving letters I do want to come to you just as soon as you can let me for I think we ought to be together. Have you a place from where you can get the money to send for me to come on? (Answer for sure.) I wrote to Mr. Baylor to know if he would help me dispose of my things at West View but have not heard any thing from him don't you know Mrs. Trafod told me that Sam Myers said if I sold my beauro at a sale he would give $3.00 three dollars for it so you can see I don't like to think of selling it for nothing you may say. I will have to go out there before I start and see what is best to do. I will tell you something of Mattie the latest thing is she was in Aunt B's room & wanted to stay but I took her up and started over here & she said "dirty cool room"   I did not understand her & when I brought her in she flurished her hand & said "see dat" there were some dresses on the bed & some things laying a round & it did look some what tumbled up but who would have thought she would have noticed it. Yesterday she told Addie to "hush"   I said "I will whip you if I hear you say that again"   she looked at me and said "Mama you better hush"   I frowned and looked at her then she said "Nussin [nothing] Mama Nussin [nothing] look dare dem pools"   she had piled some up & tried to call my attention from her she is so cute. She is the fondest little thing of the boys you ever saw she often starts to Colonadie [Colorado] I will get the Tobaco as soon as I can & send it to you   where is Billie you don't speak of him any more. Dont forget to get me a few table boarders. I can get me a set of cups saucers plates & some other dishes for $2.00 (two dollars) and pack them in with my feather bed that would furnish a table real neatly   I have been pricing them. You try & get some puffs in the paper about yourself. I have not gotten the papers yet but look for it I will

send you the B[ridgewater] Journal & Register as soon as I get
the money I sent you a letter to Staunton to mail yesterday by a
Mr Page who was going there. How did your mine turn out? Will
you get anything for it? So you have not gotten out of the old
way of "wanting it" at night. Never mind you wont have to suffer
much longer, will you?   Your loving wife & write often so will I
Aff Maggie Brown
answer every question

Charles to Maggie

Bonanza Col.
March 25th 1881

My own Love
   I have not gotten a letter from you since I wrote, but take it
for granted that you have written, and the letters have
miscarried. Well the house is under contract. I am to give forty
dollars for building it and will go and show them where to build
and they will put it right up and then I'll get us a stove that will
cost me forty dollars with twenty pieces. The cheapest that I
have seen (No8).[56] The town is getting a boom and I am
beginning to get a good practice with the prospect in the future
getting a better. Our house will not be a large one but it will (I
hope) be comfortable   Think that you will have plenty of good
friends here. All of my friends are anxious for you to come, one
old lady, says that we must come down to the valley this summer,
and spend a while with her in a visit and I expect that we will go,
for I am afraid that you will find it irksome here in the
mountains, am getting right popular in my practice. And I think
that if everything holds out as it has begun Ill make money here.
Oh! If I could have had a thousand dollars when I came here I
could have been worth ten today   well all I have to say is, that I
have done the best I could, and that was just get along, It makes
all of my friends here mad for me to tell them how Jim Dinkel
has talked about me. One of them that knew Jim says that he
could never get along with any one, that went in with him. Met a
man from Hayden Creek today says that the place is dead, think
that I got away from there in time, I have three of four cases on
my hands now that are right sick one of them is a county case the
county Dr put him into my hands, with the understanding that if
I would take him at a low rate, that he had some thing better in

store for me. He talks of putting up a hostpittle here and I think that that is what he ment. Well my love are you not getting tired of this suspense? You have no idea how much I long to have it ended, and then my own darling we will be happy and Oh! how I long for that day of bliss. My prayers are that we may soon be together am not afraid but that we will get along but if we have plenty to live on and can be with [letter smudged] then all the time I'll be happy at least. Am so much afraid that my <u>little</u> babe will not know me when she does come   Are those dear <u>little</u> blue eyes getting any better yet? If not think that the change will suit her. Mr. Adams one of my friends says that his wife will start about the first of April, and he wants me to go in with him and hire a trap to go to the depot with him <u>to meet our wives</u>, dont you think it a good idea? think that it <u>will</u> cost less and be more comfortable

Have you sent me any tobacco? Write soon to your Affect H.

C. A. B.

Maggie to Charles

Bridgewater [Virginia] April 3d/81

My dear & <u>best</u> of husbands

I received a letter from you Thursday en' and had just sent one off that morning to you & then last week I wrote to West View to see what could be done with my furniture & was in hopes I would hear by today & be able to write you but have not so will write anyway hoping I may soon be able to bid farewell to this mode of communication we can talk to each other. Well dear the family have been very much afflicted with sore eyes   Aunt Beckie has been confined to her room for four or five days with them & cousin Jake left to go to an uncle of "Cousin Beck's" with his sore expect they are swolen shut by this morning. He is as attentive to him as ever. The girls heard today at church that Mr. Nesot Vanlees was dead   he went to church in good health yesterday & was paralized and died that night.

My love I thought I would ask you if I had not better buy me a pair of shoes here before I come out   can get splendid box toed shoes for $2.50; but I have not enough to do that with soon. They are talking of going to H[owardsville] this week if so I will see what I can do for a dress; but you see I have to go up to town on the train & that will cost .75cts. & then if I go to West View I

will have to pay my way out and back from there. & I only have
$8.00 had to return some money to Cousin Jake that he had to
spend for med' for Mattie & then had to pay for Dr. Jones'
perscription and return to uncle H some stamps & bought me a
package of Simmons Liver regulator to keep off those headaches
which it does so you see where it has gone & where it has to go.
oh! I do wish my furnature was disposed of. This morning Neddie
had a hymn book & told me to sing Mattie spoke up & said
"Mama can't sing" I am very much afraid she will be disfigured
for life   her eyes look so much [like] Mrs. Gilkins (you know her
she lives somewhere near Pamas)   The lower lid seems like it is
turned inside out: this morning there was a thick bloody spot on
it but I am like you   hope she will get better with the change   I
did not get my paper last night do you send it or does it come
from the office? I have writen to Charlie Shuff to get him to find
out the correct times I can get a ticket to Poncha Springs. You
said that Man's wife was going to start the first of Ap. I cannot
come you see before the first of May. How far will I have to
travel by stage   I would be just delighted to see you at the depot
when I stop. If I bring two trunks how much will it cost to take
them over to Bonanza   I have very few clothes & think I can get
my feather bed & all I have in two trunks & have them both
checked but will have to pay something extra on one. Can get
two good zink covered trunks for $14.00 that will hold all.

It is a good thing that I gathered the violets last en' for they
are buried under the snow now what will you think when I tell
you cousin Jake & I sat on the same chair this morning. There
was so much room on the chair that he said "I can sit there too."
So down he <u>floped</u>. So you see how it is not me on his lap. No sir!

Hope you have gotten your tobacco. Yes I will have to pay for
that so wont get my dress now but if I have time to get it just
before I leave & have it new. Will try to get this in the mail
tomorrow   Your loving wife

Maggie Brown

Mary Brown [Charles's mother] to Maggie

New Hope [Virginia]
April 14th 1881

Dear Maggie

I received your postal am sorry to say I can see no way to send

for you to Fort Defiance   If I can possibly go to staunton I will
meet you there the first good day after the 25th   it has been a
long time since I ventured that far from home. I have been
feeling badly all winter seldom got out to church   I would like so
much to see little Mattie expect she has grown very much and
has learned to talk; Tell the girls I think they might write to me
if they cant come to see me, would like to see them all and see
Annie in her new home, dear girl I always loved her so much
Mary Ella is still at Tispersville   will not be at home before the
middle of May   It had been three months since Charley wrote to
me and I was feeling very uneasy   could not sleep the night
before I received your postal, poor boy he has a hard time. I wish
you could all get together again. Give my love to the folks there

Affectionately
Mary Brown

Charles to Maggie

[c. April, 1881
Bonanza, Colorado]

My own Love
    I hardly know what to write to interest you. Rec'd a letter
from you night before last with flowers enclosed. You don't know
how much I appreciated them   they reminded me so much of
home and my loved ones. I can only compair them to your
innocence & purity [letter torn]
    No married woman is impure as long as she is true to her
husband, and I have no fear of my loved one being other wise. I
feel perfectly confident that she is true to me, and I [letter torn]
. . . this country that would induce me to be anything else. Did
you notice the article in the paper about me, it was only a joke,
the Editor is a friend of mine, and we are always teasing one
another. I send by todays mail a view of the post office and this
part of main street, my office is in the post office, practice is
improving am getting about ten or twelve dollars worth of
practice per day & I think most of it is good, but am getting no
money just now. Have one house up and it will take about twenty
dollars more to finish it, but hope to be able to build another,
nearer to my practice, the one that I have built has cost me near
two hundred dollars, but I only [letter torn] . . .
that laid up for after awhile I can get more for it, and if I can get

one put up here, I can rent the one that I have up for about
fifteen dollars per month and then I think that you would be
happier down here than up above. There are five Drs in town and
I get more practice than all the rest put together and there is
every show of me holding on to it, if they empty one of the
others, they come back to me. The paper I send you is paid for in
practice. I have it sent every day. It is a daily. The town is
growing very fast and there is every reason to believe that we
will have a large city here, that is something like Leadville—
property is high some of the lots on main street are worth twenty
five hundred $2500.00   You can see from the paper that the
mines are improving. Write to me love and tell me all of the news
that you can think of for every thing is going on well here, and
the goose hangs high, and I begin to feel that I will get some of
that <u>little thing</u> soon. Kiss my little babe and my big babe and
give my love and respects to all of the family.

C. A. B.

Charles to Maggie

Bonanza Col.

April 16th 1881

My own Darling
    I have not been neglecting to write to you, have been busy all
the time and not able to write during the day and no place to
write at night. Oh! how I long for a home that I may go there at
night and rest, but love the home is coming for the house is up
but not quite finished. I have to paper, and seal over head, and
put batting over head over the cracks of the siding. When I get it
done it will cost me about two hundred dollars and then the stove
cost me twenty five and when I get the bed I'll feel that I am
getting ready for you, am laying aside the money for you to come
out on. There is between forty and fifty dollars in the till now,
and plenty more due me, the town is growing very rapidly, and of
course my practice is getting better, did seventeen dollars worth
of practice to day and I think all of it is good, but may lose some
of it. Don't you think that you could get ready to come out where
you are just as well as at S[taunton]? Do not like for you to go
there. They will regret the way they are treating you some of
these days. I don't love them any two well for it Bill Dinkel has
been here for several days and runs after for advice and

assistance, but he don't know that I know that he as well as Jim wrote those tales about me. He can't say anything about me here, he might get his foot in it. I have two many friends here, think he is ashamed of what he has done   he seems to think that I deserve all the practice that I get   has been sick himself since he has been here and came here, he is doing his own cooking, and I don't think that it is much good, he came up and I took him up to the boarding house with me, and gave him his supper   he seemed to enjoy it, altho he had had his supper. Don't you think that Jake could send me some good tobacco? He knows what I like best. Charlie has not sent me any yet. My virtue is all right and I think that it will remain so for I do not care to meddle with any of the women that I see here but I look forward to something nice soon. I know that it will be the best in the world, so I am satisfied to think of how nice it will be and go and jack off. Now don't blame me for I do get awful hard up some times. Get 3 grains of red precipitate and an ounce of lard and rub them well together and apply to the edge of M's eyelid twice a day—tell Fannie that she could get 35 cts for her eggs and 45 cts for her butter if she had them here, milk 15 cts per qt. Write me all the news. Jim Dinkel has returned with his wife and all the appertinances thereunto belonging, consisting of her brother sister and his sister &c   love to all the family[57] And a thousand kisses to my darling wife and babe—ordered the paper to be sent to you every day.

Write soon to your affect Husband
C. A. Brown

Maggie to Charles

Bridgewater   April 24th 1881

My love of a husband

I have written two letters to you in the last week but have burnt both so will now try to write one that I can send right off. I rec'd yours of the 16th last night and it gave me so much joy to read it & to think you are so near ready for me to come. Send the money you have & I will come right on. Send it as soon as you get this for I know you will have it if you have from $40.00 to $50.00 now I know you will have enough for me to come.

I was taken sick this morn' so see, I must hurry up.[58] I will see which is the cheapest rout. I have spent all the money you sent me getting med[icine] for M's eyes, me a dress, M. a pair of shoes. I will need very little more in the out fit a shawl. M's dear little eyes are no better. Will get your remedy & try it. Oh! my love, I want to come & make a home for my darling to rest in and one that he will love to come to.

Cousin Jake took me in his buggy to church today   the rest went in the carriage. He takes me where ever I go. They are all very kind. I shall write to Staunton to find out the price of a ticket but don't you wait to here from me before you send the money. If it will take you away from your practice to come to meet me do not take the time. Just so I see my darling at my journie's end is all I will ask.

I got a letter from your ma. She said she would try to meet me in S[taunton] but if you don't want me to go there I will only go there long enough to get the things I have there. My clock is at Uncle Will's and some other things. I have been receiving some papers, two last week & three letters all come in the same mail. Your ma seems very uneasy about you. Write to her.

There is some such cheap calico at $6^1/4$ cts. per yard at Alamongs, I would like to get some of that. What do you think of it?

Cousin J. & I have just had a tussel over your last letter. He said you always told him every thing. He and Lee are getting ready to go to B[ridgewater] now so I will have to close. You must ever save all you can for I do so long for the love of my dear husband.

Write soon & send the money for if you have accumulated any since you wrote, why you have enough. & remember my condition.

Your most loving wife, M. M. B.

Charles to Maggie

Bonanza Col
May 5th 1881

My own Darling

I expect that you are out of humor with me for not writing sooner but I have many causes for not doing so in the first place I have been waiting to get the money for you to come on. I know that you will say that I said that I had it well so I thought, but it was a case that I had for the county and I am waiting for the draft which will be forty five dollars and I have on hand ten dollars which will make fifty five & then I am looking for a check of fifty in a few days and I wish to send it all together and then I know that you have plenty to come on. Money seems to come in very slow every one seems to be so hard up there has been no sales in the camp yet, but there will be soon and then things will brighten up. The town has grown considerably and you will see quite a town here when you come and my practice has grown too. There are five Drs in town and I get as much to do as all the rest yes twice as much, I book an averge of fifteen dollars per day and at night when I come in I am so tired that I cant write am so tired and nervous tonight that I cant write so you can read it. Am sleeping in the drug store now and can't go to bed untill late and all is confusion so that when I write I have to wait untill all is quiet. My greatest consolation is that when I get my loved ones that I'll have a nice quiet home to go to and rest and have some one to love and care for me. I think that I have my house in the wrong place & will move it down here before you come, probably next week and then we can be together more—I can't see the lines on this paper so [I] just write at somewhere. I am sorry that you did not take our babe to Dr. B. at first for you know that I think more of his knowledge than both of the others—I think that I am going to make money here, made one long trip today that I got thirteen dollars for, that is I got an order for that much lumber some that I will need in my house, and expect that I will have to go there again—

Am going to send Uncle H. a nice present when I get you out here but have not the money to spare now. Give my love to all of the family and tell them that I'll never forget them, for the kindness that they have shown my loved ones. Hope that you get the paper regular, you will be able to see my name in them often now. Did you see the first babe in Exchequer on the third? Now please don't think hard of me for not writing oftener for I know that I deserve it. Good night love God bless you. Love to all of the family

Affect Your H
C. A. B.

Maggie to Charles

Bridgewater [Virginia] May 22nd [1881]

My precious husband

I have not gotten a letter from you since I wrote but think you

must have been disappointed again, so I will write any way.
Although I can't hardly hold the pen steady enough. I never was
sicker in my life than last night & yesterday all day   I thought it
was sick-head-ache. but my bowels run off too   I fainted twice
and threw up 4 times. I blame my cources [menstrual period] for
it   I am sick every three weeks & then so much & so long   I
sent & got some Elixir Vitriol to take a week or so. I have no
apetite atall. do hope the change will be for the better. Mattie is
broken out thick with the measels but I can't make her think she
is sick enough to stay in this room   she is running about on the
poarch an in the kitchen all the time & seems to be so well. The
rest all lost their apetite but she has not. I do hope she will get
through all right

(May 23) I wanted to finish this yesterday & get it mailed in
the en' so it would go off this morn; but cousin J. went in the
morn' in place of evening as usual. They rededicated the
Lutheren church there just had it remoddled will have conferance
there this week. the season is just splended now but nearly all
the corn that is planted will not come up all the people around
that did not take special care of their corn had it so frozen that it
would not come up. One piece of ground here they have had to
lay it off three times & plant. Cousin Hanna & Mr. W. were over
yesterday eve' she always enquires very particularly about you.
She has gained 30 lb since she was married. Mattie is more
fretful this morning don't know what is the matter with her. oh!
my dear darling husband I do want to come to you so so bad & do
little things for my love that I know he wants done & my fervent
prayer to God is that all may come out right that I can come in a
few weeks any way. Be sure to write me where to come to, and
all you can about traveling. If Nellie goes in a few weeks I want
to go so much. Now dear think of me often & know that I love
you ever so much. M. has just come to me with my tooth brush
for me to put some water on it for her to "clean her teef"   she is
cleaning them any way   she is so cute. Write at once love to your
devoted wife

Maggie Brown

P.S. They always send many kind wishes & love to you   I will
add a line more before I send this off our little darling has gone
to sleep & I just looked at her and pushed back the hair off her
head and she looks so much like her dear papa   I just kissed it
and imagined the best I could that it was you   oh! I love you so
so much.

Milly (Mrs. A. B. Gillespie), Charles's sister to Charles

Longtown Panola Misp[59]
May 22nd 1881

My dear Charley

Where are you now and what are you doing? I have not written to you for sometime because my writing time seems to be filled in answering home demands in the letter line. Is Maggie with you now & have you a comfortable home for her? Tell me all about the baby. I hear from home occasionally and often from Willie [Charles's brother] My school here will not close before the 22nd of July. My class is doing right well. I think my health was unusually good until a few weeks ago—I was closely confined in the sickroom of a young lady with measles and much fever (except when at schoolroom) it affected my stomach and I have had very little appetite—since billious & so on.

Dr. Hardy is very attentive and kind to me and I do not lack for any kind of attention. I feel rather dispirited because I am not making as much as I think I ought, at least not near enough to meet the demands upon my little income—but still I know that the widow's God will bless honest endeavor, and submission to his control. Mary Ella [Charles's other sister] is at home now which is a great source of relief to me—for the care of Ellie was too much for Ma. It seems queer to see Spring so far advanced at this time of the year—yet they say things are more backward by two months than usual. We have beets as large as a tea-cup early peas are gone second crop coming our potatoes ready for use & so on. Mosquitoes and fleas are outrageous. Longtown is built in a grove and as there is no running water pools are deep for stock these two causes combined make insects very troublesome. As I look now from my chamber window I see mosquitoes like bees swarming. the soil is very fine   They never use fertilizers. How did you stand the cold in Colorado? I hope you will be able to take good care of your family where you are and to build up an estate besides. Prompt attention to business combined with economy always insures success. No man ever went out into the world around with those two requisites and failed—a few failures stimulate—such as one to persevere until success comes causes effort.

Write to me and let me know all about how you are situated. I have no plans matured for next year—do not expect to go home—

cannot afford it. How glad I would be to see the General
Assembly in session at Staunton. Mary Ella expected to go—I
expect this day (Sunday) is a big day there.

Aff. Yrs

A. B. Gillespie.

Maggie to Charles

Bridgewater [Virginia] May 26 1881

My dear Husband

I have not gotten a letter from you for two weeks today. Don't
you feel mean? I received two of the Enterprises this eve' of the
19 & 20th in them I see you have what is called an enteligence
office   I realy think I ought to be geting the money to go out on.
I do want to come so bad. Don't be affraid that any flattery I
might receive will turn my head (I see the Enterprise is given to
it.) for I am somewhat used to it. I create quite a sensation when
I go to B[ridgewater] but that don't put any change in me for my
husband don't care any thing for me & what need I care for what
others say about me. My dear I said today to F[annie] if you
could just come up to the turnstile and see Mattie going accross
the poarch on a stick horse to see "papie" with her head reared
back and the little golden (not red) curls shining you would just
eat her up. I tell you in a few years she will be a head of us both
for she is so quick now. Today we were in here the "school rooms"
& she came in from the kitchen & knocked on the door & said
"Opie door" I let her in & she did something wrong when I
reproved her, she said "I want go to Kitchie   Beckie want me."
then answered "who! well!" just like Aunt B. was calling her. I let
her go after that cute trick. The other night she slaped me & I
said "why Mattie" she [said] "nussin" then saw me look cross she
said "I pattie you Maggie" I do think she can turn things off the
cutest I ever saw. Dug & I are talking of going to Staunton
Saturday if we can get the buggie. Will come back Sunday eve'.
They all think Dug will cut Charlie out   I don't <u>think</u> he will do
that but I do like Dug so much have given him Mattie. They
tease me very much about her liking the men so much say she
takes it from her "mama." I will finish in the morn' then will be
able to tell you if I can go to S[taunton]   I don't think we will go
to S[taunton] tomorrow as Willie came home unexpectedly a few

hours since & will only stay a few days   I don't know when I will
go now. Write to me often if you have not the money to send me.
     Much love from your ever affectionate wife
                                        M. M. Brown

Charles to Maggie

                                        Bonanza Colo
                                        June 5 1881
My own Darling
     I am so sorry to say that I failed to get the money to send for
you but do not think it will be long. It discourages me so much,
the house is all right all but the carpet and chairs, and that will
be very easy, money is dreadfully scarce here at this time. The
mines are not being worked at this time and no one seems to
have money but there are some good sales being made and when
men of money get hold of the mines then there will be money
distributed. there are men going off every day that are owing me
money and I canot get it but darling you may depend upon it as
soon as I can get the money you will get it. Our house is sixteen
by twenty feet square, with two windows in front and one door
between and one door at the end to the left as you enter the front
door, the windows will require curtains two by five feet. Will put
a cloth partition on the right for a bedroom but will do that when
you come   will get a tent to put in the rear for a kitchen, have a
first rate cook stove and a nice little heating stove for the sitting
room, you may think the heating stove is useless but the nights
are always cool. The house is on a hill over looking the town of
Bonanza and the only objection that I have to the place is that I
will have to have all the water hauled until we can have a ditch
made to convey the water to the lot and there will be several to
help do it is one of the most quiet places in the town. It is going
to be the place for private residences, there are some here now
there is such a hubbub in the business part of town that you
would be scared all the time. All I want is to have my loved ones
with me, and am not afraid of any one spoiling her by flattery,
have two much confidence in her. I get awfully discouraged some
times but always pray to God to help us to get together soon.
     Billie is working our mineral claim as hard as he can and hopes
to strike pay mineral next week and it may be that he will have
to go still deeper, but we have two claims that I think more of

and as soon as he gets mineral I think that I shall send him to
work on them. He is one of the best work men in the camp. And
I think one of the best boys in it. Oh! Darling if I only had you
with me I should be so hapy, and do hope and pray that I will be
but a short time, we could live on what it cost me to live and
then we would be so much more hapy. Tell our little one that
papa does want to see her ever so much. You say that you love
me ever so much you can't love me more than I do you. I think
that there is no other woman in the world as good and as sweet
as my darling babe. And if Dug, ever wants to come out here it
will not be long before I can help him, wages are good here when
work can be gotten, and I can always get it for my friends. I
shall try and write oftener have been waiting for the money and
put off writing, thinking that I would be able to send it, Write me
a sweet letter darling just like some of the last they do me so
much good   Love to all and a kiss to you and M.

affect. Yours C. A. B.

Charles to Maggie

Bonanza Col
June 23d 1881

My own Darling
   I have been feeling pretty good this evening. I had to send for
a draft so that I could send you the money and had to wait untill
I got it, and did not like to write untill I did get but now I have
got it and will enclose it   Money is very hard to get and I was
afraid that I would not get enough to send you but when you
wrote that you had part of it I was surprised. The town is getting
awfully dull because there is no work being done and the most of
the people are leaving town, but there will be plenty here after a
while for the mines are good and they will build it up, but we will
have to live awfully close for some time, but it will have to come
all right after awhile, if our house is not furnished nicely it will be
comfortably fixed. I am truly glad that our babes eyes are better
for I think the change will cure them, but how did you get the
money? We will have to pay it back as soon as we can. I [will] not
forget the person that let you have it. Oh! I am so glad that you
are coming at last. But now I must tell you how to get here—in
the first place try to get a ticket to Mears Station D.&R.G.R.R.
[Denver & Rio Grande RailRoad] and if you cant get that get one

to Salida on the same road, and if you cant get that then get one
to Canon City and when you get them get one to Mears Station,
and when you get there, there will be hacks coming to this place,
and I shall tell the men to look out for you, for I will not be able
to go myself and if your trunks cost too much on the hack send
them over by freight wagon and if they wont let you fetch all of
your trunks through on your ticket send it by freight and get a
receipt for it. You had better fetch your lunch basket with you for
every meal will cost you 75 cts on the road; when you get to Kas
City your ticket should take you via the Santa Fe road to Pueblo
[Colorado] and not by Denver and then you would touch
Cincinnati, St. Louis, Kansas City, Pueblo, Canon City and South
Arkansas, and Bonanza where you will find one of the most loving
pair of arms to meet you that you ever saw and they will always
remain so, for I think that you are one of the sweetest little
wives that ever lived and when you come I can swear that I have
been true. You will find that this is very rough country tho and I
am a little afraid that you will not be satisfied but we must make
a raise in this country some where before we get back. Try and
get here by the twentieth of next month and I will be ready for
you then, and I think that You will be ready for me by that
time.[60] Start on the fifteenth and you will make it then. Write
three days before you start and tell me when.   Affectionately &
                                        Lovingly
                                            C. A. B.

Maggie to Charles

                  Bridgewater [Virginia]   June 26th 1881
My dearest & best of husbands
    I received your sample of ore & letter Thursday night was so
glad to hear you had everything in readiness for me & $50.00 on
hand know when you get my letter of last week you will send the
money for me to come on. . . . If I get the money any way soon I
will start today a week. Cousin Jake & I were at Mt Crawford
yesterday went in his two horse buggy he passed me off for a
young girl. . . . My darling if you have no engagement (now mind
if you have none) I would be so glad for you to meet me some
where on the road   I don't mean this side of Cannon City   Get
Billie to have the house warm for us I want him to board with us
& would be so glad (after I come) if he would build a cabbin near

our house so of nights when you go off and stay so late he will be near enough for a protection. This is my greatest dread to going out there staying by myself so much then after being here where if I am sick they wont leave me by myself at all   I tell Fannie she is spoiling me. They all think Charlie is a great fellow & I don't contradict them for I know he is one of the best & dearest fellows I know I go about a good deal & no body comes up to my old darling & I want to see you so so much I don't think if you wanted to see me near as badly as I do you you would   I wont say it for I know you do nearly I am almost willing to have a boy for you but if I start Monday I will be clear of all & I don't want to get in "that way" [pregnant] at once. . . .[61]

Your ever loving & devoted wife
Maggie Brown

Maggie to Charles

Bridgewater July 4th 1881

My own darling:

I wrote to you today telling of our babe's sickness but I must write to you again for I feel that if you are not here or we there we can be some comfort to each other. I fear that we will soon be alone, & no babe. Oh! the thought chokes me. She is my companion as well as child but, dear, the omniscient one may take her to save her from future trouble. Now, if she dies, she is safe. She was rashanal a while this morning but looked so pinched and thin when the fever was off that it distressed me so I just exclaimed, "Darling, are you going to leave your mama?" She looked up & said, "No, me leave you—be back in a little while."[62] About sundown last eve she commenced passing blood and slime. Now, this is 1 o'clock the next day and the discharge is like that of a rotten boil. Uncle H. thought I ought to have her baptized so I did. Mr. Lose came up & did it. I saw Mr. Wilson at a conference but thought if we could raise her right until she was old enough to choose for her self, would let it a lone but as it is I had it done & feel better satisfied. None the less do not give up for I will not leave a stone unturned to save our babe, & if she has to go I will fly to my only love with all speed. But, Darling, let us hope for the best. Others have to lose, we must too. Darling, bare up, I have good kind friends to support me. I will pray for you. I tell you this so you may be prepared for anything that may come. I am trying be become resigned but it is only trying, I fear.

Cousin Jake has gone for the Dr. again, this will be twice he has been here today. If he comes I will get his candid opinion & tell you. The Dr. says the symptoms are against her recovery.

Be of good cheer is all I can say; it is for the best, be as it may.

Your loving & clinging wife,

M. M. B.

Maggie to Charles

Bridgewater July 9th 1881

My own precious husband

I received your invitation & card last eve' it just showed how far off you were   the difference in our feeling on the 4th you no doubt were having a nice time (I don't blame you if you did) & I was sitting over the cradle of our darling all that day thinking what a short time I would have her with me & seeing her lying there sitting in pain & I so perfectly helpless to relieve her   the Dr. had dispaired of her Oh! how could I give her up it would not be so hard with you for you have not watched the growth & development like I have   she is so lively so affectionate & so smart can say one verse of "Twinkle little star"   she is the image of my darling husband more especially since she has been sick her eyes & brow & mouth are true to yours. Darling I dont think we can ever be thankfull enough to Dr. B. for his kind and constant attendance to her or how we can ever compensate him: yesterday I told him that & he said "I just want to get that little babe well" but he has given so much medicine. He said when he first came to see her eyes that he would not charge for any thing but the medicine. This morning he said if he could see more moisture about her tongue that he would say she was out of danger some of her passages (most of them) for six days have been of nothing but blood & slime & every hour. If it pleases God to give her back to us we ought to be very thankfull & try to live to please him. I do thank him from my very hearts center that he has been so good & kind as to raise up so many good kind friends I feel so undeserving & will some time murmer but He is good & will forgive. The disease Dr. says is "Typhoid Disentery"   I received a letter from Millie [Charles's sister] told you on a card what she said about the heat   she said I should not take any thing but a valice not a snack basket that toling Mattie & it & change cars after night I would find as much as I could manage. That when ever the cars stoped boys came in with nice milk and dough nuts that was sold cheap that with a cup of coffed occasionally would be all I would want. The Dr. says if Mattie improves moderately that we can go in a months time. I will pay him out of what I have & by that time you can send me some more money $20.00 will be plenty. I will give you a bill of all I will spend that I know of now 1 packing zinc trunk 2.50 1 other $7.50 one pair good button shoes $3.00 1 valice $3.00 1 shawl $5.00 you see it will take all of my ($60.00) but 1.50 cts to buy a ticket to Cannon City. The reason I do this is because if I start with our little delicate babe I want to be so I can make [ending of letter lost]

Charles to Maggie

> Bonanza Col
> July 10th 1881

My own Darling

I have not written lately because I thought that you would not get, but I have just gotten your letter telling me that our babe was sick, and I will now write but do not think that you will get it, at least hope that you will not for I am in hopes that our babe is well e'er this for I do not see why the symptoms that you describe should keep her sick very long. God grant that she is all right. You don't know how anxious I am to have you with me, and I think that the time is not far distant when I shall clasp my dear babe in my arms. I cant think of a greater blessing. There is a man waiting to do some work on the house & I will not be able to write any more before mail time—but will write again by tomorrows mail.

Love to all & a thousand kisses for you and M.

> Affect
> Your Husband
> C. A. Brown

Charles to Maggie

> Bonanza Col
> July 14th 1881

My own Darling

I am truly glad to hear that our loved one is improving. I was

terribly blue untill I got your last card telling me of the
improvements don't start too soon with her. I am anxious to see
you but can stand it for her sake. I am so anxious to see you
both, and then just as you were about to start for our darling to
take sick, then the probability of never seeing her, it almost
killed me but thank God she is better. Now love write to me and
find out what route you will come and what it will cost. You can
tell the Dr. that I am terribly short of money, but will have some
before long and as soon as I get it I will send it to him. Times are
very close here, and it is almost impossible to sell any property
atall. I have some good property but cant sell at this time. If it
gets better soon and then I can sell to some advantage. Have
been fixing up the house inside, and think that I can make it
comfortable, but will not be able to put a carpet in it just now,
and we will have to use the floor as it is and it is pretty rough at
that. Money is so scarce here now that it is impossible to collect,
in fact there is very little practice at this time there are some
sales being made now and the probability is that there will be
plenty of money. There are very few sales being made any where
in the state and the consequence is that the times are hard all
over the state but if we can get together we can make shift untill
they get better and probably the mines that I have will be worth
some thing then I may sell one of them this fall but do not want
to do so untill next spring. I have thrown up all but two, one of
which is being worked at this time. I only own a fourth interest
in each but I would rather have a small interest in a good claim
than to have a doz in bad ones of my own. The contract is for
thirty part on the one that they are working and by that time
they will strike mineral. The way the thing is done is this: we
struck what we call a lead of mineral bearing quartz & probably a
small trace of silver in it then the deeper we dig on the lead the
better the oar gets some get it at ten feet and some have to dig
an hundred feet, & the deeper they dig the better the mineral.
Now my love I have perfect confidence in your good sense and
feel confidence in the good management of our loved one. Write
often and tell me how M. improves. Affect

Your Husband C. A. B.

Charles to Maggie

Bonanza Col
July 19th 1881

My own Darling
    I am so uneasy about you, even more so than I was about M.

for then I thought that it was only some attack of indigestion and
since you told me it was typhoid & that you were sick, it makes
me sick to think of it, and if I could get any thing for the
property that I have I would come home at once, but every thing
is so dead at this time that I could not get any thing for it and
the probability is that I could not get enough to come home on,
am afraid that the thing will not start any more untill next Spring
altho most of us think that it must come this fall, there is no
money in circulation at this time and I don't know how I am to
raise money to send to you, but it must come after a little, and
we will live in hope if we die in dispair, No, I have not had the
money to go into partnership in the P. O. Drug Store, but I have
a fourth interest in fifty town lots, and have three in my own
name, and a fourth interest in two good prospect holes, one of
them has a tunnel thirty feet long and the other has a shaft thirty
feet deep and I consider them both good, but I don't think any
thing of those that I dug on last winter and it will cost me two
dollars and fifty cents per foot for every foot that we sink on the
two that we have, but I have eighteen months to do that in, and
if I don't sell out by that time I think that I will be able to do my
best on it with perfect ease, at twenty five dollars for gear. Now
I have told you all of my business, and I tell you frankly that I
cant get any money out of it at this time, but have no fear of not
making some thing out of it by next spring in the mean time we
can make a living if I can collect money enough to send to you;
you see the men are so hard up that they leave without paying,
but the law is being fixed so that they must employ us or do
without any thing, and we can demand the cash, it will not allow
a druggest to fill a prescription unless it is signed by a physician
that has a certificate signed by the state board, and they are
scarce. The weather is very warm here in the middle of the day
but cool at night. How is it there? There is scarcely any sickness
here at this time. Now my love keep up a good heart and we will
make it all right. The darkest hour is always just before the day,
don't be afraid of me I am always true, and will always be so, for
there is no other woman on earth that I could love half so much.
Keep me posted love and love me true. Affect

Your Husband
C. A. Brown

Martha Magdalene (Maggie) Keller Brown and Charles Albert
Brown, Virginia (circa 1878). All photographs, unless noted
otherwise, are used courtesy of the Special Collections, Zimmerman
Library, University of New Mexico.

The Brown's Poncha Springs home. From left to
right: Judge Rose, Mrs. Rose, Mattie's playmate
Lou Mon (?), Maggie Brown, Mrs. Mon (?), Mattie
Brown, and Charles Brown.

A view of Poncha Springs (1882), Colorado before it
was destroyed by a series of fires (1883).

Martha Amelia (Mattie) Brown, with Towser Appleton, Rincon, New Mexico (1885).

Mary Augusta Brown, born June 1, 1894, Rincon, New Mexico. She was to be the Browns' only child to survive to adulthood.

A mountain outing by Maggie and friends. This could have taken place in either Rincon, New Mexico, or Villa Grove, Colorado. Maggie is at far right.

3

Bonanza, Colorado:

August, 1881–September, 1882

*T*his is a very strange country & I see many strange things.
[Maggie to Pa, September 5, 1881]

That is the way with this country—one day flourishing & the next
just the reverse. [Maggie to Pa, March 1, 1882]

We are young and may make something out of this country but I
don't want to end my days here. [Maggie to Pa, May 7, 1882]

Hustle and optimism set the tone for new mining camps, at least in
boom months. Mountainsides were stripped of timber to build mining
shafts, cabins, supply stores, saloons, and houses of ill repute. Then,
if the times became dull and mines stopped producing, what had been
a hive of feverish excitement became a ghost town—the hastily erected
frames deserted. Mining towns promised fortune, not permanence.
Thus, when Maggie Brown moved to join Charles in Bonanza, Colorado, she foresaw a brief stay. Yet she brought energies to create a
warm home for whatever time the hope of a "boom" lasted. The gran-
deur of the mountains, the flourish of the camp, and above all the
presence of Charles cast optimism over Maggie's first letters from
Colorado to Virginia.

As ensuing months brought a flagging economy, the tone of Maggie's
letters changed. Uncomfortable with Charles's eagerness to move to
yet another boom town, Maggie begged Pa for Virginia news that might
entice Charles to give up the West and return home. Increasingly

impatient with dirt floors and walls that bent with the winds, she wanted a real living room with a fireplace, a parlor with a bay window. Between August 1881 and September 1882, Maggie herself became a battleground of east/west tension. There is turmoil in the letters of this section—turmoil characteristic of the hope and despair of families on the mining frontier.

As soon as she and Mattie could safely travel after Mattie's near fatal bout with typhoid dysentery, Maggie boarded a train for Bonanza City, Colorado. Her trip, describing a great arc, took her from the soft hills of Virginia, through the exploding urban jungles of Chicago, St. Louis, Kansas City, and Denver and then on to the scenic marvels of the Rocky Mountains. Some thirty years later, Maggie confessed to Virginia friends that her first view of a place like Royal Gorge in Colorado was as vivid then as the minute she was first stunned by it. Engineer Thomas Ingham's 1880 description of Royal Gorge creates a memorable picture:

> The grade is steep. The river below is full of rapids, and is a milky, raging torrent. The massive walls of granite, which narrow up to from twelve to twenty feet, form a scene which is a constant wonder and delight. Nature here seemed to be set on its edge. The gigantic walls of vertical strata, rising in places to most two thousand feet, have a grandeur about them hard to describe.[1]

Rickety trestles, however, were the rails' scant support across such steep gorges—a hazardous route. At Pueblo, Colorado, Maggie's train had to be re-routed: five bridges had washed out. "In the midst of darkness and hard rain," the switch was made. Later Maggie wrote Pa of the "kind conductor" who guided her through purchasing a new ticket, shifting her luggage, and comforting little Mattie. But the new route posed new hazards. This time a huge boulder, part of a sudden landslide, had to be blasted off the track. After a three-hour delay, the train finally steamed off, with Maggie gazing in "perfect dread" out of the windows into the darkness, wondering what other terrors lurked. Again the kind conductor calmed Maggie with an interesting notion: road walkers with lanterns were stationed every two miles—their job, to signal danger. The night terrors eased at 4:30 when the train pulled into Mears Station, where Maggie disembarked and then reloaded her belongings and Mattie onto a mail wagon "without any cover" and took her seat for the forty-mile, twelve-hour ride "in a constant drizzle and rain" to Bonanza.

As the traumatic night faded and Charles's "pair of loving arms" neared, Maggie took comfort in the showers and the creaky wagon. What she could see of the countryside delighted her: rolling hills covered with green grass, steep mountains, low clouds hiding their soaring peaks. Finally, about five o'clock, in the still-trickling rain, the mail wagon rumbled into the little mining camp. And there at the post office, in front of about fifteen or twenty men, Maggie saw Charles, waiting for her.

Though in later years Charles seemed insensitive to the sharp changes he asked of Maggie, on her arrival in Bonanza, he buffered her adjustment. Instead of taking her on her first night to the strangeness of a cabin which *she* would have to transform into a warm home, he took her to the welcome of an already warm hearth, that of George Rose and his wife "Mrs. Rose"—whose larger-than-life adventures later supplied Maggie with a stream of "Mrs. Rose" tales with which to regale sedate Virginians.[2]

Up on the hillside overlooking the rest of the town was the cabin Charles had prepared for Maggie—"a little birdcage of a house," furnished with a "nice new stove," a carpet, new dishes (better, Maggie emphasized to Pa, than they ever had in Virginia), a rocking chair, and for little Mattie, a high chair. Amid the clutter and desolation of the mining camp, Maggie's quarters gave her a touch of the East.

Maggie's front porch looked down upon the mining camp. Nicknamed the "New Leadville," Bonanza probably echoed the description Helen Hunt Jackson wrote of the shanties of the real Leadville in 1879:

the town's houses are all log cabins, or else plain, unpainted, board shanties. Some of the cabins seem to burrow in the ground; others are set up on posts, like roofed bedsteads. Tents, wigwams of boughs, wigwams of bare poles, with a blackened spot in front, where somebody slept last night, but will never sleep again; cabins wedged between stumps, cabins built on stumps, cabins with chimneys made of flower-pots or bits of stove pipe . . . cabins half roofed; cabins with sail-cloth roofs; cabins with no roof at all . . . it looked all the time as if there had been a fire and the people were just dispersing, or as if townmeeting were just over. Everybody was talking, nearly everybody gesticulating. All faces looked restless, eager, fierce.[3]

The inhabitants of these jumbled constructions were a motley crew—a hodge-podge of southerners, yankees, blacks, whites, and foreigners from Scotland, Ireland, Wales, China, and Australia. The ingrained class distinctions of the old South softened in Maggie to a generous egalitarianism. Except to disparage anyone who was "too yankee," she seldom alluded in her letters to social rank. She did not nurture the supercilious posture that, for example, Mary Hallock Foote took when she refused to exchange visits with the townspeople of Boise, Idaho (circa 1880), considering them boring and socially inferior.[4] Although Maggie did point out behavior that shocked her (gambling, drinking, "playing baseball on Sunday") what she emphasized was the kindness people showed her. The kind people, whatever their background, formed an indispensable network with whom she found the social interplay of tea, talk, and planning—the structure for joint reflection on events and needs. In the West where men went off for long stretches, women in waiting became their own society.

The initial excitement of mountains and mines buoyed Maggie so that for nearly six months she projected onto Colorado enough of Virginia memory to stave off facing the radical differences between eastern and western lifestyles. In her early days in Colorado, Maggie was essentially a tourist, intrigued by geography and population. To Pa and the "children," she described curiosities she found: the burros packed with great bundles far larger than themselves; the strange climate that would freeze water left by the embers overnight, yet would warm so in the daytime that by early afternoon she could sit on her front porch with Mattie playing on the floor at her feet. Signals she had learned in Virginia for predicting weather failed in Colorado: she went to bed one evening "with the moon shining bright, not a cloud in the sky" and awakened next morning to a foot of snow. The strange weather affected even the proper course of rituals. It seemed somewhat sacreligious to Maggie that in January the ground was so frozen men had to dynamite it to "dig" a grave. And the wind, as all the West comes to know, grew into a presence, driving them at times to shelter in a sod house. The very altitude itself leveled demands on her. At eight thousand feet, cooking a pot of beans took hours longer than it had taken in Virginia.

Weather and altitude, of course, she could not send home; so cactus plants, buffalo teeth, and jack rabbit ears had to illustrate for Pa and the children what curious things came out of her strange new country. She did try to give the Rockies a touch of Virginia, planting acorns she had brought from Virginia on the slopes to go with the indigenous cottonwoods and scrubby pines.

But despite her own resilience and general support from Charles, life in Bonanza soured for Maggie through a combination of stresses that sapped her energy and her hope. Health and fortune fell apart. Though her age did not name bacteria and allergies, Maggie and little Mattie suffered their attacks: toothaches, sore throats, mumps, mountain fever, headaches, and general distress. Added to these strains was Charles's improvidence as a husband. Though he had a good reputation and patients, he seldom collected fees. He outlined endless new projects, however, seeming to invest greater energy into speculation than into actual work. Maggie had to square up to a distasteful reality: the little family could starve if it depended only on Charles.

Dr. B. always has some new project on hand but as he has no money to put in anything he does not lose anything but "chin music" & you know that is cheap with him. He has a hospital scheme on hand. Now he is talking of building a house down on our other lot & running one there but I fear this is only talk. [Bonanza, March 1, 1882]

New schemes fired Charles's enthusiasm as if the mere act of speculation was an end in itself. He trafficked in lots and mines both in Colorado and New Mexico: buying, selling, trading—above all discussing and projecting. Apparently, though, nothing ever paid off.

As Charles juggled western possibilities, Maggie constructed plans for returning east. Fourteen of Maggie's fifteen extant letters to Pa during her year in Bonanza discussed ways to support the family in Virginia: purchasing land at new railroad junctions, farming, hosting a vacation spot for western visitors to the old South (westerners, Maggie was convinced, longed to see Virginia). As the mine and the nugget of gold represented Charles's dream of success, the fireplace, the bay window, represented Maggie's.

Maggie, however, was not as intent on returning East as Charles was on staying West. At times she could envision a future in Colorado. Some of her schemes called for Pa and the children to move to the Rocky Mountains. For Maggie "Virginia sick" meant "lonesome for family." Their presence, more than a given place, was what she missed. Her wish to be with the Virginia family took added urgency late in October 1881, when she heard rumors that Pa's wife was leaving him.

What Maggie had hoped was only a "black undercurrent" turned out to be true. The widow "Matt Spangler" whom Pa had married, hoping to have a mother for his three young children, in fact loathed the youngsters. Relatives claimed she chased Dannie (age fifteen) around the yard with a pistol, forced W. J. (age eight) to serve her special meals, and by herself engaged in quixotic tilts with imaginary intruders. Her bizarre behavior faced Pa with two choices: commit Matt to a "lunatic asylum" or divorce her. Matt's response was to stuff Pa's dray wagon with as many of his belongings as she could and leave town.

Despoiled, he said, of his household goods and his reputation, Pa initiated divorce proceedings and moved himself and the three children to a rented apartment in Howardsville, Virginia—all this under the eyes of scandalized relatives who judged he "acted badly." If the Virginia relatives frowned on him, Maggie championed him. Nothing but comfort and admiration for him threaded through her letters. The turmoil in the little family, however, unsettled Maggie. Feeling responsible for the motherless family, she begged Pa to join her in Colorado.

The problems in her Virginia family gave a bleaker cast to the already bleak turn of the Colorado economy. Not only was Charles's poor management at fault, the whole area was becoming depressed. With the playing out of the Bonanza mines in 1882, the camp turned to a ghost town. Maggie wrote:

> There is no money in the bank & so very little in town. I saw in the paper tonight that "It was reported that there was a man in town today with fifty ct. in currency" but (the editor said) "I don't believe it." [August 1882]

Maggie's next letter was a cry: "Oh! pa, What are we to do?" [September 9, 1882]. At that point Charles's new excitement was a little place some forty miles southeast of Bonanza called Poncha Springs. Rumor had mines there producing; in addition, it was a mineral springs health resort as well as a railroad junction. For once Charles seemed to be gambling on a sure thing. Still his record of failure muted Maggie's enthusiasm for another western move.

The letters of this section show subtle changes happening in the Browns' family configuration, an initial blurring of the traditional male/female roles. The process is rewarding to observe. While the West is credited with liberating women (primarily because of the quick spread of woman suffrage), the truth is that some of the West's seeming breakthroughs for women, like voting rights, were plays for political power rather than drives for equal rights.[5] It was the East before the West that rallied to the ideology of feminism. Maggie Brown responds to economic emergency by assuming certain of her husband's decision-making postures (she speculated with lots, attempts opening a business). She does these things, though, as a survival tactic rather than as a stand for women's rights. One may suppose that much of the independent posture of western women, like Maggie's, preceded theoretical discussion.

The old South culture had grounded Maggie in the cult of domesticity. Without challenge, she embraced her role as nurturer, a pious, submissive, symbolic civilizer—guardian of the hearth. These were her tasks while Charles took the role of protector, warrior (if need be), aggressor, decision-maker, and bread-winner. The family direction took the shape he gave it. Thus *he* moved west. *He* sent for Maggie and Mattie when he was ready. *He* invested family money in mines and real estate. *He* shifted the family residence.

Such division of labor was initially a survival strategy.[6] When there was a baby to be breast fed, small children to be watched, detailed food preparations to be made, vast stretches of rocky land to be plowed and sown—life worked more smoothly with work arenas clearly marked. But when a man like Charles failed continually to make headway in economic crunches, a woman like Maggie assumed, little by little, the powers he let slack. Without consciously theorizing that she was, in fact, moving into man's domain, Maggie "did what she had to do" to help the family survive.[7] In the Bonanza demise, as Charles gambled on mines and brought in scant money from medical practice, Maggie wrote Pa about her own projects: she planned to use *her* income from *her* lots to finance her brother Danny's move west (a move she saw as beneficial to both families). To Charles's proposal to traffic in Mexican drugs, she said an emphatic "No." She and a female friend, on their own, opened a short-lived boarding house. None of this behavior was done as defying Charles; it was simply a natural response to need. It evidenced, though, independent personhood.

Maggie did not, as did eastern feminists of the time, assume more assertive behavior in a conscious push for women's rights. It is not meaningful to try to analyze her letters for evidence of how a liberated woman copes with the exigencies of the "masculine" west. Maggie did not feel bound by cultural proscriptions against women arguing with their husbands' decisions. Her definition of self was larger than the images the twentieth century sees as available to nineteenth-century women. She did have attacks of insecurity, but they did not stem from a problem with whether she was acting as a real woman should act.

Even as she began assuming parts of traditional male roles (decision-making, investment of money), Maggie identified herself in terms of beauty and sexuality. To the end, she cared that Charles should desire her body. It distressed her to become stooped and wrinkled and to lose her teeth—these diminished her sense of her femininity; to make family decisions, to earn and invest money, to ride a horse, to climb on a roof—such behaviors she took in stride. They posed no threat to her essential feminine self.

A final reflection on the letters at this juncture must address the issue of credibility. Because most of the information about Maggie's and Charles's western experience comes through letters written by Maggie, it is critical to assess Maggie as a reliable source. Several aspects of writing must be considered here. Public writing voices and speaking voices are never the same as the inner voice from which the public writing and speaking comes. The public product is a monitored voice, an edited version of the free flowing process of the mind.

For purposes of assessing "truth" in Maggie's letters one must ask how closely her written voice approximates her inner voice. It is important to know, too, the degree of self-consciousness imposed on the thinking and the phrasing of the final product. Do Maggie's letters honestly depict her feelings or do they fabricate a personality behind which the real Maggie hides? Are they stiffly selective about content? Is the style a self-conscious imitation of the model rhetoric the nineteenth-century woman was exhorted by grammar books to cultivate? Can we discover more than mere facts from Maggie? Can we get the sense of presence, a sense of an event being felt in her mind that Elizabeth Hampsten argues is the unique contribution of personal documents to history?[8] Was Maggie letting genuine emotion surface, or was she controlling herself so that only the "acceptable" was exposed?

There are certain marks of spontaneous writing: a rambling sentence structure that engages in dialogue with itself—correcting, modifying, digressing. Ideas are triggered and organized by emotion rather than expository logic. The writing recreates the immediate emphasis of speech, using in place of tone, pause, and gesture printed signals like underlining, exclamation points, parentheses, dashes, and creative combinations of these and other punctuation marks.[9] When such patterns occur in personal documents, they point to an unselfconscious quality of expression. Such writing may be inaccurate from an objective view; still it signals subjective honesty.

Most of Maggie's letters reproduce her spontaneous inner voice, ideas she is coming to understand in the very process of writing. A New Mexican friend wrote her years later in Virginia: "I was so glad to get all your letters. You write just as you talk and it seems just as if I had had a talk with you" [June 5, 1904].

The few instances in which Maggie wrote formally serve to emphasize the spontaneity of her ordinary writing. Most glaring are several didactic notes she sent "the children" in Virginia—severe, formal admonitions to proper conduct. In writing to Charles and her father, Maggie permitted her words to flow with her emotions. When calm and happy, she organized chronologically, events ordering her process. When distressed, she let her words tumble out in waves of free association. An immediacy characterizes her letters. She interjects as an inner uncertainty flashes ("Oh! Pa, what are we to do?"). She interrupts her writing process to attend to a present need. ("Dr. B. has just come with a qt of Oysters for which he gave $1.50 so I will have to stop & help him cook them"). She underlines and makes asides:

There is another man who wants Dr. B. to go to Mexico & take charge of a $2,000 dollars wroth of drugs but I say no! I think I will prevail.

By the way, yesterday Mattie said, "I want to see my gampa." I tell you I do.

A lady died (but no patient of Dr. B's).

(Now I will tell you a little secret & you keep it) if Dr. B. should make his raise it is to be mine.

For the twentieth-century reader, Maggie's letters can be taken as minimally censored responses to the galloping changes of the mining frontier. While larger history finds little place in her letters, personal time, family time, ring vitally true—touchstones for testing current myth against past reality.

Letter Texts August 1881–September 1882

Maggie to Pa

Bonanza, August [1881]
Saguache, Co., Colo.

My dear pa & family

I am at home at last arrived here Saturday eve after many
trials at least after I reached Pueblo where a tellegram was
received that 5 bridges were washed out from that place to
Leadville City where I had to have my baggage checked & get
another ticket to South Arkansas but there was a very kind
conductor on & as it was raining so hard & so dark he attended
to it for me so after a few moments we started on & got about a
mile & a half when the train came to a stop they said it would
have to go back to Canon City as there was a large bolder & land
slide on the road so we did and they went up with an engine &
chains to drag it off but it was so large it had to be blasted off.
Well after three hours we started on & I was in such perfect
dread all the time it realy made me sick & the Conductor saw it
and told me not to be uneasy that they had road walkers every
two miles with lanterns to signal if there was any danger. Well at
4½ o'clock we got to South Arkansas when at six I took the train
for Mears Station & there found a mail wagon without any cover
(but it was all to be had) so took my seat for a 40 mile ride in a
constant drizzel & rain for Bonanza, but pa I did not mind that
for all the lovely country I ever saw I saw that day. These are
called Rocky mountains. Their tops may be Rocky but I could not
see them that day for the clouds   I could only see the beautiful
round roles covered with lovely green grass & at the bottom a
stretch of meadow about a mile wide over to the mountain on the
side of which we were going along the hole of 14 miles more like
this then we got into the valley & did not enter the mountains
until we started up this gulch on the each side of which Bonanza
is situated & my house is up above all overlooking the town
which is a goodeal larger than Bridgewater. Now we drove in
about 5 o'clock and at the post office in front of about 15 or 20
men there stood Dr. B. not knowing us until we came to a dead
stop. He took M. & told the driver to drive to Mrs. Rose's where
we were real kindly treated & staid until Sunday morn when he
brought us up home, which is just a little bird cage of an affair

nice new stove, carpet on the floor, nice new dishes better than
we ever had in West V[iew] set of chairs one a rocker M[attie] a
rocker & high chair bed sted with mattress & spring wash stand
with drawers & drop handles & other little things I am nice fixed
than I have ever been. I will be real happy if you write to me
often for Dr. B. is doing very well.

Dont let the children for get me. I send you a picture of
M[attie] but she has a frown on her face her eyes being so weak.

Give my love to all & write at once. Your ever loving daughter

M. M. Brown

Maggie to Pa

Bonanza, Sept 5th [1881]
Saguache Co., Colo.

My dear pa

I have written you several letters & a card or two but have
received no answer but think it is because you are too busy. But
my dear pa, I would be so glad if you would only write me a card
every week to say you are well. It would be a great relief.

I will send you some stamps so the expense will not be on you.
My object in writing today is to tell you how we are getting along
at present & our future prospects. I think it will interest you &
you are the one I feel like ought to know. Well, Dr. B. averages
about $5.00 per day in his practice, now has an interest in 2 good
mines & where his office is over the P.O. Drug Store, the
proprietor, Mr. Adams, is going to run for County Clerk & it is
more than likely he will be elected. If so he wants Dr. B. to take
the whole charge of the store & if he does he will have to have
some help, spoke of Dannie [Maggie's brother in Virginia who
would have been about fifteen years old in 1881] to Dr. B. D. is
as old as Dr. B. was when he went into business. He said, "Well,
if your pa will send D. to school this winter & I am able I will
pay his fare out if he will let him come?" Now, pa, we both feel
like helping you & this is a good business & D is very apt & I
think he will soon learn & be able to send something back to you.
If this place takes the rise it did last spring we will (or I) will be
able to send for Dannie myself for I have two lots on Main Street
that I will sell. It has cost us $22.10 for the three weeks we have
been here but we have lived better & it is easier for us to live at
that rate than the way we lived in West View. Now, pa, be sure

to answer this. The election is in Nov. then we will let you know more definately. There is another man who wants Dr. B. to go to Mexico & take charge of a $2,000 (two thousand) dollars worth of drugs but I say no! I think I will prevail. Give my love to one & all. By the way, yesterday Mattie said, "I want to see my gampa." I tell you I do. Now write soon & often to your aff. daughter.

Maggie Brown

I wrote this letter yesterday but did not send it off so will now answer your dear letter, the only one I have gotten from V[irginia] but one from the Dr.'s sister Mary Ella. I must tell you here what a complete change there is in them. If I were their own sister they could not make more fuss over me & M[attie] why they keep her in clothes.

You spoke of pears, Dr. B. brought me 51 cts. worth the other day & it was seven pears, or 2 lbs. Everything is sold by the pound here. Apples 20 cts. per lb. I wish you could have heard us laugh when you spoke of a garden. We could have a better garden on "Eliots Knob" than here. You can hardly put your foot down without putting it on a rock & then up here it is so steep. To give you some idea of it I will tell you about the house. It is 16 ft. wide & is sunk 3 ft. in the back, & it is 8 ft. up to the front door. We are on the side of what is called Copper Gulch. It is only wide enough for a road & Creek houses are built over the creek. After the town begins to grow more all the private houses will be built up here. The most of the town is situated along Kerber Gulch. Now, the San Louis valley commences about 2 miles from here & that is very fertile. One man down there off of 10 acres of potatoes last year cleared $4,000 (four thousand dollars.) We got 70 cts. worth of potatoes & it was not quite a peck. Everything necessary is canned. I bought a can of Pumpkin the other day to make some pies, eggs 5 cts. apiece & chickens 75 cts if you can get them at all. I took a horseback ride the other day. Nearly every lady has her own horse. I had Mrs. Adam's.

Very few observe the Sabbath there is no church yet all ladies & gentlemen I have met are very nice.

Well, I will now write a letter to dear little sister. Give my love to all & remember me to Emma S. [sister-in-law of Pa's current wife, Mattie Spangler]. I will send the stamps. Now don't think hard for it may not always be convenient for you to get them, being so far from the P.O.

Maggie to Amelia Jane

My dear "little Sister"

I was delighted to get your letter so will soon try to answer.
Mattie is on the floor with a roll of paper on pasteboard and has
got the little "kittie" running through. She is very well & her
eyes are nearly well.

This eve while we were at supper there were three "burros"
came to the porch. They brouse around on the hills & mountains
& eat bread crusts. I threw some out & while they were eating I
put M[attie] on the back of one of them   Now I will tell you what
they are like: Jackasses, only smaller & the Jacks are blue & the
Jennies are black with white across & around their eyes. Their
ears are not as large as a mule's ear. They are used to pack
things up in the mountains. You would laugh to see one packed
with great bundles bigger than they are on their backs.[10] The
men drive them in front. This is a strange country & I see many
strange things. In the morn I will get you a cactus & send you it.
Just get some dirt out of the meadow & stick it in & it will grow.
These around the house are too large to send by mail. I will go
up on the mountain farther & get one. Then you will have
something that came off the Rocky Mountains.

You write often to your loving sister

M. M. B.

Maggie to Pa

Bonanza Saguache Co Colo

Oct 4 [1881]

Dear Pa

Your letter with the childrens I received last week with much
pleasure   I am very glad you are going to let them write to me.
I hope they will improve by it. I have put off answering so I
could write you something definite about our movements   we are
going to move downtown nearer the office   Dr. B. thinks it will
pay, but we are to leave our house and rent one we may be able
to rent ours to some one   this is only a box house & the one we
get will be log & three rooms. Dr. B. has gone to his claims this
morning   there is a man from Cal[ifornia] that he is trying to sell
one to, but I won't consent to his selling one it is called The
Sedalia   it is only 35 feet deep & is showing mineral so I want
him to sell his interest in one & sink the S. deeper. I get right

"Va sick" sometimes but I have some very kind friends here   one
a Mrs. Rose seems <u>very</u> kind has given Mattie several little
things the other day we were down there & last spring [the
Roses lost their little girl, Mattie's age]   the first death in the
camp & the first Dr. B. has lost since he came out here but they
seem to think a great deal of him. I expect we will send you some
specimens of ore by this mail. Now I must write to my brothers
& sister. With much love to your wife & your dear self I remain
your loving daughter M. M. Brown

Maggie to Dannie

Bonanza Oct 4 [1881]

My dear brother Dannie
   I received your letter with pa's and am very glad you have
such a good crop of broom corn & hope you will make it up & sell
your brooms & raise money to pay for your schooling this winter
you are getting to be a great big boy & you must try to improve
yourself whenever & where-ever you can   I know you have the
brain if you put it to work in the right way some how I feel like
we will all some day be proud of our brother Dannie. We do live
on something like a pile of rocks but the soil under the rocks is <u>so</u>
rich I feel like it is a pitty that things can't grow for that. I
brought some acorns along with me & am going to plant them on
our lot just to see if they will grow. There are no trees here but
the cotton wood & something like pine it is nearly all dead. the
Indians killed it before they left, but there are no Indians close
here   we seldom hear of them.[11]
   Now I will write to A[melia] J[ane]   you write to me & I will
answer your letters   Your loving sister
                                              M. M. Brown

Maggie to Amelia Jane

Bonanza Oct 4 [1881]

My dear sister
   I received your letter and was glad you had gotten your cactus
all right now you must not keep it too wet better not wet it atall
if there is any danger of it freezing   they grow tall then but it is
so cold they only grow around here. Mattie is playing with our
bottles two black ones & 2 white   the black ones she calls her
"niger babies"   she wraps them up & talks to them   she talks

right plain   there is a gentleman in town by the name of
Henderson he has a confectionary store & he makes a great deal
of Mattie & gives her Gruber peas [peanuts] when she goes there
yesterday morning I went there & she did not want to come
away said "wait mamma   Miss Henesy full my pockets"   I asked
her what to tell you for her she said   "Tell her me got a little
niger babe"   her [Mattie's] face is as round & fat as can be.
There is a little girl that comes up to play with her near your age
when I left [13 years old]   but a goodeal smaller now I suppose.
Well I must answer W. J.'s letter I know he will look for one so I
wont disappoint him get pa to read my letters to you   you write
the next time pa writes all of you must

Your loving sister
M. M. Brown

Maggie to W[ashington] J[ames]

Because W. J. is Mattie's uncle, though he is just eight years old,
Maggie plays at writing this letter to him from Mattie's point of view,
hence "Unkley."

Bonanza Oct 4 [1881]

My dear little <u>Unkley</u>
   (I suppose your letter was written to Mattie   I will answer for
her) Me likes it very well out here there is some little Jacks &
Jennies that come to the door & want me to give them bread
they are not any taller than you are & the Jacks are awful ugly
but the Jennies are right pretty   I [I is then crossed out in
original] me is a fraid of them but mamma puts a crust of bread
on a fork & me gives it to them then. I reckon you want to know
what they are used for   well the men can take them up into the
mountain where a wagon cant go so they pack a sack of flour (50
lb) & a role of blanket   a tub & sheet iron stove coffee pot frying
pan & tin cups then they start off driving the Jack in front & you
would laugh to see the little thing going a long with a bundle on
its back a good deal larger than it is. They are very gentle you
could catch any of them & ride them. Now my dear little <u>Unkley</u>
you must write to me often your letters are so interesting. Oh
yes there is a little girl (not the one I wrote to A. J. about) that

comes up to see Mattie that looks so much like you. I feel almost like I had my baby brother with me   she is only 5 years old.

Kiss all for me & tell them all to kiss you for me too
your afft niece   M. A. Brown

Maggie to Pa

Bonanza
Oct 31st 1881

My <u>dear pa</u>

I have not heard any thing from you for some time so I thought I would write to you.

I thought when I came out here I would not hear the distressing reports that were coming to me all the time I was in Va. I hope the last has no foundation. I got a letter from Va. since I heard from you, saying Uncle Fritz [Washington Keller's brother] had gotten a letter from your wife saying she was going to leave you. Now I hope this is not so if not I will never trouble you with any thing more I hear. And trust to <u>you</u> to tell me anything that might happen if serious. We are having some cold nights now the water freezes in the glass at the bed side every night but we have very warm days   yesterday & today I have had the door open all day   I am feeling very well, but walking is very hard on me   you could not go at your usual gait here. Since I wrote to you I have been up on Round mountain a point much visited here for its good view   started from here at 10½ o'clock & went to the Belle of Colorado mine & took dinner there about 2 o'clock reached the top of the mountain   it is about 200 ft above timber line we saw the Continental division or where the waters flow East & West, all the mountains as far as we could see are covered with snow but the one we were on & a few near to it. I got very tired & Dr. B. told me if I did not ask to take any more such trips this fall he would take me to Mt. Antonia that is some 12 miles from here & in the Continental D.   it has commenced snowing on all the mountains near now so I dont think I will say anything. Horse back is the only way the ladies & gents ride here & the horses are very sure footed. I papered my house last week. I do wish you could step in & see how cosy it looks. . . . Dr. B. has just come with 1 qt of Oysters for which he gave $1.15 so I will have to stop & help him cook them.

Nov 1st

Last night when I stoped the moon was shining bright & not a cloud in the sky, when we awakened in the morning there was a foot of snow on the ground. Pa have you any chestnuts close to you if so I wish you would send me a little pack full by mail you can send 4 qts. that way they are 75 cts per qt. here. 4 qts would only cost 64 cts. I will pay the mail   I want to try to send A. J. a set of furs for a Xmas gift; don't say any thing to her a bout it so she will not be disappointed if I am not able to send them. I have a heep more to write but will wait until next time. Give love to <u>all</u> & kiss the children for me. Much to your dear self from

                              Your aff daughter M. M. Brown

Nov 2

Dr. B. has just brought up bear stake [steak] the bear weighed over 450 lbs.

Will Hanes to Charles

                                        Nov 14th, 1881

Socorro, New Mexico

Dear Friend,

   I hope you will excuse the hasty lines I dropt you from Gunnison[12] as I have not heard from you I dont know whether you received them or not. I am in Socorro as you see we had 12 inches of snow last Friday but the present warm weather is melting it very fast although Socorro is nearly 100 miles south of Santa Fe the nights are very cold. There are some very good mines about here Gov. Taylor has brought some they have a Stamp Mill with 150 power engine also a larger smelter[13] there is very little going on at present   few of the mines are working but not many. I met Maj. Blakely yesterday he is from the Miner Hill M Co.

   Is there any thing new at Bon[anza] and is there any chance of selling our prospects if you could do anything with them I would give you what you asked for your trouble. I dont know weather I am owing any thing or not but I will make it all right if you let me know   I am in pretty close circumstances at present.

   Hoping you and your family are blessed with Health and prosperity I am

                                        Yours Truly
                                        Will

Please address
   W. C. Hanes
      Socorro N M Terr.

Maggie to Pa

> Bonanza, Saguache Co.
> Dec. 25, 1881

My <u>dear</u> pa

I received your letter the middle of last week. I had written some to you before I got it but had not finished so when I went to finish, Mattie had gotten it and cut it up. She has learned to use the scissors right well & is cutting all the paper she can get. I was not at all well when I got your letter & alone. Dr. B. went to Saguache (the county seat) as a witness on a trial last Monday & did not get home until Friday night. Would not have gotten home then if he had not walked. It was 20 miles the way he came. Mattie & I have been right sick with sore throats.

This is Xmas but the dryest I ever spent in my life. I do hope I may never spend another out here. The children of the Sunday school had a Xmas tree last night but Mattie could not attend on account of our throats. I will write the children what all M[attie] got. I do hope you may have success with your broom business.

The climate is just splendid here now. This is Xmas & only one snow & no cloudy day, or rain. Have not had a rain since two weeks after I got here. I came in the rainy season. It is not so very cold, only freezes after night. Well, it is cold all the time but we do not feel it. The creeks that run through the town are frozen solid all to a space about a foot square at the bottom, they will stay that way until near June. Well as I have no news I will close my letter to you & write something to the children. Write just whenever you can, of course as often as you can. With much love

> Your devoted daughter
> M. M. Brown

Maggie to Dannie, Amelia Jane and W. J.

My <u>dear</u> brothers & sister

I will write to you all in one letter but you must <u>all</u> write me one. I enjoy W. J.'s letters very much, am glad he <u>can</u> <u>write</u> to

"Sister Maggie" so when I get a letter directed by pa I now look for 4 letters. It used to be only 3.

Well, the Sunday school had an Xmas tree. Mattie got a doll, an iron & stand, a bag of nuts & candy & a package of popcorn. A little friend of hers (a little girl that looks so much like W. J.) gave her a beautiful French doll with white hair. Cousin Charlie got a whistle off of the tree. This little girl is 7 years old, is very sweet. She is the only child. Her name is Edith Dobson. She slept with me while Dr. B. was in Saguache.

I got a letter from Fannie Wynant the last of Nov. and she said they were going to send us a box: Turkey, apples & butter would start it the first of Dec. but we have not heard anything from it I fear it was lost. I got a letter from Aunt Betsy Coyner who lives at Colorado Springs. She said I would not find an Uncle Harry out here, no indeed, nowhere often. You all write soon.

Give love to all, your aff. sister
M. M. Brown

Maggie to Pa

Bonanza Saguache Co Colo
Jan 22/82

My very dear pa

I cannot refrain writing to you this beautiful Sabbath morning it is so bright & warm just like spring I am sitting with both doors open & Mattie is sunning on the poarch playing with her dog, but to give you an instance of how cold it was Dr. B. sat up one night reading until between 11 & 12 with a good big fire in the stove until he went to bed   I had a half gallon in bucket full of water sitting on the stove and at 7 o'clock the next morning it was frozen sollid. I have not much of interest to write for this is the dullest time of the year they say with mining camps   the grown [sic] is frozen so hard unless the mines are a good depth they cannot be worked last week a lady died & (but no patient of Dr. B.'s) & the groun was so hard it had to be blasted every foot of the way. Pa this place reminds me very much of Pattonsburg now it is just as calm not a bit of wind then some times it blows very hard

I commenced this Sunday & it is not finished yet. Dr. B. came home for dinner & I had to get it ready then go to Sunday School which is half past two Dr. B. has the bible class & I have a class of boys. I have had company every day since. I am invited out to tea tomorrow so I thought I would try to finish today.

I hope your are moved & settled but I have been so uneasy about you. The last letters I got from you Dannie said you had so much rain & you had just gotten home I have been afraid you took cold & was not able to write. I have had a Drum New Year paper to send you for two weeks but thought every day I would get a letter telling me where to direct   I will not send it until I am certain to direct for it is a nice large paper & I want you to get it. I will send W. J. an almanac with scenes some I past through those I mark are the ones now let me hear from you soon & as often as you can   Kiss the children & Give love to one & all

Your <u>devoted</u> daughter

M. M. Brown

Maggie to Amelia Jane

Your letter was also duly received & with pleasure. I recognized the hand writing with which it was commenced that too with pleasure. Pa has his two sons & ma her daughter for company   I have my daughter & she is a heap of company. Her papa got her a little (silver plated) knife fork & spoon for a New Years present & she is so proud of them the last thing she said before she went to bed was to tell "Gam pa" she had them. I have been suffering with tooth-ache but am too big a coward to have it pulled. Well you must write again soon your letters are all so interesting I like to get them

With love to you & all your aff sister

M. M. Brown

Maggie to Dannie

Bonanza Jan 30th/82

My dear brother Dannie

I was very glad to get your letters it had been so long since I had gotten one. I was surprized to hear you say you went over for a load of things I suppose you are almost a man but it is hard for me to realize it get pa to measure you & tell me in your next [letter] how tall you are   you ought to see the sleighs they have here for coasting   they are two small sleighs fastened together with a board six feet long but the front one is loose & they guide it that way. The other day Dr. B. was starting down town &

when he got to the road two men had a sleigh just ready to start so he got on & they took him to that store which was about as far from the school house (West View) to Wiseman's store   they go very fast

Well I must close with love   your aff sister

M. M. Brown

Maggie to Pa

Bonanza Saguache Co
Jan 30th [1882]

My own dear pa

I was so glad to get your letters this eve' I wrote one last week & sent to Fluvanna P.O. but suppose it will be forwarded I will send the papers & Almanac to W. J. from Mattie   the scenes I past through coming out I marked. I think W. J. did just splendid in writing. The childrens letters are so interesting. I got a letter from cousin Jennie Cullen the other eve: I had written to see if there was still an opening for a Dr. & she said there was, both at Bealton & Midland there was a small piece of land just two miles from both places that could be bought cheap & the R.R. was selling lots in Midland for $5.00 (five dollars) ($1/8$ acres) have you ever been to Midland & if you have how do you like the looks of the land. Embry at Bealton asks $140.00 (one hundred & forty dollars) for this land so you see land has gone up.

Well as it has not been long since I wrote you a letter I have not much to write & have to write to my brother & sister. I will close with much love from your devoted daughter

M. M. Brown

Maggie to W. J.

My dear brother W. J.

I received your dear little letter & was so glad my baby brother is learning so fast. Your name was real good   Mattie has not forgotten her "little Uncle" yet & I am not going to let her either.

Write again soon to your aff Sister

M. M. Brown

Charles to Pa

Bonanza Colorado
Jan 30th 1882

Dear Cousin Wash[ington]

I was glad to read the letter that Maggie received this evening
from you dated 23d. Write often. We're always glad to hear from
you, and I am well pleased to know that you have gotten to your
new home and you may not be surprised to see us back there by
fall if things look up here this spring as everyone expects I shall
sell out and come back. I have property enough if I can sell for
any thing like their value   I can get me a very nice little home
back there. Have already instructed Dan Lullia to buy me a small
piece of land in his neighborhood on 12 months time, and I think
that I can pay for it in two or three months; times are very dull
here, but I can always get more money here than I could back
home, but I can't say that I like it here. There is too much
yankee about the people, and then we have every thing to buy;
can raise nothing here. The altitude is too great only nine
thousand three hundred and seventy feet above sea level, and
consequently the seasons are too short for raising any thing. We
have always plenty of snow but not deep snow, from 1 to 6 inches
deep, and plenty of wind. The air is dry and that is the reason.
Mining pays well for those who have money to carry it on. but if
a man has no money, he had just as well leave it alone. The
mineral here lays in leads that run perpendicular in the ground,
and it costs some thing to get down to good mineral. On top the
oar is nearly always mixed with rock that makes it run so low in
silver or gold that it does not pay to work it, but as it goes down
the rock begins to disappear, and more mineral comes in untill it
all becomes mineral. The piece of oar that I sent you out of my
claim was the first mineral that came out, and that was twenty
seven feet deep. It is now only thirty feet and it costs $100 per
foot to sink on it so you see I have to go slow, but as soon as the
snow goes off up in the mountains I shall begin work again if I
can raise the money to spare. The lead is three feet and a half
thick. Some of them are as wide as thirty six feet, but when they
go down on them they will close up. A mine has to be from one to
two hundred feet deep to pay for working. Maggie and Mattie are
well. Maggie never suffers from any thing now but tooth ache
and she will not let me pull it out. Mat is fat and saucy. She says

"tell Gam Paw." "I's got a sork" (fork) "and poon" (spoon) and then went to sleep. She is a good baby and a great deal of company to us. Was glad to see that W. J. has undertaken to write. He will succeed if you will encourage him. Don't forget to plant plenty of water melons for I expect to be there to help to eat them. Maggie will finish so all I have to say is God bless you.

Respectfully,
C. A. Brown

Maggie to Pa

Bonanza, Mar. 1st/82

My <u>dear</u> pa

I received your letters nearly a week since but have been so busy I could not write. Today a week ago, I went in partnership with a lady friend to start a boarding house but only run 5 days and found we were about to come out "the little end of the horn," so we closed. That is the way with this country—one day flourishing & the next just the reverse. Dr. B. always has some new project on hand but as he has no money to put in any thing he does not lose any thing but "chin music" & you know that is cheap with him. He has a hospital scheme on hand. Now is talking of building a house down on our other lot & running one there, get monthly practice & bring the patients to the house, but I fear this is only talk or he will be undermined by some other physician. There are some awful mean people here. Will do <u>any</u> thing for money, & you know how Dr. B. talks about his plans to any body. You all write about so much rain. I have not seen a drop of rain for more than six months & may not until next August. That is the only month we see any rain. The wind is blowing very hard now. Week before last we got up and left the house about 12 o'clock at night and went into a log cabin that is covered with dirt & would stand as long as any house in town. The wind came very near tearing all the paper off that night & I notice the house was sprung some by the way the door shuts.

I don't think I have told you how our house is built. It is 16 × 20 ft. 7½ from floor to joists. No scantling except in rafters joists & under the floor. The planks run up & down with strips nailed over the cracks, then lined with common bleached cotton. It is sewed together over head & tacked to joists & around the sides it is just lapped & tacked. This is the way Dr. B. had it fixed when

I came but since I have had it papered around the sides. Can see the sun shine through any time. Soon we would freeze in such a house in Va.

Well, "pappie" dear, I commenced this letter more than a week ago but have been real sick since with what is called here "Mountain Fever," am a little better & improving. I expect, if I continue to get better, we will move day after tomorrow. Dr. B. has succeeded in getting enough names to justify him opening a hospital so we will have to rent a larger house until he is able to build.

I bought me a sewing machine last week. Hope to make something on it. Tell the children Sister Maggie is not well enough to write this time but will soon. You be sure to write whenever you can & I'll do the same. We must not count letters.

With much love to all & your own dear self

> Your aff. daughter
> M. M. Brown

Pa to Maggie and Charles

> Glendower P.O.
> Albermarle Co Va

Mar 26th 1882

My <u>Very Dear</u> Daughter & family. Your letter dated 1st of this month but mailed on 20th was received last night. I do not know when I ever was so anxious to get a letter from you   it has been so long since we got a letter that I was really uneasy about you was glad to know that you were all well except what you call mountain fever & hope you are all right now & that the Dr. & you will be successfull in your new enterprise am very sorry you had to move out of your house at night. I think I would build strong houses if I was there. I was not satisfied the way they builded houses in Larned Kansas. But I guess the log house you moved to was all right as it was covered with earth. Will now tell you something of myself & family. First will tell you that we have never had as much rain & snow before in the same length of time. & consequently never had such bad roads   the truth is they got so bad that people had to quit trying to travel on them & I could not finish and am not done yet. I got out of broom handles & could not get to Charlottesville for them so I just had to do nothing. The weather & roads is all right now. But the Sawmill at his place broke the main cog wheel & Mr. Dillard who all the property here belongs to could not get any body to put them on but the casting was such a bad job they would not do & I will now have to go up to Howardsville & have the casting made. The man at H'ville wants me to come up & make some patterns for him. I expect to go up there tomorrow. I have 100 handles on hand now & plenty of good broom corn & when I get through jobing will pitch in to the broom business. We have planted potatoes some early rose & some I got which was brought over from Ireland the potatoes from Ireland cost me 2 dollars per bucket & the Early rose $1.75 I saved some oats which cost 65 cts per bushel. We planted some corn onions sassifrass lettuce & all early vegetables have cabbages & tomatoes peanuts up. The wheat crop is looking very fine & grass is beginning to grow. Tell the Dr I will plant some water mellons & Sweet potatoes for him & will try to save a few pears & apples for him too. Tell him to sell out as soon as a good chance presents itself write soon & let me know how you are getting along this leaves us all well except myself I fell off of a head block at saw mill yesterday & hurt my side very much it is improving & I hope will not interfer with my work. I had to take D. A. out of school to help on the farm but W. J. is going & A. J. is learning her lessons at home & so will D. A. continue his studies will get them to write in this letter. Your ever loving Father W. J. Keller

Amelia Jane to Maggie

My Dear Sister
    I was very sorry to hear that you was sick. We will soon have lettuce to eat. We have planted some peas beats and parsnips. The peach trees are blooming we have fruit trees of all kind it is very windy here now I will be glad when March is over Ma told me to ask you what dryed apples were selling at out there. Ma rheumatism very bad. Pa is talking about buying a evaporator. Well I must close my badly written letter Amelia

Maggie to Pa

Bonanza, April 2d 1882

My dear pa
    I received your ever welcome letter tonight & I hasten to reply because I want to hear from you again soon & that your fall is

not anything serious. I have not been well since I wrote to you
before. Have had the mumps & it seems to me like I have been
sick every way anyone could be sick   Dr. B. is getting very much
discouraged about it & says as soon as he can raise a thousand
dollars he will start me back & he will come in the fall. Now, pa,
from what you say I like the place you are on. Now will you see
if the title is good & the very least it can be bought for for cash
& if there is any running water & all you can write about it you
do.

(Now I will tell you a little secret & you keep it.) If Dr. B.
should make his raise it is to be mine & if he makes anything
after I am gone it is his but he is real homesick too.

I hope you will have good crops & good health & above all that
it won't be long until I see you, but I fear this is vain hope. The
town is getting right lively now & I hope we can sell well enough
to come back together. We are haveing splendid weather now, but
very dry & nothing green but the trees are beginning to bud &
the ice on the creeks is melting . . .

Indeed, I must cut your letter short & write to the children. I
have not written to them for so long.

Your ever devoted daughter,
M. M. Brown

Maggie to Amelia Jane

My dear sister

I was very glad to get your dear little letter & wish I was
there to help eat the nice fresh vegetables you will soon have
there. There has been some lettuce in town but we did not get
any. Tell your ma I will enquire & see what she can get for apples
& let her know . . .

Write when you can. I am always glad to get your letters.

Your aff. sister
M. M. Brown

Maggie to Dannie

My dear brother,

I was also glad to get your letter. Aunt Bet had sent me a
Charlottesville paper & I saw something of the murder you spoke
of. I get a letter from her about once in six weeks.

I am sorry you had to stop school but you must do all you can

to help dear pa. I have been uneasy about him since he wrote of
his fall. You try to be as much of a man as you can & you shall be
rewarded. Your letters are all read with much interest by all of
us. Mattie says she does not want me to take her away from her
pa. Give my love to all & as to W. J., why did he not write—dear
little fellow.

Your loving sister
M. M. B.

How far did you say the R[ail] R[oad] was from that place? The
fruit is what takes my eye.

Although the following fragment letter has no signature, the handwriting is unmistakably that of Will, W. C. Hannes, who wrote Charles
from Socorro, New Mexico, November 14, 1881. This letter confirms
Charles's range of mining interests. The "deal," though not spelled out,
suggests Charles was already contemplating a move into the mining
regions of New Mexico.

W. C. Hannes to Charles

Fairview April, 10/1882

Dear Friend Dr.
    Since writing to you I have been prospecting in the Black
Range[14]

[segment of letter missing]

certain four letters & postals were received after being in Socorro
a great length of time. I am in new camp 120 miles south west of
Socorro and we seldom receive any mail which was forwarded. I
was in Socorro some time ago and met Capt. Stearling & P
MacCardo and several other Bonanza boy's. from there I went
down the Rio Grande prospecting

[segment of letter missing]

but returned went down the Rio [Grande] again about 65 miles
and came back to the Black Range, it is so long since you
[segment of letter missing]

lawyers out here I dont know if power of Attorney will help you
anything or not, I think six months is a long time. I would take
300 cash for my interests in the B. B. and if the Silver Chief is
allright tell Sam Love he can get my third cheap if he wants it. I
may be in Bonanza in 2 months but am not sure if power of
attorney will do any good now   write at once and I will try to
send it. You can have 10% commission for your trouble but I want

Maggie to Pa

Bonanza May 7th/82

My <u>dear dear</u> Pa

I <u>just</u> received your long looked for letter I was getting uneasy
about you for fear you were sick but was very glad to hear you
were able to work. But don't work too hard for when we do come
to Va I don't want you to be broken down   one thing you can
calculate on is a place by our fire side if we ever have one and
when we get a home the door is <u>always</u> open to you my <u>dear</u> pa[15]
I feel as though the affection I had for both parents is centered
on one I talk and plan so much for your future with us that I
think some times Dr. will get jelous but he does not and coincides
with me in all. No I am not coming back until he can come too.
This is a very fluctuating country   we may have money in a week
& it may be months. The town is in a balance now it may go up
or down if up we will hold on and see, if down we will sell & get
enough to go some place else to try our luck. Dr. B. got about
$75 (seventy five dollars) worth of practice last week & about $30
(thirty dollars) in money. He has some lots (5) in the next town
one mile from here that he will take the deed out on them this
month & they are making arrangements to have the RR come up
there soon. We thank you very much for your plan. Like it very
much   you keep your eyes open about all farms & as soon as we
get the money will send it to you to invest for us. If we make a
raise & you don't see any better bargain than the "Omahundra"
farm we may get it & if you get any leasure time work on the
house in neat stile for us   we furnishing the lumber & pay you
by the day. If you had come to Denver when you went to West
View 1871 you would have been independently rich. We have an
old Virginian boarding with us   he came to Denver in 72 owns a
nice house & two lots, got $5 per day supertending the building
of Senator Hills house & I know he was a second class carpenter
in Va. he has a family of a wife & 5 boys   he is about 40. His
name is Croswell from Pulaski Co, but we are young and may
make something out of this country, but I don't want to end my
days here   we had thought of going to New Mexico but Dr. B.
has written to a friend there & we will not decide until we hear
from him. Hope you are at home and [letter torn] of many
brooms. Give my love to each & all of the children & wife for me,
by the way I must tell you how we cook beans in this high

altitude. I put on a pot full at one o'clock yesterday cooked steady
until 10 last night & are just getting done 3 o'clock in the
afternoon. "How high is dat." Write again soon to you ever loving
daughter.   M. M. Brown

Pa to Maggie and Charles

Howardsville, Albermarle Co Va
June 7th, 1882

My very Dear Daughter & family. I am here again. This will be
two weeks for this time & then I am going home to make some
more brooms. I made 170 when I went home the other time &
sold them all. I do not remember if I told you what I am getting
for my work here. Mr. Bateman who is the gentleman I work for
gives me two dollars per day & boards and lodges me & pays me
for the time it takes me to come from home & the time it takes
me to go home. It is not as much as I can make at the broom
business but he cannot get any person who understands making
patterns as well as I do & he begs me to help him out of a tight
place now & then. . . . I am tolerable well. My work is not hard.
I have a hand hired on the farm at 40 cts a day & I board him.
The children are all well except W. J. he has a stone bruse on his
foot & it hurts him very much. I am puting out a big crop of corn
broom corn, potatoes peas & some water & muskmellons
cantelopes &c the season is a little backward for spring crops
owing to the cold weather but wheat never looked better & is
very near ripe, grass is very fine too. Corn is selling for $1.20 per
bushel flour $7.50 per barrel hay 1.00 per 100th, broom from
$2.00 to 3.50 per doz bacon from 12 to 10 cts per lb   I would be
very glad if you & the Dr could send about 300.00 three hundred
dollars in here to buy the Omahundra farm I would like to fix up
the place for us it would make us a good home & I could do well
there. I got a letter from your Uncle Fredy he is still hard up
little Fred left him & is gone west left 4 months before his time
was out & took 25 twenty five dollars of money with him. I must
close excuse my delay in writing as I was too busy. write soon to
your

Aft Father W. J. Keller

Maggie to Pa

Bonanza, June 25/82

My ever dear pa & family
   I received your letter a few days ago but was so busy all week

I did not have time to write so I stayed home from church this morn to write to you. We have a very nice young presbyterian preacher. He is a real nice little fellow & very energetic. I have heard him preach about three times. He has been here near two months now. This is all the preaching I have heard since I left Va.

The summer has come on us with full force. The sun shines warmer here than in Va. We have had shipped vegetables since the middle of May: tomatoes, lettuce, onions, & cabbage. Now are getting apples & peaches but I want you to send me some fruit packed by your own dear hands. They come wrapped in paper, each apple & peach separate. Now if you pick them before they are quite ripe & wrap them up that way they will be all right when they get here. I would like for you to send me about 25 lb. of mixed fruit but will have to send you the money & get you to prepay the expenses to ensure it getting here, for they sent me a box from Uncle Harry's for Xmas but they did not prepay & about two weeks it came back with the Turkey spoilt. . . .

Dr. B. says he does not know when he can send you the money but it may be a short time & it may be in the Fall but property is gradually improving. He is doing very well in his practice just now but it is no use for us to try to lay up anything out of that. He will have to sink one of his claims deeper before he can sell & it costs $10.00 (ten dollars) per foot, a hole 3 1/2 × 6 1/2. I told him I would be willing to spend another winter here if we could send you $300 or $400 this fall. I know how you take care of property that you rent from anybody & if we were to buy that you could live on it and fix it up or if you did not, I would want you to fix it up any way for what would be your taste would be mine. Can you tell us what kind of houses they are and how much would it cost to finish them up & put a bay window in the parlor?

Well, I will close for this time. Write soon. We always have a fight for your letter, we both want to read it first. Kiss my dear brothers and sister & love to all for me.

Your aff. niece [sic] M. M.

Brown

Maggie to Pa

Bonanza, July 2nd, 1882

My dear pa

I wrote you last Sunday but having you in my thoughts all

week & this being my birthday, I thought I would write to you again. I am 28 years old, not far from 30 but I don't feel over 23 or 24.[16]

I want to come back so bad & feel as though I can hardly stay here until I can come. Do you think I could do anything there by keeping boarders? I think there are a good many here that would come and spend the months of May & June for those—or April or May, they are the worst months we have here. Two of my friends go from here to Denver to spend those months & it costs them about $35.00 per month. I could raise all I would need & only have groceries to buy. Would buy cows, have chickens which sell 75 cts. here just large enough for us to make one meal off of. You and Dannie & W. J. could run the broom business & A. J. & I the house. We have a great wrong to undo that is to get those young minds in the right channel again & believe their father & see [he is] a virtuous gentleman   I have no selfish motive in this. What can I do? I am away from it & if I was selfish I would have let that letter go unheeded but I felt it my sacred duty to let you know of the black undercurrent, and minding the love & respect of those that ought to hold you dearest of all human beings. But, my darling pa think there is one that is going to take care of us all. Last week I was nearly heart-broken all week. I felt as though I could not stay, but my dear, kind husband said, "My dear, you could not do anything if you were there." So I could not. So we will have to trust all to the Lord. "Two wrongs never make a right" so if I was to come back it would not be to lower your wife in the children's mind, but to bring out your own true manly character. I am going to write the children a letter & if you think it advisable you can give it to them. They are making great preparations here to celebrate the 4th but I have not done much nor will I. They are going to have a big picnic & dance.

Now dear pa do write soon. Give my love to all.

Your most devoted daughter
M. M. Brown

Pa to Maggie and Charles

Glendower July 3d 1882
Albermarle Co Va

My Very Dear Daughter & family
Your kind & long looked for letter came to hand this morning it

was received at the P.O. Saturday but as did not call in person
P.M. would not send by the children or any one else. I am much
oblige to you for all you have said. But in reference to your last
sheet will say that my wife is not responsible for her conduct as I
am perfectly satisfied she is a lunatic on the subject of jealousy
she imagines she sees persons around the house & on the
premises when no one else can see or hear a thing. Mrs. Spangler
her sister in law came up to spend 7 or 8 days & she went home
satisfied that Matt (as they all call my wife) was crazy. She is
something better now but I have noticed simtoms of lunicy for 3
or 4 years or in fact ever since we were married. Out side of the
subject of jelousy she is tolerable sane but her whole mind is
disease & impaired more or less. Her health has not been good
for some time past & she has lost some 30 or 40 lbs flesh & is
quite lean to what she was. I have a very great burden to carry
in the way of family trouble. I am not nor can I live as I used to
but as it is I must try to bear it somehow hoping for relief
sometime. I have said enough on this subject & more than I
should have done but as she had written to you I thought I would
say something on the subject & will say here that her
derangement was the cause of my leaving home as much as I did
for she seemed to be better when I was away than when I was at
home. Miss Emma Spangler is staying here now & is using her
influence to keep my wife's mind off of the subject of jealousy. All
the Spanglers & neighbors see how the poor creature is suffering
& all are doing what they can to benefit her or to keep her mind
right. Never did I think when we used to live oposite the Lunatic
Asylum & could see & hear the poor lunatics there that I would
have to live with one or have a wife in the institution myself &
from what I see before me I am sure such will be the case & you
can better immagin my feelings than I can describe them. She is
very kind to us all & will cry over us when she sees us want any
thing & she has nothing to give. I am very glad you have a fine
dress   hope you will enjoy it & be a good wife to your husband &
a good mother to your little child. The wheat crop is all harvested
& is very fine the corn is looking very well too we have a very
fine season here our garden is splendid had plenty snaps peas
onions more than a month since & have cabbage potatoes &
tomatoes & quite an abundance of blackberries & the apples are
just getting ripe. Will try to send you some thing some of these
times. Our water & musk mellons are doing fine. Would be so

glad to have you & the Dr. here to help eat some with us. I will send this
so D[annie] is out plowing corn & W. J. is thining corn in the orchid & A. J. is getting dinner. Wife & Emma are gone to Scottsville & I will close this letter hoping you are all well & happy. God bless you all is the prayer of your aff father W. J. Keller

Maggie to Pa

Bonanza July 20th 1882

My own dear pa

Why have I not heard from you   I am so discouraged that I don't feel like doing any thing have no energy so much depends on our communications   it is my greatest source of pleasure, for I am not very happy out here. I am so sick of this gulch although there are some kind people here. I have not much to write only to beg you to write soon to your ever loving

Daughter
M. M. Brown

Maggie to Pa

Bonanza, Aug. 7th [1882]

My own dear pa,

I received your letter & wrote you only a card. Will now try to write a letter. We are having summer awful hot here & has been so warm for about two months. Suppose you are having it good & hot there. I can sympathize with you when you were in Kansas for I am getting awful Va. sick. I was so amused at Dr. B. today. I said, "When I get to thinking about old V[irginia] I can hardly stay [in Colorado]" He said, "That is so when we get back we will be contented to stay." It is the first time he has said that but he is getting along splendid here, is so successful & is getting a good sum of practice. But money is very tight just now & he cannot collect anything just now. Men are coming in every day now who represent millions & there will soon be a general looking up. Dr. B. wants to go on a prospecting trip soon. I hope he will & strike something. We took a ride up on a mountain last week. It was 12,000 feet high, or altitude, & I got some Buffalo teeth out of a skull we found up there. I am saving up all such things to bring back.

I commenced this yesterday. Will now finish & get it in the morning mail. I have just made up my light bread, will have light rolls for breakfast. Wish you were here to eat some with us. I hope it may be God's will that I can be permitted to make some for you before too long. But our hope is so often deferred that I get very low spirited sometimes. You take the best care you can of yourself so I will not see an old man when I come back. I don't know what I would give to hear you whistle "old Dan Tucker." I will just have to stop. I can't write any more. I am getting too homesick & it will only make you feel badly.

Give much love to all & tell the children to write soon to their sister for I do love to hear from my darling sister and brothers.

Your own loving daughter to hear from her dear pa soon.

M. M. Brown

The following brief note would be typical of summons Charles received as mining physician, delivered probably by messenger on horseback.

W. A. McEntyre to Charles

Columbia Mine Colo
Aug 17th/82

Dr Brown
   Dear Sir
I want you to come down hear this evening
We have a very Sick man hear. I think he has Mt. fever.
Yours &c
W. A. McEntyre

Maggie to Dannie

Bonanza Saguache Co.,
Aug. 19 [1882]

My dear brother
   I am glad to hear you are always glad to hear from me. I know my Brother Dannie has a good kind heart if he has a rough exterior & his sister often thinks of you & wishes I could do something to lift you all up out of poverty & I wonder why it is that those who use their money for selfish purposes prosper & if I had some I could make so many happy. I hope you succeeded in driving away bad luck & Had a nice time.

You always write whether I write to you or not for I love to get letters from

I must write to A. J. now. Your loving sister

M. M. Brown

Maggie to W. J.

My <u>dear</u> little baby brother,

Well I will tell you about your little niece. She has a little kitten & a grey hound pup.[17] You never saw one, I don't think. It is a mouse color & has long sharp nose & small ears. If he lives until we come to Va. I am going to bring him with me. You write again. I can read your letters.

Your affect. sister,

M. M. Brown

Maggie to Amelia Jane

Bonanza, Saguache Co., Colo
Aug. 20 [1882]

My sister

I was <u>very</u> glad to get your letter & love to hear from you. You must write often for we are the only two girls & we ought to confide in each other & I do wish you were here, or we there. But you will have to be pa's support & comfort. I think he thinks a great deal of you & you must not be so afraid of him but tell him all of your troubles. He would like for you to come to him & be free with him.

How are you off for clothes? & how is W. J.? Dannie and pa now write me the truth & don't be afraid so if I can help you, I will but we will have to have new clothes this winter. Dr. has not gotten anything new hardly since I came & we have to wear very heavy underclothing here in winter.

Now, you write often and all the news. I will have to close. I have written so much & it is getting late & I have to get up soon tomorrow morning as I have to wash. Write me how tall you are in your next.

your ever loving sister
M. M. Brown

P.S. So all you children must cling together & all to pa so if I come back I will find all at once.

Pa to Maggie and Charles

Glendower P.O. Albermarle

My Very Dear Daughter & family

Your letter to hand. I am in a great hurry to start to
Howardsville & can only write a few lines. But will say give your
self no trouble about the old woman killing me for I do not think
she will do any harm I am going to get a divorce as soon as I can
get money & time for I will not be the husband of such a bad
woman. I will now close & let the children finish & I may write
from Howardsville soon I stay two weeks at a time. The children
are all well & happy as larks as we were all at Sunday School
today together but when I am not here they all go anyhow. Try
to be cheerful & happy your self it is no use to grieve about any
thing I am well & go to church whenever I have a chance I lead
prayer meeting at Howardsville every 3rd week as there are 2
others who lead meetings thereabout write soon your

Aft F

Maggie to Pa

Bonanza, August 29, 1882

My dear pa

I am not very well but feel like writing to you. We are rather
blue now. But all that come west get blue when money is hard to
get. There is none in the bank & so very little in town. I saw in
the paper tonight that "It was reported that there was a man in
town today with fifty ct. in currency" but (the editor said) "I don't
believe it." We live in hopes of times getting better every day.
There was an old miner, a friend of Dr. B. that collected some
money the other day & he got Dr. B. to go with him to trace up
some leads and stake them so today Dr. B. went to sink them.
We get 2 ounce ¼ at no Expense. one is the "Washington," & the
other "Lady Jane." Dr. B. names the last and we the first. The
flow (that is the rock found on the surface & what they go by to
find a lead) is the richest this old man says he ever saw & he has
been to a good many camps in Colo. Dr. B. received a letter from
old Mr. Atkinson & he said he saw Aunt Bet at the Depot going
to Churchville where you would meet her.[18] How is this? I hope
now things will work all right. She is getting right old & childish
but she can keep your clothing in order & be a guide to the
children. She had written to me repeatedly for your address but I

did not know whether you wanted me to give it or no so did not, unless it was in the last. I have forgotten whether I did, or not. Dr. Brown has had a good practice offered to him at Poncha Springs some 50 miles from here.

Sept 9th

Dear pa, I commenced this letter some time ago, but was interrupted & so did not finish. The bank has suspended payment & it was thought broke. We can't tell yet for certain whether it is or not but things look very blue. Although Dr. B. has booked already this month about $30.00 (thirty dollars), he has not gotten near $7.00 & all he has to do to lose his men is to dun [to ask repeatedly for payment of a debt] them & they are off. There are 5 Drs. here & about as many people as in Churchville, but two of the Drs. are talking about leaving. If they do Dr. B. will stay here, if not, he will go to Poncha Springs.

Oh! pa, what are we to do? I hope against hope all most—think if we can just make it out from Spring to summer, from Summer to fall. Now it is if just until spring. It was thought the Exposition of mineral at Denver would help the camp out, but it has not. It is thought the winter will be very hard here—the draught. The date this letter was commenced, we had 2 in of snow and ice froze in the house. Just think of it in Aug. snow & ice but now the sun shines very bright & warm during the day.

The men are come back that went to sink the assessment the day this letter was commenced. They only worked on one, the "Lady Jane" & it was all we ask. They sunk a 10 foot hole that will hold it until next summer & where it is it will soon be covered with snow. I went up there with the Dr. the last of July & there were still drifts 50 feet deep from last winter. I did not mention I had received your letter last night. I don't think you could do better with the children than you have if you can keep them with you, take good care of your self & let us hope to meet as soon as we can to part no more until God may call some of us to Him. All that keeps me up is hoping for the future.

I will now write to A. J. & D. A. & Aunt Mary. I owe them a letter anyway. This leaves us all well & I hope it may find my dear pa well. Now pa write often and let me know how all are getting along.

Lovingly,
M. M. Brown

Maggie to Dannie

Bonanza, Sept, 1882

My very dear brother,

I received your letter with pa's. I was not so much surprised to hear Aunt Bet was there for we had gotten a letter from old Mr. Atkinson, the school teacher & he says he had seen her on her way there. My dear brother, I would like very much to have all of you out here, or we there, but it is no place for young boys or girls to be raised. It is very wicked, they play base ball every Sunday. No, I hope you may never take it in your head to come West unless you get rich & just come on a trip & go back to Va. It is the prettiest country I have seen yet. You and pa do all you can together & try to hold out until next Spring & I hope then we can all unite once more. You & pa write <u>often</u> & keep me posted as to what you are doing & where you are. With much love

Your sister,
Maggie Brown

Pa to Maggie

Glendower Albermarle Co Va
Sept 3d 1882

My Very dear Daughter

Your letter came duly to hand for which accept my hearty thanks. I sent a copy of the statement to your aunt Betty Jordan & if agrees with her recollection will send you a similar statement. I sent for Uncle Gust to come over in his little wagon & take Aunt Bet (who is here) & Amelia Jane & W. J. over to the Vally with him. My poor wife is so <u>vulgar</u> I cannot let her have controll of the children or stay where they are any longer. I want to get Aunt Mary Shuff to take A. J. & Uncle Gust to take W. J. until I can make some other arrangement for them. D. A. & I will stay here until the crop is gathered & broom corn is worked up & then I do not know what I will do but hope something will turn up to better my condition. We have a splendid season now & my crop is doing first rate. My wife is staying in Scottsville at Dr. Anderson's with Miss Emma Spangler. My wife took it in her head Emma's womb was out of fix & made her go there to be treated & <u>sure enough</u> she has been treated & that pretty badly for she is now so low she cannot sit up in bed. They scarified &

sarenged [syringed] her & fooled about her womb until she has
spassums & cramps pretty near all the time.[19] I am much oblige
to you for calling my attention to the matter of A. J. condition in
life [approaching the age to begin her menstrual cycles] & have
turned it all over to Aunt Bet & will tell Aunt Mary so I hope she
will still have the care of a Ma.[20] I am truely sorry that my
circumstances are such that it is necessary for me to break up
housekeeping & to put my Dear little children out among friends
a thing which I was trying to avoid by marrying. I do not know
how I will come out of the things she took[21] I have made out a
bill for them in dollars & cts. I am going to Mr. Gallups where
the goods were left   I may write more when I come back.

Well I am back I spent a very pleasant evening the family has
about 9 boarders & I like them very much though I think the
boarders are a heep of trouble. They only pay $15 fifteen dollars
per week & only stay about 5 or 6 weeks I must say I like this
part of the country better than any other that I have seen. I have
taken in since I came here & done work to the amount of $250
dollars as follows.

Wages at———	$ 71.92
Brooms nett	121.55
Work on—& sawmill	90.50
	282.97

I find by looking over my book that I was not big enough in my
guess the broom business is all right & if I can get a good hold on
it can make it pay. Yours, with affection &c

W. J. Keller

4

Poncha Springs, Colorado/Villa Grove, Colorado

October 2, 1882–February 24, 1884

A volume of smoke came from a building on the opposite side of the street & I screamed fire within 20 minutes seventeen buildings were in ashes. [Maggie to Pa, November 22, 1882]

I live in hope of things getting better if not God help us we were never as poor in our lives as now. [Maggie to Pa, November 22, 1882]

If I do stay here two years longer I will be lost body and soul. . . . I would give 5 years of my life if I had never seen this state. Now we have been married 7 years nearly & getting worse off every year instead of better. [September 30, 1883]

Grim, gloomy, desolate—the period of September 1882 to February 1884 ground down Maggie's hope in the West. Supportive letters from Virginia friends trickled to almost nothing, the only mail coming from Pa—and that fraught with court trials for divorce and insanity. Despite a few moments of financial upswing, Charles's coffers banked nothing. Natural forces unleashed rampant destruction: fire, avalanche, disease. In his final letter of this period, Pa gently teased Maggie that he was sorry to learn he must now have a daughter some sixty-five or seventy-five years old—older than himself. She "wrote" old; her picture looked old.

The first twenty-six letters of this time period were written during the Browns' stay in Poncha Springs, Colorado [September 30, 1882–

April 1883]. Initially, Maggie exclaimed over the natural beauty of the Poncha valley, particularly the mountain streams rushing through the town. In 1880 surveyor Thomas Ingham described his first approach to Poncha Springs, the road Maggie and Charles would have traveled:

> The descent down the Atlantic side of the [Poncha] Pass is even more abrupt than on the Pacific side, and the stage rattled down the sharp pitches at a pace that is anything but quieting to the nerves of tired passengers. However, an hours ride brought us in sight of the great valley of the Arkansas, and we rolled into the little town of Poncha Springs. Here there are fifty or more newly-constructed houses, hotels, restaurants and business places, situated on the South Arkansas River, a few miles above its junction with the main branch, and which appear to have been mostly built within a year. The celebrated Poncha Springs are within a mile, and are quite a resort for bathers and health seekers, as the hot soda and iron waters are considered very beneficial.[1]

Town leaders took unusual measures to enforce sobriety. Every deed to property in Poncha Springs included a clause prohibiting sale of intoxicating liquor. For the West the proportion of saloons to other businesses was small. It would seem, then, a happy combination of natural beauty and civic responsibility, yet soon after their move, Maggie read the scene as discouraging.

In Poncha Springs Charles replaced a physician who had been netting between four and five thousand dollars a year. While protesting that he was determined to make money in the West, Charles pressed few patients to pay their bills, and in the course of his stay in Poncha Springs netted only between four and five hundred dollars a year. In addition to his medical practice, Charles spent considerable time with his mining concerns in Bonanza, frequently riding horseback the forty miles to check his investments, leaving Maggie lonely and apprehensive.

Life in Poncha Springs, Maggie soon realized, was uncertain at best. A sudden gust of wind could revive a smoldering campfire whose blaze could catch and turn a street of wood shanties into an inferno. Maggie wrote harrowing accounts of fires. In terror, she watched one fire destroy seventeen houses in twenty minutes, her own house saved only by a sudden wind shift. The flames, though, came close enough to blister the varnish on her wash stand. Three weeks later, Maggie and Charles woke to more cries of "Fire!" and a young boy running out of his burning cabin, his very hair ablaze. Maggie noted to Pa that that made four major fires in one month, each fire rekindling for her the trauma of her mother's burning death. Fire eventually succeeded in destroying Poncha Springs as a settlement; the little town had neither the money nor the resilience to rebuild continually. By the summer of 1883 the population was depleted.

But during the previous winter it was cold that loomed a deadly threat to Poncha Springs. In January avalanches thundered down mountainsides burying men alive—traveling men, like Charles. "One man leaves a family—and is under 100 feet of snow" [February 3, 1883]. It was easy for Maggie to visualize herself a widow to the fierce weather. The saloon boys added their threats of violence to the natural disasters. There were fights among the saloon crowd and there were hangings. A night knock at Dr. Brown's door was often a call to repair an "awful-looking, bleeding" wound from a pistol shot.

In addition to such environmental tensions, Maggie had to face another kind of trouble—poverty. Poverty did not humiliate Maggie nor lessen her sense of worth, but it angered her. Furious, when at Christmas she had not even money for stamps to mail a letter to Virginia, Maggie vouched she was ready to steal (or at least to take in washing) to stem family losses. The real crunch in the poverty, though, was the reality about Charles it forced Maggie to confront. He was a bungling provider, an unproductive speculator whose goal was not a steady income (that he could have managed in Virginia), but a "lucky strike." Undaunted by his failures, he sank money into mines even while he scarcely knew how he would pay for his family's next meal. He was the Virginia gentleman, forgiving his debtors (as if he had surplus wealth) yet attending scrupulously to his own debts. Quick in the theoretical, he was naive in the practical, gullible—an easy mark for slick "friends."

Physically and emotionally spent, Maggie suffered chest colds, headaches, toothaches, and feared she was developing a chronic heart condition. As letters from her Virginia friends slowed, Maggie panicked that she was being forgotten, cut off. In her depression, she made Virginia her one hope, writing and remembering it as a womb, a garden, a place of healing. In some fifteen of the twenty-nine letters Maggie wrote, like a refrain, of apples, chestnuts, persimmons, "chinkpins," peaches, melons, snapbeans, black-eyed peas, ginger cakes. She wanted life-giving rains that came weekly, not yearly. The fertility of Virginia symbolized all she lacked in Colorado.

Compounding her distress were Pa's personal troubles. Losing the judgment in his divorce proceedings against his wife, Pa was forced to sell even the few belongings she had not stolen when she left him to give her the money awarded her by the court. Maggie was outraged with the woman and beset with concern for Pa. As the oldest child, she felt she should shoulder responsibility for the little family in this disaster, nurturing them as she nurtured Mattie and Charles. The dilemma was frustrating: Pa refused to move west; Charles, to move east. Financially, Maggie could salvage nothing to send Pa. Then in the throes of this family turmoil, the Poncha Springs economy, torn by natural disasters, collapsed.

It would have been the perfect time to move back to Virginia. But Charles entertained no thought of going back to the "Old Dominion." His dreams wandered ever west: Utah, Idaho, Montana, Oregon, Washington. What he ended up doing, though, was merely shifting the family from the burnt-out Poncha Springs to another Colorado town, Villa Grove. More of a farming than a mining area, Villa Grove housed a warm community whose people had requested Charles as their physician. The town's proximity to Bonanza (about ten miles) allowed Charles to continue to check his mines from which he was still expecting his "lucky strike."

At first Villa Grove improved conditions for Maggie. The women, delighted to welcome her as neighbor, asked her to go walking, invited her for tea, treated her to homemade pies and fresh milk. And on Sunday there was a bona fide church to attend. Maggie's first impression focused optimistically on "good kind friends."

Villa Grove, however, did not change Charles. From his stream of grateful patients, he collected next to nothing. He collected literally nothing from his Bonanza mines; in fact, by September 1883 he had lost every one of them because he could not afford the yearly assessments. The Colorado mining code demanded annual proof of labor on all mining claims, and the amount of improvement (only twelve dollars for mines the size of Charles's) had to be officially recorded in a sworn affidavit. Failure to comply with the regulation resulted in the mine's being reclassified as public territory.[2] Charles could not muster even that mere pittance.

To furnish the bare essentials, Charles and Maggie took odd jobs. By late fall Charles was shingling the Methodist church at $2.50 a day. Maggie, then five months pregnant, was rising early to help a neighbor cook for a team of brickmakers in exchange for the family's board. It was a dramatic crisis: Maggie in the throes of a difficult pregnancy, dragging herself to sweat over a hot wood stove, Charles hammering shingles—projects that, for Maggie, stamped their lives with melancholy failure.

> I don't see any likelihood of times ever being any better. I feel if
> I do stay here two years longer I will be lost body and soul. . . .
> I would give 5 years of my life if I had never seen this state.
> Now we have been married 7 years nearly & getting worse off
> every year instead of better. [September 30, 1883]

About the pregnancy, Maggie felt ambivalent: she loved the unborn child; she resented Charles who would be no more provident for the new infant than he was being for Mattie. The strange wilderness was not the place to give birth. A spoor of tired sadness trailed through her letters:

> Suppose you are at home now with the family, & having a nice
> time. I almost envy you all the pleasant times you have together.
> I think it is so hard to be out here and going through with all
> kinds of hardships & not have a friend to turn to being deprived
> of seeing our friends is the hardest of all. . . . If I can't write
> more cheerfully I had better close. I know you would rather not
> get any letter than one of this kind. [September 30, 1889]

In mid-November, a full three months before she was due, Maggie was taken with hard labor pains and after twenty-four hours, she brought forth a dead child. Then she hemorrhaged and almost died from the blood loss. It was Charles who assisted at this stillbirth and cut the umbilical cord of his lifeless infant. Did he link his uncompromising determination to stay west with the tiny body's failed life?

Maggie's letter to Pa a week after her ordeal was unbearably still: no anger, no resentment, no despair, no sorrow. Her handwriting was faint, as if no strength pressured the pen. Before this time, Maggie had not mentioned her pregnancy to Pa (possibly to keep from adding to his already heavy worries). Her message to him then was in a voice so limp that it seemed she had taken all she could, as if events had finally whipped the protest out of her.

For weeks she was listless, lying most of the day in bed; when she walked it was with a stoop because straightening up sent sharp pains through her. She mentioned no one other than Charles who cared for her during her recovery, although it is hard to imagine that her "good kind friends" deserted her in such need.

By Christmas, Maggie was mending, but the family finances had dropped to nothing. "Not a cake or nut did we have & not a cent of money" [January 5, 1884]. She confided to Pa that he should write even when she did not because there were times when she was too low-spirited. By January Maggie had rallied enough to make bread to sell. But she was a faint image of the feisty young woman who had traveled three years before from Virginia to set up housekeeping in Bonanza.

At some time during 1883–84 Charles negotiated with a Ralph Widmer, of Rincon, New Mexico, to become partners in a drugstore in Rincon, a newly opened railroad junction. Widmer's February 17, 1884, letter gave Charles the "go ahead" to move with or without his family into the territory of New Mexico. The mining excitement sparked by the letters of Will Haynes from the Black Range, surely more than pharmacy, fed Charles's imagination and drew him into the "terra incognita." New Mexico promised him a wide sky and wide possiblities. This next uprooting promised Maggie, however, little except more loss.

The New Mexico territory was "foreign" to the rest of the United States. Albuquerque's Judge Franz Huning was not joking when in 1880 he wrote of the need to educate easterners who held wild misconceptions about New Mexico, like thinking steamboats docked in the Rio Grande at Santa Fe.[3] Pa claimed he could not find Maggie and Charles's new location on his map, while Dannie teased they may as well go to China where things were also rumored to be opening up.

In reflecting on the letters of this section, a reader may gain an added dimension by attending to the "sense of presence" of the writer. Such things as word choice, phrasing, use of example, repetition give access to the personality beneath the document. Maggie's attention, for example, to detail, to the natural drama of life around her, to the implicit moral lesson in daily events, accords with her tendency to behave practically, to focus on getting things done in the here and now. In addition, the didactic tone she assumes in her letters to the children shows she took seriously her obligation to edify the young.[4] Maggie made parables from what she observed. After Dannie wrote her about an accident he had had with a gun, she wrote him a warning story about the hazards of firearms:

On Sunday about 5 weeks ago a young man about your size but older came to the door with his hand all bleeding & about to

faint. He had been fooling with a pistol and shot himself right
through the hand about an inch from the last joint & broke the
bone. It looked awfull but Dr. B. dressed it & it is getting along
finely, *you must never fool with fire arms*. [November 12, 1882]
[emphasis mine]

When she wanted to dissuade Pa from sending Dannie to live with her
and Charles in Colorado, she recounted an example of the dire end
men in the West could come to, even in the family of a good Christian:

Today there was a funeral parade of an old lady that realy died of
a broken heart. She was a perfect christian taught the bible class
in our little s[unday] s[chool]   last fall her son a man about 28
was arrested for cattle stealing & about two weeks ago was tried
& condemned. The dear old lady came to town & tried to find out
all about it, but every one kept it from her so she went up to the
county seat & there found out the truth & it is said took pluricy
& only lived a day or two   God took the soul & has perhaps
saved her from seeing him hung but it is to be hoped the death of
such a mother will have a good effect. *This is no place for boys.*
[emphasis Maggie's] [February 11, 1883]

Both pieces of writing craft fine stories, having just enough conflict,
suspense, and detail to hold a reader. Maggie's keen eye captures the
drama of everyday life. These stories, however, like countless others
Maggie wrote, were told not to entertain but to teach, to emphasize
a point, to give evidence. A far cry from the nineteenth-century stereotype of the mindless, pleasant female, Maggie was almost the committed evangelist, driving home her lessons through emphatic example.
Her writing reinforces the behavior we know of her—her firm practical
bent, her shouldering of responsibility.

Rarely in letters to the Virginia children did Maggie display the
spontaneous emotion characteristic of her letters to Charles and Pa.
With the children she marked grammar and standard punctuation (com-
mas and periods were notably absent in letters to Charles and Pa).
Like formal maxims, the letters to the children admonished good behavior and high ideals:

This is a hard world to get along in without an education but if
you are ever so poor & have a good education you will be
respected. [to Amelia Jane, March 4, 1883]

I do hope you may read & profit by them [books]. The greatest of
our men have had no better opportunities than you. Although you
may never be a great statesman, you can obtain a great deal of
knowledge that will be of use to you in any station. [to Dannie,
April 23, 1883]

Charles, too, strove to edify the young, and in his counsels also underscored his own commitment to the southern code of the gentleman.
To Dannie he sent concise guidelines on how to write a good letter:

I am really glad that you are improving in your writing but you
must try to improve much in your composition, so that you can
write a long and nice letter. The way to do that is to get a piece
of paper and from day to day write some thing on it that you
wish to write and at the end of the week get your paper and read
it over carefully and select from it all of the matter that you think
will interest the one you are writing to. Write to me in this way
and I will answer. [January 30, 1884]

Charles, following his own advice, then wrote Dannie (who wasted
little energy on things other than hunting, fishing, and adventure)
about a recent rabbit hunt. The letter illustrates something basic about
Charles. His outlined process is, above all, gentlemanly, concerned
with the other person. There is no emphasis on parading erudition, on
impressing. The focus is on entertaining the reader. In great measure
Charles was the embodiment of the gentlemanly code: he forgave debts
while scrupulously paying his own. He wrote Virginia for seeds, plants,
vegetables, and tobacco to share with western friends. He stressed to
Maggie the importance of a good reputation.

    In their content and style, the letters of this unit show how Maggie
and Charles reacted to and felt about their frontier. The events they
were experiencing were not unlike situations they could have encoun-
tered in the East. What made the disasters different on the frontier
stemmed precisely from that: they happened on the *frontier*, on that
edge between civilization and wilderness. On the frontier there were
few of those reliable presences—family, friends, organized religion—
that civilization offers as ready support in times of crisis. On the frontier people like Maggie and Charles were thrown on their own to create
new survival strategies. New life scripts had to be written, casting
new characters for the new environment. In the letters of this section
we note, for Maggie, a recasting of herself as a realist. She squares

up to facts of poverty, estrangement, and death. In Charles we see a pronounced move to become the dreamer. He skirts the fact of loss, and pitches into the dream, the gamble, the new possibility. As a young husband and wife, they are beginning to write different fictions and to see each other as characters not quite right for each other's plots.

Letter Texts October 1882–February 1884

Maggie to Pa

Poncha Springs
Chaffee Co., Colo.
Oct 2d 1882

My own dear pa

Here we are at Poncha Springs 40 miles from Bonanza but as different as if it were several thousand. I have only been here two days. Dr. B. came two days before me with the household goods. He has gone right into practice. The day before he got out of Bonanza the Bank & two other business houses broke. The Dr. that has been practicing here is going back to get married & then this may be a nice town next summer as there are very fine hot Springs here.

This place is rather in the valley & just beautifull little streams of water running on each side of the street 5 feet from the houses. The water is out of the South Arkansas River. We have very fine drinking water too.

We are close enough for Dr. B. to attend to his claims in Bonanza. He has had all of the assessments done for the next year. There is talk of a very fine hotel being built next Summer by the Arkansas hot springs company. If they do build it would you not come & get a good job at from $4.00 to $5.00 per day? I believe this would be a good place for a broom factory, so much water & the corn could be raised on any of their ranches here. The ranches are thick around here. We pay 50 cts. for brooms here.

I have not heard from Aunt Mary's or Aunt Bet since you wrote. I am anxious for them to write so I can hear how they are getting along. You write to us often. I believe if we had staid in Bonanza this winter we would have starved. Everybody was getting out that could. Everybody considered us fortunate to get away.

Give much love to Dannie & much for your own dear self & write <u>soon</u> to your aff. daughter

M. M. Brown

Maggie to Pa

Poncha Springs
Chaffee Co., Colo.
Oct 11th, 1882

My own dear pa & family

I received your <u>welcome</u> letter & the children's last eve. It was forwarded from Bonanza. I have written one letter since I came here. I like it very well so far. But Dr. Brown lost his first case Monday morning, a little boy 2 years old. He saw it for the first time Sunday eve about 3 o'clock & it died Monday morn' about 4 o'clock. They seem to think he did all in his power to save it. The family is a very nice family from New Hampshire.

We still hear from Bonanza things are very quiet now. It is very cold this eve it has been snowing on the mountains all around all day & down here tonight we have not gotten our house banked yet & the floor is very cold with large cracks between the planks.

I have not been well for some time. We did think I had heart disease. If it was, I could not stay long for no one can live up this high with it & B[onanza] was near 2000 ft. higher than this place so I am a little better here   two healthy looking men came to Bonanza last Spring, went to bed well & the next morning they were found dead. Dr. B. examined them & found it was heart disease which I don't suppose they knew they had. I have heard that in the early days of Leadville there would be 8 & 10 a day of such deaths but now people do not rush up in the high altitude so fast.[5]

The young doctor that was here went away last eve he has been here since last Jan. & has made between $4,000 & $5,000 (four and five thousand dollars) but I have no idea Dr. B. will do as well he is such a bad collector & the people soon find out how easy he is & take advantage of it. But he pays for everything he gets & so it has been hand to mouth all the time. As soon as we get the money you shall have it. I send you some stamps. Dr. B.

wants you to send through the mail as many black eyed peas as you can with them. He has promised an old ranchman he would get some & let him try them.

Pa, if Aunt Mary can't take A. J. you try to keep her with you until I can come back, or take her with me. Nellie Eskridge [see letter November 7, 1880] was talking of going back to Va. to spend the winter. If she does & you would let A. J. come I would try very hard to get her out here. Give love to all & I hope you will succeed with your suits [the divorce proceedings] and all will in the end come right. Dear Pa, bare up the best you can. I wish I could be of some comfort to you but this is all I can do to love you & hope to be able to do more.

Your aff. daughter

M. M. Brown

Pa to Maggie and Charles

Glendower [Virginia] Nov 5th 1882

My <u>Very Dear</u> Daughter & family

Your postal card & letter ordering black eye peas came to hand in due time & this morning got the cloak which I sent for A. J. with the [letter smudged] bout. I must tell you that one of the warrants was tried yesterday (Saturday) for the horse & the case was decided against me before the magistrate so the old <u>Monster</u> [Pa's wife, Mattie Spangler, whom he was in the process of divorcing] has my horse & wagon for which I never received one cent. There is still some property which is not decided but will come off in 3 weeks but I will have her tried as a crazy woman as soon as I can which will be in some 8 or ten days. Will then know what course to take if she is not insane I will never have anything more to do with her & if she is insane I will try to take care of her as best I can of course she will never have controll of my family or be allowed to have anything to do with them in any way. We are having fine weather no frost of any consequence our tomatoe vines are still fresh & bearing abundance we have picked our apples but the crop is very short & all wine saps my broom corn is very much damaged by being let stand out too long seed is very good though will get up a lot [of] peas & a few chestnuts soon & perhaps some apples too. D. A. and W. J. have something like a peck of them (chestnuts) will pick out the largest & send to you. You referred to the money question in your last letter & am

in need of some money just now & it would come in very well. I
am very much pleased with this section of county. . . . I am glad
you are pleased with your new home would be the gladest in the
world to see how you are fixed hope you will do well & that you
will enjoy good health   I am <u>very</u> well in deed & so are all the
rest. W. J. had a boil on his knee which kept him from school for
a few days but is all right now. I am puting in a Mill dam for the
gentleman who owns this place but orders for brooms are coming
in so fast I expect to go to making brooms as soon as I get done.
I have at it for two weeks & it will take me a week more   I am
in more trouble just now than I have ever been & I never had as
good prospects as I have now but I will get out somehow soon
write soon & let me know how you are getting along. You
mentioned in your last postal card that you had just written a
letter & you had written all the news   I am of opinion that it
never came to hand   next letter tell us what the date was. The
postal you wrote last came quicker than anything I ever saw   it
was dated & mailed on 28th Oct & we got it on 2d Nov about ½
past 3 o'clock P.M. & it came ten mile in hack from Va Midland
R.R.

> Yours affy W. J. Keller

Maggie to Pa

> Poncha Springs, Chaffee Co., Colo.
> Nov. 6th 1882

My dear pa

I wrote you a card & sent A. J. a package last week I said I
would write a letter in a few days so as I was prevented going to
church I thought I would write to you although I have very little
to write—and that not very cheerful. It has been 4 months since
I have gotten but one letter from V[irginia] & that was one
forwarded from you to me from Bonanza about two weeks after I
got here   I feel some times if you & the children were with us I
would never set on V[irginia] soil unless I got able to go back to
some of the Springs for a season. I have written letter after
letter to Mattie C[alhoun] & have not received one since last
Spring from her. The same way with Uncle Wynant's family. <u>I
may be able to survive without them.</u> We are just having lovely
weather now   our worst is generally after Christmas.

Times are very dull here now but the old spring property burnt down last week. And now the town is trying to get it & if it does the town will greatly improve. This leaves us well. Do write to me soon, it is so disappointing to receive <u>nothing</u> from <u>anybody</u>

Give love to all & much for yourself

Yours aff.
M. M. Brown

Dannie to Maggie

Glendower, Virginia
[undated]

My Dear sister

I believe A. J. an Pa have told you all the news. But I will tell you that it is geting cold here now I have gathered all the apples. My dog run a squirrel in a hollow tree the other day and I cut it out and it bit my thumb to the bone and I give it to my dog and she pulled and give me fits and I could not get it losse untill I broke its Jaw tell cusin Charley that there are lots of squirrels here and I have a splendid dog to tree them well I must close my badly writen leter. My thumb is geting beter he fairley made me hop thats all I can think of

Your affectionate bro
D. A. J. B. I. L. Keller

Maggie to Pa

Poncha Springs
Nov. 12th [1882]

My dear pa & family,

I was delighted last night by Dr. B. bringing me a letter from you & all the rest   I am so sorry you are having so much trouble but hoping you will come out all right & when it is in our power to help you we will. Our plan is if we can sell anything to send you enough money to buy you a comfortable place & let it be yours for your life time. If you can make enough to keep yourself & the boys & educate them more, well & good   would even take A. J. with me but, pa, I do feel as though I would begrudge that woman that has caused you so much trouble the bread to keep life in her vile old carcas. She may pretend insanity to get a living out of you & let what she has gotten go to her relations untrammelled.

We had a picture taken of the house & ourselves, with three of our friends & Mattie's little play fellow   Mattie is standing by her pa but she turned her head & I am afraid she spoilt it. We won't get them for a week but will send one as soon as we can.

If you have not sent the apples, do not for we can buy them cheaper here than the express will be from there but I would be very glad to get the chestnuts & peas. You could send them in different packages & through the mail, four pounds in a package.

It snowed yesterday & the thermometer stood at 10° below zero this morning—the coldest we have had it this fall, but we will have a heap of nice weather before Xmas.

Dr. Brown talks every now an' then of sending me back on a visit if he gets the money to buy a place there for you, but he says he is not going back until he is rich nor do I think he will. If we can get A. J. with me we could keep boarders & make enough to keep ourselves. . . . A. J. mentioned having chicken pie the day she wrote. We have only 4 since we been in Colo. & 2 of those were given to me. I have not bought M[attie] a dress since I been here. I have only had to get her aprons & shoes.

Well, I must close & write to the children.

> Your aff. Daughter
> M. M. Brown

Maggie to Dannie

> Poncha Springs
> Nov. 12th 1882

My dear brother

I hope you have recoverd from your wounds from your battle with the squirrels. One Sunday about 5 weeks ago a young man about your size but older came to the door with his hand all bleeding & about to faint. He had been fooling with a pistol and shot himself right through the hand about an inch from the last joint, & broke the bone. It looked awfull but Dr. B. dressed it & it is getting along finely, you must never fool with fire arms.

I thank you ever so much for the chestnuts you are gathering for me. With love, your sister. Write soon.

> M. M. Brown

Pa to Maggie and Charles

> Glendower Albermarle Co
> Va

Nov 19th 1882

My <u>very dear Daughter & Family</u>. Your very welcome letter

came to hand in four days after being mailed. Was glad to notice
a more hopeful & cheerful feeling in you hope you will continue to
do well. In order to settle the old womans claims on everything I
ever had I got Mr Dilland to get out a Landlords warrant & got
the constable to sell everything except what the law allows me.
Mr. Dilland bot[sic] everything & left it just as it was. . . . My
suit will come off for the house hold property on next Saturday &
if nothing prevents will have something to write to you about it
next Sunday. I have 3 very fine hogs to kill & 1 sow   she is same
age of the 3 I am going to kill & will make good meat to wards
Spring. I do wish you could send me enough money to buy a
small home where I could settle on   I know I can make a good
deal more than a living I have about 65 to 75 bushels corn now &
enough broom corn to make about 2000 two thousand brooms. I
have two 2 barrels flour crop & lots of beets parsnips cabbage &
lots else. I can get plenty of homes for very little money. I have
all my plows & harrow [a heavy frame with spikes or disks, used
for breaking up and leveling plowed ground] & harness all I need
is a team & wagon. I am as you say. I do think she is the
meanest creature ever God let live if she is not insane but she has
acted in other ways like some of the inmates of the L[unatic]
assylum does. She would run her poor old self out of breath in
broad day time with pistol in hand after the sluts [used here
meaning "bitch," female dog][6] God knows there was not a human
being to be seen & yet she contended they was. I know just as
well as I live that she is insane & I will have her tested before I
am done with her. I have been very busy on the Mill dam for 24
days & just finished yesterday at dinner will send peas &
chestnuts this week. Will let children fill in the other side of this
sheet write soon Your ever affectly

W. J. Keller

Amelia Jane to Maggie

Glendower

Nov 19 1882

My very Dear Sister
    We received your welcome letter and were glad to see that you
all were well. Aunt Bet was making my cloak it fits me splendidly
it has a cape to it. My hair is allmost to my waste. Aunt Bet got
a letter from Cousin Mattie and she said that she had written to

you twice and has not gotten a letter from you since Apr. Pa says
he does not know how he can get a long with out me and his
business is so he does not know what he will do. I hope it will not
be long till Cousin C[harlie] will be rich so you all will come back
to Virginnia   Your sister AJK

Maggie to Pa

> Poncha Springs
> Colo
> Nov 22 [1882]

My dear pa
    Yesterday morning I sat down & marked some views of the
house that were tak[en] a week last Saturday of this house & last
eve' about 3 o'clock I was standing in the door looking for Dr. B.
when a volume of smoke came from a building on the opposite
side of the street & I screamed fire within 20 minutes seventeen
(17) buildings were in ashes[7]   the best part of & center of the
town it was with the greatest exertion our house was saved the
street is about 40 ft wide but fortunately the [wind] came up &
took the blaze the other way but the heat was so great as to
blister the varnish on the wash stand through the window & it
sat 3 ft from the window. The house was white but it is brown &
every window light in front is broken. The post office Drug store
& the large white building you will see in the picture a millenery
store hardware & three dwellings & other large building that
were not injured or occupied   it caught in a house that was used
as a lodging house but the person that owned it was absent. The
town was about dead & now I suppose it will die. I tell you times
are awfully dark for us & we have not a cent & dear knows when
we will get anything   Dr. B. say if it gets any worse he will go
to Salida & work by the day that is six miles from here. He
exerted himself so much that he has an awful cough from it. But
we thank God we were left our bedding & clothing & shelter.
    I commenced this 22 now it is the 25th   I received your ever
welcome letters this morning that were written the 19th. I am so
glad our communications can be exchanged so rapidly   I live in
hope of things getting better if not God help us we were never as
poor in our lives as now   but the old adage says the darkest hour
is before day. I must stop & not say anything more so dolefull.
Hope you will out sit those that are trying to put you down. The

picture is not good of Mattie because she moved her head just as it was about done. If you look at that slope in the mountain just behind the house that is Poncha pass where the rail road goes the grade is 130 feet to the mile & some times heavier the pass is 8 miles long. The picture of the town was taken from the foot hill back of our house   it does not show the town very well but it shows the valley. I will write to the children the next time which will be soon. Give love to all

Your aff. daughter. Write soon
M. M. Brown

Those dark places in the Valley are pinion trees something like pine that large building off to itself to the right is the brick school house

Maggie to Pa

Poncha Springs
Dec. 10th 1882

My dear pa

I was disappointed in not getting a letter from you last week as you said you would write Sunday. I would have written sooner but was waiting for the chestnuts. The peas came all right but the nuts have not come yet. Many thanks for your trouble & the peas.

There was another fire this morning but it was three blocks from us   burnt up a dwelling & stable. A young man was sleeping in the house & got up and made a fire & went back to bed & asleep & when he woke up the whole ceiling was on fire. He barely got on his pants & out the hair on his head nearly all burnt off. This is four fires since the last of Sept. I am uneasy all the time. Things are at a stand still now. If the whole town burns up I don't know what will become of us.

Mattie is an insistent [incessant] talker & can ask more questions than a doz other children. The other day she was sitting on her little chair & her pa & I were reading and she was talking to herself & said, "Oh! I wish I could go back home." I asked why. "Oh, to see pa." I asked her what to tell Grandpa. She said, "Tell Gampa I loves him 'round neck."

Since I started this letter I have had two teeth extracted & took ether. It took a half pound to get me under the influence of it but then I knew all that was going on & did not feel the pain but one tooth pulled so hard & tore up the gum so I have not been able to eat anything solid since. Oh, pa, I am so homesick or rather V[irginia] sick, but Dr. B. will <u>not</u> come back. I know he could do as well there as anywhere but he has too much pride to come back & have the people taunt him. It will be 3 years in March since he came & we are really no better off than in Va. I don't say half I feel to him for I know it will do no good. He dreads the Jordans more than any one, so don't let on to them or Aunt Bet but that we are doing fairly. Tell Aunt Bet there are no flees in Colo. they have never been seen here. I have been disappointed in not getting a letter last or this week. Suppose you have gotten the picture. Tell the children I will write to them soon.

You write soon, I find <u>so</u> much pleasure in reading your letters although they have been sad lately. But they are from my dear pa for all that.

With love, your daughter
M. M. Brown

Maggie to Pa

Poncha Springs
Dec. 25th, 1882

A Merry Christmas to <u>all</u>

My dear, darling pa

Your letters & the children's are duly received. You spoke of wishing you could send me a Xmas present. Your dear letters are equal to a very handsome one. Xmas caught us without a cent of money. If my husband's credit was not good I don't know what would become of us but as soon as he gets any money he always goes around to pay his bills so if he has none they trust him. The way we are living reminds me of the first winter we went to West View & you were sick. This country has nothing but its fine climate to recommend it in my estimation but that is just fine. We have had just about 4 inches of snow all put together. From the first of the month up to this time it has been just like the month of May only no rain, all sunshine. Today it is snowing a little. We may have a deep snow. Dr. Brown has not had on his overcoat but 3 times this winter.

I have gotten two presents, a box of paper & envelopes, & a lady that lost a little babe & I sat up a good deal & she gave me a set of nickel plated flat irons. They are the patterned iron with over handle.

Mattie got a set of blocks off of the Xmas tree & a pair of stockings. She is not at all well, has a bad cold & the poor little darling has sick head-ache too. She has had it about 4 times since we came out. I do not have it so much. I hope the children were visited by old Chris Krinkle. They must all write what they got. I don't get any more letters from W. J. he must not forget me. Dr. Brown was in hopes up to Xmas that he would get some money & send some to the children but he did not. We love them just as much as if we could give handsome presents.

I will write to the children in my next. Give love to Aunt Bet & all. Tell her she don't think much of me now since she has gotten with the other children.

Your loving daughter
M. M. Brown

Maggie to Pa

Poncha Springs
Jan 9th 1883

My dear pa

I received your card in today's mail but too late for me to answer so will write & send in tomorrow's mail. I wrote to you a few days since: hope you will get it then you won't be so uneasy. I have gotten over my other sickness. Have had a very bad cold on my chest am just getting so I can talk loud again   I was very disappointed that your card was not a letter. What did old "Chris" bring the children? Mattie just got a little candy & an apple.

Ask Aunt Bet if she can't bake me one or two ginger cakes & put in with the persimmons. There are a great many here that don't know what they (persimmons) are. The chinkpins [chinquapins: nuts found in Virginia, akin to chestnuts] were quite a curiosity, only two out of all the people I showed them to ever saw any before.

Dr. Brown has gone out to kill some rabbits. Did I ever send D. A. any jack rabbit ears? If not I will send him a pair. the Jacks are too strong to eat. Write soon and a letter this time. Give much love to one and all & a large portion to yourself. Your most affect. daughter M. M. Brown
P.S. Why don't the children write?

Maggie to Pa

Jan. 21st 1883
Poncha Springs

My own dear pa

I have received two letters from you since I wrote one. I hate to give my reason for not writing but will be frank with you. I wanted to write last Sunday but Dr. B. said wait until we get some stamps so I waited & no stamps yet so I will write & get one if I have to steal it. No, we have not had enough money in the last month to get a stamp. If I could take in washing to help along I would do it, but if I did Dr. B. would not get any practice for people are so suspicious any way for fear they will employ a quack or some one that is not any account. they take the one that makes the best show. Dr. B. left one of his best claims in Bonanza to have the assessment worked by a man that owed him $60.00 but he failed to do it & it was jumped the first of Jan. If they are not worked up to that time they are jumpable[8] that has discouraged him so much. I am in favor of his going out near the Utah line & taking up a ranch there. the climate is more mild & all kinds of fruit & vegetables   he can take up 160 acres by preemption & 160 by homestead so you see he could take up a plenty. Now, pa, if he was to do any thing of the kind would you come out here? We would have done something of the kind long ago but Dr. B. said he did not want to have any thing to do with your wife. Broom corn can be raised over there in abundance so in one season there could be enough raised to keep us all busy at making brooms all winter. It is on the line of the Denver & Rio Grande R.R. which is now within 40 miles of the Utah line   since Dr. Brown came out the Road has gotten out there.

We have now received Mattie's card telling of the small pox in Uncle G. Steven's family & Annie's death. Oh! pa, be careful. If it comes near you, use a heap of acid cream tarter & get Bromo Chlor-alum & use as a disinfectant.

M. M. Brown

Charles to Pa

Poncha Springs
Jan 21st 1883

Dear Friend

If I can sell everything that I have in this country next spring,

I will take all of the money that I can raise & scrape and go west of here in a warmer climate and locate a home off of some of Uncle Sam's lands where we can raise anything we want. I can locate 320 acres, which will make us a good home that is for all of us and there we can raise broom corn by the Ton and grapes— and if you will husband all of your strength and money I want you to sell every thing that you have and come out and locate right by me so that we can have a large place and help each other & I think in a few years that we can have one of the nicest homes you ever saw where we can raise any thing from a Blackeyed pea to a bunch of grapes and not depend on rain to make them. We are among some of the highest points in the rocky mountains and it is too high to raise anything here worth talking about   but then we will be on the Pacific Slope where there is very little cold weather except in the mountains. and until we can get a start we can kill wild meat until we can do better, I think that you Dan and myself can make a nice home and make money at the same time   after we can raise a crop of broom corn we can work the ranch in the Summer and make brooms in the winter. I shall not write to you to come unless I think we can succeed. Am truly glad that you are rid of the <u>old man of the sea</u> [the wife Pa just divorced]. I think now that your life will be happier than it has been for some time. Give my love to the children and Aunt Bet. With much love I can now only ask God's blessings upon you all

Truly Yours etc

C. A. Brown

Maggie to Dannie

Poncha Springs
Jan 21st, 1883

My dear brother

It has been some time since I wrote to you & A. J. so I will now write to you. It made my mouth water when you spoke of persimmons. I know they are delicious now. You have had splendid luck getting Rabbits. Dr. Brown went hunting last week but only caught or killed a rabbit. My dog, a greyhound, just a pup, got after a Jack Rabbit but he got in the bushes & the dog lost him. The first one Dr. B. kills we are going to send you the ears. Well, my dear brother, I will close & write a letter to A. J. You write whenever you can.

Your loving sister

M. M. Brown

P.S.   Dr. Brown says he is going to write to you soon.

Maggie to Amelia Jane

Poncha Springs

Jan 21st 1883

My dear Sister

I received a letter from you with pa's & will now try to write
to you. It has been very cold here & now the wind is blowing
very hard but it is not so cold. Where we are living is a very nice
yard & I think in the summer I will have some flowers. How do
you like to go to school. You must study hard & make a fine
woman.

Tell pa if the smallpox gets anywhere near he had better stop
you from school, but he will know what is best to do about that.
Give my love to dear Aunt Bet & take good care of her for she
loves you all <u>very</u> dearly & might over do her strength. You are
well off to have her in the house. Kiss little brother & tell him I
can read his letter but to improve all he can. Write soon to your
loving sister

M. M. Brown

Maggie to Pa

Poncha Springs

Chaffee Co.

Feb 3d/1883

My dear pa

I received your card about two hours since but suppose by this
time you have received my letter explaining why I did not write
for <u>two</u> weeks. If not, I will tell you again we had not a cent of
money for over a month & the day before I wrote my last letter,
Dr. Brown pulled a tooth for which he got $1.00 & went & got me
50cts. worth of stamps so I wrote <u>as soon as</u> I got the stamps. I
knew you would be uneasy & it made me feel very badly. I <u>will</u>
<u>try</u> to keep enough on hand to get a stamp any way. Dr. B. would
not let me borrow one from the Post office   it is only a few steps
from the door & we had no excuse but <u>poverty</u>.

I sent the children some pictures a few days after I wrote the

letters. Suppose they have gotten them & a card accompanying
them.

Around us have been some awfull snow slides but still no snow
here. We can see it on the mountains & all around but not here.
The main line of the Denver & Rio Grande R.R. runs by here to
Utah. About 65 miles west of here there have been some terrible
drifts & slides. This morning a train went by with 4 cars & 3
engines on the front, had a snow plow on. Under one slide 60
men are buried. One came down the mountain & knocked an
engine & 3 men off & buried them & 2 more slides buried one
man each. One man leaves a family & is under 100 feet of snow—
will not be able to get him out until next summer. That is all
about 50 miles from us.

Mails are very irregular now it goes west, lays in the snow
bank & then we get it. A young man at the next town wrote to
Dr. B. Monday night & he got it Friday & it is only 15 minutes
ride on cars in sight.

I received your papers with thanks. On that letter was one
each to the children from me & one from Dr. B. & self to you.
Write soon & let us know if you got it. I will write as often as I
can.

Your loving daughter
M. M. Brown

Maggie to Pa

Poncha Springs
Feb 11/83

My own dear pa

I received your welcome letter's last even so will answer right
at once although I have four other letters to write to Va friends
one is from Cousin Anna Wise   I think I wrote you some time
ago of Uncle H Wynants death. In this last letter she tells me of
the suicide of Mr. Ben Long a man that has worked for Uncle H.
of 12 years & lived in the house on that little farm of Uncle H's
just above there. He hung himself in the barn & his son found
him there no one knows the cause as he appeared all right   John
Shuff has been so kind in writing to me he did not know my
address at first so sent a letter to Staunton for them to direct
then I wrote to him & he wrote all the circumstances he could or
knew. Mattie C[alhoun] has also written to me. Their affection is

indeed great but today there was a funeral parade of an old lady
that realy died of a broken heart. She was a perfect christian
taught the bible class in our little s[unday] s[chool]   Last fall her
son a man about 28 was arrested for cattle stealing & [she] tried
to find out all about it   but every one kept it from her so she
went up to the county seat & there found out the truth—& it is
said took pluricy & only lived a day or two   today that son was
at her funeral under the sherif God took the soul & has perhaps
saved her from seeing him hung   but it is to be hoped the death
of such a mother will have a good affect. This is no place for
boys. Dr. B. says he is going to write to you so this may have to
lay until tomorrow   I will write to the children soon. You write
when ever you can. I do hope I can come home next summer   I
am getting home sick
Your everloving daughter

M. M. Brown

Maggie to Pa

Feb. 16th/1883
Poncha Springs

Dear pa

I know you think I have neglected you shamefully for not
sending off any letter sooner but have thought Dr. B. would
write his letter for me to put in with mine. But he has been real
busy for the last week but only going to see one man but he lives
12 miles from here so you see it takes a day for him to go there &
back & yesterday morning he started for Bonanza which is 40
miles & will not be back until Sunday or Monday.[9] It is reported
very dull there, but all the mines that are working are doing
well. I expect we will go back in a month or two. Pa, is that a
fruit country around you? & have you your watch yet? I have
been thinking to ask you these questions some time so will now.

You write soon. I suppose Dr. B. will write when he comes
back. He went horse back. He is keeping one now for his feed. It
costs him $1.00 to hire one to go only a mile & it only cost him
about $2.00 per week to keep this one. It is bed time so I will
close with love to all.

Your aff. daughter
M. M. Brown

Maggie to Pa

Poncha Springs
Feb 21st/83

My dear pa

I have not received an answer to my letter but as it has been about a week since I wrote, I will write again. This is the only sheet of paper I have & Mattie has been writing on it [The original was covered with penciled swirls and scrawls.] but hope you will excuse it. The people are very anxious for him to come back, but the <u>snow</u> is still there & very cold. The mines are doing splendid. One <u>mine</u> was bonded for $20,000 (twenty thousand) dollars & 22 sacks of ore paid the bond. A sack holds about a peck. Just think of a peck of rocks being worth nearly 1 thousand dollars. Dr. B. took a very deep cold while there & is not atall well.

Small pox is in Salida[10] the town six miles from here & it is reported that a lady at the upper end of town has it. She spoke to R. B. Monday to vaccinate her family but he has not been able to get any viras yet. He has not been vaccinated for 7 years. Mattie never, & I can't remember when I was. It is so warm here now I hope it will not make much headway. I am sitting with the doors open & not a spark of fire & it is half past 4 o'clock.

We are very anxious to come back to old V[irginia] any way but I would like if we ever get able to have you spend a winter here just to see what a winter is here. Well, we have no winter to speak of. I wish you could see the washing I did today, 44 pieces & all big pieces. Cold is the making of me   I am still lean but <u>oh so tough</u>.

Charles to Pa

Poncha Springs Colo
March 3d 1883

Dear Friend

You asked me to send you some papers giving some information concerning the country that I spoke of going to. It is just this there is not a paper that is published by the Rr's that I would believe any thing that is in them, but I have talked to men that have been there and from what they represent the thing to be it must be a good thing and there is a man gone from near here that I know well and he said that he would write back full particulars to his wife and she has promised to give me all the points. The place I speak of is western Idaho or Eastern Oregon & Washington S.[11] If everything works well I wish to sell every thing that I have and go in a wagon, if I fail to get off by the middle of June I shall make my arrangements to come back to Va. in the fall, but if I do go I shall send all the money that I have to spare back to you, so that you can come and bring the children. I think that we all would be better satisfied if we were together, we could work into each others hands. It is hard for one man to get along in this country by himself, and if we could get together we could take up about 640 acres of land, and the time will come when that land will be available. When I get further particulars I shall write you more fully on the subject.

I am going back to Bonanza in a very short time, to sell every thing that I have there. When we leave here we will write you. We are all in pretty fair health. Mattie is growing very fast, and getting fat and saucy. You would hardly know her.

This country does not suit me and I am anxious to leave it before I came here there was plenty of money to be made here, but now the whole state is dead and no one seems to have any money and I came out here to make money.

I suppose M[aggie] has written all the news and I will close. Love to the children Aunt Bet and your Self—

Truly your friend
C. A. Brown

Maggie to Amelia Jane

Poncha Springs
March 4th 1883

My dear Sister

I wrote to pa a few days ago & thought of writing to you then but had not the time.

I see that you & Dannie & W. J. are improving & hope you all will make good use of your time. This is a hard world to get along in without an education but if you are ever so poor & have a good education you will be respected. So you do the best you can & improve in every thing.

Mattie has a doll nearly as large as she is. I sent to New York for it. It only cost 80 cts. & it is indestructible. It is the second doll I ever bought. It is wearing the same dresses she wore when we left Va. You write soon to your aff. sister

M. M. Brown

Maggie to Dannie

Poncha Springs
March 4th 1883

My dear Brother

I have written to all now, but you. I am so glad you all have the privelege of going to school this winter. It has distressed me no little to know that you were growing up without an education and we could not in some way help you & I know that pa was not able. I felt as though I would be so glad if I could return in some way the money my dear, fond father spent on me. But I have not, except by loving him all a child can love any one.

Soon my dear brother you are growing so fast physically I hope you will try to develop your mind as far as your opportunity will permit. The Dr. got a very smart letter from his niece who is going to Coe's College Cedar Rapids, Iowa. She will be 16 this summer, but she has gone to school a great deal & has nothing else to do, but you can work and study too.

Well, I must close with love to ask you to write soon.

Your aff. sister
M. M. Brown

Maggie to Pa

Poncha Springs, Chaffee Co., Colo.
March 11th 1883

My dear Pa

I have received your letters a day or two since & will now answer. I have written two letters in the last two weeks   this will be the third   I hope you have gotten them by now   a sick-head-ache coming on so I will try to write some letters.

We are both getting home sick. Dr. B. thinks if he can raise enough money to buy the Omahundra place he will come this fall or send me back with what he can raise & make a payment & the Dr. will stay & make the money to make the other payments. He is such a poor collector and we can get along on just so much & he don't try to get out of that   maybe if I was away from him he would have to "russel" more & send me some. I think the small

pox has subsided. For the last two weeks we have had sunshine
& no wind, consequently lovely weather. The wind is blowing
some today. If this weather continues long we will go back to
Bonanza. Dr. B. can do well there but he takes such a cough in
winter when the place is a sheet of ice and snow.

Well, I must write to the children. You write soon. Your letters
are such a comfort, they are so cheerful now & you gaining so
much makes me think I will see a dear young pa if I come back.

Your affectionate daughter
M. M. Brown

Maggie to Pa

Villa Grove Saguache Co
Colo
[late March or early April, 1883]

My dear pa

I wrote to you last week but thought as I got a letter from you
& the children I would write again. You have no idea how sad it
is to hear of the news of our dear friend & acquaintances   since
last spring there has been nine of our friends & acquaintances
died 3 in the Stout family   Uncle Harry   Mr Long   their cousin
Sgt Mellon   2 at Aunt Marthas & aunt J Smith it all makes me
feel as though I must go home. Mary Ella wrote to Dr. Brown of
his aunts death & that his mother was in very feeble health. You
don't know how glad I am that my dear pa is so well as long as
you are well I can start to wait for better times & come home
better off. But if you feel that you are giving away be sure to let
me know for I will try to see you again

Bonanza is about dead the small pox broke out there & I
suppose it will finish it   we hear from there every day how
people all pass through here from there in going & coming
Dr. B. ought to do well here.

A lady called yesterday (whose husband ran last Fall for
senate) & insisted on Dr. B. & i coming to S[unday] S[chool]
school & Dr. B. being Superentendent. I like her very much. she
says she thinks providence sent Dr. B. here. Said she and the
other ladies of the town had been discussing him for two weeks.
It was a week Thursday since we came. Friday Dr. B. sent D. A.
a pair of Jack rabbit ears   Mattie Dr. B. & I took a little walk &
chased up 2 Jacks & one cotton tail   Dr. had a gun & killed one

the ears of which he sent D. A. I sent off some Pinon nuts
yesterday. I must dress & get ready for S. S. as Mrs
Casstarphan (the one I spoke of) said she would come by for me
at 3 o'clock.

Write soon to your very loving daughter

M. M. Brown

N.B.   I will write to the children next time.

Maggie to Pa

Villa Grove, Colo

April 9th, 1883

My dear pa

I did not write yesterday as usual. In the morning Mrs.
Barrett, the proprietress of the Hotel came up for me to take a
walk with her before I got my breakfast dishes washed. Well, I
just left every thing and went[12]   Then she had to have us to in to
dinner, so after dinner & some chat, it was s.s. time & Dr. B.
was elected Asst Superintendant & me Secretary   we have 34 in
attendance.

I think if Dr. Brown can hold out here against the Bar room
"outfit," he will do well but they like those that drink & gamble
with them   [he] stayed at home Thursday night & started Friday
morn' at 7 and got home 10 o'clock P.M. tuesday until 6 o'clock
P.M. Thursday, he rode 106 miles Saturday eve & went 60 miles
all the time right round here. There is quite a number of <u>good</u>
ranches. Well I have plenty of time to add to this before mail
time tomorrow so will now bake some light rolls which I wish you
could help eat.

Here it is the 13th of April & your letter not finished yet. I
have been scrubbing this morning & am so nervous I can scarcely
write but will try to finish this so it will go in the mail.

Dr. Brown just brought in your letters of the 8th. I am so glad
you all seem so cheerful & happy & the children doing so well

We have had quite a small pox scare here but have not found
out yet if it is small pox yet or not. Dr. B. was authorized by the
county clerk to go & investigate the matter but the Dr. who first
had the case would not let him go. So the county Dr. was sent for
& he had a hard time to get in & then said it was only veriloid
[varioloid is a mild form of smallpox that occurs in people who

have been vaccinated or who have had it previously] if it was at
all   so you see we are no better off than before.

The products of this Valley are principally hay, potatoes & oats.
The people do not depend on the rain which only comes once in 12
months. They irrigate from the creeks. We have had beautiful
weather up to the last 4 days & the wind has been trying to blow
the houses over but doesn't succeed.

I will write to all of the children in a few days.

> Your very aff. daughter
> M. M. Brown

Those nuts were from New Mexico

Maggie to Dannie

> Poncha Springs, Chaffee Co. Colo
> [should be Villa Grove]
> April 23/83

My dear Brother

As I have not written to you for so long I will now try to
write. I am so glad you are all doing so well. Pa spoke of getting
you some good books to read. I do hope you may read & profit by
them. The greatest of our men have had no better opportunities
than you although you may never be a great statesman, you can
obtain a great deal of knowledge that will be of use to you in any
station. The storms you had there the first of the month must be
passing here now. The snow is deeper now than I have seen it
any time this winter & that is about 3 inches.

I am so glad that you are so much help to pa & hope you may
continue to keep on.

Well, I will write to A. J. and W. J. Write soon. I do enjoy
your letters so much.

> Your loving sister
> M. M. Brown

Maggie to Amelia Jane

> Villa Grove
> April 23d 1883

My dear Sister

I have just written to D. A. so will write to you. I know you
think I am not going to write to you any more. You are so kind to
write to me. I am so homesick this eve' but I have very kind

neighbors. This eve I stepped over the fence & she gave me a $\frac{1}{2}$ gal. of sweet milk & a pumpkin pie. It helped out with the supper. You must not get discouraged about not getting the prize at school but try the next time. Give my love to Aunt Bet although I don't often mention her in my letter she is very dear to me & I often think about her. I suppose you have moved from the Glendower farm but you have never said when. If so, what kind of house are you living in & will you have a garden spot? Write to your loving sister

M. M. Brown

Maggie to W. J.

My sweet little Brother

"Sister Maggie" gets every one of your letters & will write to you. If I ever come home I am going to bring you a magpie. It is a pretty bird & can be taught to say anything. Write soon.

Your loving sister
M. M. Brown

Maggie to Pa

Villa Grove
May 2/83

My dear pa

I received your kind & <u>ever</u> welcome letter a few days since. I commenced writing to you all when I wrote to the children but was interrupted & before I got at it again Mattie was taken sick & then she and I just got better when she took a relapse & my dearest neighbor's husband went off on a law suit & she would have me & Dr. B. come & sleep at her house so we are just putting up here. People are so kind & if I only had good health as I had six months ago, I would enjoy my kind friends more.

I will get some thing and send to you to plant. If that old woman had any thing I could get at I would let Aunt Bet enter a suit of slander against her. Any body can vouch for Aunt Bet's character. I am so uneasy about you. I am afraid she will hire a negro to kill you she is so mean. I will try to write more Sunday I am feeling so badly today.

Your loving daughter
M. M. Brown

Maggie to Pa

                          Villa Grove
                          May 12th/83

My dear pa

I received your welcome letter & dear picture today for which receive my hearty thanks. The picture is very much like you 10 years ago. I do hope you may keep your health & strength until I can come & spend many happy years with you. Pa, I do get so home sick sometimes I can hardly stand it   just think of it   I never was over 8 months without seeing you before & now it is more than two years. I know you think I am older & ought to stand it better but I have the same heart in me although it is some what hardened against the thrusts of the world but over sensitive to the love of my own dear loving pa.

Well, tonight we are having a rain   the first since last April—a year, that is to say, a rain. It may have sprinkled a little last August or Sept. but only a sprinkle.

Mattie & I have not been well for some time but both of us are feeling better now. Will there be much fruit this year? Be sure to write me in your next. When ever I speak of going home & the fruit there, so many tell me they want to go. My next door neighbor, Mrs. Hillis, is 24 & has 3 little ones. Says she never saw apples or peaches on the trees but if her husband makes a strike she is going to Va everybody wants to go.

May 20th. I was interrupted & have not finished this letter yet but I have been so miserable this week I could not write. If I can't write a cheerful letter to you, I don't want to write any. Some time ago I dreamed that old woman had you stabbed. So be careful of your dear self. I received Aunt Bet's & the children's letters and will answer soon. I want to get this in the mail today & which leaves in less than an hour & I must close for this time & hope to write soon. I do appreciate the letters from home so much & will do the best I can. I am looking for a letter from you in a few days.

                          Your ever loving daughter,
                          M. M. Brown

Amelia Jane to Maggie

                          Glendower Alb Co Va
                          May 27/83

My very dear Sister

We did not write to you last Sunday because pa was not here,

we received your kind and welcome letter. I wish you was here
there is going to be a great deal of fruit of all kinds strawberrys
is turning now   on our way to Sunday school D. A. found some
ripe ones in the chirch grave yard   there is a great many   I do
wish you were here and hope you can be here when apeles
cherries and peaches are ripe   there is no fruit here where we
live but one peach tree and it has some on it about as large as
your thumb but where we lived last year the orched is full of
appels and the people that lives there have a daughter about my
age and she says I must come up and just help my self when ever
I want to and her mother says the same. Well I must close and
leave the other for the next time. I remane your loving sister

A. J. Keller

Dannie to Maggie

My very Dear sister
   they did not leave much room for me to write in but I will tell
you what I can. It is getting pretty warme now and dont rain
much now that is all the room I got
Your aff. bro. D. A. K.

Maggie to Pa

Villa Grove
June 24th 1883

My dear pa
   I received your letter & the children's the first of the last week
but I have been too sick to sit up long enough to write a letter. I
can't tell what is the matter. I have such a pain in my chest & my
heart beats so fast it almost takes my breath. Dr. B. says he is
discouraged   what seems to help others does not have any effect
on me. My hand is so tired now I can hardly keep on.
   Dr. Brown says he thinks if he has got more than enough to
come home on this fall he thinks he will come. He says if I get
through this summer he will be thankful. What do you think of
his coming? You asked what was the business of this place. It is
the terminus of the Denver & Rio Grande R.R. or the branch
intended some day to go through this valley. Now it consists of 3
saloons, 1 grocery store, 1 dry goods store & 2 houses of ill fame
& 1 hotel. Gamblers are in the majority—1 livery stable. Mattie
& her pa are both well.

I suppose the sooner I close this letter the better it will be for you for I know if I keep on writing you will try to read it.

Give much love to the children & tell them I will soon write to them. You write soon & often. Your letters have been & always are such a comfort to me.

> Your most loving daughter
> M. M. Brown

P.S. I direct this to Glendower because I don't know if Batesville is in Albermarle or not.

N.B. Dr. Brown told me to ask you if we could raise enough money to make the first payment on that Glendower farm & come home would you help make the next payments & for you to find out how much would be required for the first payment. I think we all might buy a home & all have a home to go to when we feel like it. Now, pa, do find out as much as you can about it. He & Dannie could attend to the farming & you go on with your business & he could practice also. Write soon to your ever loving daughter

> M. M. Brown

Maggie to Pa

> July 8 1883
> Villa Grove, Colo

My dear pa,

Your letter of the 1st just received   I will try to get this in today. You spoke of being uneasy about me   & you had not gotten my last letter in which I wrote of being sick   I am better in some respects & want you to know it. You spoke of the place where you are being such a poor place for worship of any kind. Some people out here would get offended if you were to ask the blessing at the table where they were. Keep your eyes open for a little home but I want fruit if it can be gotten on it. People think it very smart if they can "beat" an honest debt here & say "I am just that much a head." Dr. B. is as thoroughly disgusted as I am is always making plans for what he will do when he gets to Va. & one thing we can have a family alter [altar] of our own   I am afraid you are not well having to take bitters get some Iron & take it. Well I will close. I will direct this to Glendower as you

spoke of going to Cumberland Co. Write soon to your most aff
Daughter

M. M. Brown

Pa to Maggie and Charles

Trent Mills
Cumberland Co
Va

July 29th 1883

My Very Dear Daughter & family. I have not heard from you
for a long time & I have been very uneasy about you for when
you wrote you was not well I hope you are well now & in good
heart & cheerfull. I got a postal from home a few days ago & all
was well they said they had gotten a letter from you but did not
know my postoffice & did not send the letter but I expect a letter
at the P.O.   now will get it in a day or two. I am at this place
putting in all new machinery in a mill for Mr. Bateman & a man
by the name of Edward Willson   it is a big good mill I have been
from home two weeks last Thursday. The people here think I am
the best Millwright that ever was   I am doing my work well &
gives entire satisfaction   & I am treated very kind & much
respect shown me   the people are of first class & all have invited
me to visit them they say they like to hear me talk for you know
[I] cant sing but I can do my share of talking. I am invited out to
dine to day by 3 or 4 parties. I have not lost more than 2½ days
in 5 months & Dannie I expect is making brooms as fast as he can
I sent him 500 broom handles & wire & twine to make them up.
Aunt Bett & the childdren are getting along splendid. They have
plenty to eat & to wear & all seem to be quite happy except
when they think of you being so far from us. I do wish it was so
that we could see each other now & then at least & I hope the
time will soon come when it will be so   I will not be done with
this job for 2 or 3 weeks more & I must write to my little
precious family today as this is Sunday & I write to them every
week. The above was written before breakfast & I have just
finished eating & will now try to finish writing. Will say that this
country is a good one the mill is on what is called Willie river
which flows into the James some 15 or 20 miles below here & is
navigable for small boats which is a very great advantage to this
country in shiping produce to market as there is no R.R. nearer

than the Richmond & Alleghany which runs on the canal toepath
on James river which is reached by everything that is good when
managed <u>right</u>   peaches are beginning to ripen muskmellons
watermellons watermellons tomatoes apples plenty of all kinds of
fruit. The season is a little dry just now & corn & tobacco is
suffering for want of rain. I must close & write a little to the
other children & perhaps to Uncle Burt Jordan. God bless you my
<u>Dear Daughter</u>

your aff Fr
W. J. Keller

Maggie to Pa

Villa Grove
Saguache Colo
Aug 5/83

My <u>very dear</u> pa
     I have <u>just</u> received your letter will write so this can go out by
the same mail yours came in on. We have had quite a hospitle
here for the last week. We rented our front room to a man & his
wife & she was confined today 3 weeks since & had convultions
but is now up. I have had the whole care of her since & not being
well myself has been <u>very</u> hard on me but I am better than when
I wrote you before. This morning I had tooth-ache & Dr. B. is
<u>very</u> much complaining. He went down for the mail & when he
came back said he "had something he thought would be good for
my tooth-ache" & handed me your letter. Your dear letters are
not near long enough. I just look over & over them to see if there
is any thing I have not seen. I had a mess of snaps the other day
& they reminded me of home. We will have peas today. They are
raised here, but oh I do want some fruit so bad. I have had
apples once but they were shiped green & not much good. Dr.
Brown has been very busy for the last month was in Bonanza
from last Thursday week until Monday. By the time you get this
I suppose his mother & sisters will be in Corinth, Miss. Milly is
principal of a female College there   We got a letter from her two
weeks ago saying they were going the first week in Aug.
     I don't suppose you have gotten my letter speaking of the
Glendower farm or any place you think we would do well to buy
us also sometimes.

Hoping to soon hear from you again I will close & write to the children.

Your most aff daughter
M. M. Brown

Maggie to Dannie, W. J. and Amelia Jane

My dear brothers & Sister

I am glad you write to me if pa is not at home for I feel very lonely sometimes & your letters are great comfort to me & hope some day I may see you but now I think it will be a long time so don't look for me until you see me. It cost so much to live here that it seems like I can never see where the money is to spare to take me home.

I will have to close with a <u>kiss</u> to <u>all</u>. & ask you to write soon.

Your loving sister
M. M. Brown

Maggie to Pa

Villa Grove
Saguache Co Colo
Aug 15, 1883

My <u>dear</u> pa & all

I received your short letter of last Sunday a week as I am all alone tonight with Mattie & don't want to retire so early I thought I could not employ my time better than in writing to you.

I don't know when we will come back. We are thinking of building a house here (a log house) we have been paying $15.00 per month to rent but now it is reduced to $12.00 it just keeps our nose right to the
[section of letter missing]
I curl the back in three curls & plat the front & back. She [Mattie] is cross eyed but for that she would be a very good looking little girl. I was just saying today if we went back to Va in fruit season I reckon we would make hogs of our selves & die eating so much. We are getting some apples now 11½ cts per pound, peaches 20 cts per pound. Well I will close for this time.

All of you must write to me for I am so glad to get your letters
Your most aff sister M. M. Brown

P.S. Dear Pa   have gotten two letters from you in the last two
days   oh! they are so much comfort to me
Your ever loving daughter
M. M. Brown

Maggie to Pa

Villa Grove
Sept 2/83

My very dear pa

I said when I wrote or sent the letter last week I would write
in a few days but one thing after another prevented until today:
now I will not get it off before tomorrow.

We were out berrying the last of last week. The berrys are the
most delicious raspberry a bright red. I got a bout 5 gallons but
this is all the wild fruit I have seen. You spoke of getting a letter
from Miss Keller [Pa's ex-wife]   I do hope you will not let her
work on your sympathies & get you to take her back again. She
is so envious seeing you are getting along so happily without her
rather than take her back take her at her word. Suppose you are
at home now oh! ever I wish I was with you all but don't know
when that will be. Dr. Brown is getting a better hold here every
month he stays & when he gets well established & can lay up
something I am coming back & you & me will select a place & I
will come back here & we will both stay here until we get our
house in Va paid for. I wont tell you what our prospects here are
for fear they might fall through like so many do. I wish you
would make me a small whisk broom & send by mail. I am glad
Dannie is doing so well with his brooms. Hope he will be able to
go to school this winter & improve his time. Just think of it I will
soon have a girl big enough to go to school. Dr. B.'s sister Milly
is principal of a femail school at Corinth, Miss.[13] they have all
gone there to live but Will [Charles's older brother, the family
drifter] they don't say anything about him. Have not heard any
thing from the Wynants for some time. Suppose the place is sold
by this time   Cousin Anna Wise wrote to me last spring that it
would place in the summer. It is very sad to think of the changes
that have taken place in the two short years I have been here.
Well I must close as it is time for me to get Mattie & my self
ready to go to Sunday school

Write <u>soon</u> & a long letter to your <u>ever</u> loving daughter

M. M. Brown

Maggie to Pa

Villa Grove

Sept 30th/83

My very dear pa & family

I suppose you think I have forgotten you but not so I have been very busy this week I could not write. My next neighbor's husband has taken the contract for making brick for the new school house & she is boarding the hands so got me to help so I do what I can & she boards all of us for pay so you see this is some help if I just keep well is all I ask   & I have been real well. Get up at half past 5 o'clock in the morning   I bake the bread suppose you are at home now with the family & having a nice time. I almost envy you all the pleasant times you have together. I think it is so hard to be out here and going through with all kinds of hardships & not have a friend to turn to being deprived of seeing our friends is the hardest of all. I don't see any likely hood of times ever being any better. I feel if I do stay here two years longer I will be lost body & soul. Any thing good is laughed at & some times I think it will distract me.

Dr. Brown will lose all of his claims this Fall. He will not be able to have the assessments worked out & so all he has put in the ground is gone & that will be the case as long as we stay in this state. As soon as he gets a few dollars ahead into some prospect hold it goes. Then it is nip & tuck to get bread to eat. I would give 5 years of my life if I had never seen this state. Now we have been married 7 years nearly & getting worse off every year instead of better.

If I can't write more cheerfully I had better close. I know you would rather not get any letter than one of this kind. You write to me & all of the children I do enjoy their letters so much. I will write to them soon. Give love to one & all & ever so much for your-dear-self

Your aff daughter

M. M. Brown

Mrs. George Rose to Charles and Maggie

Rosedale, Poncha Springs

Oct. 30th, 83

Dr and Mrs Brown,

   Dear Friends

I have looked anxiously for you or an answer to my short letter of some time ago and wandered what had come over the spirit of your dreams that you dident write. Had come to the conclusion that you had eaten all the chickens in the country and couldent find any more for us.

But am glad to hear from you at last and also real glad you can send us some even at the price.

Please send the one dozen and more if you can get them. Mrs. B. isent it about time you were coming over to make that proposed visit? I wish you would come and bring Doc with you. I have not been out of the house for almost a week and have not shut my jaws together in that time, have just suffered untold torture with my face, have got to have a tooth out and Geo. says I cannot take chloroform or ether and I dont know what to do am, miserable will commit susanside or something.

This is Registration day and Geo. is on the Board as usual so I have to do the writing. Miss H. is here yet but expects to go home the last of this week.

Tell Mrs. Hills that Katie Sprague is over at Berts, staying for a while. Has rheumatism and takes a bath every day. I havent seen her, for I havent been able to go out myself. Do write and tell me how you get along. Am always glad to hear from you.

Ever your friend and well wisher
Mrs. Geo W. Rose

Mrs. Quaintance was over and spent last week with us

Maggie to Pa

Villa Grove Nov 5th/83

My very dear pa

I have received two letters from you & one from the children since I wrote but one the first was missent. You direct[ed it] to "Villy Grove" & it is "Villa"   there is a Valley Grove in the state. You spoke of my letters being so changeable. Well I will tell you how it is. Dr. Brown will have a patient who owes him a good bill & is able to pay & we make our calculation often on getting it & the man will leave the country & not pay or get out of doing so some way & often he is out of the house here he has to pay all of his bills. Now a man got his hand all mashed in a mill & sent for Dr. Brown to bring a buggy & bring him down here. Well he did & the man boarded with us & I waited on him   we both did all in our powers to make him comfortable & don't you know all the

time when he was able to get out of the house he was talking
about Dr. B. & said his hand was not treated right & at last he
went up town & got drunk & came down & we could not do any
thing with him & he got mad & went to the county seat to
another Dr. People think it smart to "beat" a man out of a bill so
this is the cause of my letters being so changeable. I have had
only two dresses since I came out here & the same number of
shoes & hats but we hope for better times! oh I must tell you
Dr. B. has turned Republican but I tell you it is for policy. I am
heartily ashamed of it but if he can make any thing by it let it go.
He has gotten a nomination already. The office of coroner, but
there is not much pay in it but he is after the county
physicianship that pays & is given by appointment & the county
commissioners are Republicans.[14] I sent the children some Pinion
nuts last week. They are not cooked some went for on Sunday
Dr. B. went for a load of wood & M[attie] & I went for nuts & we
nearly froze had to build 4 fires. Pa you asked me what I thought
of sending A. J. to that young lady & taking music   why I dont
think you could do better.[15] I wish you would take the family to
H[owards]ville any way. I think you all would be happier. If the
spring dont bring us something better we are going to come back
if we can get enough to come on. Dr. B. says if he just could rent
a farm & he & Dannie could run it & in winter make brooms he
says he will learn & you just keep on at your work & make home
with us he thinks more of you than of his own family. If we stay
here we will have to send our child off to school. I would not send
her to such [rest of letter missing]

Maggie to Pa

Villa Grove
Nov 25/83

My dear Pa
   I have just received your card. Will try to write you a short
letter no more to send off in this mail. Since I wrote the last
letter I have been seriously ill   I was 6 month gone with
pregnancy when I wrote & very foolishly went to help a neighbor
tack a comforter & sewed up four long seams on the machine &
thereafter the waters broke. Well I went that way for a week
some times up & some times down then I was taken with hard
labor which lasted 24 hours & I was delivered of a still born child.

After birth it took Dr. Brown one hour & a half with the aid of
ice & water to stop the flooding under which I sank once. Of
course this left me very weak   then my milk gave me a good deal
of trouble & I took thrash [Perhaps Maggie is referring to thrush,
a fungus infection of the digestive tract.] but it was checked
before it got very far   I am sitting up but very weak & so poor
you would not know your own child now & pa some times I think
my lung are going to be weakened by this   I am stooped & it
hurts me to straighten up. I doubt if you can read what I have
written so I will close & write more when I get stronger   I wish
you would send me some persimmons for Xmas they will be good
then wont they. This leaves us all well but me & I hope to be
soon   Mattie has had the toothache & Dr. Brown a deep cold   he
took shingling the Methodist church where he worked for two
weeks & got $2.50 per day. He stood the work very well until he
took cold.

Write soon & a long letter. Love to all & much to yourself from
your devoted daughter

M. M. Brown

Maggie to Pa

Villa Grove
Jan 5th [1884]

My dear pa

I have been thinking & waiting for every mail in hopes you
would write but I have been disappointed every time   well I
never in all my life spent such a dull Xmas not a cake or nut did
we have & not a cent of money   I went over with a friend of
ours to spend Xmas week in Poncha but got sick & had to come
home   I went to take the bathes at the hot springs for the pain I
have in my side & have had for the last 18 months the bathes
cost 75cts a piece but Dr. Ried said I could have them free being
a Drs wife   but I never got to take a bath. Hope you all had a
pleasant Xmas. Times are still very dull but we live hoping for
better. It has been very cold here 14 below z'o   Matties Grand
ma [Charles's mother] sent her a flannel dress so she is very
comfortable for the winter but Dr. B. is wearing this black coat
he got in the heat of the summer I have a flannel dress too that I
got from a woman that owed him. I want all of you to write to
me   I enjoy the letters from home so much   Don't wait for me to

answer any letter   sometimes we are so low spirited that I think it better for me not to write.

Give much love to all of the family & _much_ to yourself. Write a long letter to your ever loving daughter

M. M. Brown

Maggie to Pa

Villa Grove

Jan 30th [1884]

My very dear father & _all_ dear ones at home

We received the persimmons & the dear letters. The persimmons were some molded but very good any way we had just moved & I have been fixing up is the reason I did not write sooner. I am also baking bread for the public so that keeps me busy we had to do something so as I could not wash I thought I would try that   I am feeling very well now. Dr. Brown heard of his mare he bought a few weeks after he came to the state. She had a colt that spring & when it was six weeks old lost her & colt & never could hear of them again until about two months ago he heard of her & finds out she has now a colt & is with fold [foal] with a blooded colt   the one that was with her when lost was also a blooded horse   he will be 4 years old in July if we can get her that will be a great lift but will cost about $15.00 to do so. We are going to make every effort to get back as soon as possible. Times are very hard all over the state.

We have been having cold weather since Xmas   it is not so cold now but the wind has been blowing all day & will all spring that is a great objection to this country

I baked today & will wash tomorrow so I thought I would write to you to night   I wish you would send me a paper when ever you can   we enjoy them _so_ read everything in them. I wrote to Mattie Calhoun before Xmas   I told her that when they all met in Middlebrook for them to write me a line _all_ of _them_, as a Xmas gift but not _one_ word have I heard   you can ask them for me why it was but _I_ wont write.

You write soon to your loving daughter

M. M. Brown

P.S. Dr. Brown wrote to Dannie he enjoys D's letters so much he will always be a boy   I mean Dr. B.

Charles to Dannie

[Villa Grove
Jan 30, 1884]

This is for D. A.

Dear Dan

I am really glad that you are improving in your writing but you must try to improve much in your composition, so that you can write a long and nice letter. The way to do that is to get a piece of paper and from day to day write some thing on it that you wish to write and at the end of the week get your paper and read it over carefully and select from it all of the matter that you think will interest the one that you are writing to   write to me in this way and I will answer.

Some men came and got my dogs whilst I was at sunday school last sunday and went hunting and they caught two jack rabbits one of them was a very large one. There is very little to hunt here except rabbits. I killed (11) eleven the last time I was out. Write soon. Affect   Your Bro   C. A. Brown

R. Widmer to Charles

Rincon, N.M.   Feb 17 1884

R. Widmer

Dr. Brown

Dear Sir

Your note came duely to hand. Have house ready for our drugs. If you wish to bring your family with you, do so and move in with us as we have a large one with plenty of room one mile from town.

This you could do until you [section of original missing]

Dr. Brown I find that doctors in this territory need have a certificate from a board of examiners in Santa Fe to practice— that is I am told by reliable persons that this is the case. I do not know the names of the two examiners but they are in Lauteede, and you will have no other trouble than the mere delay of stoping off. A Commercial ticket the agent here tells me cost 5 cts per mile while the regular price is only 6 cts. and although he said he could get you such a one for a thousand miles he further stated that he thinks it [section of original missing]

Pa to Maggie and Charles

Glendower
Albermarle Co Va.
Feb 24, 1884

My Dear daughter & family
Your letter came to hand in due time found us all well. Am very
glad you have gotten well but sorry you have grown so old, not
that sick headache is less frequent but to think I have a daughter
so much older than I am. I suppose from your letter that you
must be some 65 or 75 years old by now. Why don't you & the
Dr. have your likenesses taken & let us judge for ourselves. I am
going to have all the children's likeness taken as soon as get
where there is an artist. I hope you will realise all you antisipate
in New Mexico. Get the Dr. to send us a R.R. map or some kind
of a map that will enable us to locate the place to which you are
going   we cannot fine it on our map.[16] D. A. says they are having
a big time in China & suggsts if you cannot make it in New
Mexico perhaps you can in China. He is very much put out about
your not coming home to Va & Aunt Bett had a big cry the night
I got your letters. But all 1 can do is to commit you to God who is
more willing and more able to take care of and provide for you &
in my prayers with my little family I never forget to ask him to
take charge of you. So when our bed time comes which is about
nine or ten o'clock I read a chapter or two & then offer up a
prayer for us all   I will keep on praying & trust all to God   I
will not send the whisk brushes now but will wait until you get
settled again. Write when you leave Villa Grove & when you get
to your new home. Love to all
    May God bless you all

Your most affect
Fr. W. J. Keller

Amelia Jane to Maggie

Glendower
Feb. 24, 1884

My very Dear Sister
    We received your kind and welcome letter   I was glad to hear
you was so much better sory to hear you all were going to
Newmexico instead of comeing home but I hope you will come
home soon Aunt Bet says she does not suppose she will ever see

you again. We have had some very bad weather. Our hens have
been laying very well for two or three weeks and we got 18 cents
per dozen   we have not set any yet. I told pa the other day I
was going to set the first hen that goes to seting I love to raise
little chicks   last summer I raised 4 little chickens in the house
I sold enough of chickens to buy me a pair of slipers and kept me
4 to lay and raise off of   have you any chickens   well I must
close as it is geting late write soon to your loving sister

Amelia J. Keller

5

Rincon, New Mexico:

February 21, 1884–November 10, 1885

She [Maggie] said if she came home could she live with you [Pa] Cousin Charley is getting so wicked that she cant stand it every thing she says nearly he just telles her to go to the D———l. [Amelia Jane to Pa, August 17, 1884]

Saturday night about two o'clock a Mexican came for Dr. Brown & said that "Pete shoot Harry" When Dr. B. got down there Harry was dead, shot in cold blood. Rincon is a hard place! [Maggie to Pa, September 3, 1884]

Dr. Brown is in debt for what we had to get to eat he is almost in rags & I am no better. I think our corn will die there has been no rain for more than six weeks . . . Saturday the Thermometer stood at 110°. [Maggie to Pa, June 22, 1885]

In the bitingly cold winter of 1884 Charles Brown fled the depressed Colorado economy and joined a disorderly rush of other adventurous men spilling into the El Dorado of New Mexico, recently connected to the rest of the United States by the railroad. Rincon was one of the southernmost junctions, strategically located to give Charles access to mining activity.[1] There he could cover his speculations by ranching and practicing medicine among the Anglos and Hispanics of the area. With little advance warning to Maggie, he went down to Rincon, leaving her again a woman in waiting while he set up arrangements for a home and a business with his old Bonanza mining camp buddy, Ralph Widmer. Anxious and resentful, Maggie readied their belongings for shipping. She also had to raise ticket money for herself and Mattie.

While Maggie packed boxes, Charles wrote her letters packed with the folklore of New Mexico, most of which he cited as fact: mysterious legends of Montezuma's promised ghostly return to the Pecos, perpetually burning cult fires, and the miraculous Indian resistance against the Spanish at Starvation Peak. He marked the "splendid ranches" between Santa Fe and Albuquerque but he said nothing of the "alkali, cactus, desert scrub and sand" he crossed over between Albuquerque and Rincon—the Journada del Muerto where early day settlers on foot and horseback left a string of graves and unburied bones.

When Maggie finally joined him, she saw what he had failed to describe. Rincon was harsh: barren, craggy earth beaten by sun and whipped into fine, sandy dust by the ever-present gusting of dry hot wind. Some fifteen houses were scattered like dice tossed over the bare earth, each a one-story adobe rectangle, scarcely two or three rooms large, with only slits for windows. Barbed wire fencing surrounded some of the houses, marking yards which were flat bare patches of earth dotted with scraggly desert sage or tumbleweed. The Rio Grande, which snaked along but a mile or so from Rincon was a western, not an eastern river. Though it created a ribbon of fertility, it was an unreliable water supply—as prone to dry up as to flood. Rincon was a stark contrast with the Virginia home Maggie had left: a stately two-story antebellum building whose porch roof was supported by white Greek columns, with a yard shaded by spreading oak trees. Cultivated flower beds nestled close to the house; a wrought iron fence bordered the trimmed lawn.

The move from Colorado to New Mexico demanded rigorous adjustment. It was *frontier* with a new edge. Interacting in New Mexico in the late 1800s were several vigorous cultures: the Pueblo, Apache, and Navajo Indians; the Hispanics; and the newly arrived Anglos. Complicating the sociology, the Anglo settlers ganged into factions: miners (boisterous and often criminal), farmers, cattlemen, investors, eastern "barons," and "badmen" of every stripe.[2]

While much of this diversity polarized the territory, some of the factions worked together to stimulate economic growth. In a single year (1880–1881) the railroad had laid one thousand miles of track, creating a boom of towns all along its routes: Raton, Springer, Las Vegas, Albuquerque, Las Cruces, Deming, Silver City. The trains brought in heavy mining equipment and took out what the mines produced: gold, silver, copper, lead, magnesium, and zinc. Along the train routes lumber and livestock industries also flourished. In the mercurial fashion of the West, New Mexico became, temporarily, a site for speculators and dreamers. By 1881 Albuquerque and Santa Fe, advertised as America's "foreign country" and "the most curative climate," drew tourists and health seekers.

The eastern tourist or tubercular patient felt easier about venturing into New Mexico in the 1880s because for the moment the relentless force of the U.S. Army had stemmed the rebellions of the feared Apaches and Navajos. In 1864 the Navajos had been rounded up, humiliated, and literally starved into submission in Fort Sumner.[3] By the 1880s Geronimo and his Apaches had been corralled in Fort Apache, Arizona. His last heroic flight for freedom in 1885 was halted by pursuing military who outnumbered the Apaches ten to one. With the Indian fight against white interlopers staunched, Anglos spread through the territory. Despite the influx of United States citizens, the New Mexico of the 1880s was not Anglicized. Predating Anglo settlement by hundreds of years, Indian and Hispanic cultures had left their pronounced mark on language, food, art, religion, social structure, land and water law, and even world view.

The territory was rife with conflict. The government was so embroiled in political machinations it could hardly function. The Santa Fe Ring, a set of lawyers, politicians, and businessmen, ran the territory and were becoming scandalously rich from covert deals in land, ranching, mining, and railroad development.[4] In 1881 territorial governor Lew Wallace resigned, contending he was powerless to act in the face of the Santa Fe Ring's tactics. In the central part of the territory sheepmen (primarily Hispanic) and cattlemen (chiefly Anglo) competed and brawled.[5] Protestants and Roman Catholics clashed over religious and educational policies. And notorious Lincoln County erupted with the murder and violence of its vigilante system of justice. The turbulence emphasized the Browns' distance from Virginia.

Although there were sections in New Mexico (like the southeast nicknamed Little Texas) in which Anglos predominated in the 1880s, Doña Ana County, in which Maggie and Charles settled, was one of the most Hispanic parts of New Mexico. Indeed, after the 1848 signing of the Treaty of Guadalupe-Hidalgo, which ended the United States war with Mexico, some of the inhabitants of New Mexico refused to become American citizens and moved across the Rio Grande into what is now southwestern New Mexico to preserve their Mexican citizenship. However, pressure for a southern railroad route forced Congress in 1853 to negotiate the Gadsden Purchase, which made that section

U.S. territory. Still, even after the purchase, the area kept its Mexican character.[6]

Rincon, part of Doña Ana County, demanded that Maggie and Charles find new survival skills. Critical among these was a new concept of *water*, one wholly different from that held by Virginians, one the Browns never really grasped. Promotional pamphlets of the 1880s did, indeed, mention, in asides, that the "greatest garden spot with the richest alluvial soil in America if not in the world" depended totally on a complex system of irrigation.[7] But such oblique notice about irrigation meant almost nothing to the average easterner. Prospective farmers like Charles from Virginia, where "the early and the latter rains rarely failed to come" and where fields were, in addition, amply watered by running springs, brought to the arid Southwest little notion of the problems of irrigation. The East envisioned but one "normal" climate— humid and moist. The reluctance of the eastern-based federal government to legislate funds for western irrigation projects was a result of its sheer ignorance of the needs of the arid West.[8]

In the West even those who comprehended the reality faced problems. In New Mexico the system of water rights and waterways, begun as early as the Pueblo settlements in the thirteenth century, increased in complexity with each new wave of settlers. The waters of springs, streams, and rivers belonged officially to all the people of New Mexico—a situation opposite that of Virginia where water (following British common law principles) belonged to the person over whose property it flowed. In New Mexico, theoretically, anyone had the right to tap into a body of water. But over the years a series of controls were developed to establish rights of priority to water. Though by 1883 a legal formula designated who along a waterway had priority, court challenges abounded. Diversion ditches added to water rights litigation. These man-made canals had right of way across any property directly in their path, a setup ever ripe for dispute. In addition to these conflicts, there was the ever-present haggling about responsibility for upkeep of the connecting ditches. When optimistic Charles wrote Pa that he and Maggie were in, *"if properly irrigated,"* some of the most productive farm country a person could ask for, he hadn't the least concept of the complexities demanded by "proper irrigation."

New Mexico's fascination for Charles was not ranching but mining. From his first days in Rincon, Charles speculated and followed the doings of the "boys" digging the nearby mines of White Oaks, the Black Range, and the Organ Mountains. The job he got within a few months on the railroad took him regularly to Deming and Silver City,[9] where

banks were flush with mining fortunes, and where every street corner
sported miners in from the hills with tales of new strikes. Charles kept
in excited touch with these accounts.

Ranch-bound, Maggie wrote letters to Pa that were set in a small
bleak world; she seldom mentioned the drama surrounding her—the
range shoot-outs, the political coups, the Hispano-Anglo tensions. She
did note that Rincon was a "hard place." "The sun," she wrote, "never
shown on a worse set of people than Rincon contains."[10] It was the ash
heap of her dreams. The wild ambiance threatened her eastern values
and offered little that Maggie could classify as "refinement" to pass to
her daughter Mattie, then nearing six. In place of dolls and upper class
Protestant Americans, Mattie was playing with rabbits, horned toads,
ponies, and goats, and was speaking either Spanish with her little
Roman Catholic Mexican playmate or western slang ("you *bet* I would!")
with passing cowboys.[11]

Along with everything else in that grisly atmosphere of the Southwest was the unknown world of Maggie's new neighbors, the Mexicans.
Though according to railroad promotion pamphlets for New Mexico, a
"quiet, orderly, law-abiding, frugal people,"[12] they were suspect to
class-conscious Maggie. They spoke a different language, ate different
foods, and practiced a different religion. Their standard of living, too,
seemed different: to Maggie's eastern eyes, trained to judge class by
clipped lawns and picket fences, the New Mexicans were poor. Their
adobe homes, with floors of earth bound with sheep's blood, offended
Maggie's Virginia expectations of what a proper house should be.[13] In
measure, she identified the Mexicans with the blacks whom she labeled
a lower caste than herself. There were differences, though. After the
Civil War the Virginia blacks were free, angry, and often rebellious,
and they frightened Maggie. The Mexicans were gentle and friendly
and confusing. Maggie could not relegate them to a serving class stereotype because many of the government officials and landowners in
Rincon and Las Cruces were Hispanic. A key frontier crisis was the
shattering of ancient prejudices and the consequent reassembling of
world view.

Most aspects of New Mexico, though, intrigued rather than threatened Charles and Maggie. They wrote Pa and Dannie about tarantulas,
centipedes, Indians, and the curious language. Charles bragged about
eating *six* hot chiles at a meal (no small feat), and he put some "real
Spanish" in one of his letters: "*no mass, a mass poko tempo.*" There
were so many horned toads in the Rincon area that its section of
railroad line was known as the Horny Toad Division.[14] Maggie mailed

home to Virginia a live "horned frog" with precise instructions for keeping it in the driest of places in the hottest of sun. She also sent Mexican coins, piñon nuts, and western hats. The diverse nationalities in Rincon surprised Maggie. She told Pa she had purchased a small carved egg from an Arab's bazaar and that a "Chinaman" did her washing. Numerous Chinese had labored on laying the railroad tracks and remained in the area after the lines were completed.

For all their efforts to come to terms with New Mexico, personal conflict between Maggie and Charles ricocheted through the letters. Part of the tension came from Maggie's battle with premature aging. The dry heat wrinkled her skin. Her mouth sank in after she had front teeth pulled. Her shoulders sagged, hollowing her chest. When she sent a picture of herself to Virginia, Pa and Amelia Jane wrote, distressed at her worn, haggard look.

The sexual excitement and intimacy she and Charles had shared in the Colorado years eroded. Since the stillbirth, anxiety over new pregnancies may have led her to reject Charles. Depression settled over Maggie. It may have been the relentless wind, sun, and isolation; it may have been Charles's plans to build an adobe house for his mother and sisters (whom Maggie despised) in the cottonwood grove next to his and Maggie's ranch. Whatever the cause, after the Browns had been in Rincon but six months, Maggie sent a furious note to Pa accusing Charles of becoming so wicked that she wanted to leave him, return to Virginia, and support herself and Mattie by taking in sewing. Six more months in Rincon, she claimed, would kill her. Slaving harder than she had in her life, she felt broken and old.

Interestingly, when Charles gave up his project to move his Virginia family to New Mexico, Maggie's attitude to him somewhat softened. Still her outlook on life in Rincon remained bleak. She wrote Pa detailing Rincon's crime and low society. One night Charles was summoned by a Mexican who just cried, "Pete shoot Harry." Pete was a saloonkeeper and gambler; Harry, a gambler. When Charles got to the saloon, Harry was dead, "shot in cold blood," the sheriff lolling casually by making no arrest. Then Maggie told about "Rollers," men who lurked in the night shadows waiting for a victim with money whom they could roll over and rob. This was Rincon: "3 grocery stores, 1 dry goods store & 5 saloons, the vilest place on earth." Christmas 1885 found Maggie, Charles, and little Mattie, as in Colorado, without money even for a cake or nuts. The winter months, even under the big blue sky, were a struggle for Maggie. She wrote Pa repeatedly of homesickness and invested Virginia culture with exaggerated perfection.

But spring brought a modicum of hope. In March Maggie began raising chickens, and by April she had over one hundred. Charles set out four thousand grape slips in addition to acres of corn, peas, and melons—anticipating a big fall harvest—*if* the rains cooperated and came. With no sense of how to irrigate, Charles and Maggie watched in dismay as the sun dried up their sprouting crops. By May all they had were parched fields; the one sprinkle of rain had dampened the ground scarcely half an inch. Woefully, Maggie and Charles began to understand that they would have to have some means of irrigation if they were to be Virginia farmers in the Southwest. But there was no irrigation ditch nearby and a windmill (the means of irrigation most used in the Rincon/Deming area) cost $250, which they did not begin to have.

In June 1885 as if more problems were needed, there was an Apache scare. Fleeing the ever-tightening confines of their southeastern Arizona reservation, Geronimo and a band of some ninety Apaches made a fierce, desperate run for the Sierra Madre Mountains of Mexico, leaving panic in their wake. From the American point of view, that southwest section of New Mexico had already had its surfeit of terror from the Apache people, so the U.S. Army pursued them hotly. Maggie and Charles watched several nights behind barricaded windows with rifles and guns, while flashes of gunfire splintered the neighboring mountains.

Summer dried up Maggie's hopes completely. The whole region was hit by drought. Not only had rainfall been minimal, but the river itself had changed course. There was wholesale movement from the area. Desperate for money, Charles offered his ranch for sale, but no one wanted the poorly irrigated acres.

Letters from Virginia during the period dramatize the differences between "arid" and "verdant." While Maggie bent to the constant, dry, whipping wind, the baking sun, the scorched, grassless earth, and to long stretches with only six-year-old Mattie for company, her family wrote from Virginia glowing descriptions of peach orchards, fields of blackberries and grapes, flowering locust trees, green pastures watered by cool springs, houses with shade trees, fine rains, abundance of fresh vegetables, yards covered with "grass as fresh and green as can be," and pleasant visits with dear friends. Buckling under the contrast, Maggie looked out at her Rincon ranch with its wasted fields, symbolizing to her the barren western dream.

Maggie begged Charles to go back to Virginia. But Charles refused to return in defeat. The West was dealing him bad cards, but he insisted on staying in the game. In the late fall of 1885 the Atchison, Topeka & Santa Fe opened its Needles Run between Albuquerque and Mojave, California. Charles was taken on as mail clerk for eight hundred dollars a year. Albuquerque rumor talked about gold and silver deposits along the new run. Surely Charles was interested. But while the job rescued Charles, it trapped Maggie. For weeks at a stretch, Charles would have to live on the train. Whether Maggie stayed on at the Rincon ranch or moved to Albuquerque, she would be a widow to the railroad. She balked and decided that this was her time to take Mattie for a six-month visit to Virginia.

Rather abruptly, in November 1885 Maggie and Charles went separate ways, each perhaps naively expecting the new direction to be a kind of bonanza. But Maggie's hopes for what she would find in Virginia were as unrealistic as Charles's hopes for what he would find in California.

The letters of this section dramatize the cognitive dissonance raised by the frontier.[15] Maggie and Charles, in New Mexico more than in Colorado, were in a situation where their familiar southern cultural guides for behavior and thought did not work. The confusion about irrigation was a practical instance. The southeast looked regularly to the sky for water; such an expectation in New Mexico proved disastrous. Analogous problems made social and emotional issues confusing. Anthropologist Clifford Geertz says, "It is in country unfamiliar emotionally or topographically that one needs poetry and roadmaps."[16] The unsettling of Maggie's accepted cultural scheme of things made her reexamine her code of values. She, more than Charles, had to address the process of assessing old vision and shaping new. Perhaps Charles's dissonance was less because Old Virginia values were in some measure what he wanted to escape.

It was in elemental needs and behaviors that value crises surfaced for most frontier settlers and certainly for Maggie. In that line between wilderness and civilization, new and old values clashed. And only the ones deemed most essential to survival formed part of the new existence. A brief reflection on some of the manifestations of tension highlight the essential strain of the frontier.

For Charles and Maggie, the frontier did not offer (as Frederick Jackson Turner claimed it did) escape from the "bondage of the past." On the contrary, Maggie's and Charles's relations with their families in Virginia reinforced the family network. For a southerner, any family member's location in a place made that place "home" for all the rest of the family.[17] The frontier did not diminish this obligation of hospitality.

Family was an unquestioned value. Pa was urged by both Maggie and Charles to move West. The invitation was genuine and enthusiastic. He would have brought with him a pleasing combination of love of the old and trust in the new. Pa posed no threat or test.

Charles's family, on the other hand, posed both because their presence stirred guilt and resentment in Charles over values and expectations he eschewed. When Charles's family sent him $800 to buy them land and build them an adobe house in the cottonwood grove next to him and Maggie, they presumed a definition of family that made such proximity usual. Even in the face of Maggie's keen dislike of the Brown women, Charles, given his southern code of honor, could not gainsay his mother and sisters' request to move to New Mexico.

A complex psychology, however, tangled Charles's relations with his family. There is a distinct possibility that Charles misrepresented his fortunes, citing his pipedreams as flourishing successes and never admitting his dismal failures. If such was the picture the Virginia family received, no wonder they wanted to move West. Yet Charles, after agreeing to set up a homestead for them and taking their money, mismanaged it. Not too gently, they accused him of losing the $800 they had raised. It was an expensive price for Charles's contradictory impulses. His southern code obligated him to relocate his family with him; his adolescent resentment and shame could not tolerate their scrutiny. Perhaps he *had* to mismanage the money. Had he built them the house, they would have arrived and witnessed his miserable failure. The pressure of the extended family rankled Charles. Still, rather than confront the problem, he presented a face of compliance with the tradition and blamed his lack of compliance on economic vagaries. He did not break from the bondage of the past. He let distance camouflage his problem. His crisis was unproductive in that it held dissonance at bay and thus failed to generate a clarification of values.

A tension positively resolved is illustrated by Pa and Maggie's adherence to the Protestant ethic as a clearly articulated source of social and emotional support. The late nineteenth century was a period of militant evangelism. Itinerant Methodist preachers viewed the West particularly as a field ripe for harvest. Strident theological debates were frequent, and rigid interpretations of the Bible enforced. In this context Pa's religion, as indeed Pa himself, stands singularly untouched by repressive theology. Pa's belief system stressed faith in a God who cared for human beings and who connected them despite distances. Such was the heart of Methodist theology (which most fundamentalists

ignored): "that all true Christian religion is social religion, to be expressed through Christian love, doing no one harm but instead good."[18]

The humanitarian impulse should have fitted in a church anywhere;
however, the dearth of Protestant communities in Roman Catholic New
Mexico made the strange new world even stranger to Maggie. Pa
understood and encouraged:

> If it is a little hard to attend to it [religious observance] now it
> will all come right at the close of life which will soon come round.
> Be found at your post & if the summons should be sudden &
> without warning that it may find you as it did your dear Mother
> all ready. You can wield an influence over the people by whom
> you are surrounded that will do immense good. I hope to hear
> soon that you & the Dr are good workers for the Master.
> [February 22, 1885]

Even when Maggie could not reproduce her southern Protestant church
circles, she could hold as paramount value the personal rituals that
informed the theology. Pa's reminder to her of his night prayers described a practice Maggie could reproduce in New Mexico without a
church or a minister.

> All I can do is commit you to God who is more willing and more
> able to take care of & provide for you & in my prayers with my
> little family I never forget to ask him to take charge of you. So
> when our bed time comes which is about nine or ten o'clock I
> read a chapter or two & then offer up a prayer for us all I will
> keep on praying & trust all to God. [February 24, 1884]

A crisis in values not so successfully resolved for Maggie was the
discrepancy between the eastern world she wanted Mattie to be part
of and the southwestern world Mattie was assimilating. Mattie played
with Mexican children and spoke Spanish. The Mexicans, to Maggie,
were a step beneath her in social class. Unlike the southern blacks
whom she feared, the Mexicans were "a simple people" who could be
"managed well if treated right" [March 23, 1884]. Mattie's playmate
was a humiliation. In the typescript, Mary Gose emphasizes Maggie's
initial sense of shame at her daughter's friend: "In that land of entirely
uneducated Mexican peons Mattie was seven [years old] with a little
Mexican peon as her sole playmate."[19] Maggie could not accept what
she perceived as social inequality; yet she was proud that Mattie could

speak Spanish, the little friend's language. It was an unresolved strain; the Mexican friend would not be one written to from Virginia.

In another way Mattie's behavior precipitated a crisis in values for Maggie. Mattie liked traditional boys' activities more than she liked those of girls. The demure Amelia Jane, steeped in the Virginia tradition, wrote Maggie about clothes, hair styles, baby chicks, gardens, girl friends, and delicate embroidery designs. Mattie, in contrast, was a wild thing, described by Charles as "full of mischief." In addition to her Spanish, she was also adept in western slang. She had two little kids (goats) that she had full care of and that she was trying to train to pull her small wagon. Other key parts of her world were her kittens (some of which she negotiated to sell), her dog, chickens, and rooster.

An anecdote in Mary Gose's typescript describes Mattie's western enthusiasms:

> Mattie always had some wild creature that she caught and tied a ribbon around its neck. She had to have a pet. It could be a rabbit or a horned toad or a bird, anything else that she could tame. One day she called, "Oh, Mummie! Here's a great long thing and it's swallerin' my wabbit." It happened that a visiting neighbor heard her so he dashed to see, calling Mattie to come back into the house. He found, under the front doorstep, a huge rattle snake with a blue ribbon sticking out of his mouth. There was a hoe handy and he killed the snake. When he pulled the snake out it was six feet long and had numerous rattles. My mother [Maggie] said she was so weak with fright she didn't know what to do, but Mattie was inconsolable at the loss of her pet.[20]

Mattie lived free from gender restraints the traditional southern culture would have imposed on her. It seemed a happy loss for Mattie, but an upsetting one for her mother.

Finally, the letters of this section show Maggie herself breaking out of southern propriety. Refusing any longer to resign herself to a stoic acceptance of fate (as her tradition would advocate), she lashed out in anger at Charles's improvidence and rather than follow him to Albuquerque, she raised money for tickets for herself and Mattie to visit Virginia.

This period ends in pronounced discord. Both Charles and Maggie opted to flee rather than to continue the struggle to resolve crises in Rincon. Charles followed one of the new paths for the American Dream—

the new railroad line from Albuquerque to Mojave, "the Great Needles Route," while Maggie followed another American Dream to an Eden of memory, which for her was Virginia.

Letter Texts February 1884–November 1885

Charles to Maggie

Rincon, N.M. Ter.
Feb 21st, 1884

My darling Wife

I reached this place this morning at 4 o'clock. You will arrive at the same hour in the afternoon, as I had to lay over in Pueblo for 12 hours, but I sold Flora[21] for $45 in cash. I found by looking at Smith's books that she was nearly 17 years old. And the colt was very small and really of but little value. After I sold her I got my clothes which I think you will like, and got your things, all but Mat's Doll and I could not get one at the house that I got the rest at, and did not have the time left to go elsewhere, for I just had time to make the train. I intended to send one from here but they are all china, but she shall have a nice one when she gets here.

Now I will tell you of my trip. After a rough trip we got across the mountain to Poncha [Springs] where I met Mr. Rose, but Mrs. R. was better and I did not stop. So when I went to get back on the train, Mr. Towser Appleton [the Browns' dog][22] hesitated too long about getting up and the train came off and left him. He kept up with us for about a mile and then went back. Forgot to give Mr. Rose his jam and left it with Mr. Casmino for him.

My trip was extreamly interesting, passing over the old historic grounds. The first that I saw was a peak called Starvation because years ago the Indians ran an hundred and fifty Mexicans on the top of it and starved them to death there. It is a flat topped mountain to your left as you come on the way and if you will watch close you will see 2 Crosses on top of it.

The next of interest is the ruins of the old church that Montizuma took his flight into from the Spaniards 450 years ago, and around the old church there was a great battle fought in which the Indians were conquered and Montezuma captured by the Spaniards. This place is from 15 to 20 miles from the first, on the right side of the road, and not far from the top of Mt. Glorietta.

Saw plenty of the Zuni [incorrect identification. These would have been Pecos Indians] Indians at one of the stations. They have a city not far from this station that was founded not long after Montezuma's death and I understand that they have kept a beacon fire burning ever since his death. when he went away he told them to keep up the fire until he returned. It is burning now but where, I do not know.[23] At this Zuni City we first came to the Rio Grande, the valley of which is very rich, and much of it under cultivation by the Zuni. Below came some splendid ranches. You may tell Barton that if he wants land he can get plenty about 3 miles from here, and there is plenty of water in the river that can be gotten easily. The Texas Pacific have been holding the best of it but I think their right has passed out of their hands. The sooner he can start, the better. Will write to him soon.

Expenses—

Ticket at V.G.	12.05
" " Pueblo	34.65
Supper at Salida	.50
Bed, Breakfast & D. Pueblo	.75
Lunch at La Junta	.30
6 other lunches on road	1.00
Bed & Break. at this place	1.00
	50.25

Have only seventeen (17) dollars left, and as soon as I get my license will send what is left to you. Don't pay any that you were not obliged to pay, the prospects are good here.

Just as soon as you get money enough, come right on. We can make arrangements. The people are anxious for me to stay and willing to help me all that they can. Will send particulars next time.

Kiss my babies and think of me often. God bless you both.

Affect.
C. A. Brown

Charles to Maggie

Rincon New M.
Feb. 25th 1884

My dear Wife

Rece'd your welcome letter today and sent you a telegram

telling you not to sell the stove. The fact is that they are very high down here and very scarce and hard to get. The freight on all of our stuff will cost twenty ($22.10) two dollars and ten cents which would be less than the sacrifice by considerable. Better get them ready and ship at once. But after I think about it wait for a few days. I may have them sent for express if I can get it as cheap as freight   the agt here seems to think that he can fix it for me and they will be safer. Begin to like this country.[24] It looks awfully barren all round but the river bottoms are very firm. I have an idea of taking up some land myself. They raise almost everything that any one would desire. . . . Have not got the goods up yet and my license has not returned from Santa Fee [probably spelled phonetically to follow the Anglos' pronunciation] am getting impatient. Keep all the money that you get for we will need it.

The water is not as cold as that at V[illa] G[rove] but I like it it has iron in it from the iron in the sand. My bowels are all right and my weight is the same that it was there, 165 lbs with chances for improvement. If Mr. B. does not have too much load he may bring our things with him. The W[idmer]s have nothing to cook on and it is hard to get some thing to eat. I want to see you awfully but dont want you to come yet you will be all right when you do come. Rincon is smaller than I expected to find it but there will be plenty to do, and every one is anxious for me to stop here for I pretend to them that I may take the store some where else and now if they ask such high rent that we dont like to give it and are trying to get them down and I am pretty certain, that we will get it cheaper. . . . Groceries are near about the same here as they are there but I can get the rent cheaper & Quick. Love to all Many kisses to yourself & Mattie. Will write soon again

Affct
C. A. Brown

Charles to Maggie

Rincon N.M.
Feb 28th/84

My darling

I wrote you the day before yesterday   am sorry that it takes letters so long to get to you. . . . Am feeling splendid as health is

concerned, but there is considerable delay about the house   we
have not opened the goods yet but when you get ready to come
there will be a place here at the ranch for you. . . . Have you
gotten the things from Pueblo yet? I left them at Wilson &
Bosmunds to send by mail. Kiss Mattie & yourself a thousand
times for me for I miss you so much. The country is new yet I
think you will like it. Write often

Affect Yours &c
C. A. Brown

Charles to Maggie

Rincon NM
March 7th 1884

My own dear Wife
   I rece'd your card and two letters today and God only knows
how grieved I am. The only thing that I can do is ask you to wait
until I can take in the money here the people are anxious for me
to do well & are doing every thing that they can for my interest
and must get some money now pretty soon. The trouble about
the house has been about the price of the rent but we are in it
now with the goods opened up and are now taking an inventory
and will get done by tomorrow evening. I am determined to
practice here for cost or its equivalent only I could get the money
of Mr W. but he has none and will not have any before I can
make it myself. Cheer up my darling and lets work out of it the
best we can   it will not be long. It makes me sick to think of our
troubles, but God will help us out some way. Our lot seems to be
a hard one, but oh! my darling bear up for my sake for you know
that I am doing the very best that I can. The only house that I
can get that is fit to live in is the back part of the store a nice
room 15 × 25 feet nicely papered with 2 windows, which is in the
contract for my purpose to live in   it will not cost much to put up
a house and mean to do it as soon as I can. This is a better
country to live in than Colorado. There is great need of a newer
depot here on a small scale & I have been intending to get a
small stock for you, and let you run it. There is a very good
chance for Mr Boggs to run a small grocery store in the other
half of it. The man talks of putting in groceries himself but I
don't think he is able. Please tell Mr Barton that the land that I
spoke to him about had been taken but there is plenty of R.R.

land here.[25] And if he will watch the proceedings of Congress upon the Texas Pacific affair   there is apt to be plenty of that <u>Vacant</u> soon, and I think that he could risk coming for I am satisfied that it will be vacant. He asked about game tell him there is only ducks and quails and not many ducks at this time of year   the climate is as good as I ever saw. Foundations and stakes are not recognized among the settlers here. Plenty of timber on the bottom lands and that is the only kind that is worth locating.

Now my dear please for piety sake bear up. Have we not been in tight places before and has not God helped us out.

Hope our babe has gotten well by this time kiss her for me and many to you, and May God bless and protect you both.

Affct CABrown

Charles to Maggie

Rincon N.M.
March 8th/84

My own darling

Rec'd your nice letter today and am truly glad that you feel in a better spirit about the trouble that we are in and to tell you the truth am rather anxious for you to stay for a little while longer as the small pox has broken out in a Mexican town about 3 miles from here and I have heard that there is one or two cases in this town but do not know as the Mexicans do not have any Drs for small pox. Will have plenty of good virus in a few days and will vaccinate a large no of both white and Mexicans[26]

You asked me about going to Will Steels party. Of course if you wish, I have always considered my wife a lady and a lady never does any thing that she thinks would be wrong so all that I have to say is use your own judgment about such things. We will have plenty of melons of all kinds this summer, but I am afraid that the vegetable line will be small, as there is so few planting any. This climate is lovely and when we get started right we will enjoy it.

Have not time to write more will write again soon

Much love to both.

Affect
CAB

Pa to Maggie and Charles

Glendower
March 23d 1884

My Very dear Daughter & family

I am so glad to know that you have made another trip safely.
But really from your letter it seems that you are going from bad
to worse. I want you to tell me all about how the people make
their money so I will know what chance the Dr. has to get some
of it. I have allways found that where people are making money
is the place to go to get some. I want you to send me the note
the Dr. received which was written in Spanish or some other
Spanish writing & let me know what kind of Drug Store he has to
keep for his friend & in fact give me all the facts relating to your
new home. I hope you will do well. I will send you some garden
seeds though I have none of my own as I did not have any garden
last year & will not have any this year as I will be from home
most of the time. I cannot get any sweet potatoes but will send
some broom corn seed 3 varieties Dwarf, Tennessee ever green,
California golden. Tell the Dr. to plant them some distance apart
so they will rise. I have some whisks made but they are too large
to send in the mail but will make some small ones in a day or two
& send to you. Aunt Bet will send ginger cakes at the same time.
Your letter was 7 days on the way   did you get our last letter
before you left Villa Grove? We wrote on the 9th of this month. I
hear nothing from the vally & can tell you nothing about our
kinspeople. I am paddling my own canoe now I can do better
among strangers than among my kinfolks as strangers have no
envious feelings to wards me. I have enjoyed myself very much
with my family this winter & all have been very well & are now
for which I feel very thankful. Be sure & send us a R.R. map or
some kind of map so we can locate you[27] Write soon & a long
letter. Kiss little Mattie for me & tell her to Kiss you for me.
Give the Dr. my very best wishes. love to all
May God bless you all.   Your Afft Fr. W. J. Keller

Maggie to Pa

Rincon New Mexico
Mar 23 1884

My dear pa

I thought I would write to you but found this was all the paper

in the house so you must excuse it. I do feel so far away from you all. I almost get sick some times when I think of it, but I am going to work awfull hard this summer & try to make money to come back to see you all this fall. I think Dr. Brown has a better show now to make money than he ever has since we have been married. There is fewer Yankees[28] here than any place we have been. The Mexicans[29] are a simple kind of people & if they are treated right they can be managed very well. Suppose you have gotten the map & papers   I think if I could make the money I could afford to spend it that way [reference to above project to make money for a visit to Virginia]   Dr. B. runs the store gets half the profits & divides up his practice gives them half Mr Widmer gives one fourth ¼ of his half for the rent of the store room the practice included so you see there is two other parties interested in getting up a practice besides Dr. B. They both are acquainted too makes a difference. Sunday is observed more here than in Colo no stores are allowed open on Sunday altho' we have no church. Having nothing more to write but lots of love to all I will close. Tell Aunt Bet not to grieve too much I hope to see her again in a few months   it may be a year but as soon as I can. Can't you send me the picture of the whole family
Will write to the children <u>soon</u>

> Your ever loving daughter
> M. M. Brown

Commissioner of Immigration, Kansas, to Maggie's father

To W. J. Keller, Esq.
CO. Glendower, Albermarle Co Va.

> C. B. Schmidt, Commissioner of Immigration
> March 23, 1884
> Topeka, Kansas

Dear Sir:

Referring to yours of recent date, asking for information in regard to the South-west, I take Pleasure in forwarding in separate package, by mail, printed matter descriptive on the country reached via the Atchison, Topeka & Santa Fe Railroad.

If you wish to be further informed with regard to any particular locality, or, if you are in search of an opening for any particular kind of business, I should be pleased to give, as far as I am able, such further information as you may desire.

Yours truly,
CBSchmidt
Comm'er of Immigration

Maggie to Pa

Rincon, New Mexico
Mar. 29th, 1884

My own dear pa

How would you like to make us a visit? I think I have struck on a plan that it wouldn't cost you anything to do so.

We, with several others, want some good cattle, some good milk cows & a few good Durhams like those cousin Meg Keller had. Now you see where they can be gotten & how much they will cost & what you could charter a car through to this place for.

Now if they can be gotten there we will have to have some one to come with them & see to them. Now if you would come it would not cost you any thing to come or go & then we would see you. That is worth all the cattle.

This is if we get the money we want now you see & if we do you will hear from us at once. You let us hear from [you] as soon as you can. Try to get cows with calf, if possible. You see what the cows will cost & the cost of the car, then we can tell what they will cost per head. Dr. Brown has sent in his application for R.R. physician & if he gets it, it will bring him in about two or three hundred dollars a year & get a free pass from El Paso to Las Vegas.

We just received the garden seed & your letters of the 23. Will write to the children another time. Thank you very much indeed. Write often because it takes so long for the letters to come through.

With _much_ love to _all_, your most Aff. Daughter
M. M. Brown

Will send you by this mail a picture of Depot. That dog is our grey hound. I brought him from Villa Grove with me. Dr. Brown is standing at the corner of Depot with his hand on his dog's head.

Pa to Maggie and Charles

Glendower [Virginia]
April 5 1884

My Dear Daughter & _Family_

Your letter dated Mar 29 came to hand in due time, was glad to

hear from you. I sent to the agent at Topeka & got maps & descriptions of the country along the R.R. I will look around & see what can be done about cattle & will send to the same agent for terms of freight. I sent 4 whisk brushes to you some time since hope you have gotten them. I sent in my last letter my <u>love</u> & kind wishes to my little <u>Grand Daughter</u> (if I have any) though I have not heard from her for a long time & I am not sure that I have a grand child but hope I have in your next please let me know if you can & how she is getting on   tell her if you see her that I will send her a little present some of these times for a remembrance of me & as you have an artist who takes good pictures try & send me the likeness of the whole family & as soon as I can get to where an artist is I will have all our pictures taken & send to you   I got the picture of Rincon Depot Greyhound & Dr. Brown   I like it splendid I would like to have such a <u>dog</u> as that I guess you prise him very much as he is a relic of Colorado   did you take little Mattie with you from Colorado or what has become of her? I would like to know. I will finish my brooms this week & will soon be out of work   I am not sure what I will do with my family it does not suit to leave them here & D. A. & I away but will know in the course of a month or so. Nothing would give me more pleasure than to visit you & Mr. Bateman has a Pattent air bolt for flour mills which I like very much & he wants me to canvass the western states for him. Let me know in your next letter what kind of mills is out there & how the wheat looks &c &c. Good night God bless you <u>all</u>
Your aff

> Fr. W. J. Keller

Maggie and later Charles to Pa

> Rincon, New Mexico
> April 12, 1884

My dear pa

Your letter of Mar. 29th received. Well, I will ease your mind & tell you I did bring Mattie with me. She often says things I think I will write to you but when I go to write, I forget them. The other day she was playing with her kittie & she said, "Kittie, I am going to send a note to God to put finger nails on you."

Dr. Brown is doing better than in Colo. We have very little love for Colo. If we can get a ranch here we will take one up.

I think you could do well to take that man up & come out. If
you come out I may go back with you, but if Dr. B. can do well
here, we had better make this our home

Maggie is feeling a little badly and asked me to finish this, just
went into the back room to lie down and rest. We are having
some March wind today and it makes us all feel a little chilled.

There is a mill near here that needs fixing up badly, and I think
you might dispose of one of them [the patented air bolts Pa
mentioned Apr. 14, 1884] there, but I'll speak to the man the next
time I see him. Am under the impression that you could do well
here on a ranch. All of the land is claimed but you could buy out a
squatter and make a homestead of it. There is plenty of them
that will sell for little or nothing and the land is as good as it can
be found anywhere, but it can only be cultivated by irrigation.
There is plenty of water in the river to for that but it has to be
gotten out in ditches first which is the heaviest expense about a
ranch here.[30] But after you have it out the ranch is always worth
considerable money and you don't have to depend upon rains
which are very seldom here. The climate is of the very finest,
plenty of tolerable good drinking water, healthful except small
pox which is to be found only among the Mexicans. Have not
heard of any white people having it except one—they all
vaccinate, and the Mexicans don't believe in it expect that Ma
and the Girls will come out here this fall or Summer if you and
your family were here I think that I could make this my future
home. It is the only country that I have liked since I came west.
I intend to rent an acre of land to raise me a garden on, and then
will have plenty of garden stuff for this winter.

Well, I left this for Maggie to finish but she is taking lessons in
cooking on a Kerosine Stove. It seems to work all right. She is all
right now. Tell Dan the boy he spoke of in the picture has a
poodle in his arms. *No mass, a mass poko tempo.*[31]

Write soon again. Love to all from

All affect.

C. A. Brown & family

Maggie to Pa

Rincon Apl 11 [1884]

My dear pa & family

Dr. Brown finished other letter so I will try to write a few lines now. I have some Mexican coin. I will send you all for keep sakes the 50 cts piece is for you & the 25 cts for Aunt Bet & the 12 cent for DA & the 10 for A. J. & the 5 for W. J. Last night a lady came in & I in conversation asked her her father's name. Mattie spoke up & said "Keller is my ma's pa's name he is my Grandfather" I hardly thought she knew your name we always speak of you as pa she says she will write to you. I think we will have water mellons this year if you don't come out here I think I will try to make money some way to come home this fall I would be willing to work very hard this summer to see you all this fall.

We have so little to write about we can't write long letters.

Will enclose Matties letter she says she is writing to her "Grand Father" & telling him "I am nice & good & mind you" & he says all right I am glad of it.

Give love to one & <u>all</u>   Write soon

your aff daughter

M. M. Brown

Pa to Maggie and Charles

Glendower

Albermarle Co

Va

April 20, 1884

My Dear daughter & family,   Your letter of the 12th just came to hand. I sent you 4 whisk brushes did you get them & how do you like them & I am done working on brooms   I finished yesterday & will go to H.ville this week. Mr. Bateman wants me to come up there & live but I must first make arrangements to suit. I will see how everything is before I go. Tell the Dr. to be sure to let me know about the mill he spoke of in his letter & of all the mills if run by water or steam power and what kind of flour they make. I would not be surprised if he would send me out there but it will be some months yet   I am much oblige to you for telling me about Mattie   can't you send us her picture & yours & the Dr. too. Write soon & a long letter. How are you getting on studying Spanish   I think the Dr. closed his letter in Spanish. No mass a mass poko tempo   love to all

W. J. Keller

Dannie to Maggie

[April 20, 1884]

My dear Bro [sic]

The weather is different from what it was last winter when I made so much fuss about the rain it is fine now. we finished up our brooms yesterday. We expect to move to Howardsville but are not certain. I believe I would rather go out to N.M.   have you seen any Pueblo houses since you been out there and are there any Apache indians[32]   I got after them ducks two weeks ago and killed finest one I ever saw and two days later I killed two at one shoot   I have been looking for a hawk all day to day (Sunday) but he dont seem to want chickens as bad when I am looking for him as he does when I am not he come about one hundred yards from the house to day   I am going after some pheasants next week   I am going where there are some wild turkeys and I might pop at them if they try to bite me [even] if it is against the law to kill them I aint going to let them kill me.

Your Affec Bro D. A. K.

Maggie to her brothers and sister

Rincon, New Mexico
April 23, 1884

My dear brothers & Sister

I will write to you all in one letter. It is getting very warm here. The trees are putting out leaves. I send you by this mail a horned frog from New Mexico & the egg is of olive wood, made in Jerusalem & bought by me from an Arab. We have quite a mixture of people here   a Chinaman is doing my washing[33]   This frog don't require any thing to eat or drink, neither will it hurt any one but I don't like to handle it. The lady that gave it to me brought it in her hand. I hope you will get them all right. Be sure to write if you do. Things are looking very well for us now.

I must close for this time. Give my love to all & all write to me.

Your loving sister
M. M. Brown

P.S. Look through the little knob on the egg & you will see a picture.

Maggie to Pa

> Rincon, New Mex.
> April 30, 1884

My dear pa & family

I suppose by this time you have gotten the money; also the frog. Tell me what you all think of them. Well, I suppose New Mexico will be our home. Dr. Brown's mother wrote from Miss[issippi] (where she has been for a year) that she would as leave make New M. her home as any where so would send him a Draft on a New York bank for ($800.00) eight hundred dollars to build them a house. Now I will tell you the kind of house it will be. 30 ft. × 32 ft, 1 floor, 4 rooms, ceiling 10 feet, the material adobe or brick 16 in. × 8 in. & 4 in thick. They are mixed with straw and just dried in the sun, then the house will be plastered inside & out. It will be in a grove of cotton wood trees as large as large oak trees. They will all be here in six weeks if we can get the house done. In our walk this eve we brought home some flowers & Mattie took one & put on her hat & started to the P.O. with it to send to "my little Uncle." I would send it but it is too large to send in a letter.

I hope something will turn up that it will suit you to come out. I am still in hopes I can come home this fall. If you all were here I would be contented to live here too, but it is a bad place to raise boys. But I hope my brothers will never be led from the path of honour & duty to God & man I feel like the child of My mother & Father will never go very far astray

Give my very best love to all & much to your own dear-self, from M. M. Brown

Maggie to Pa

> Rincon, New M.
> May 9, 1884

My dear pa & family

I received your letter & A. J. & D. A.'s but none from W. J. He was too sick, I know, to write. I am so uneasy about the little darling. Don't let the Dr. give him any calomile & very little med. of any kind if it is fever. You write so often about something being the matter with W. J. he must be delicate. My prayer is God may spare me to see you all once more.

You put the Frog in a box with dry earth in it & set it in the hottest sun you can find. Have the box 10 × 18 in. & 6 in. deep. give it blossoms off of trees, flies, etc. to eat. I don't know how they come into the world. We thought that was a young frog   I have seen them larger. We can get plenty of frogs but no more eggs just now.

Pa, just as soon as W. J. gets better, have the picture of the family taken & send it to me. I can't write more just now.

Love to all. Write soon & often now, my dear little brothers & all

yours lovingly

M. M. Brown

P.S. I thought you had this letter long since. Found it in some old papers.

Maggie to Pa

Rincon

New Mex   June 6 [1884]

My dear pa

I received your letter some time since, but have not written because I thought the mail would not get through if I did write there has been awfull washouts on the roads no mails or anything for a week & most likely for a week more but I will write to let you know we are all well & poor as poverty & likely to be all our days. Dr. Brown's mother sent him $800.00 (eight hundred dollars) to build a house & he has put it all into a mud house & nothing to show for it he has had 7 or 8 men working all the time & at least half standing around watching the other half. Oh pa I get so discouraged sometimes I feel just like giving up. Now when they [Charles's mother and sisters] all come I know there will be great dissatisfaction   I just want to come home & stay until all of their money is gone & I wont have to bare the blame of spending any of it. It wont take them long to get through with it. This time last year they had about $8000.00 eight thousand. Now they only have $3000.00 so you see they wont have it long. Hope little W. J. is well now. There is a goodeal of sickness around here but everybody treats themselves.

Write soon to your ever loving daughter

M. M. Brown

Pa to Maggie and Charles

> Howardsville
> Albermarle Co
> Va

June 16, 1884

<u>My Very Dear</u> daughter & family   Your letter just came to hand to day. I am truly sorry you have the blues so bad. I am sure I cannot advise you what to do except to be patient & do the best you can & be as cheerful as possible & still hope for the best do not be discouraged. I would be more than glad to have you with us though we have nothing very inviting or very pleasant but what we have we enjoy as much as any person can. I went home last Saturday & took A. J. a hat all trimed it is white straw trimed with flowers & a pair of gloves that was long enough to reach to her elbow all cost $2.50 two dollars & fifty cts. A. J. is <u>real pretty</u>. She never looked better than she did yesterday. I am real proud of her & she is smart too & is very fond of me & so all the children. W. J. is all right now we went out to get some cherries to eat & we enjoyed them hugely. I am as fond of them as ever & can eat just as many. Harvest is going on now in earnest   we had a fine rain the last three or four days & everything is looking fine. I expect the children to write to you as usual & give you all the news   I have none. Goodbye
May God bless you all is my constant prayer.

> Your affectionate
> Fr. W. J. Keller

Pa to Maggie and Charles

> Howardsville Va
> Albermarle Co
> Va

July 20, 1884

  My Very Dear
daughter & family
Your letter of 10 [July] went to hand we did not write last Sunday as usual for we were just on the eve of moving & thought we would not write until today & then give you all the particulars. You gave us a very good discription of your house & grounds which is very nice & hope you will do well. I want you to send up a centipede & terantula   I never saw either. We still

have the frog & its box. I will try to give you a discription of the house we live in. I rent from a widow named May. She is very much like Aunt Lizzie White   I give her $2.50 two dollars & fifty cents per month. I get one very large room in basement & one small one & one on 2nd floor & one on 3d floor & use of hall on 2nd & on 3d floors & use of yard for wood & fowls we have 13 hens & one rooster & a whole lot of little chickens. The house has an L to it the lady uses two rooms in the main building   the L which is 1¹/₂ stories high with three rooms in it. I hope we will get along all right with her. D. A. & I will start for Cumberland in the morning if nothing happens will write to you from there next   God bless you all   Yours & c

W. J. Keller

Amelia Jane to Maggie

Howardsville Va
July 20, 1884

My very dear Sister
   We received your most welcome letter. I would not like to live out there on account of those centipedes for I would always be uneasy   I hope you all will come home soon. We have moved to Howardsville   I like it very well and I think I will like it better after I get acquainted   I hated to leave Glendower very bad. We stayed one night and a day and a half I went and stayed all night with one of my girl friends and I had a very nice time. Where we live now there is a large yard and nice locast grove   there is one buck eye tree in the yard and three maple trees. We moved a setting hen on 17 eggs pa and D. A. carried her in their hands every bit of the way up here and we pined her up to make her set and she broke 6 of them [eggs]   she set till last night and we let her out to feed her when we fed the other chickens and she left her nest so W. J. had the fun of breaking them   every bodys chickens are dieing with the cholera except our's I am a fraid they will take it.
   I must close as I have not any news. I remane your fond Sister Amelia J. Keller
   excuse bad writing and mistakes

Dannie to Maggie

Howardsville Va
July th 21, 1884 [sic]

My dear sister
   I havent wrote for so long that I have forgot what little I did

know about heading a latter but we have moved to our new home
H.ville   Pa and I will leave for Cumberland tomorrow expect to
be gone three months that will be the longest I ever stayed away
from home. We had a tough time coming up here we slod half the
way but didn't loose any thing as it hapened but smashed a chair
it was the roughest road I ever saw. I cant hunt now like I use to
at Glendower thats one objection I have to H.ville   the hills are
too bare. H.ville is on two rivers rock-fish James and the rail
road runs through it from Richmond to lynchburg. There is no
news now games too scarce here but I will tell you I had a
present of a swarm of bees there is about a half bushel of them
they are working fine now or at least they was the last time saw
them thats all I know and more too

> Your Aff Bro
> D. A. J. B. I. L. Keller

P.S. Write soon

Amelia Jane to Pa

> Howardsville
> Aug 1d. 1884

My very dear pa
    Do pleas write for sister Maggie and little Mattie to come home
I believe she will die out there. Aunt B and I both think she looks
nearly as old as Ma did when she died   I want to see her once
more and if she comes I believe Cousin Charly will come after
while.
    Write soon to your fond daughter

> Amelia

Amelia Jane to Pa

[When Pa was away from Howardsville working in Batesville, Amelia
Jane either forwarded Maggie's letters to him or, as in this one, if she
feared the forwarded letter became lost, summarized the contents in
a letter of her own to Pa.]

> Howardsville
> Aug 17 1884

My very dear pa
    We received another letter from sister Maggie   I sent it to you
and directed the envelope to Trents Mill   Mr. Bateman says it is

rather unsertain wither you got it or not, so I will try to tell you the most important part. She said if she came home could she live with you   Cousin Charley is getting so wicked that she cant stand it   every thing she says nearly he just telles her to go to the D———l. She says she is liveing on fat middling meat and irish potatoes. she says she is so bound up she don't know what to do and she asked him to get her a little fruit all she got was a cussing she says if she don't come home she will go elsewhere for she don't believe she can live six months the way she is living she works as hard as she can she said if he had remained the man she marriad she would have been another sort of woman but as it is she is as much broken as and [sic] old woman when she is not middle aged and he cares nothing for her since she has broken so. She says she can take in sewing to support her and Mattie and she knowes she will not have to work any harder any where then she does there.

Pa do please write for her to come home I am afraid she will die if she does not come home   Aunt B says she could not see a feature any thing like her [in the photograph].

We are all getting along very well indeed the old rooster died all the rest look better as I have no news I will close my badly writen letter.

I remane your loving daughter.

A. J. Keller

P.S. Give my love to D. A. tell him I would like to see him.

A. J. K.

Amelia Jane to Pa

Howardsville
Aug 25, 1884

My very dear pa,

We received your most welcome letter. I said I thought maybe sister Maggie and Cousin Charley had a quarrel, though you know Sister Maggie has changed mightly I don't think it agrees with her out there I wish you would write for them all to come home she would be so much happier if she was at home. Mrs May is not at home now, she went to Fluvanna with those ladys that were at Captain Bragg's she said she did not know when she would be back. She might stay two or three months. So we are by our selves she went Friday. We are all getting along very

well. You told me to tell you who all had been to see us the
Misses Spencers have been here very often to see Mrs May and
us both Miss Bragg and Miss Oliver the ladys that Mrs. May
went home with Miss Nannie Sugg Miss Emma Bertis Mrs Lion
and her sister Mrs Johnson. Mrs Clay and Miss Selic are just like
home folks I go with them to milking every evening. I have been
to Sunday school every time there was any   I have been to
preaching 3 or 4 times since we have been here. The neighbors
have been very kind we have had vegitable all the time. We got a
letter from the old woman [pa's ex-wife] she has another
traveling fit in her head.

Please excuse bad writing and mistakes as W. J. is writing and
is asking me questions all the time he will tell you the rest of the
news. He goes with Mr Clay to water his horses nearly every
eavening when I go milking he has two horses and a coalt   W. J.
rides one of them.

As there is not any news I will close with much to you and
D. A. I remane your loving daughter

                                        Amelia J. Keller
I havent got any thing for W. J. pants yet he needs them I cant
find anything home that will do

Amelia Jane to Maggie

                                        Howardsville
                                        September 3, 1884
My very dear sister

I know you think I have for gotten you nearly every day for
two or three weeks I have said I must write to Sister Maggie. I
sent your letters to pa   him and DA are in Cumberland we are
here by our selves   Mrs May the lady we live with went to
Fluvanna on a visit we have neighbors very close so we are not
afraid. I wish you all would come home there is a splendid
opening here for a Doctor ever body I have seen nearly says they
wish Cousin Charley would come home there is a gentleman here
they are nearest neighbors he says he would sell Cousin Charley
this place and I know it would suit you all better than any place I
ever saw the house has nice rooms in it painted nicely outside and
in a lively front porch nice front yard fenced off from the back
and back yard two stables one right new one   oarchard nice large
garden and a very large paster lot a nice well the water is bearly

as cool as ice water every thing is so convenient   they keep two
cowes and one or two horses WJ helps him bring the cowes and
takes the horse to water nearly every eavening   I go with them
to milking sometimes   I like howardsville very well we go to
Sunday School every Sunday that there is any to the rosebuds
meetings   I have not joined yet. The protracted meeting
comenses here next Sunday. Our chickens have been dieing with
the cholera it is the first time our chickens have had the cholera
since we came this side of the mountain   I think the reason of it
was we moved in with our chickens when Mrs May's was dieing
with it we lost 4 hens and one rooster they are nearly well we
had six or seven hens sick three got well some of our frying sized
chickens have been taken. We still have the body of the little
horned frog it and the box is a great curiosity.

   We are all well and getting along very well by our selves. As
there is not any news I will clos with much love to you all I
remane your very fond Sister

                              Amelia J. Keller

P.S. Kiss sweet little Mattie for me

Maggie to Pa

                              Rincon, New Mex.
                              Sept. 3d 1884

My dear pa & all

   I received yours & Dannie's letter commenting on my picture.
Every one that saw it said it looked like me then, but now I am
feeling better & have improved some what.

   Things are moving along a little smoother now. Dr. Brown is
doing well in his practice. He seems to have the confidence of the
people. Sunday a special train was sent up from Rincon (a half a
mile from the house) to take him to Upham [a section of sidetrack
on the AT&SF RR, about 20 miles northwest of Rincon] a station
17 miles from here to see a sick woman. He got there at 9 o'clock
A.M. & came back on the regular passenger train at noon. He
left the woman doing well. I was taking dinner at the conductor's
house & then after dinner he had to help take a freight train up a
steep grade of about 25 miles & his wife & babe & Dr. Brown,
Mattie & I all went with him there & back. Made 50 miles for
Mattie & I & 84 for Dr. Brown & not costing us a cent. He can
do well here. But it is such a hard country. Saturday night about

two o'clock a Mexican came for Dr. Brown & said that "Pete
shoot Harry." (Pete was a saloon keeper & Gambler who last
Spring came near dying with an abcess in his side but Dr. B.
brought him through all right) & "Harry" was a gambler. When
Dr. B. got down there Harry was dead, shot in cold blood.
Rincon is a hard place! A man don't dare go through the streets
with $10.00 (ten dollars) in his pocket after night. "The Rollers"
just knock them down & "roll" them over & take the money. The
officer was standing by when this man was shot & never said
"arrest him!" So he got away.

There is 3 grocery stores, 1 dry goods store & 5 saloons, the
vilest place on earth.

My precious pa, write when ever you can. I all ways look
anxiously for your letters. They are such a comfort.

Much _love_ to _all_ and much to your own dear self

> Your aff daughter
> M. M. Brown

Charles's mother to Charles

> Staunton, Va.
> Sept. 15th/84

Dear Charlie:

I have not written before because I was too much concerned
about what to do for ourselves and because I could not determine
what is best to be done about sending more money to New
Mexico. I cannot agree with you that we ought always to act
hastily. I can see now, as the others do, that it was a rash thing
sending the money to have the house put up. Now I do not think
one rash act ought to be followed by another. We think it would
be a safer thing to lose the eight hundred [dollars]. Maggie does
not want to be tied there [This suggests that the strategem
Maggie used to protest the Browns' moving to Rincon was to
publicize her discomfort with New Mexico as a permanent
residence.] Suppose you advertise the property get what you can
for it and be free to go where you please or perhaps you could
trade it for the drug store. It seems to me if you would bring a
little business talent to bear upon it you would be able to do
something. If the eight-hundred is lost, it would be easier for us
to lose that then fourteen hundred.

We came to Va. [from Mississippi] and were much troubled to

know what to do till we decided to come here and take boarders. We have the house full promised but there is only one room occupied at present. We do not know yet how we will do—but it was the best thing we could think of.

The family do not want Billy Stout [Charles's footloose older brother Will] to go to New Mexico nor do I. He would give you a great deal of trouble. I have no idea that he will go.

I have so little time for writing that I must close.

Now try to be reasonable and consider well this matter. There is too much risk in hastening to be rich.

With much love to Maggie and Mattie I am

Affecly

M[ary] O B[rown]

Maggie to Pa

Rincon, New Mex.
Sept. 21st, 1884

My Precious Pa

Yours & D. A.'s letter of the 14th just to hand. Those letters are the greatest of pleasures to me & I fully appreciate them. I wrote last week to A. J. to ask the price of the place she spoke of in Howardsville. It is the place next to them.

Dr. B.'s people are treating him very badly. He thinks more of your little finger than all of his Sisters and brother. D. A. spoke of chills. Oh, beware of a country that has them. Although you have been so well, if you were to take them you would soon go into consumption. I hope we will see each other soon some way & I hope too you will see a better looking woman than that picture.

I will send you two papers each have an account of the crimes committed in this town. We are going to a funeral of a little babe this eve. I must close & get dinner over so we can go.

Write whenever you can & D. A. also

With much love from all, your loving daughter

M. M. Brown

Maggie to Pa

Rincon Dona Ana Co
New Mex Nov 27/84

My dear pa & all

I received your letters & card a few days since I do appreciate the kind tokens of remembrance on those cards & think them very pretty. I had thought of not writing until Sunday but I am alone today a thing very different from what I had expected   a conductor's wife & myself were going to have a thanksgiving diner together & a little dance here to night but last night Dr. Brown was called to go about 25 miles from here to set a mans leg a "cowboy" he was rounding up cattle & the horse fell on him. A "cow boy" also came for him it is the biggest ranch in New Mex between 50,000 and 60,000 acres in it & about 16,000 head of cattle. He wont be back before tomorrow. He will also get a free pass over the Rio Grande division of the A.T.& S.Fe R.r. [section of letter torn] the first of Jan 1885 running to Jan 1886 this will take him over between 400 & 500 miles of the road.

I would be delighted to get a picture of the family for a Xmas gift   I will go with Dr. Brown some time after he gets his pass & have our picture taken every one says I am looking so much better. The hot weather came very near being too much for me.

Dont you think you could come out this winter

Well I believe I have written all I can think of   will write to the children soon.

Your loving daughter
M. M. Brown

Maggie to Pa

Rincon Dona Ana Co
Jan 11/85

My dear pa & all

Your letter of the 4th just received. Suppose you have gotten my letters by this time. Please never put off writting again unless something does happen Well it does hurt me to think my brothers & Sister have so changed I would not know them if I was to meet them face to face. DA is the only one I can see any resemblance to the children I saw last   Aunt Bets is so good I am glad to get it. Mattie has forgotten all about Va. but she had a doll named "Amelia Jane"   I have put the pictures all in my big Bible. When we get able I will have our picture taken & send to you all I only wrote a short note to Mattie C. is the reason I said nothing about Mattie. I dont think it looks well for a parent to always be bragging on their own flesh & blood. But I feel if it was God's will to take my babe all that is sweet to me on this earth is connected with her. How tall is A. J. D. A. & W. J. & what is their weight each. They all are fine looking but dont suppose there ever was a family that every one is so different from the other none of them look any like I did do they!

I want to come home I could not keep back the tears when I saw them. . . . Now A. J. looks so sad. When I went to have a picture taken I always had a broad grin ready never had any thing to make me look sad   my childhood hours were happy oh! so happy.[34]

I must close with much love & many thanks.

I will write to each one soon. It is so near bed time now. Your ever devoted daughter

M. M. Brown

Maggie to Dannie

Rincon, Dona Ana Co., N.M.
Feb 1/85

My dear brother

I will try to write you a few lines. I have written to pa & A. J. Saturday. I received a letter from you all but W. J. You have all grown quite tall. Suppose you will be as tall as Grandpa Jordan? I hope you are growing in knowledge as well as physically. Now is your time to learn while you have no cares. A smart man can go any where & feel easy. He may be dressed in rags but if he be an intelligent man he will be respected.

We are having the most delightful weather. In all of the papers we see accounts of such cold weather & the very coldest night we have had the ice has only been 1¹/₂ inches (one & one half inches) thick. All sunshine & so calm. I don't know whether I can persuade myself to come back to rain snow & mud or not. If there was good society here this would be the home for all of us. But there is so much wickedness & no good. I think some time the sun never shown on a worse set of people than Rincon contains   we are a mile & a half from there now. I will send pa Dr. Browns picture as he insists on it know he will take a great deal of pride in showing his daughter & son-in-law as soon as we get able we will have better ones taken.

Write Soon all of you Much love to all

Your aff Sister
M. M. Brown

Pa to Maggie and Charles

Howardsville
Alb Co

Feb 22nd 1885

My dear daughter & fam

This is our time to write to you. I just came home from church & ate my dinner & now am writing to you & while I am thinking about it I see there is the "Christian Advocate" which I send you in this mail that there is an appropriation for a Rosebud School in your town & Wm J McCorkle [Methodist minister in Virginia, good friend of Kellers and Browns] is sent to El Paso 77 seventy seven miles south of your place. Now dear daughter try & do all you can to assist in the good cause be at all the meetings & tell the Dr to be sure to help all he can. I just know you & him could most carry on a Sunday School by yourselves. Please keep up your religion if it is a little hard to attend to it now it will all come right at the close of life which will soon come round. Be found at your post & if the summons should be sudden & without warning that it may find you as it did your dear Mother all ready. You can wield an immense good. I hope to hear soon that you & the Dr. are good workers for the Master. Go right on & do your best both of you are very well qualified   good education & the Dr can sing very well I wish I could hear him now. I was very fond of his singing. A. J. is writing & will give you all the news. love to all   Your Afft Fr.   W. J. Keller

Amelia Jane to Maggie

Howardsville Albe Co Va
Mar 24, 1885

My dear & only sister

We received your very welcome letter was very glad to hear you have as many chicks as you have for we have not any at all. All 3 of us are still going to school & our teacher will teach 6 months and perhaps 7 seven the weather has been very bad for spring. D. A. says he thinks we will soon have another Xmas. You think it is glorious out there now. I expect it is but about midsummer it will be so warm you can hardly stand   so I wish you would come home now before you fall off like you was when you had your picture taken. I hope your hand is well. I do not know whether WJ will write any or not   I told him he must

write to little Mattie. I will write a few lines to her   I will
commence the correspondence   I will close this one.

> Your loving sister
> Amelia J. Keller

Amelia Jane to Mattie

Dear little Mattie.

I told W. J. he must write & I will write too. I suppose you
have a great many pets. W. J. wants to get a pet pigeon they live
around here he will try to get them out of the nest and tame
them   he has a pet opossum   we have only one dog and one cat
WJ has one hen I have two.

As times are very dull I will close with much love to one and
all. I remane your ever devoted Aunt

> Amelia J. Keller

Pa to Maggie and Charles

> Trents Mill
> Apl 12th 1885 Colemansville P.O.
> Cumberland Co
> Va

My Very Dear daughter & family
It has been some time since I wrote to you & I expect you are
scolding me like anything for my failure to write but you must
not be so particular with me as I have to work every day have
not time to read papers or books & not much time to write   I
have only wrote once home since I came down here & I have
been here over a month & have heard twice from home. All were
well. I am puting a dam up for the same man I worked for last
summer & summer before last. I will get it done about the 15th
or 16th of this month & will then commence the forebay which
carries the water from the canal or race to the water wheel. The
canal or race is about one & a half miles long & the dam in middle
16 ft long the walls are of stone & was put up some 50 or 60
years since but was never completed til now. They need a
temporary dam to throw or turn the waters in races   I suppose
the children wrote to you regularly as I told them to do all are
going to school & doing very well   I miss D. A. very much down
here as I have no body to stay with me of nights. We have had a
very cold spring it snowed some yesterday (11th) & is very chilly,

but still I have my usual health I weigh 131½ lbs one hundred &
thirty one & a half pounds which is a little more than usual
[Washington James Keller, born September 24, 1823, would have
been sixty-one and a half years old in April of 1885.] I have no
news to write   hope Wm. P. Mccorkle has been to see you & that
you had a happy meeting. Write soon & often to your
Most Affet   Fr.
W. J. Keller

Maggie to Pa

> Rincon
> April 19th/85

My dear pa & family
    I wrote one letter & left it in the window but cannot find it as
the wind is blowing east you may get it but for fear you do not I
will write again have been trying all week to find time but we
have so much to do planting & attending to what is planted we
have not had a rain for a month but the corn planted last week is
up will have peas in another week or by the first of may anyway
I suppose you think it is getting very warm here but not so we
are sleeping under two blankets the same we had all winter
except 1 quilt. I have 87 little chicks & one hen on 17 eggs & one
[on] 15 I will not set any more this spring the gnats & mosquitoes
will get bad in a month or so & they are hard on little chicks. The
trees are in full leaf & grass 6 inches high we have also 4000 four
thousand grape slips in the ground to set out next fall. If we can
just get water on the place to keep them growing after they are
set out a wind mill would do the work & it will cost $250 two
hundred & fifty dollars. You see we cant get that much together
& it has to be cash the man that is breaking up the ground is
Mexican that had a sick child & he is doing the work in pay for
Dr. B's attending to it. I must close for this time. You write often
I will do so as often as I can   I am trying to sew some & all
together keeps me quite busy.
Much love to all your aff daughter & Sister

> M. M. Brown

Rev. Wm McCorkle to Maggie

> El Paso, Texas
> April 21, 1885

My Dear Mrs. Brown:
    Your kind form of 16th just came duly to hand. I was surprised

to learn that the Doctor had received no reply to his very cordial
and greatly appreciated letter. I was fully under the impression
that I had answered it long ago; but it may have been one of
those cases in which a very honest intention passes into memory
as an act performed. But really I had hoped to be able to pay you
a visit ere this. Nothing has prevented but an unaccountable
delay in the transmission of certain drafts that are due me by the
Board of Missions. Among all the friends I have met these many
years past, my association with none has been more cordial and
pleasant than with your self and Dr. Brown; and I know of none
whose presence under my own roof (had I a home of my own)
would give me more sincere pleasure. I can never forget those
old days in West View—days in which our friendship was
cemented alike by mutual joys and by mutual sorrows. Yes, the
greatest sorrow that came upon your young womanhood, and
under whose express gloom you and your dear husband took upon
yourselves the holy vows of wedlock,—was a keen sorrow to me,
as though your mother had been mine; and the viewing of her
sad, yet triumphand death has been an inspiration to me in all the
years of my ministry. "I am so glad that I have a Jesus—" oh,
how those dying words have rung in memory, now making me
thankful for the comforting presence of Divine grace

My time has been very fully occupied here. I have to hold a
night lay, five services every week, and sometimes more.
Teacher's meeting, prayer meeting, chair-meeting and sometimes
a church social in the week; and then Sunday School and two
services on Sunday. That with pastoral visiting, "filling the
hopper for Sunday's grist," &c., keeps me very busy. Sometimes
in allay I hope to get up to see you and the Dr. I will write you
the week beforehand, so the Dr. can blow my horn and gather
the tribe together. [closing of letter missing]

Pa to Maggie and Charles

> Howardsville Alb Co Va
> May 17th 1885

My Very dear daughter & family
as this is our day to write I will do my part but we have not
received a letter from you since we wrote last but hope to get
one soon. We are all well except myself I have a sort of broncal
infection which troubles me sometimes but I still attend to

business. Our spring has come but it is very cool & dry. We never had a better prospect for fruit of every kind than we have now peaches everywhere if the bush or sprout is not 3 ft high it is full of peaches, chincapins, black berrys & other kind of fruit all grow together   I go along the old fence now & can see good ripe peaches & amaze   the chincapin bushes & in some places can get blackberrys & grapes (I mean the season)   our yard is full of locust trees which is higher than the house & the house is 3 stories high & they are covered with bloom every person says they never saw as much bloom in their lives   our yard is covered with grass as fresh & green as can be. I believe I have written all I can think of & will leave the rest for the children. My love to all. Tell the Dr. I would like to see a letter from him   I know he could give me some news if he would try. I tell my friends I used to take great interest in Colorado when you all was living there but as you have left Colorado & gone to N. Mx I am now interested in N.M. our minds & affections will follow the object on which they are placed & that is why I take so much interest in your country. God bless you all (good bye)

Your most affect Fr
W. J. Keller

Amelia Jane to Maggie, Charles, and Mattie

My ever dear Sister & family

We have not received your letter though as it is time to write to you I will write any way. The weather has been very dry for some time, though it is very pleasant. The locust trees are just as full of bloom as can be   I will send you a boquet   it is for the whole family   most of it is for Mattie   tell her I say the rose & honeysuckle is hers the rest is your's & cousin Charley's. W. J.'s squirrel loves those pinon nuts you sent us better then any thing we can give it. We had a very good Sunday School this morning. I hope it will continue to improve there are enough children in the village & neighborhood to make a very nice Sunday school. As there is no news, I will close with much love to one & all   I remane your ever loving sister.

A. J. Keller

Maggie, then Charles, to Pa

Rincon, N.M.
May 25/85

My dear pa

I hasten to write to ask you to get some Tincture of Iron &

take 15 drops (to be increased to 30) 3 times a day before eating. It has always helped Dr. Brown & I think it will help you.

You said in one of your letters you were going to get a piece of land the day after you wrote but you did not say anything about it in this letter. Did you get it? If so, describe it to us. I have a very bad headache this eve. Cannot write more now. Dr. B. says he will finish this.

Your loving daughter
M. M. Brown

Dear Friend

As there is space left for me to write upon, I shall endeavor to write to you some and as M. has not told you anything but med. advice, I shall try and tell you how things are on the ranch and around it. In the first place there has been more rain here than there has been for years and every thing looks nice and green. My corn is knee high and looks healthy and green, have about fourteen (14) acres out. My water mellons are very fine also. I planted what was left of the black eye peas that you sent whilst I was in Colorado and they arc up. Had one sack of broom corn seed left & planted them also, and it is looking nice, but was unfortunate with my tobacco seed. I had no water and gave them to a Mexican to plant & he flooded them with water and none of them came up. They [the Hispanic neighbors] only understand raising corn, mellons, chili or red peppers & onions. [Here Charles suggests that raising tobacco calls for an esoteric knowledge peculiar to Virginians.] By the way, you ought to see us eat red pepper. I eat about 6 or 8 pods at a meal and don't think any thing of it   am very fond of it.

The Indians are on the war path in this country now.[35] There was a large gang of them passed about fifteen or sixteen miles of us yesterday, going to Mexico and probably go into Arizona and considerable mischief, but they have passed us and will not come back, as they know that the soldiers are after them. The Indians are said to have about fifty bucks besides the squaws & children and there is about six or seven hundred soldiers after them. [It is not clear whether Charles's disproportionate numbers of pursuers and pursued was honest miscalculation or a conscious exaggeration so that Pa would not fear for their safety. The proportion was more ten to one.]

Mattie is growing very fast now and is very healthy and full of mischief. She has a little Mexican boy that she plays with and is learning Spanish very fast. She has two white kids that she expects to break to a little wagon when they are large enough.

My wife has now about one hundred young chickens, mostly Dominicks [a black and white speckled breed of chicken]. They are all doing well. I sent you a small pamphlet giving some light upon this country and it is most about true.

> Love to all from all
> Affect. C. A. Brown

Maggie to Pa

> June 9
> Rincon
> Station, New Mex., 1885

Dear Pa & family

I received all of your letters yesterday. You did not say how your health was. I am very anxious about you all the time. We had a very pleasant visit from our friend W. P. Mccorkle. He came up Friday & stayed until Monday preached 3 sermons. There was only 6 Saturday eve at 11 o'clock Sunday & perhaps 15 Sunday night Mexicans & all. He thinks he will try to come up once a month & preach for us. I expect his wife up to spend a month with me some time this summer. We have had quite an Indian scare. The Apache Indians got off their reservations & did a good deal of murdering but never got accross the river or within 20 miles of us but we put adobes in the windows & were fixed for them. One night we watched all night with pistols rifel & shot gun. Our corn is looking fine but am afraid if we dont soon have rain it will be stunted. It has not had but one rain on it since it was planted & it strikes Dr. Brown about the waist & the stalks are at least 1½ inches one & a half inches in diameter. Wm Mc Corkle brought Mattie a quantity of nice fruit. California fruit is coming in to El Paso now.

You all write soon again

> Much love to all from all

your ever aff daughter
  M. M. Brown

Maggie to Pa

> Rincon, New Mex.
> June 22/85

My dear pa & all

I received your letter of the 15th Saturday. I can't help being

uneasy about you & I want to come back to be with you. If you
were to write me you were quite ill I could not come for we have
no money at all   Dr. Brown is in debt for what we had to get to
eat   he is almost in rags & I am no better. I think our corn will
die there has been no rain for more than six weeks except last
eve a <u>very</u> light shower passed over with some hail but it did not
wet the ground ¹/₂ an inch deep   for the last 10 days there has
been a hot dry wind blowing that was so hard on the corn Friday
& Saturday the Thermometer here at the house stood at 110′
from 10 o'clock in the morning until 3 & 4 in the evening at 9 it
fell to 75 & was a good night to sleep. If our corn fails I can't tell
what we will do this winter. There is <u>so</u> little practice. Dr. B. is
painting a roof for the man we owe. Are you taking the iron now
don't neglect it for I know it will do you good you <u>must</u> take <u>care</u>
of <u>yourself</u>. the cough may not be serious but I would rather you
had none. Is your land in a swampy place? if so shun it although
the boys & A. J. may be strong & healthy now they would not be
long if they were to take the chills & fever that you so often find
in those lowlands & you would not stand the chills 6 months. The
natives have chills a good deal here. Well I will try to write to
the children this week. Give love to all   tell W. J. Mattie is
having a good time with her kids today   she is learning to talk
Spanish real fast if we dont know what they say I just call Mattie
up & she can nearly always tell me & when she is playing with
the little boy she talks it all together.

Write soon & dont <u>forget this letter</u> before you write.

Your ever aff daughter
M. M. Brown

Maggie to Pa

Rincon New Mex
July 18 [1885]

My dear pa

I suppose you have gotten my letter but have not had time to
answer   I will trouble you with some more questions if we could
get the land we want to sell and come back. Now what will a
house on concreat (of which Dr. B will send you the dimensions)
cost we also want a cement roof (it is more pleasant in summer &
less danger of fire) close rafters & corse coard on them close
together 12 windows, 6 with glass 24 × 36 & 6 with 4 pains

12 × 36 in. swung on cords to move up & down, 6 doors in the 2
halls with side lights, 2 chimneys & fire places & 2 flues a poarch
the whole length of the front 72 ft & 42 ft in the back? What will
2 horses & good wagon & a no 1 cow cost. We want to know what
all these things will cost before we give up what we have   we
are holding it at a certain price but am afraid we cannot get it so
we want to know what we can afford to take   our corn is a
failure it is cooked. We want from 100 to 150 acres of land. We
want to come back. Mattie ought to be in school   she will be 7
years old the 23 of this month if she was there she could go with
W. J. & A. J. so well. Some times I think you dont want us to be
near you but I can't help wanting to be there. I thought we might
have our houses in sight   if you don't want to live with us. Can
Dr. B. get any practice there   he says he will work in the house
as carpenter. You show him how   would you   if you work for us
you shall be paid the same as anyone else would pay you. It
would be best to get the windows & sash all ready to put in the
glass in them or not as you think best. What would it cost do you
think to clear off the land. I know you are out of patients now
with this letter of questions but you know it is best "to look
before you leap"   we have had our experience at that now. We
expect to make that our house the rest of our days so we will
make it comfortable at once. I never want a two story house &
there is less danger of wind in them also [The one story house
sturdy against wind suggests western influence.] Dr. B. made a
mistake in the front windows   they are to have only 2 pains in
each window 24 × 36 in. The roof slopes to the back. [section of
letter torn] You make the calculations what this will cost & let us
know. Your ever loving daughter

M. M. Brown

P.S. We want the kitchen & Dining R at right angles from the
back door 3 doors 6^1/2 × 2^2/3 3   4 windows 12 light   10 × 12
cement roof also [remainder of P.S. torn]

Maggie to Pa

Rincon, New Mex.
July 27, 1885

My own dear pa & all
    It has been two weeks since I got a letter from home. Hope
Dr. B. will get one today. I have just been looking at your dear

faces. I have them all on one page in my Bible. I often look at
them   I am getting so homesick. I really get sick at heart when I
think how far separated we are. Dr. Brown got a letter from his
sister Millie saying his mother was quickly nearing "The other
shore." She has been sick since the second week in Jan for some
time not able to use her hands. Dr. Brown says if you get any
worse he will sell out and we will come at once. Now, don't fail to
write if you get very weak. I don't want to come to just see you
die but want to enjoy some of your good council & society. If you
were Dr. B's own father, he could not think more of you. Let me
hear from you soon & that the house can be put up cheap. I will
finish when Dr. B. comes. Why don't the boys write to me any
more. I mean my letters for all   they must not expect me to
write letters to each of them. Have just gotten yours & the
children's of the 19th. I thank you very much for your kindness in
answering my questions   in what county is the land? Is there any
practice there for Dr. B.? Hope you will get my letter before you
leave. Write soon. Love to one & all.

> Your aff. sister & daughter
> M. M. Brown

P.S. How far is that land from a R.Road or Station? Pa, you said
there was "plenty of land & low at that." Now what can it be
bought at per acre? We must make our calculations the land so
much & house so much & then the trip back the furniture & all
must be considered when we sell this.

> Affly,
> M. M. Brown

Maggie to Pa

> Rincon Dona Ana Co NM
> Aug 10 1885

Dear pa & family
   We received your letter & A. J.'s today. We are offering our
place for $2000 (two thousand dollars) every thing for this
household & Kitchen furniture & chickens. We have fully decided
we will buy land & put up a house as we mentioned   I do not
want a two story house so you let us know what a house like the
plan will cost. If you please you know, if we come back & have
any money it is so offered to be spent if not invested at once. Of
course we will have to look around some & the first thing to be

bought would be a team & some kind of light veical to travel in. It is still very dry & warm here the corn looks as it had been frosted yellow & dry. It is raining now so we will have a little corn yet out of the past planting which is in silk now. The first is all gone. Out of the $2000 dollars we will have to pay some debts we owe here our expenses home & until we get to house keeping again & furnish our house & farming impliments & so we will not have more than $1000 to put in a farm & house.

Write to us soon again about the house as we are anxious to hear. I commenced a letter to W. J. will finish it & send it. I enjoy A. J.'s letter's so much   I will be happy when I can get back with my brothers & sister. I left A. J. almost a babe now she will be a companion & D. A. too. I expect Dr. B. will get jealous when I come back I will be so glad & happy & love you all so much but he loves you too. I will write to A. J. in a few days.

Your ever loving daughter
M. M. Brown

Maggie to Pa

Rincon, New Mex.
Aug. 19th/85

My dear pa

Dr. Brown has gotten a letter from Millie telling him of his mother's death. She died the 9th of this month was buried in Bridgewater.

Today at dinner Mattie said, "Mama, will you take your cooking stove to Va.?" I said, "It will cost more than a new one to carry it." Then she said, "Will Grandpa let you stop with him till we get another?" I told her, "I suppose so." She is very talkative and we think sweet but not pretty as her eyes are badly crossed from those sore eyes she had before we left Va.

She is right sick now with flux. I thought this morning she was better but this eve she is right bad again. Think if I keep her quiet she will soon be well. She is so full of play it is hard to do so.

Write soon. We are all ways glad to hear from our dear folks at home. Do you spit any blood?

Your most loving daughter M. M. Brown

Maggie to Pa

Rincon NM Station Sept 11 1885

My dear Pa & <u>all</u>

I received your dear letters day before yesterday. Told Mattie what you said about the present she said "He dont have to." She meant you did not have to send her one for her to know you loved her. Dr. Brown wrote to the chief surgeon to know if he could get a pass for Mattie & me. He wrote he would pass up to Kansas City & a return also if we wished to come back soon, but we cant raise the money for the rest of the way which will be about $50.00 fifty dollars. The regular fair from here to Kansas City is $40.00 for 1 ticket and half fair for Mattie which would be $60.00 sixty dollars so you see the pass would cover more than half the fair. Dr. B. has written to his people for the rest of the money but I doubt he gets it they treated him badly enough before his mothers death & now I can hardly think they will let him have anything now.

Yours lovingly,
Maggie Brown

Maggie to her Virginia family and then to Pa

Rincon N.M.
Oct 17/85

My dear ones at home

I have not received a letter from you for so long about two weeks now. You are all constantly in my thoughts now more than ever I have received my pass to Kan's City good until Dec 31st 1885   I am trying every thing I can to get enough money to pay the rest of the fair but it seems like trying is all I can do. I just feel like this that home is so near & yet so far. I think about going home alday & dream about it at night just think the last time I saw A. J. she was about the size of Mattie a little bit of a girl. I do think if God is kind enough to let me ever see you all again I will spend most of my time in looking at you & trying to realize you are my dear Brothers & Sister & Dear Sweet pa I just feel like if I do ever get with you I will never come so far away from you again. Dr. Brown is trying to get a Government position which if he does he may come back next spring for me, but you know such appointments are very uncertain. He must get something besides his practice or we cannot get along. It is getting quite chilly now in the eve we have to have fire. Give my love to one & all write often to your loving Sister & daughter

M. M. Brown

P.S. Tonight at Supper I asked Mattie if she would know any one back there she said "You bet I would"   I asked her who she said "grand pa." She also said "I am just as anxious to see them as you are." she is a great talker & uses a great deal of this Western slang.

Our circumstances are very unsettled   now we cant tell what we are going to do. I am fix-up my old clothes & Matties so if Providence will permit we will be able to go on short notice. I will close with much love to all at home   Write soon to your aff daughter M. M. Brown

Mattie to her grandfather [dictated to Maggie]

Rincon N Mex
Oct 18/85

Dear Grand pa
    I am comming back   I hope you are well   I had some little kittens & I sold them. I had some kids & they ran away. We got some chickens I got some little girls here I play with—we got a house built mitey near at Rincon   Papa hasn't come home stagering yet. Thats all. oh yes I got a cat & two dogs & a chicken named Nellie & nice prettie rooster name of Jim. (This is Mattie's letter just as she dictated it   she came to me & said I want you to write a letter to Grand pa   Mattie says I got a friend here that likes me lots Mrs. Sangre from Colo   I hope you will come out here some day & make a visit to us. My love to my Uncles & Aunts & Aunt Bets & lots to Grand pa

Your little Grand-daughter
M. A. Brown

Maggie to Pa

Rincon, N.M.
Nov. 7/85

Dear pa & family
    I have very little to write. The Chinkapins have not come yet. It is a little cool here have had frost for some time a few needles of ice were on the bucket of water at the pump for a few

mornings. I see the account of Stuart Koiner killing another man
in Staunton. Will send you the paper with an account of that &
my old Sunday School teacher's mysterious disappearance. Jon M.
Carroll. Poor Stuart's money did not give him much enjoyment. I
suppose he had a fearful temper & never having controlled it he
has gone crazy.

This is Sunday & we hardly know what to do with ourselves on
Sunday. Bro. McCorkle has only been up the once. He said if we
could get the people to pay his fare up here $5.00, he would come
the fifth Sunday in every month but there was not enough to do
so. If we had been able we would have done so ourselves.

It is very dry the dust is about 6 inches deep. You must all
write soon to your loving daughter & sister

M. M. Brown

Maggie to Pa

Rincon Nov 10th/85

My dear pa & family

We received you & A. J.'s letters a few days since. Dr. B. has
an appointment to serve as R.R. mail Dr. from Albuquerque
N.M. to Mojave California. It will take him from home at the
time & the pay is $800.00 eight hundred dollars per annum but a
friend of his Col. Clay Taylor who is now acting as Special Agent
Gen'l Land office has resigned & has advised Dr. B. to send in his
application for same   it pays $1500.00 fifteen hundred Dollars per
anum besides all traveling expenses & $3.00 for board when out
on duty. It is for this we want Hon John S. Barbons
endorsement. If you can get some of your influential friends to
recommend him   you can refer them Judge J. W. Stout H.St
George Luckas. Hon J. T. Ham's & Cha's L Oferek as to his
standing there &c. Don't mention the present appointment. We
will get ready to come home as soon as possible. This is all at
present. Be sure to attend to this at once as Col Taylor's
resignation will take affect the 20 of this month.

Your most affectionate daughter
M. M. Brown

6

New Mexico/Virginia:

November 19, 1885–July 7, 1886

*O*BITUARY: DIED—At Rincon, New Mexico, of Scarletina, Martha A. only daughter of Dr. and Mrs. C. A. Brown, June 17th, 1886 age 7 years, 10 months and 25 days. [newspaper clipping]

Now part of the camaraderie of the railroad brotherhood, Charles sped along on his "iron horse" across the stark desert stretches of New Mexico, Arizona, and California. In the past five years he had been miner, carpenter, housepainter, farmer, circuit physician, and mail clerk—a typical checkered career of a westering man. It was part of the vagary Maggie feared.

Disenchanted with Charles's unflagging optimism, Maggie boarded her eastbound train for Virginia, where her hopes lay. Her ride was fearful as well as hopeful. Returning without Charles, she had to steel herself to meet the questioning eyes of inquiring friends. To them she must appear proud and successful. The giftless Christmases, the uprootings from one shanty town to the next, the parched crops, the played-out mines, her smoldering anger at Charles's improvidence— all had to be camouflaged. When she embraced family and friends, she had to give the illusion of the wife of a man who was making it big in the West.

The initial task of creating such a front was mitigated by the sheer thrill of going home. Yet little in the visit made it the return to Eden Maggie had fantasized. Other than the consolation of having Mattie from the start enrolled in a genuine school, the visit confronted Maggie with disappointment after disappointment. The Virginia of her dreams did not exist. There were no "children." The sister and brothers Maggie had continued to call "the children" were all in their teens, the two boys taller than Maggie. There was no family home, only a rented place. To support the family, Pa and Dannie traveled to distant parts. Amelia Jane, W. J. and Aunt Bet did the best they could, and stayed beholden to kind neighbors for company and counsel.

And Pa, while energetic, sensitive, and kind, did not fit into Maggie's imaginative memory of him. When she criticized his haphazard discipline of "the children," Pa accused her of interfering with the way he ran his life. Their quarreling smashed one of Maggie's sacred illusions. After only a few weeks in Virginia, Maggie was writing Charles that she was ready to return to New Mexico.

New Mexico itself was not what she desired, but represented escape from confronting the real Virginia. While she defended Charles to his family and friends in Virginia, she accused him in her letters. From the start, she suffered a foot inflammation whose pain and restriction seemed to her Charles's fault, somehow connected with the dismal poverty of Rincon and his railroad job. As he had done during her waiting to join him in Colorado, Charles again assured her of ticket money coming any minute yet procrastinated with its delivery for four months.

Charles's railroad adventure was glamorous at first, his job as mail clerk, one of the better assignments: "The men on the speeding trains got extra pay and the additional rewards of travel and excitement. They were the aristocrats of the postal service."[1]

Conscious of the historical transition they were effecting, a deep sense of pride united the men who worked on the nineteenth-century railroads. In addition, "the peril and thrill of their work united them as men who understood constant dangers of gunslingers, fires, washouts, falling bridges, runaway trains, and wrecks."[2] These men had a sense of the sweep of the United States as had few others of their day.

For Charles, his first trip across the hundreds of miles of desert was amazing, while repeated crossings of the treeless expanse grew dull. "Desolate," "nothing but desert," "awe," "grand," "black," "ugly"— Charles recorded his initial response:

Well I have been out to Mojave and I think that country the most desolate that I ever saw. From Needles to Mojave there is nothing but desert, not a living thing to be seen except at the section houses and they are few and far between. There is two extinct volcanoes that is interesting. One of them about two miles from the road with miles and miles of lava all around. It impresses one with awe to see it standing there amidst the great desolation that it has produced, grand black and ugly. [December 8, 1885]

While Maggie struggled with her Virginia disillusion, Charles became disenchanted with a West that did not have Maggie in it:

I did not write you since I came in this time because my bowels have been troubling me and I was too nervous to do so. [December 31, 1885]

   Am sick of this separation and life is "too short" to stand it. [March 9, 1886]

Often his handwriting showed marked stress—letters erratically shaped, slanting now left, now right, the *t* cross, usually a perfect balance, becoming a diagonal slash. The scrawl was not the result of writing on a moving train, because he pointedly apologized the times he wrote in transit. And at those times his penmanship was not chaotic. He may have been drinking. Sometimes the most erratic script wrote about random ideas—quite a departure from Charles's usually well-patterned thought.

   Adventure and speculation agreed with Charles; an angry separation from Maggie did not. He was having remorse for their unsettled life. In addition to these gnawing regrets, Charles discovered the Rincon property was vandalized and the Widmer pharmacy was also in jeopardy. Suddenly he felt pressed to return to Rincon. With perhaps an inner apology to Maggie, he negotiated a transfer to the Rincon–Silver City run, for which he had to pass a qualifying exam in Deming. Once he passed (with one of the highest scores ever made he boasted to Maggie) he readied the ranch for Maggie's return and studied ways to irrigate the fields. Preparations took him from March through May.

   Leaving Virginia this time, Maggie felt less regret in the good-byes but also less excitement for traveling west. Neither direction held much hope for her. By the time Maggie and Mattie arrived in Rincon in late May 1886, Charles was making regular train runs on the new route— his schedule allowing him but one night home every two weeks. Once again Maggie was the isolated woman, seven-year-old Mattie her sole companion.

The empty ranch house echoed her inner feeling. Bereft of an idyllic
Virginia, she gazed out at the desert stretches beyond the spare cottonwood grove. Whether she like it or not Rincon was her home. Yet
Rincon, especially without Charles, was only the dry wind-swept desert of "mud houses" and tumbleweed.

The June weather blazed over 100° each day. Mattie cried from the
heat, so every evening Maggie let her run to the pump and splash in
the cool water before getting ready for bed. Maggie must have watched
Mattie with sad affection, the little girl who had been privy to much
of Maggie's adult heartache, a confidante as well as a daughter. Mattie's
sudden illness, then, in mid-June first panicked Maggie and then dragged
her into sick despair.

Fever, rash, headache, stomachache, and vomiting consumed first
little Mattie's strength and then her reason. By the third day she
babbled incoherently. In desperation Maggie prevailed on a neighbor
to telegraph Charles on his train run. Charles seems not to have comprehended the seriousness of his daughter's illness. He stayed on his
run, simply telegraphing prescriptions. It was Maggie who watched
day and night as Mattie's condition worsened with alarming speed.
Something warned her that the illness would be fatal. At 2:30 A.M.,
June 16, Maggie wrote Pa a melancholy letter:

> While keeping a lonely vigil over my darling I will write to you
> for I cannot sleep . . . Dr. B. thinks it scarlet fever & if it is it is
> in a most malignant form   she has not been rational since noon
> yesterday. Dr. B. can only be at home about one ½ hours in the
> middle of the day. He has asked for a lay off. . . . if God just
> spares her is all I ask but I have my fears she is so much
> reduced, not a mouthfull of anything has been [in] her stumak
> since Sunday.
>
> I can't write more now pray for me if I should lose her I will
> need them.

Whipping along on a train, Charles struck Maggie as more duty-bound
to his job than to his own child. (Mary Gose felt Maggie believed
Charles's presence could have saved Mattie and never forgave Charles
for his absence.) On the afternoon of Thursday, June 17, 1886, Charles
finally got to the ranch and Mattie's bedside, present for her last
struggling hours. She died at ten that night.

Numb in her grief, Maggie prepared the little body for burial. Tend-
erly, she dressed Mattie to look as natural as possible, laying her a

little on one side with her doll in her arms—a posture of sleep, not death. On Mattie's breast she pinned mementoes of Virginia: dried flowers Amelia Jane had sent, a brooch given by a Virginia cousin.

The obituary was in turn stark and saccharine:

DIED—At Rincon, New Mexico of scarletina, Martha A. only daughter of Dr. and Mrs C. A. Brown June 17th, 1886, age 7 years, 10 months and 23 days.

In the tradition of the time, the announcement eulogized the brunette Mattie's golden hair and her peels [sic] of laughter mingling with the "half a score of mocking birds" in the "spreading branches of the forest trees that surround her western home"—far-fetched for the craggy barrenness of Rincon.

Through Mattie's bouts with other illness Maggie had anticipated that this child would never reach adulthood. The fear of losing a child was not, for a nineteenth-century mother, idle or morbid. Child mortality was common. Maggie's own mother lost six children; Charles's mother had lost four. Yet the fact of commonality did not dilute the terrible fact for Maggie.

The letters pouring from Virginia and from Colorado and New Mexico did assuage Maggie and Charles's grief. A friend, Mrs. Sangre, from Raton sent word that she was coming down within the week to stay with Maggie. But it was a barren earth that surrounded Rincon for Maggie. The ranch held intolerable memories; thus, after Mrs. Sangre left, Charles rented a house in Deming where Maggie stayed while he continued his railroad runs. The Methodist church there ("a nice brick one") held a memorial service for Mattie.

During the Fourth of July celebration, fire ravaged a major part of the town, causing some seventy-five thousand dollars of damage, destroying many of the best buildings. Yet to Maggie, the saddest loss was not the structures but "a little girl about five years old went up in the burnt district & got in to the hot ashes & run a hot nail in her foot from which she died of lockjaw" [July 7, 1886]. It was as if Maggie's life, too, had been gutted by fire, and the center of the devastation was the loss of a seven-year-old daughter.

For the twentieth century, death is a taboo. For the nineteenth century, adults and children alike lived in the shadow of death, which was seen as life's major event. Children's literature, for example, was often a pulpit for beliefs about death. Stories emphasized that life is guided by God, eternal love, and wisdom. The death of a young person was a reward for the child's exceptional religious sensitivity. Every event of life and especially death was seen as a result of God's fatherly concern; every tragedy, felt to couch hidden blessing:

> Accidents, disappointments, suffering, even death, occur for reasons that may be obscure but these events can teach the virtues necessary for the establishment and maintenance of a satisfying life and a stable society.[3]

Nineteenth-century death was a community experience, particularly in the South. People still died in their homes surrounded by relatives, making the process of dying a vivid part of people's lives.[4] The separation of the frontier disrupted such communal mourning. But as Maggie and Charles discovered, the distance did not stop the impulse, the usual gestures of grief and sympathy now being translated across the miles through the mails. The letters that came to Maggie and Charles made palpable the support of the Virginia community.

After a death, grief must be worked out by the survivors. This grieving involves a painful admission of the intense distress connected with the loss so that the bereaved may readjust and become open to new affection.[5] Part of Maggie's and Charles's working out of their sorrow came from their actual writing over and over to friends and relatives the details of Mattie's sickness and death. Another part of the healing came from reading the expressions of sympathy.

The letters show how the Virginia community "processed" death. First they acknowledged the hard reality. Repeatedly the letters emphasized the fact of death, almost brutally stressing "dead," "death," "the unbearable pain," "the pain too great for mortal person to endure." They talked of Maggie's "empty arms," her "crushed and bleeding" arms. Loss was painted in detail. Mattie was gone. Her beauty and loveliness, her bright ways, her delicate, affectionate, sensitive nature—all these things gone forever from Maggie and Charles.

Yet the letters moved beyond the dark pain to a ritual outpouring of solace. In refrains of Biblical cadence, the letters recalled images not only of resignation but of hope—spelling out the theology taught from the pulpits of middle-class Protestant churches of the nineteenth century: God is good. As a tender, loving Father, a good Shepherd, he does nothing not for the best. He loved Mattie, and because she was, indeed, so special, he wanted her early for his own loving arms. Who could know what future misery his early call saved Mattie from?

This same loving God also cared for Maggie and Charles and would someday reunite them with Mattie in eternal bliss.

Admonitions to good living were the final part of the messages. To be sure they were ready when their time came to join Mattie, Maggie and Charles must renew their efforts to make the world into God's image. Whereas, while Mattie was alive, they concentrated on doing good for her, now they must do good solely for the love of God.

Almost like verses to a chorus, the letters repeated personal testimonies, detailing similar grief, assuring Maggie and Charles that others, too, had felt keen tragic loss, but had risen to acceptance and understanding. Charles's sister Millie, for example, confessed to feeling "so rebellious" when she lost her little girl Mamy:

I have been where the very billions of sorrow overwhelmed me but God was with me all the time though I could not see it then— now I know it and believe and feel that everything God does is right and well. [June 23, 1886]

Realism marked the letters, counseling Maggie to talk or write about the gamut of her grief and to seek comfort in friends. The psychology they advocated was sound even by twentieth-century standards: realistic admission of pain and rebellion, followed by a gradual move to build a fresh life.

That Maggie tried to internalize the counsel of her friends is clear. In a letter to Pa she echoed the words so often written to her:

Pa dear, I am not rebellious, but feel thankful we had her the time we did have her with us. She has escaped much for this world is full of unforeseen troubles. Now they are all over with her. She has only gone before. [July 3, 1886]

Collecting Mattie's things, folding and packing them into a small trunk, Maggie tucked away her memories. She let herself begin showing affection to the little son of the people with whom she stayed in Deming. In such quiet, small gestures of pained movement, Maggie took up her life again.

Perhaps nothing the West had taken surpassed the total loss of what the process of life itself had snatched. Maggie's response here, as with the stillbirth, was to bend to the blow. After Mattie's death, she stopped clutching at Virginia for solace and faced life as it came stark to her in the West.

Letter Texts November 19, 1885–July 7, 1886

Charles to Maggie

UNITED STATES POST OFFICE,
Albuquerque NM
Nov 19 1885

My dear Wife

I am all right will start out on my first trip in the morning at 3
oclock. Will sleep in the car tonight. My cough is improving
think I will be well in a few days.
I do so hope that you will get through all right. And I pray God
that he will guard and protect you both and write to me soon.
Kiss my babe and give love to all of them at home.

With much love I am most affect.
Husband   C. A. Brown

Charles to Maggie

Albuquerque N.M.
Dec 8th 1885

My own Darling

I have rece'd three letters from you since I wrote, but have
been out on the road and did not have time to write. My intention
is to write every time that I come in from a run so that you will
know that I am all right. Well I have been out to Mojave twice
and I think that that country the most desolate that I ever saw.
From Needles to Mojave there is nothing but desert, not a living
thing to be seen except at the section houses and they are few
and far between. There is two extinct volcanoes that is
interesting. One of them about two miles from the road with
miles and miles of lava all around. It impresses one with awe to
see it standing there amidst the great desolation that it has
produced, grand black and ugly. They have some new oranges on
the market at Mojave but they are high yet and as soon as they
are cheaper I wish to get some if the freight is not too high. I
received the tobacco before any of your letters, and it was just as
good as a letter for I knew you were safe at home.

My cough is all right. [section of letter missing] Was to see the
foundry man of this place and he told me that they were
intending to enlarge and in all probability your pa could get work
there as a pattern maker and he thought he could make from one

hundred and twenty five to thirty dollars per month and that I
should come again and he could tell me more.

Give love to all and kiss Mattie for me and always remember
me as affectionately

Yours
C. A. Brown

Charles to Maggie

Albuquerque, N.M. Dec 15th 1885

My own dear wife

I received two letters from you on my return last night and
will answer as well as I can all that I know about the ranch. . . .
I get awfully lonesome, when I am off duty thinking about you
and my babe, tell her that I am glad that she is doing well at
school. Kiss her for me and do not forget to remember me in your
prayers write to me often. Will enclose the Rx that you ask for
they should not neglect to keep the bowels open. Kiss yourself
many times for me and do not forget me. I got cold last night in
bed, and felt like I would like to be in old Va for a while. Daisey
is with pup from an imported blue gray hound. I think that they
will make nice pups cannot write more for I do not know what
else to write. Affect.

C. A. Brown

Charles to Maggie

Albuquerque N.M.
Dec. 31st 1885

My own Darling

I did not write you since I came in this time because my bowels
have been troubling me, and I was too nervous to do so, but they
are very much better now, and I think I shall be all right for my
trip tonight.

Hoy says things are all right, since Mr. Sickels sent me word
that some one broke into one of the back windows, he does not
know what is gone. He fixed up the boards again. I shall go down
next week and see about things. And think I shall get him to live
in the kitchen.

When I come back I shall be able to write you a good long
letter for I shall go on to Rincon before I write. Kiss the babe for

me and tell her to learn to read and I will get her a burro to ride
when she gets back.

Give much love to all of the family and a thousand kisses for
your self.

As ever
Your Affect. Husband
C. A. Brown

If I can get a young man from Va to put up as much money as I
have in the ranch so that I can stay there and work, will it be all
right with you? Of course he would put up money for his share of
my labor.

C. A. B.

Charles to Maggie

Albuquerque, N.M.
Jan. 29th 1886

My own darling

You must not get so discouraged, things will work out all right
yet. They are coming slowly and surely. Wrote to Weston, asking
him to go to our house & live and will go down on the fifth. Have
been so much pushed that I could not go before. The snow
blockades are a little rough on us. We have to make our regular
runs and then when we come back double back with some one to
help them out with some big thorny mail and the consequence is
that we get very little rest. I thought you knew what my position
was. I am not a regular mail clerk until I pass my final
examinations which I will do in April and after that time I shall
get eighty dollars per month instead of sixty six. Am afraid that I
will have to let the Xmas present pass and give it to you this
summer and instead send you the money. I received the shirt and
whisk and am ever so much obliged. Tell W. J. that I shall send
him some thing nice for the nuts he sent. The P[ost] M[aster]
here says that W. J. must think that I am very lazy to pick them
out for me. The cold weather has broken and we are having some
very fine weather. And the last day I was in California I think it
was one of the most beautiful days that I ever saw. I road all day
with my air door open and when my days work was done sat
down and admired the view. There are a lot of old dry lakes on
the Mojave desert and one week before it had rained very hard
and at the time that I past through there there was about 3 or 4

inches of water in them and not a breath of air and it was most
lovely. It was one of the most perfect mirrors that I ever saw.
You could see mountains that were miles off reflected to
perfection. Yes our run is long and tiresome but the country is
lovely. Give much love to all of the family. Tell your Pa that the
foundry has changed hands but I shall try and see what I can do
with the new man. Much love to Mattie and a thousand kisses to
my beloved wife. Affect.

C. A. B.

Charles to Maggie

Albuquerque NM
Feb 12th 1886

My own Darling

I have not gotten a letter from you this time and there has
been two mails since I left but it is all right. I suppose it has
miscarried. When I wrote last I forgot to tell you about Daisey.
She had six pups on the first of the month, and out of the six
there is five dogs. The little bitch only lived a day or two, but the
rest are doing well. There is two beautiful blue ones, and I shall
keep one of them for you, but I really do not know what to do
with it. Yesterday evening I took out an accidental insurance
which will cost me six dollars per month for four months and then
the year its paid for but it takes effect at once and if I am hurt &
have to lay off I will be paid fifteen dollars per week & if I am
killed then will be three thousand dollars coming to you from the
Hartford Accidental Insurance Co. The weather here is very fine
now and everything is lovely. I am very tired when I come in, for
at least two days. I am getting fat 164 lbs now and not done
growing yet. [Charles was 5'11½" tall.] Now and then a button
gives me to understand that I am getting fatter. I had to pay
some things that I did not expect one of the men died here & we
had to all chip in and help his wife out as he left her with out any
money and a long ways from home, but I think my outside
expenses are about over now and I shall be able to do better. I
would have gone down and seen that foundry man for your pa but
I have been so tired lately when I come in that I have not done it
but I shall attend to it for him as soon as I can. Give my love to
all of them and tell my babe that papa wants her to come fast.
Have you gotten your money yet? Would like to have done better

but I could not. With much love and many kisses to you and the babe

Your most Affect.
Husband C. A. B.

Charles to Maggie

Albuquerque N.M.
Feb 19th 1886

My dear Wife

. . . I feel almost satisfied that I will soon get down on the Rincon run and then if I run from Rincon to Silver City think I can get my lay off at home which will be one day. Today got a letter from chief clerk and he told me that he would put me there as soon as he could make me an opening so far he has treated me very nicely. Oh if I could only have my loved ones with me I should feel better. Do not think there will be any trouble about me passing my final examination. What do you think of your Valentine? Is it not pretty as well as useful. Think you ought to kiss me for it any way. God bless you. I wish you were here & give it to me   I know it would be ready. Give much love to all of the family. Kiss my babe and my dear wife & may God bless you both is the prayer of your loving husband.
C. A. Brown

Charles to Maggie

Albuquerque N.M.
Feb. 28 1886

My darling Wife

There is so little for me to write about that I hardly know how to start my letter . . .
There is some talk of increasing the work on our run and putting on some men which means an increase of pay to us & if we get this I shall remain where I am and keep house in Albuquerque, but unless they do I will be apt to go to the Rincon & Deming run—and then I can see you every day and probably after they make that Silver City branch a [junction] they will put on two men and then I think that I can get a day lay off at Rincon—but of course this is only speculation. Hope by this time that you have gotten your shoes and your heel is much better. No it is no laughing matter to me. It makes me feel that you should have

had shoes long ago. Hope that your head aches are much better
and that you will be in better health when you come back. Am
much gratified that Mattie is improving. After she gets a start
she will go much faster. Don't be discouraged about her. Kiss her
ever so much and tell her papa is proud of his little girl and
wants to see her ever so much. Give my love and regards to all of
the family, and a thousand kisses to yourself, and write soon,
your most affectionate Husband

C. A. Brown

Charles to Maggie

Rincon N.M.
March 19th 86

My own Love

I am afraid that I will be disappointed in getting any post for
you and, all that I can do is to send you all the money that I can
spare on the first and let you wait a month longer and then I can
send you forty or fifty more which will make in all from seventy
or eighty. The train is moving and I cannot write any more just
now write to morrow   affect

C. A. Brown

Charles to Maggie

Albuquerque N. Mex
March 19th 1886

My own Darling

I intended to write to you when I returned from Rincon but I
got here at 12 oclock and had to go out at four and it left me no
time. Well the man that broke into the house is in jail and has
been indited and I think will tell who the rest of them are and I
hope that we will be able to recover at least part of the things. I
have sent in application for transfer to the Rincon and Deming
road and by the time I pass my final will get the transfer, and
then we can be close together and can see each other every day
and then I am satisfied that I can get you a pass easy from Kas
City and think it will be from St. Louis. Am sick of this
separation and life is "too short" to stand it and after I get you
and Mattie out here and settled again I shall make every
endeavor to get your pa out and I think we between us can
manage to do so.

I think that after awhile we will be able to get an eighty off of Hoys place and that will make our place in better shape and more valuable. . . . Am real sorry that your foot is not well really do not know what to recommend, but think you should take [writing unclear] something like the one enclosed.

Hope that Providence will let us be together soon for oh! I am so lonely   With much love and many kisses to you and Mattie and respects to your father and the rest of the family I remain lovingly your husband

C. A. Brown

P.S. Tell your pa not to forget the goats one male and two females, kids if he can get them.

C. A. B.

Charles to Maggie

[This is one of Charles's letters in which his handwriting lapses into an uncharacteristic pattern of erratic loops, sudden slants and sharp diagonal t crosses.]

Albuquerque, N.M. April 1st 1886

My own Darling

In the morning I start to Rincon to take charge of the run from there to Deming & after I pay Hoy all that I owe him, I send you money to come out with and I think it will be on the first of the month and I feel soon that after a short time I shall have every other day at home. It seems strange to me that you have not gotten my letters as I have written regularly, but don't you think hard of me for I have had a pretty rough time but now expect to be some what better. The chief clerke will be out for some time soon and I shall ask him then to get you the pass that I ask for and he will do the best that he can for me cenlairily [sic] get it from K.C. and probably from St. Louis. I am just sick to see my land once more and thank God the day is not far distant. Tell Fanny if she will just come out with you I will show her what double and twisted love is and also give her her share of it too. Would love to see them all once more but am afraid that will never be but give my love to them all and say God bless them for me. Tell Mattie papa wants to see her ever so much. Rece'd your present and appreciate it so much but did not know that it meant my birthday [Charles would have been thirty-seven; Maggie,

thirty-two] untill a friend suggested that it might mean that. You
spoke of the twenty seventh (27) then was the first time that I
knew that I had a birth day. Well kiss you for me and always
remember that I am yours truly and faithfully,   Good night

C. A. B.

Charles to Maggie

Deming N.M.
April 4th 1886

My own Darling

This is my first night in this place—and I can hardly tell how
much I like it. I went around to the Bubras. They are both living
here in the same house and Al is in the same old swan and six.
The babe has good eyes and in fine health, running around and
talking, looks just like Al. Will not have time to write much
tonight as I must go study for my examination. And the most
that I can say is that I am anxious for you to come & next month
I shall send you the money. Old Delores that used to live with
Mrs. Hoy wishes to live with us for her board and clothes. What
do you think? Do you want her? If you and Mattie were with me
I should be satisfied—Give much love to all of them, and a
thousand kisses for you and Mattie—Affect

C. A. Brown

Maggie to her father, sister and brothers

[Maggie, still in Virginia, has left Howardsville where Pa and the young
people live and is visiting relatives in Staunton.]

Staunton, V[irginia]
April 9, 1886

My dear friends at home

I arrived here safely the 7th. Received 2 letters from Dr.
Brown while in Farquier. He was well. In his last he had gotten
his transfer to the run between Rincon & Deming. Would go
down the 5th of this month. Have received no answer since he
moved. I had very bad weather to visit but they took me all
around. Suppose the James [River] was booming at Howardsville.
Hope it took the whiskey shops & old Bateman off together—I
can't help but associate them.

How is the Temperance thriving[6] hope all is going well & my

brothers will always be staunch members. By the way, Dr. B.
says he will live in Deming. I will send W. J. his hat mark. It is
not nice but I will make him a nicer one someday. My foot looks
better is nearly well but am afraid to put on a shoe.

How is the school getting along? Write to me here. I sent word
to Uncle H. I would go there tomorrow if they come for me but
all of my letters will come to Staunton.

Love to all. will write more another time.

Affectionately your Sister & daughter

M. M. Brown

Pa to Maggie

Howardsville

Albemarle Co

Va

Apl 11 1886

My Dear Daughter

As this is the first chance we have of sending mail out from our
place [because of the flooding of the James River] we will not lose
our opportunity of so doing. First will say W. J. & I got home
from Rockfish safe & did not suffer much cold. I felt sad to think
of our parting & when we got home we missed you & Mattie so
much & when we sat at table your vacent seats made us all feel
lonesome & sad. You did not tell us in your letter how your foot
was hope however it is well. A. J. had written to you but as you
think I must not see her letters to you of course I will not know
what she has written & I will not know what I must write so you
will have to excuse my short letters   I must however differ from
you as to who is the guardian of childrens plans & engagements.
While I do not suppose she would willfully ignore my right to
know anything that concerns her present or future welfare I
think as I am the person who has the right & whose duty it is to
watch with an anxious care over those who God has given me & I
think I know my duty & God being my helper I will try to
perform that duty I must not forget to tell you that I have not
gone down to my ranch yet but will go soon & will see about the
goats. "Dick" [a bird that seems to have been a gift from Maggie
and Mattie] has just come in from out doors & is flying about in
the room. We all feel very near to the "bird" as a relic of Maggie

& Mattie. I hope I will get to see you before you leave somehow or other. Give all the friends my love

Yours as ever
W. J. Keller

Amelia Jane to Mattie and after to Maggie

to Mattie

from her Aunt Pet

My Darling Little Mattie   they all are writing to your Ma   I thought I would write you a few lines. I cant tell you how much I missed you after you left. I was so lonesome I felt like I could not stand it I wish you and your Ma was home I do hope you will come back before you go home   I expect you are having a nice time we have plenty of peas and every time we have them your Grand Pa wishes for you. Dick is getting a long very well I will stop

Your Aunt Pet

Sister Maggie   My school is getting along tolerable well I started with seven. They do not attend regular   the flood had something to do with that. I did not teach the two days it was so bad. I think I will make a little something if not much.[7]

Charles to Maggie

Deming New Mex
April 13th 1886

My own Darling

I have been intending to write for three days and I have been so much pressed for time that I would not do so and now in the car whilst the train is waiting upon a delayed train I shall write. Between my duties in the car and getting ready for examination, it makes me jump, but if I had you and the babe here I would not care. By-the-way your mockisons [sic] have been ordered ever since you wrote for them and are not done yet the indians take there time about doing any thing of that kind and that puppie I could not take care of him and gave it to one of the R.P.C.s [railroad post clerks]   I think after we get fixed up again our hard times are about over, but oh! How much I do want a nice home and think for the present we will have to use a wind mill which I shall be able to get by fall put up a tank with it and water our grapes and crops from a hose and tank upon a wagon.

The ditch has about fell through. Every one seems to be anxious for you to come back. Have written for your pass and hope to get it by the first of the month. What did your pa do about the goats? We must not give that up for there is money in them. [See] what you can do about a cow for this fall.   Everything looks quiet at the ranch. Trains coming   Much love & many
kisses affect
C. A. B.

Amelia Jane to Maggie and Mattie

Howardsville Abl.Co
Va
April 18th, 1886

My ever dearest sister & Niece
     . . . Sister Maggie I do not want you to go way out there again. I hope something will happen that you will not go back & Cousin Charley will come back to Va. The yard is just beautifull now. The flowers are in bloom & everything is so sweetly perfumed with apple blossoms. Aunt Bet says kiss little Mattie for her & I say so too . . .
Your ever loving sister   Amelia J. Keller

Charles to Maggie

Deming N.M.
April 24th 1886

My own Darling
     Have been intending to write for three days but thought I would wait until I stood my examination so that I could send you the paper which I rece'd this morning but I feel satisfied that I will not get any pass so you find out what you can get a ticket for good for thirty days to Los Angeles will send you from seventy to seventy five dollars on the first of the month will have to borrow forty of it but can pay it the first of June as you can see I passed by a large majority one of the best examinations that he has had. He says that the rail roads refuse to give passes because the rates are so low that they think we ought to be able to pay our fair. You ought to be able to get the ticket for 25 or 30 dollars— But so you come back it makes no difference. I must have you here. You will live on the ranch and in a short time I shall be able to spend half of my time with you. Oh how much I would like to

see you. I just get sick with lonlyness. The only time that I feel like I was near home is when I go into Mrs. Hoys. . . . Mrs. H. says that she wishes to see you ever so much. Well I don't its some one elses all the time that wants to see you. Kiss our little darling and tell her papa wants to see her ever so much and she must think of him often. Give my kindest regards to all of the old friends and tell them I would like to see them, but never expect to see them there, that they must come out here. . . . With regards to all and much love and many kisses to you and Mattie I remain as ever Your loving and

Affect. Husband
C. A. Brown

Maggie to Pa

Staunton   Apl.26/86

My dear pa

Yours & A.J.'s letters were received in due time. . . . I received a letter from Dr. B. this morning. He cannot get my pass so I will have to stay a month longer. Mrs. White [Aunt Lizzie] says she is going to come over to see you this summer. Try to have things fixed up nicely by that time. I asked her to go to New Mexico but she said she thought she would go to see you & the children   I hope she will I know it would be a pleasant affair all around.

I am about out of paper will get some & write to A. J. & the boys. What is my dear old big brother doing? I do love my <u>big brother</u> so much—if he is big [Danny measured well over six feet in height.] he appreciates love as much as any & it don't hurt him to let him know it. Now, do make an effort to come over.

Your aff. daughter
M. M. Brown

Charles to Maggie

Deming N.M.
May 3d 1886

My own Darling

I am so sorry that I could not send you the money to come out on the first of the month but it may be for the best. Mrs Sickels has moved to Rincon and the children have scarlet fever. Geo. was at Mrs. Hopkins all day before yesterday and the next day

he was taken down with it   but I hope that it will be all over by
the time you come. I spoke to the P. M. at this place and I think
he will let me have some money in a few days and I will add that
to what I have and send it to you. I wrote to Dr. Hogeboom
[chief surgeon of the Atchison Railroad Employees Association]
and he promised me the pass and I shall write at once and tell
him what I want and for how long, but you know that it will only
be from Kansas City. I am perfectly satisfied that you would not
like to live in Deming and in a very short time I shall have my
lay off at Rincon and have one day off with my loved ones   oh!
My love I do want to see you and Mattie everything seems to be
working to our benefit now and I think we will be more
comfortably fixed in the future. I shall send you all of the money
that I can raise and trust to your judgment as to how to spend it
and how much to spend. Our home looks lonely now but I hope to
see it more cheerful soon. Hope that by this time you have
received my letter enclosing my examination but my final
appointment has not yet come. They seem to be pushed with
work in Washington and may not send it before the fifteenth and
my pay will not increase untill I get it and then it will be eighty
dollars per month. You old darling I wish it was a thousand for
your sake. I am so glad that your foot is better. Don't you get
sick, but come back to me in good health for you are the only one
in the world that I love. You are everything to me. If Millie will
be contented to stay on the ranch I will do all in my power to get
her up a school but not in Deming. It is one of the worst holes
that I have struck yet. The weather is getting warm and every
thing is looking fresh and green but there has not been a drop of
rain yet and the dust at this place is fearful but on the river it
looks nice. Write often to your loving husband—C. A. B.
Give my regards to all enquiring friends and tell them that I am
floating yet.   CAB

Maggie and Mattie reached Rincon in late May. The following letter,
written at two thirty in the morning as Maggie watches beside a fever-
ridden Mattie, sets a stark stage for the tragedy of the next days.

Maggie to Pa

                              Rincon NM June 16 2 1/2 A.M.
                                   [1886]
My dear Pa
    While keeping a lonely vigil over my darling I will write to you

for I cannot sleep. Our darling has taken sick Sunday (13th) after
noon she said "mama my throat is so sore I can hardly swallow"
I called her to me & looked in her throat which was very much
inflamed & swollen then in a few minutes a high fever came on &
an eruption down her back looking something like measles by
nine oclock she complained of headache & until 12 that night then
she complained of pain in her stumac [sic] & throwing up every
thing I gave her to opperate on her bowels   well up to this time
we have been unable to brake the fever & she is broken out thick
Dr. B. thinks it scarlet fever & if it is it is in a most malignant
form she has not been rational since noon yesterday. Dr. B. can
only be at home about one ½ hours in the middle of the day   he
has asked for a lay off. I have my house hole duties & her both to
attend to but if God just spares her is all I ask but I have my
fears she is so much reduced not a mouthfull of anything has been
in her stumack since Sunday.

I can't write any more now   Pray for me if I should lose her I
will knee [sic] need them.

Your loving daughter
M. M. Brown

OBITUARY.

(Communicated)

DIED:—At Rincon, New Mexico, of scarletina, Martha A. only
daughter of Dr. and Mrs. C. A. Brown, June 17th, 1886, age 7
years, 10 months and 23 days.

Mrs. Brown with her little daughter had just returned from a six
months visit to Virginia, and her home had only been gladdened for
a few days with the sunshine of Mattie's presence when she was
stricken down with the dread disease that so suddenly and unexpectedly took her from the warm and loving embraces of "mama"
and "papa" forever. For only a few brief days did she renew her
acquaintance with old familiar scenes, enjoying her childish sports
of a year ago, her golden hair shimmering and darkening in sunlight
and shadow, as fawnlike she tripped from place to place with bound-
ing step; her joyous shouts and peels of merry laughter mingling
with the notes of half a score of mocking birds, that from the spreading branches of the forest trees that surround her western home,
welcomed her return with their sweetest songs.

The last Sabbath she spent on earth she played Sunday school

with the neighboring children in the shade of the great trees near
the house, and as she sung the familiar hymns and the music of her
voice floated through the open windows to our ears, little did we
think that before another Sabbath dawned, the sound that we heard
would be transformed to the seraphim song.

Yet so it was, on Sunday night she was taken sick, and at 10:45
p.m. of the following Thursday, again she left the familiar scenes of
her childish years, this time never to return. But all is well. It is
well with us, it is well with the child. We mourn, it is true, but not
without hope. By faith we look away beyond the darkness of this
suffering life and behold her in the children's choir around the golden
throne of her Redeemer and Savior, who, while on earth, assured
us that "of such is the kingdom of Heaven." By faith we look away
beyond this vale of tears and behold her, a bud from earth trans-
planted to bowers celestial where it will bloom and flourish forever
in the paradise of God. By faith we lift our bleeding hearts and tear-
dimmed eyes from earth, and behold her as she is, "not dead, but
only gone before."

The harp is broken, and we mourn and weep. But blessed joy!
the sweet childish strains that but yesterday trembled on its strings,
to-day are heard in heaven. The Lord gave, and the Lord hath taken
away, blessed be the name of the Lord. "Blessed," because He hath
promised through He takes our loved ones from us, to restore, them
and one day Mattie shall be ours again, living, glorified, immortal.
And so this sad bereavement, and deep affliction will work out for
us a "far more exceeding and eternal weight of glory."

Mrs. A.L. Sangre [See October 18, 1885] to Maggie

Raton N Mex. June 21 1886

My dear Mrs. Brown

The sorrowful letter reached me this morning telling me of our
dear little Mattie's death. It was so unexpected to me although I
knew of her sickness but hoped so for her recovery. I had
planned having a pleasant hour with you and she. Oh that I could
of seen her for I loved her so dearly. Mrs. B you and the Dr.
have my heartfelt sympathies for she was your life and light. Do
not grieve for her she has only gone before to welcome you in the
next world as you welcomed her in this.

I have decided to come to you this week if you so desire it[8]
and stay until Mr. S. is ready for me which will perhaps be a

month and perhaps by Sunday next. Monday at the farthest. If these plans suit you telegraph to A. Hawk Manager of Western Service Telegraph at Raton he will receive it and there will be no charges. Send Tel. between hours of 8 AM and 6PM   I shall expect to hear from you by Wednesday at farthest and in between time will get ready to come. I've not been well since I came here. This climate does not agree with me.

Please write me also.

I am your Sincere friend

Mrs. A. L. Sangre

Raton N Mex

Box 46

Charles's sister Millie Gillespie to Charles

Harrisonburg Va—

June 23d 1886

My dear Brother

I am so shocked, and so grieved at the news your letter brings—I am so sorry for you both, that I am utterly unable to express what I feel. My heart shrinks at the loneliness and desolation death has left to you but oh! dear little Mattie is so happy! I felt sad whenever I looked at the child that she came too late for Ma to see her, but now she will be with her forever and you know what she will be to her—think what will Jesus be! When my little Mamy died I was so rebellious she was sweeter to me than any of my children—but I have since often lifted my heart to God in thankfulness that he thought my child fit to live with him and that he took her from the ills of life. It may be that you are both nearer the home that our savior went to prepare for his loved ones than you think—& how much better to meet your child there than to leave her here. I am so afraid Maggie will reproach herself for having gone back with the child—but that is all wrong—God's power is with his love, over everything—He could have stayed the cell of death or he could have prevented her going back— God wanted the child and you must feel that he has never given you so positive a proof of his love as in that he has taken your one dear sweet child to be his own.

I do wish I could comfort you! I have been where the very billions of sorrow overwhelmed me but God was with me all the time though I could not see it then—now I know it and believe

and feel that everything God does is right and well. So will he
bring you both to submission and rest in him—With the child we
know it is well—All that your love and pride could have done for
her could never ever approximate what she now enjoys and will
while Eternity lasts. You say she was all you worked for—she
will look down upon you with glad approving eyes if you give that
work to God. Do not relax a single energy—do all the work the
dear Lord gives you to do and he will see that it brings you
blessing in this life and that which is to come—but go ahead with
duties because it pleases God—before you were pleasing
yourselves, because it was for your child, now it must be all for
God and you must try to do it better. It always helps me to work
when I try to please God and there is real pleasure in feeling that
all results are in his hands—Mary Ella and the children unite
with me in sympathy and much love. I hope to hear from you
soon again.

Ever your affectionate Sister
A. B. Gillispie

Charles's sister Mary Ella Brown to Maggie

Harrisonburg, Va.
June 1886

My dear Maggie
    So shocked and distressed to hear of poor little Mattie's
death—not death but birth into a new and beautiful life, and my
heart is bowed down at the thought of your crushed and bleeding
arms. I am so sorry for you both. I know what she was to you
and the blow is too suddenly for you to take my comfort now but
you must learn to look away from yourselves and think of the
good of the child—for truly it is well with her and do not make
yourselves miserable with reproaches. You did all that you were
able to do for her and we would all have lavished things upon her
if we had known she was so soon to take wings—but our hearts
were full of promises for the future when we will better able
[probably a reference to the school for Mattie Mary Ella and
Millie had planned to open in Rincon]—that time perhaps would
never have come—you know how disappointing have been our
hopes and this thought made me very, very sad when I looked at
the child and saw how delicate, affectionate and sensitive she
was. But there was a tenderer Eye upon her with infinite love

and pity—"I'll have this little lamb, said He, and place it in my breast." And there she is forever at rest. Be assured that whatever sorrow the future has in store for you it holds no drop for her—however you may prosper here it cannot compare with her exceeding riches. You are only called upon to part with her for a little while—soon we will all be sleeping.

When you feel more like you could write let us know all you can write about—do not attempt anything that will harrow your feelings too much. Let us know of your plans too. I do not know what we will do this winter we will have to have situations because we have nothing to live on. Sister talked of going out there [New Mexico] and teaching that school then Gussie [see March 24, 1915] wrote to her that the matron at Coe College [Iowa] expected to leave and she has applied for that place. I am trying to prepare myself to teach art and had been thinking I could accomplish enough to teach by the time your school opens there. Of course our main object in going there though would have been to teach Mattie.[9] She was too delicate to have been taught more than a little at a time.

Sister is waiting to enclose this.

May God bless you and comfort you! I know that He will in his own time and way.

With love and sympathy I am

Affectionately Your sister
M. E. Brown

Maggie's cousin Maggie Keller to Maggie

Churchville Va
June 25th 86

Dear Cousin Maggie

Your missive containing the sad, sad news of your little darlings death was received by Aunt Mary Wednesday and she sent the same to us on Thursday. We will all ever remember the dear little girl, and extend to you & Dr. our warmest sympathy in your bereavement. But as you say she was too good and sweet for this world and as God loves a shineing mark he thought it best to remove her from our midst. We often spoke of the dear little pet how smart and cute she was and how we would love to see her. And now to think we will never see her again it dont seem possible but our lives are not in our own hands. They are as

grass in the morn it flurish and groeth up and in the eve it is cut
down and dies   we all have to give up those that are very near
and dear to us and the brightest flours are the first to fade and
when once gone they can never return.

Oh! the dear little girl   little did I think when I kissed her
good by that it would be the last time I would ever have such a
pleasure oh my we were so very sorry to hear it and feel so for
you but you must cheer up and bare with it the best you can.
This world is full of sorrow and we all have our share. Aunt Mary
Uncle Will & Cousin Kettie all wish me to extend their sympathy
to you & Cousin Charlie. Bro John is not at home but I know he
will be very sorry to hear it when he comes. We have not heard
from Brother Sexton for a long time Ma will write to you soon.
Please excuse me for not writeing more this time and write soon
again

From your affectionate

Cousin Maggie Keller

God bless you & Cousin Charlie

Maggie's cousin Ed Shuff to Maggie

Staunton Va June 28/86

Dear Cousin

We received your letter a few days agow and announcing the
death of little Mattie witch we wear sorry to hear of for Mattie
was a good child and we all will miss her from this world now but
thire will be no mis her as much as her Dear Mother who tender
care has watch over for theas many years. I know it was hard for
you to gived her up but she is far better off then any of ous for
She has gown to that home of hers in heaven to live for ever
whar thire is no sorrow nor trouble thire   we mus try and learn
to lived in the way of God So when the last day come we will be
ready to gow I have written to all of the rest of the Famly   we
got a letter from Chas last week they wear all well with the
excepton of little May   She has Been varry Sick for nearly 3 or 4
weeks we are having plenty of rain now I am still loafing yet you
mus excuse me for not writting sooner but I will promis to do
Better now and to more promp ans your letters write soone all
send much love to you and Dr

Yours &C

Ed L Shuff

Maggie's Cousin Marshall Shuff to Maggie

Covington, Va., June 29th 1886

Dear Cousin Maggie

The painful news of the removal of your dear little Mattie has just reached me, in a letter from Ed, this morning, and I hasten to express my affectionate sympathy with you and Dr under so severe an affliction. Alas! How fresh in my memory is the recollection of the liveliness and innocence of the lovely departed: All that was mortal is changed now, and clouded forever. But how great is your comfort in the well-grounded assurance that the good Shepherd who "Careth for his flock—has taken the gentle Lamb into his own fold. Your Darling Child has gone to him who said Suffer little children to come unto me. And we know not, when how soon our hour may come.

Oh, that we may all meet in that brighter and happier world, where sorrow and sin and suffering are alike unknown.

That a higher than human power may console and support you under this heavy stroke is the earnest prayer of,

Your Dearest cousin
Marshall

Maggie to Pa

Deming, N.M.
June [sic] 3d,/86

My dear pa

Your dear letter of comfort was received yesterday. I have received a good many since our darling's death & it is of great comfort to know so many love the dear one. We (Mattie and I) were down to see her aunts on her papa's side & I saw they loved the child but had no idea they loved her so much. Their letters are very kind indeed.

As you see, I have left the ranch for a while. I could not stay there alone as I would have had to have done. Dr. B. might get down to dinner if the trains were on time. Then every thing seemed so lonely there without her. I am lonely any where though but would be more so there.

We are living by a lady & gentleman that have a very bright little boy who has taken a fancy to us & is a good deal of company to me. I could not stand to have a little girl around.

We will try to sell the place now & if we do & both live, we will come back & bring our babe's remains & put them near her dear grandma.

Sunday morning before she was taken sick, she came into the kitchen & asked me if she did not have two grandma angels & one grandpa. Her mind seemed to run on such things. Remember how she talked so much of dying, being afraid to die before she saw her papa. Well, she just did see him   he could be with us so little. I think she knew she was going to die. The heat went very hard with her & caused her to suffer more but I am glad she did not linger since she had to go   for her suffering would have been so great now. When she died the heat was 102! Yesterday it was 115 in Rincon & 114 here. It has been increasing ever since her death. Just one month to the day she was buried from the time she left Va. We left there the 18th of May & the 18th of June we laid her away.

Papa dear, I am not rebellious but feel thankful we had her the time we did have her with us. She has escaped much for this world is full of unforeseen troubles. Now they are all over with her. She has only gone before.

I am so glad I took her home this winter. There is a nice brick Methodist church here we will go tomorrow night, nothing preventing. We have a letter from Brother McCorkle to the preacher in charge.

I will close for this time. The flowers A. J. sent in her first letter after I came out I pinned on our darlings' breast with the little breast pin her Cousin Mattie C. gave her. She was dressed to look as natural as possible, lying a little on one side with her doll Aunt Mary gave her in her arms just as when she went to sleep Sunday night. She would have me undress her doll & give it to her when she went to bed. I can't fully realize I won't see her here any more. I suppose it is better so too.

All write soon & as often as you can
Your most loving daughter
M. M. Brown

Bruce Bowman, Maggie's friend, to Maggie

Retirement, Va.
7–4–1886

Dear, dear, Maggie,
    You and Dr. have our sincerest sympathies in your great

affliction. There was much sorrow at our breakfast table this morning (Sammie brought your letter after ten o'clock last night) as if each had lost a dear friend. Every one remembered Maggie's [sic] bright little ways and were so sorry for you. Dollie has just been to have me show her on the map where you live and to talk over Mattie's conversation with her. How lonely you are, and how happy Mattie is! No more sorrow and suffering, only a bright and glorious waiting for her parents. I know your hearts are crushed, she was your all, and I can imagine how her bright happy manner cheered your gloom and often despondency when thinking of your absent friends.

Then your every thought for the future was for her aggrandizement, but with all, you could never have given her an inheritance, such as she now possesses. Possibly as earthly prosperity arose about her she might have lived for it and forgotten her God. Now she is safe in the arms of Jesus. Close to His loving breast. You will sooner or later meet her in the great beyond. "The Lord hath taken away. Blessed be the name of the Lord." I was so shocked when I read your letter many times during the night I awoke and questioned. Why should poor Maggie lose her one treasure? We cannot tell. But I am sure it is all for the best. Poor, poor Maggie. Now, we see through a glass darkly; then all shall be revealed. I hope some kind friend can be found to keep you company while Dr. is away. Your loneliness is almost unbearable. I have thought of you often in the last two weeks that you were so busy you had forgotten your promise to write. I would wait awhile longer and then remind you of it. If I had dreamed of your trouble I would not have waited. I hope you will write to me very soon and give me all the particulars of Mattie's death where you buried her, how you dressed her, how long you had been at home whether the disease was very fatal and all your home news, everything will interest me.[10] All are well and send much love and sympathy. Hoping to hear from you soon I remain truly your loving friend

Bruce Bowman

Maggie to Amelia Jane and then to W. J. and Dannie

Deming July 7/86

My dear Sister

I will undertake to answer your letters. I thought of doing so

yesterday but it was so warm & I was so sleepy I could not. The
night of the 5th was celebrated as the 4 & there were a great
many fire works &c as a 4 of July is generaly celebrated out here.
Well some of the fire fell in some trash neare some frame shantys
owned by Chinamen   the result was a $75,000 or $50,000
thousand dollar fire   fortunately for us we were not very near &
the wind was from us   but never-the-less we were up until after
12 o'clock or rather between 1 & 2 o'clock some of the best
buildings in town were burnt but the saddest of all was a little
girls about 5 years old went in the burnt district & got in to the
hot ashes & run a hot nail in her foot from which she died of
lockjaw last night. We had quite a hard rain last night the first
we have had for 18 months cattle are dieing all over the country
for want of grass. I was very uneasy about the fire & the first
things I thought of was my loved ones little things   that is the
reason I want a little chest so I can put them all together so if
any thing of the kind should occur I could save them   I have the
picture of Mattie with the dog   but I thought you had the other I
wanted to have it enlarged. I sent one to her grand ma Brown
the same time I sent that to you if they have that one I will get it
as I have written for it we will send you one of the enlarged
ones.

Yes your letters are of great comfort write as often as you can.
I will write to the boys now

With love your aff sister
M. M. Brown

My dear little brother

I hope you will keep & treasure those little things your little
niece left & be a good little man so you will go where she has
gone. I have a little book I will send you of hers but she was too
sick for me to read out of it to her when she got it.

Your loving sister
M. M. B.

Deming N M July 7/86

My very dear brother,

I received your highly appreciated letter a few days since. Your
loving sympathy is of great comfort to think I have dear brothers
& a sister to sympathize with me. But I am sorry my brother
could not write before. You wrote us often before I came to Va

why is it you don't write now. Hope you & W. J. are still staunch
in your temperance cause & above all things I hope you & A. J.
will stay close by each other & your company be hers & hers
yours I would have been so happy if I had a brother older than I
like you but our dear pa had to be brother & pa also.
I think there is nothing in this world much nicer than to see
loving & affectionate brothers & sisters. We have received very
nice letters from many will enclose them all some time & send
them to you all to be returned for these letters of sympathy are
very dear to me. Every one seemed to love our little darling.

Write often to your loving sister

M. M. Brown

(*Above and opposite*) These three photographs illustrate the
contrast in housing and terrain between the Browns' Virginia estate
in Bridgewater and the spare, one-story adobe structures of Rincon,
New Mexico.

Miners and their loaded burros in front of a supply
store, probably located in the Deming/Rincon region of
New Mexico (circa 1888).

(*Facing page*) Daniel (Dannie) A. Keller (Maggie's brother), newly
arrived from Virginia on the velocipede car he used for his first job
at the railroad depot in Rincon, New Mexico (1888).

Interior of one of the Roman Catholic churches in the
Rincon, New Mexico area. To Protestant Charles and
Maggie Brown, the Hispanic Catholic worship was as
strange as the terrain.

Burt Ruple at a mining camp in northern Mexico. Charles and Maggie pinned hopes for a rich strike on Ruple (circa 1898).

Maggie Brown, Virginia (1917). Courtesy of Lolita Cox Smith.

7

New Mexico:

September 4, 1886–November 25, 1888

I am here all safe & sound after traveling 2704 miles, I didnt count them all my self but this is correct. . . . You ought to just see these mud houses with a garden on top of them & a ladder to go up on to chase the chickens off. Things are not as shabby as you think they are. Give my regards to who think enough about me to ask. . . . [June 24, 1888, Dannie to Pa]

For the western Browns, the time (September, 1886–November, 1888) triggered positive change—the flourishing of the Rincon ranch, harmony between Maggie and Charles, regular paychecks, a new baby, Dannie's arrival from Virginia. But for the eastern Kellers, affairs plummeted—the Virginia economy dropped, Pa and Maggie became estranged, Aunt Bet (the Black woman who had been friend and housekeeper to the Kellers since Maggie was a child) died and scandal threatened Amelia Jane. It was a sad play in contrasts.

For Maggie and Charles, the three years from Fall 1886 to Fall 1888 marked the first settled time of their turbulent marriage. What Maggie had first rejected as an austere landscape, she began to view with affection and to catch the enchantment the play of light created with the bare, craggy earth. The morning brilliance and the twilight cast of mauve and carmine over the ocher desert, the russet mesas and the dark mountains—these became magic hues that comforted rather than repelled: "Fall is lovely here indeed all the year is" [October 21, 1887].

For the first time, there was money. Charles provided a regular income: eighty sure dollars from his railroad job and random fees from a small medical practice. Maggie herself generated business from ranch produce, selling butter, milk, and bacon to customers in Rincon (1½ miles from the ranch). Maggie wrote about milking <u>my</u> cows, increasing <u>my</u> sales and investing <u>my</u> money. She invented a saddle pack for the milk container, and with her own income she employed a farm hand to assist her with deliveries.

On the frontier, women as well as men became drawn into the affairs of gains and losses.[1] Spirited women developed their economic skills, supplementing family income through inventive schemes involving a range of things from dairy and bakery produce to clothing and laundering needs. Quite often, as a husband prospected or worked for long stretches away from home, a wife directed the family business or ranch, often relishing the challenge of the new enterprise.

Commerce with the Rincon people improved Maggie's opinion of them. "I had no idea they had such nice people there." In response to a Virginia letter criticizing New Mexicans, Maggie retaliated with a spirited defense:

> I beg leave to inform [you] we are not living among savages &
> Mexicans are better although they speak a different language
> from ours & the white people with whom I visit are more
> intelligent than it was my fortune to meet while in Va: There is
> one <u>great</u> difference in this country & that is people have to
> comply with their promises or they are not thought well of.
> People are what you might call self-made. It is just according to
> how they act as to how they are received. If anyone is caught
> doing any little mean thing he is ever afterward looked on with
> suspicion. [April 14, 1988]

And when the Virginia family vehemently disapproved of the young man courting Amelia Jane, Maggie tried to lure her West with subtle hints about eligible bachelors in Rincon.

> We had the agent & a young telegraph opperator down to tea one
> day last week. I like them so much. You can have nice company
> out here. The agent looks like Ed Shuff something & the
> opperator is small but a pure blond. [September 12, 1888]

Amelia Jane's romantic attachments during this period angered Maggie. Part of her distress stemmed from the fact that one of the young men was a close cousin, who strongly resembled Dannie and W. J. There seemed to have been a cultural taboo about compounding family resemblances. Maggie justified her own marriage to her third cousin Charles because family likenesses between them were negligible. The major source of Maggie's rancour over Amelia Jane's suitors was simply Amelia Jane's reticence to discuss them with Maggie. To Maggie one of the strongest obligations of "sisterhood" was the sharing of secrets. That Amelia Jane lived in a world to which Maggie was not privy seemed to Maggie to destroy essential womanly bonds.

The small adobe house on the Rincon ranch was a far cry from an antebellum southern home: no trees, no clipped lawn or cultivated garden, no curtained bay windows. The mud roof, in the occasional times of rain, dissolved and had to be reinforced with more dirt. Still Maggie discovered that New Mexico allowed for Virginia customs. She opened a warm hearth (southern style) to guests. Maggie cooked extra portions so that anyone around could be welcome and well fed at her table. On his days off, Charles indulged in pastimes he associated with the genteel style of Virginia: he trimmed "shrubbery" (cactus) around the house, entertained, shot wildcats that occasioned his front door, hunted, fished, socialized on neighboring ranches, and participated in national and local politics.

New Mexico modified the Browns' dress code as well as their house design. While she regretted the loss of her "beautiful clothes," Maggie, unlike some pioneer women who clutched fervidly to eastern styles, focused on the practical benefits of plain apparel:

> Here on the place we just need enough to cover our selves decently. When Dr. B. comes home he puts on an old pair of cordurory pants all out at the seat and has an old pair of low quartered shoes he wears without socks. I have in the way of clothing 2 calico dresses 2 pair of $1.25 shoes & two pair of stockings & 2 skirts but fortunately we dont need much in this country if we stay home. [February 24; May 14, 1888]

As Maggie and Charles's life eased, so did their interpersonal relations. "I think I have a fine looking husband as any in town" [September 20, 1886]. "I think I have the best and most attentive wife in the whole country" [November 17, 1886]. Sharing ranch chores, joking about who milked cows best, they relaxed and became "an old settled couple." In the genial glow of those days, Maggie, at age thirty-five, became pregnant. The earlier pattern of their sexual relation suggests that the pregnancy was planned. They were willing to risk loving and nourishing another child.

It was unpleasantries with Virginia relatives that threw periodic dampers over Maggie's otherwise happy months of pregnancy (February–October, 1887). First there was Charles's family, again angling to homestead in New Mexico. Millie Gillespie (Charles's older sister) moved to Deming for a period and purchased a herd of cattle which she soon deeded to her brother Will. But the chilled relations between Maggie and Millie may well have dissuaded Millie from carrying out her plans to settle in the territory. Mincing no words, Maggie wrote to Pa, "My revulsion feeling to her [Millie] is growing" and claimed she preferred to die rather than accept a glass of water from Millie, whom she labelled, "viper."

As provoking as they were, the chilled relations with Millie were chronic; Maggie probably could not imagine a different kind of feeling for Millie. However, the coolness that began separating her and Pa was new and consequently quite upsetting. Until Maggie's 1885 visit to Virginia, a pronounced affection bonded her to Pa. It was a kind of warmth not actually unusual; historian Carl Degler found women who westered from the south were particularly effusive in their letters home to their fathers. Still, the tenderness between Maggie and Pa was a comfort and strength to them both. And the breach mattered.

Of the fifty-eight letters remaining from this time period, only one is from Pa. Yet he obviously wrote because Maggie's letters are responses to his. Perhaps Maggie preserved the earlier letters because they represented the ideal of her relation with Pa and she discarded his letters of this period because they underscored hurt and misunderstanding.

Pa's financial situation worsened and his health deteriorated during this period. His money problems mirrored the flagging economy of all rural Virginia at that time. Deeply in debt, Virginia farmers were hard-pressed to get credit and often lacked even the essentials of food and clothing. While the general decline explains Pa's financial strain, it fails to clarify Pa's edginess toward Maggie. He seemed wary of discussing his shifts of residence and employment with her and, judging by Maggie's letters, he resented her interference with any of his affairs: health, children, house, or job.

Even without Pa's words, the sharp exchanges are evident through Maggie's remarks:

I am almost afraid to make any inquiry about your affairs for fear
of being accused of presumption or [being] scolded in the next
letter. I am really sorry my solicitous feeling will be
misconstrued. [April 14, 1888]

Try to get a place with Mr. Wiseman. I only mention this. It is
not advice or anything of that kind. I am almost afraid to speak
to you as a father. You are so apt in your next [letter] to give me
a reprimand. [August 12, 1888]

Maggie's phrasing is curious. She protested: "I am afraid to speak to
you as a father." Yet, in reality, she had not been addressing him as
an authority figure but as if he were a child. It may have been her
tone of condescension that offended Pa. Whatever the inner source of
contention, the letters show a decided coolness in the previously warm
relation.

The sudden death of Aunt Bet compounded Pa's home problems and
Maggie's pressure on him. With his three young people (Dannie, 20;
Amelia Jane, 18; and W. J., 14), Pa rented part of a house in How-
ardsville; yet he was away from there for weeks at a stretch working
some thirty miles distant in Cumberland. Aunt Bet's presence as a
stable, maternal figure had given respectability to the arrangement.
Without her the arrangement opened itself to whatever the town gos-
sips wanted to infer. Maggie's southern sense of propriety bristled at
Pa's seeming unconcern for the scandal-ripe setting. With passion,
Maggie insisted that Pa must send at least Amelia Jane to live in
Rincon. Actually Maggie wanted the whole family, including Pa, to
move west. Pa's rebuttal came more by act than by counter argument:
without informing Maggie, he began building himself a permanent
house in Cumberland Valley. When Maggie discovered this from outside sources, she was angry and hurt.

So keen was her hurt that when her child was born on October 6,
1887, she refused to notify Pa herself, confessing to Amelia Jane that
she felt so estranged from Pa she could not bring herself to write him—
even about his new grandson. But Charles sent the news, and Pa
responded with happy pride, not to Charles or Maggie but with a note
addressed to the newborn James Albert:

I heard of your arrival a week or two since. I avail myself of
extending a hearty welcome to you as a citizen of our planet &
hope you will ever be as you were in your arrival "a little ahead

of time" in that case you will never be <u>left</u> by the train. Oh how I
wish I had you in my arms a while I would squeeze your little
bones so much. [October 23, 1887]

In naming her son, Maggie overlooked her current bad feelings toward
Pa and used his name James (and, of course, her brother W. J.'s) for
her little boy. James was also the name of Charles's brother James
Newton, who had died in 1862. The baby's middle name, Albert, drew
from Charles's lineage: Albert for Charles himself and for his uncle.
In the south naming was virtually a mystique and carried considerable
meaning in the family and the community.[2] A name suggested a responsibility of living up to ancestral standards and an affectionate
bonding with revered individuals. As she traced the tree of connections
in the name James Albert, Maggie felt pleased that she had properly
linked this western-born baby with his southern heritage. "Ask W. J.
what he thinks of his name sake. He is named for pa & Dr. B. & Dr.
B's brother & my brothers" [October 21, 1887].

James Albert brought joy to Maggie and Charles; yet he did not
assume the preeminent spot in Maggie's letters that Mattie had often
held. Maggie had mixed feelings about this new child. While he was a
dear new life, and the "son" Charles wanted, he was also a reminder
of the dead Mattie:

Albert is beginning to notice when I lean over his cradle. He
jumps & throws up his hand & laughs. He has blue eyes & they
are straight, but I think if he were more like Mattie I would
think more of him. [November 7, 1887]

In the winter of 1888, the persistent Maggie renewed her efforts to
move Dannie from Virginia to Rincon. The task was complicated by
Pa's resistance to losing Dannie as his co-worker in broommaking and
construction. Maggie argued that Dannie working in New Mexico could
send home far more money than he could earn in Virginia. Certainly,
Dannie was enthusiastic about moving west, but with his eye not on
wealth but on adventure. In February, Maggie sent him ticket money
from her own earnings; yet it was late June before Dannie arrived.
During the interim Maggie watched eagerly, expecting his big figure
"to loom up soon" [March 21, 1888]. Once she ran shouting welcomes
to a tall man ambling down the railroad tracks, only to discover not
Dannie but a neighboring farmer who guffawed at her mistake.

Dannie's arrival in June surprised Maggie and Charles. But both delighted in the genial fellow. To Maggie, this was her "big boy." To Charles, this was a sporting partner. Dannie wrote to Virginia with what he thought was humorous overstatement—the kind of exaggeration that emphasized stereotypes.

Ride on the train from Kann City & every nation in the world is represented there and hard costomers they are too. You ought to just see these mud houses with a garden on top of them & a ladder to go up on to chase the chickens off. . . . You think it is hot there [Virginia] but is the honest truth that there is a thermomiter here boiling over. . . . I used to jest about thermomiter runing over but I never saw it be fore. [June 24, 1888]

For a time Dannie played the greenhorn to oldtimers' legpulling. He was particularly "sanguine" (Maggie's designation) about the "100 lb catfish" he could catch in the Rio Grande. From odd jobs he saved enough to buy lumber for a boat and fishing tackle. However, by the time he had all readied, the Rio Grande (unlike any other river he'd known) had dried to a trickle. Undaunted, Dannie took up hunting. For him, New Mexico was a sportsman's paradise.

In time, practical Maggie found Dannie's idle lifestyle a concern. At her insistence he got a job at the Rincon depot, yet within ten days was let go. He dabbled with other odd work, but had nothing to call an income. He was an amiable freeloader.

It was Charles, though, who brought to an end the three years of relative peace. In the fall of 1888 he was severely disciplined for losing the key to a railroad security locker. Docked a third of one month's salary, he also lost favor with his employers and slipped in line of promotion. The humiliation did not dampen Charles's spirits. A mining boom was then firing the imagination of the "boys" around Rincon and gold, rather than humiliation or job concern, preoccupied Charles. Maggie foresaw that the period of ease was finished. And she was correct.

Letter Texts September 1886–November 1888

Maggie to Dannie

Deming NM
Sept 4/86

My dear brother
    I am indeed glad to know you had not forgotten me or how to

write your letters are so few & far between I am afraid you will wait so long some time you will forget how to write. What are you doing now? How much do you get per day. Dr. B. says he dont think he will come back to Va before he is better off & then not to practice medicine. He finds it a very nice thing to walk up at the end of every month & receive his $80.00 or $85.00 as the case may be   we want to improve our ranch & sell it for enough to come back & buy us a comfortable home in Roanoke County, Va. I wish Pa's land was in Roanoke.

Now don't fail to write me what you are doing. We must have missed any letter telling about pa going to Cumberland for we knew nothing of it until A. J.'s letter telling of the Festival saying he had not come back yet.

Your aff sister
M. M. Brown

Maggie to Amelia Jane

Deming N.M.
Sept 4 86

My dear Sister
    Your letter telling me of the Festival was received a few days since & your & DA's of the 30 was received this morning. I found me much better than usual & trying to put up some persimmons. Tuesday was pay day & went around & settled our bills then went to the Chinese Bazzar & bought me a china tea set consisting of tea pot sugar bowl & cream pitcher & 11 cups & saucers (the other cup & saucer was lost in the fire)   It was pure china bought from a chinaman & from China   also a fine sandle wood fan the price was $4.00 but we got it for $3.00 taking the set and it all at once. When I got home from Va I had not a cup to drink out of so borrowed some until I came up here then only bought two (2) until now   have been using a glass aunt Mary gave me for a sugar bowl. We had a sociable at the church last Tuesday we took in $27.00 only had a collection taken up the refreshments were free. We will join the church tomorrow if nothing happens. Well we are having an old Va rain   has been raining since 5 oclock this morning now it is 1 oclock
Write soon to your aff sister

M. M. Brown

Maggie to her family in Virginia

Las Cruces Dona Ana Co NM

Sept 20/86

My dear friends

I suppose it will be more than a week between this & my last letter. Dr. Brown was summoned down here as a witness in Mr. Hoy's land suit last Monday today a week   & I could not think of staying home a lone so came with him thinking we would only be here for a few days & I had not seen the country so I came & went over to Mesilla the old town 2½ miles from here   it is a much prettier place than this. There is an old friend from Colo living over there he is engaged in shipping fruit from this country grapes &c. The peach crop was almost a failure this year on account of late frost. I want to try to get up a package to send to you by the 27th [Pa's sixty-third birthday] but if it don't come by then it will be there soon after. We want to go home tomorrow. Dr. Brown has been on the witness stand since Saturday eve. They think he will get off today. I think I have a fine looking husband as any in town   he bought himself a new derby hat & nice fitting coat & vest the day before we left Deming. A lady friend was in & I had been trying to persuade him to buy a new hat & he said the old one was good enough   I asked the lady if he did not look "horrid" in that "old hat"? she said I could not put any thing on him to make him look "horrid." Then I called an other lady in to stand by me & she said the other one was right but I gained the day & he did get one. I am sick & tired of this place & am home sick will write a gain soon. Will go home to Deming tomorrow we think.

Your most [loving] daughter

M. M. Brown

Deming Sept. 22   I sent you part of your present today for I want you to put them <u>right</u> on. Hope you wont take offence but Dr Brown got too fat to wear them after he had them about 6 weeks so I thought they would fit you

Maggie to Pa

Deming, N.Mex.

Sept. 23/86

My own dear pa

I sent you a few things yesterday that I thought would make

you comfortable   but there is no use talking you must come out
here before the cold Nov. rains & fog sets in. Now it won't take
more than $50.00 (fifty dollars) and what good would $50.00
worth of land do us without our darling pa   now papa I loved my
babe but you can't imagine how much I loved my precious mama
always thought I loved you better than her. To think you have
that cough again   if you love me you will come to me   yes you
will. If Dr. B. keeps his position we will see about getting you
home when you get ready to go. If any of us needed $50.00 fifty
you would try very hard to get it   now you will wont you &
write me in your next you will come. Don't wait until you get
ready for you will never come if you do. Now let me be physician
& prescribe a change to a <u>warmer</u> climate.[3]   all I have written is
from my heart. I think the children can manage & get a long
without you for a little while   where as if you stay there a few
months longer I fear we will have no papa atall.

   If Mr Bateman should refuse you this & the consequence would
be what I fear   his future life will be a burden to him.

   Now pa do please say you will come.

Your most loving & affectionate daughter
M. M. Brown

Maggie to Pa

Deming NM
Sept 29/86

My dear pa
   It is more than likely we will go within the next month to the
ranch to live. Dr. B. will run from silver City to Rincon in place
of Deming to Rincon & the lay off will be in Rincon so we will
live at the ranch as our home & will save about $20.00 house rent
& fuel this winter. <u>Now</u> you <u>must</u> come   we would have a place
or room for you here or any <u>place</u> we might be for you but at the
ranch you can have a nice room with a fire place in it. <u>By the way</u>
you <u>will</u> have to bring the andirons for <u>it</u> & the one in <u>the parlor.</u>
[Maggie underlines to ensure that the significance of their now
having a parlor and other rooms with fire places does not escape
Pa.] Now if Dannie goes to Scottsville[4] it wont cost much for the
rest at home. I will write to D. A.   Now let me hear from you
<u>soon</u>

Your loving daughter
M. M. Brown

Maggie to Dannie

Deming NM
Sept 29/86

My <u>dear</u> big Brother

I <u>am</u> afraid you will be disappointed for a few weeks in getting your present [Dannie's twentieth birthday would be October 12.] but I have selected it and want to get it but we have no money and will not until after the first as Dr. B. is always paid off first. If you don't keep on writing to me after you get your present I will not send you any thing Xmas   it will improve you in the use of your pen to write every one better than the last. I think you are improving any way. Write me all about your business. How much will you get & all such things   they all interest me. I do think you ought to be doing something. I think if we get pa out here you will all come finally   I think his health would be so much better here if he don't do any more this winter than last he had better come even if he has the work   I think it would be better to leave it for I don't think he can stand the winter. Write soon to your loving sister.

M. M. Brown

Charles to Pa

Deming N.M.
Nov. 17th 1886

W. J. Keller Esq
    Dear Friend

In your last letter you seemed to think that my wife was complaining of me and was dissatisfied. Do not think so for I think I have the best and most attentive wife in the whole country. Of course she is sad and lonely at times but that is because of the loss of our darling. I think if by any means you would be induced to move to this country she would be more contented, but I do not think that she will ever be contented in Va unless we could be able to buy us a nice home when we come back and I do not know how long that will be but we are doing better now and hope that it will not be long. It has been very cold here this fall some thing that we are not used to.

No sir, I do not envy any man his wife for we are as well maited as can be.

I think that you could do well at your trade in this country as there are very few good carpenters in this country and when you find one he wants five dollars per day.

With much love to your self and the rest of the family from us both, I remain very respectfully

Yours
C. A. Brown

Maggie to Pa

Deming, N.M.
Feb 1,/87

My dear pa

I have written D. A. a letter asking him to come out & live with me. Of course this is with you what we shall do. You can see the proposition I make in his letter. I think if he comes you will come also. I will not live there [Rincon] alone or rather I cannot. I can tell this much, we are not going to have any pardners. Not even his Sister or brother, but if D. A. comes I do assure you you will not lose any thing by it. He will be a protection as well as company & my own dear blood & when I work I want to know it is for some one that loves me & I love. Now you all think of this. There may be a change made in Dr. B's run the same we have been hoping for for a year that is he will run from Rincon to Silver City which is fifty miles the other side of here. I will close hoping to hear from you real soon,

Your loving daughter
M. M. Brown

Maggie to Pa

Deming, N.M.
February 6, 1887

My dear pa

Yours of the 27th just in hand & it distresses me more than I can tell. The trouble among the family is all the troubles I have. I am afraid you misunderstand D. A. He more than likely came over to help you in all your work but thought you had better do some thing to get some money to live on first. I know you could not be much worse off than last winter a year & you did have something to do but this winter you have written of doing so little you or D. A. that I know it must be near starvation point or D. A. would do as you want him. I did not ask D. A. to come and improve our "place" but knew Dr. B. would have to hire some one or give up his place & he could afford to hire better than to give up his place [the railroad position] & I knew D. A. had no work all last winter & thought it better for him to come here than to live on you & do nothing.

He wrote me in his last letter that he was going to help you. But, pa, you persist in misunderstanding him. I wish I could make you all happy. I find out there is more pleasure in making others happy than myself.

I wrote out a list for some things for A. J. for this summer. If any girl or woman wants anything it is when she is young & I always had things to look nice in when I was young & if I can make A. J. happy by giving her anything I will go without myself & give her things.

Have not heard from the children for 3 weeks. Can't tell why. I will send this to Willis P.O. It is very cold now & awfully windy. Write soon. With much love & affection, your daughter

M. M. Brown

Amelia Jane to Maggie

Howardsville Va

Feb 14 1887

My very dear Sister

I received your letter with the edging or at least the sample. As soon as I read the letter I got my crocheting needle & thread & learned how in about 15 minutes   I think it is just lovely prettier then the pineapple [pattern] & believe The Amen thread has not come yet   I am real anxious to commence crocheting it. Pa is in Cumberland now he is doing some work for J. R. Jones the man Bateman got his land from   I do hope we will never have to live on it pa says he will sell it if he can I wish he could you know what a horror we all have toward that land.

To day is Valentine day. I received one a day or two before the time. Mr Crowder sent me a lovely one Aunt Bet says she thinks it is the prettiest one she ever saw the mottoes on the front are, first "Attribute of love." second, "Forget me not" third, "Devoted to you." & then inside there is a very nice verse. I have not received a letter from him yet. I will send you the other two patterns of his initials if [rest of letter missing]

Maggie to Pa

Deming, N.M.
Mar. 25/87

My darling pa

I have not written for so long I don't know if I can write now to suit you or so you can read. Your letter from Cumberland came duly to hand & it seems now as though you & I are getting ties that bind us each to our separate countries. I did hope we would either one or the other be able to sell out & we would spend your last years together but fate seems against us. I am afraid they are not getting along very well in Howardsville. I have not heard from them since you left. What have they to live on? Is D. A. at work? I will write to them also today. I have not written because of a friend of ours, the best & most substantial friend Dr. B. & I have had since we have been west he is worth about $75,000 (seventy five thousand)   they have a Chinaman cook but Mrs Byron wanted me to sit by her & give her her medicine so I did. and when Dr. B. & I went down in their buggy about 3 miles out of town to look at some cows Mrs. Gillespie [Charles's oldest sister, Millie] was thinking of buying, I was very much pleased with a Durham heifer, so Dr. B. says "I will get that for you this month." I came home & was telling Mrs. Byron how much I was pleased Dr. B. was going to buy me the heifer suppose she told Mr. Byron for at supper he said "Mrs Brown let me make you a present of that heifer you were talking of & Dr. B. can keep his money"   so I told Dr. B. & he says Byron shant be ahead of me so he bought me a Jersey heifer   they had been taken to the ranch with Mrs. G's cattle   they will be fresh in a month   then yesterday Dr. Brown bought me a little Poney   it just strikes me above the waist   it is as gentle as a lamb can be ridden by a lady or man   paid $25.00 twenty five dollars for it. You don't say any thing about D. A. coming out if I was dieing I would not let any of them [Charles's sister Millie and brother Will who at this time are in Deming] that are here hand me a drink of water & this repulsion feeling is getting worse. You dont know any thing. Mrs Gillespie is going to live at the ranch until she can get one. We are having delightfull weather at the ranch now. Write soon I enjoy your letters <u>so so</u> much

Your most loving daughter
M. M. Brown

Maggie to Pa

Bosque Verda
Rincon, N.M.
July 15/87

My dear pa

I have not received a letter since I last wrote but suppose you thought you would pay me back in "my own coin." I have been very busy all summer. Am milking two cows & will soon have another fresh. One of these I am milking is not mine but one I am taking care of   I will not get my chickens until next spring.

Pa, I am going to tell you something & make a request of you. In Nov. I expect to be confined [Maggie is pregnant and expects the baby to be born in November.] & want you to let A. J. come out & spend a year with me. I would like for her to come the last of Sept. or first of Oct. She will have no hard work to do as I will have a woman to wait on me & the same Mexican that lived with us two years ago will be here again & his wife will do the cooking. I just want A. J. to look after things & then if I should not get through all right I would like to have some of my own near me. There are things I want her to have if I should die. We will pay her way back & forth. My Sister has never spent a week with me in her life   I think Aunt Bet & the boys could get along very well for a while without her. Mrs. May being there in the house is not like them being alone. Let me know if you will let her come. I will be anxious until I hear from you about it.

Dr. Brown's sister should not hand me a cup of cold water if I were dying. She is more than a viper. I have good reasons for saying this. We had a fine rain a few days since things are looking fine. Write soon and tell me all you are doing. Your most loving daughter

M. M. Brown

Maggie to Pa

Rincon NM
July 24/87

My own dear pa

Yours of Sunday two weeks since was duly received. I will not wait for an answer to my last but as today is Sunday & I call my time my own on Sunday if no other day I will spend it in writing to you but since I have been milking I cannot write very well   I

am not used to it yet & it makes my hands ache. I do wish you
had some of my nice butter. I just make what we use but we
have all of the milk we can use. My Pony has a colt & she is only
2 years & a half old herself but it is a very nice little colt. I gave
it to Will Brown[5] he is so good to the Pony & has paid her so
much attention since I have had her. It is very warm here now
the thermometor is 102 now (1 o'clock) will be warmer about 3
o'clock this after noon. We had a slight shower a week ago &
planted some turnips but it is so hot & dry now I don't think they
will amount to much. I wish I had some of your fine Blackberrys
is there any Huckelberries over there if so I wish you would get
some of those negroes to dry me about $1/2$ a bushel. I can have
them sent out this fall. Mildred McCorkle [See April 12, 1885] is
with me has been since the middle of June is talking of going
home to El Paso Tuesday she is a heap of help but very hard to
talk to on account of her hearing. Will McC[orckle]'s wife was up
& spent a week I like her very much. They are very anxious for
me to come home with Mildred but I am afraid to undertake the
trip. When do you think of going home   the children seem very
anxious to have you come home. Is not W. J. a little rustler
A. J. writes so much of his working. It does hurt me no little that
we cannot be together much   but this is indeed one of the finest
climates in the world although it is so hot here & hotter in El
Paso there is no such thing as sun stroke & the papers are filled
up with people dieing all though the east with sunstroke. My
hand is getting cramped I will have to close. Write soon to your
ever loving daughter

Maggie Brown

Maggie to Pa

Rincon Dona Ana Co NM
July 31st/87

My own dear pa

   I am doubling up on you but I think there is no more profitable
or pleasant way for me to spend this beautiful Sabbath morning
than in writting to one of the dearest pas a daughter ever had. It
does hurt me so much to think our homes lie so far apart   but I
am afraid it will never be any better although Dr. B. says when
he can sell this place for enough to buy him a good home in Va he
is coming back but I don't think he could stand the wet weather

there even here when it is damp he is inclined to cough & it is so seldom wet. Then we are getting so many things around us too. We are getting fixed up real comfortably. Dr. B. was saying he wished you could come out here & sell some of those Mill bolts enough to pay your expenses anyway & make us a visit this winter. We bought some bran for our cows from the Las Cruces Mill & it is so badly bolted I cannot make good dough & some other parties that got of the same lot are sifting it & making Graham bread of it. Dr. B. says he thinks you would do well to write to the man. I will enclose you a card with his address on it. Well I must tell you I sold the first butter I ever sold Thursday & got 40 cts per pound but only had 3/4 of a pound so only got 30 cts when my other cow is fresh I expect to make more. I could sell all if I made 50 pounds for that. Suppose I wrote about Millie (my pony) having a colt. I am not feeling very well but I do all my work but washing & ironing. I was quite sick the other day & Dr. B. said "don't you get sick you are the main spring of this place" well if I do say it myself I keep things moving when they would give up if I did not push   then a few evenings ago he said I was getting more like ma every day & when I got like her he would be satisfied"   My mother was almost perfection in his eyes. I think he thought more of her than he did of his own mother   he loves all of my family so much & says if he could get you all out he would not go back. Well I must close. You owe me 3 letters now am going to have apple dumplings for dinner will put your name in the pot if you will come. Will Brown [Charlie's older brother who stayed long stretches with the Browns in New Mexico] dont drink much now [I] tell you he can eat so I keep him full of that & he don't want to drink.

Your most aff daughter Maggie Brown

Amelia Jane to Pa

Howardsville VA
Aug 3rd 1887

My <u>dear</u> pa

I received your ever welcome letter yesterday. I have not any other paper so will just write on this. I have thought the matter over about going out there to Sister Maggie   I don't see how I could go. The boys say they don't want me to go & aunt B cannot get along with out me. She is worse then she was when you were here   I believe she has some kind of fever or at least the last two evenings she has had high fevers   I think I will give her some Indian root pills to night I hope she is not taking the fever. I would like to be with Sister Maggie but I don't feel like I would be doing right to leave aunt B & the boys & you too if you don't come home often you would miss me anyway. I wish Sister M would come here. Aunt B & the boys say if I were to leave the family would be broken up. I don't want that to be the case. I hope Sister Maggie will not think hard of me. Now I have told you the very way I think about it. Mrs May says she would like for you to fix her house as soon as possible before it gets any worse   she means when you get through with your crop so you can leave it. I believe I have told you all the news for there is so little. I suppose you are still enjoying blackberry pies. I am well as usual   as the paper & news both have given out I will close with much love for your dear self. I am as ever

Your affectionate daughter   Amelia Jane Keller

Aug 6th
P.S. I don't believe aunt Bet is any better to-day   if she don't get better soon we will send for the Doctor

Your affctionate daughter
Amelia

Maggie to Pa

Rincon, N.M.
Aug. 25/87

My own dear pa

I think I have given you time to read my last letters so will answer yours of the 31st. I do love your letters so much. Dr. B. enjoys them too. We have been having some fine rains & the grass & weeds are doing finely. My cows are increasing in their milk & the weeds will make my pigs fat. I have 4 in the pen. Hog weed grows just like it does in Va. when we have rain.

You ought to see what two settled old folks we are. Dr. B. & I both go to milk. He cleans out the cow pen (which is 60 × 60 feet) while I milk he wants me to let him do it but I won't. I can get so much more than he can.

I churn about 1 gallon of cream & get 2 pounds of the nicest golden butter. Can get 50 cts for every pound I would sell but they eat nearly all. I sold a dollar's worth for Mission money.[6] Sent it to Bro. McCorkle. It was the first & only   butter I ever sold. Just give me the things I will keep things going. I have not gotten any start in chickens yet but if I live I will get them too. We have to crawl now by degrees.

Dr. B. had a nice Tom cat in Deming that he thought so much of so the other day he paid a negro up there 50 cts. to get it & when he brought him home he remarked "Now we have all of our live stock at home." We have no good dog yet. If things go on as they are & Dr. B. can be at home like he is we will soon be fixed. He is so good to help me. Anything I ask him to do he does so cheerfully, wash dishes, or pull weeds, or anything. If you come bring me some of your sweet potatoes for seed they raise very fine ones here but they are not so sweet as those we have in Va. I am getting along very well. Have not heard from home for some time. Hope they are getting along all right. Will write soon again. I love to read your dear letters.

With much love, your most aff. daughter

M. M. Brown

Maggie to Amelia Jane

Rincon NM

Sept 10, 1887

My very dear sister,

Your letter of the 2nd telling of dear old Aunts death was received last eve   Dr. B's train was so late he went on to Deming & staid all night. He threw off your letter as he went by. I had no one to talk to about you all so it made me doubly sad. Will Brown was here but I never talk to him about family matters. I am glad God spared her so long with you all. You are old enough to know right from wrong & if any one could teach it Aunt Bet could. She knew that an unblemished character was the best & most valued thing a woman could possess & the way to keep that is to keep out of loose company. Now darling sister you are in a manner alone. Of course there will be male company for the boys & you will have to be so carefull & not let there be the least cause for talk. Oh! I wish I had you with me but I can't see how that dear little brother could get along without you   he is so sensitive I am afraid it will be hard for him to get through this world. Write me all of the particulars. Did she know she was going to die & was she affraid? What form did her disease take? I was not surprized for I know at her age [around 71] it is very seldom one can recover from any thing so weakening. You children could not have known the end was so near. Did she say any thing about me. I have thought so often since I wrote asking you to come out it might have hurt her feeling me being so thoughtless as to ask such a thing after all she had done for us. I don't think I will be able to get this letter off today but will just as soon as I can. Does D. A. realize what a friend he has lost? I know she loved all of you but I think D. A. was loved the most. Now you keep this letter & when you answer read it so you can answer all I ask. Were the neighbors kind? I feel now like I would like to have <u>all</u> of you with me. I will write a few lines to the boys. Write ag<u>ai</u>n soon. Suppose Pa will write. I have written him three letters & I have only received one in the last 6 weeks. Tell him I will write to him soon again.

Your most loving sister
Maggie Brown

Maggie to her brothers

10 September 1887
Rincon, New Mexico

My ever dear brothers

I have written to A. J. answering her sad letters. If any thing you boys have lost one that you will miss more than A. J. or any of us but you are boys & can do for your selves more than a girl can now my dear brothers you both take charge of our sister to do all you can for her   I know she will do her part. She is inexperienced & very young to take charge of a house & all its cares. Then another thing don't bring any one to the house you cannot trust or that there would be the least cause for talk. A. J. having no female company now it will be hard to keep down talks. I could not sleep last night for thinking of you all. I do think it would nearly kill me for anything to happen to mar the character of any of my immediate family I do pride myself on having the most wise brother & sister any one can bost of. It is something to bost of too   I would be willing for my whole life to be spread out for the world & no one <u>dare</u> say any against it either. If we are less in power we are <u>rich</u> in virtue. D. A. you be gentle with our little brother you are a <u>man</u> now & he is so like

our dear ma in disposition so sensitive. Be good to each other &
cling together my heart is with you all,   God knows you have a
larger share in my prayers for your safety of soul. I have not
seen Dr. B. since I mailed the letter so cannot tell what he
thinks. I wish Pa would write I might write to him and he would
be in Cumberland so will wait until I hear from him before I
write you back write soon W. J. don't write & neither does D. A.
With much love & best wishes

Your devoted Sister

Maggie Brown

Maggie to Pa

Rincon NM

Sept 10th 1887

My darling pa
   Your letter with A. J.'s & W. J. received this eve   I wrote to
A. J. this morning in answer to hers of yesterday telling us of our
loss   I say our for I like you felt safe while I knew the children
had Aunt Bet with them. I could not sleep last night for thinking
of some way of helping you out. Dr. B. says he thinks it would be
perfectly safe for A. J. to come out alone for her to take a
pullman sleeper at Staunton & she would not have to change until
she got to St. Louis   I would like to have her with me better
than I can express & if she was to stay a year it would give you
all the time to fix up. I do wish all could come out here. I think
you could do better here than there. I did not say any thing in
my letter this morning about A. J. coming. I know a sisters
influence is very great over her brothers & A. J. is such a good
sister but the seperation wont be for long. I do feel so for you if I
was so that I could come I think I would try to get back with you
all for a while. I have written to Fannie Wynant to come out &
go in the Dairy business with me. This is a good place & I get
from 40 cts to 50 cts for every pound I can make. If she comes I
expect to hear from her soon & if she & A. J. could come
together they would be perfectly safe. Fannie is to furnish as
many cows as I do & we divide the profits. I will write tomorrow
to the ticket agent at Staunton to see what a first class ticket will
cost. I would [like] to have A. J. come by the first of Oct if
possible. Will close for the present & write again soon.

your <u>most</u> loving & sympathizing daughter
                                        M. M. Brown
P.S. I have just read your letter over and the sad tone of it hurts
me so   yes my dear pa yours has in deed been a troubled life but
I think the reward will be greater. I think you have born up
under your affliction so bravely but pa we all do love you so
much. I know I could not love you more. I have such kind friends
& feel some times like refusing their kindness because you cannot
enjoy it. I had two baskets of fruit sent me today   but were I to
take sick tonight [go into labor] I have no one to call on   my
friends are not in Rincon but I have no enemys there either just
acquaintances. Well good night my darling pa. May god abide
with you as he has done is the prayer of your loving daughter
        M. M. B.

Maggie to Pa

                                        Rincon NM
                                        Sept 11, 1887
My <u>dear</u> pa
    I sent a letter off this morning written after the dictates of my
selfish heart but on maturer thought think it best to send A. J. to
school this winter. You know a woman's life is very uncertain in
my condition & I have been so near death's door twice[7]   I will
not think of having A. J. come until I am through with my
trouble. It would be awfull for her to be here left alone if I should
die   & I can't think of asking so much. If Fannie Wynant comes
why A. J. can come but not unless she does. I love my sister too
much for this. Now don't you think I am right. If you can get a
<u>good</u> place for her to board & go to school why if I live I will try
to help you in that   but don't have her in any out-of-the-way
place   I am so affraid of the abominable negroes   I don't feel at
all well today have the tooth-ache real bad. Well you must write
as often as you can. I love your letters so much.
    Give my love to all
                                        Your aff daughter
                                        M. M. Brown

Maggie to Pa

                                        Rincon, NM
                                        Sept. 18/87
My own dear pa
    I have been thinking all day I would write you a long letter but

have been interrupted so much I could not. Now it is nearly time
for me to commence our 5 o'clock dinner but can get my letter so
far done that I can finish in the morning for Dr. B. to take it with
him. Now there is no use talking. You must all come out here.
There are so many ways we could help you & there it is almost
impossible for us to do anything for you. This morning Dr. B. was
talking at the breakfast table and said that if his substitute got an
appointment as acting clerk (the same as Dr. B.) he did not know
who to have appointed in his place. This young man was
appointed soon after Mattie's death—is now likely to get
appointed as acting clerk. If he is & D. A. was here Dr. B. would
get him appointed & then he could gradually work up. Well there
are so many ways he could help you all. There is a little boy in
Deming no older than W. J. getting $35.00 (thirty five dollars) per
month for delivering telegraph messages. If W. J. could not get
that place there are other places for him just as good   then if
A. J. was here I could get a good school for her that would pay
from $30 to $65 dollars per month[8] & you could do well at any
thing. There is a place near us that an old man has filed on a full
160 acres that I think could be gotten for $50.00 fifty dollars and
when we get water here that place can be watered too then I will
have my darling pa where I can see him every day. Why pa land
is increasing so rapidly here. The R.R. has bought some land
near the county seat & are advertizing this whole county   land
that sold down there this time last year for $25.00 (twenty five
dollars) per acre is now selling for $200 & $300 two & three
hundred per acre. Will Brown has filed on an hundred & sixty
acres joining the piece I want you to come & file on. He came out
here terribly prejudiced against the country even in June he said
he thought he would go back this fall we could not get him to say
for some time back what he thought of the country but a few
weeks since I over heard him say to a man he would "rather live
here than in Va 10 to 1 any one could live so much happier here &
it was the finest climate in the world." Now I think if we could all
live close together we would be much happier. Dr. B. said this
morning "If I could get your pa's family out here I would not care
if I ever went back to Va again." The other eve I was feeling very
badly & asked him if I should not get over this to   [letter torn]
                                        I dont want this to
change my plan about A. J. coming.

With much love to <u>all</u>. Tell the children to write soon.

Yours most lovingly
Maggie Brown

Amelia Jane to Pa

Howardsville Va
Sept 19th 1887

My very dear pa

I will send you all Sister Maggie's letters & let you see what she says   I wrote to her yesterday & answered all her questions & told her all I could about Aunt Bet. I told her I would do as you said about going out there if you think you can do without me I don't think I will be afraid to take the trip. W. J. says he hopes I can go just to see everything but he wants me to come back in a year <u>anyway</u>. Dannie does not like the idea of my going but if I go I hope I can learn a good deal by observation of course I will learn more about the Geography of the country than I could by studying three or four years   if I go I cannot get ready before the middle or last of Oct   I will have to have one nice dress if no more for I havent any fall dresses atall. Now you think about it I wish we could be together & talk it all over   though as Sister Maggie says "it won't be for long & by that time perhaps we will be better situated to keep house.["] I feel now like I would like to go out there, the hardest thing would be the separation but I would be going to see my <u>dear</u> & <u>only</u> sister. She thinks so much of me it seems that both of them are very anxious for me to come.

I am getting on very well. We are all well & hearty. W. J. eats more now than he has for sometime & I am glad for when you left he was so puny & was all the time mincing & would not eat regular but now he eats his meals & don't bother me any more he went out to the saw mill this morning to go to work.

I wish we had some corn meal & Mrs May was just wishing for some for her dinner   whenever you have a chance I wish you could send us some. Well I had some more of the nicest salt raising bread you ever saw. The boys say there can't any body beat me making bread. I can learn Sister Maggie that much any way can't I?

Now I will close as I have written you a long letter & you have not written any or we have not gotten any from you since you left. Now please answer this very soon.

Your affectionate daughter
Amelia Jane Keller

Maggie to Dannie

Rincon N.M.
Oct. 2/87

My own dear Brother,

Yours & A. J.'s of today week were received last night. I am so sorry I have nothing but love & best wishes to send you for your 21st birthday. I do sympathize with you so much. You try to hold out a year longer there & in the meantime I will use all my persuasions to get pa to come out here if not why by that time I will (if I live) be so fixed as to help you if we are where we can help you in the meantime we will but a year is the very out side if we both live & have our health. I do really wish pa would give up that land & come. We are trying so hard to improve our place it takes all Dr. B's salery to do it but I think by spring he may be able to help you all. Pa wrote me his plans for a house. I was really sorry to hear him talk of fixing up there but we cannot force pa to any thing if we can get him to see when it will make us all happier to give it up and all live close to gether   I think he will do so. Well I will close & write a few lines to A. J.
Your most loving Sister

M. B. Brown

Maggie to Amelia Jane

Rincon NM
Oct 2/87

My dear Sister

I have written three letters already so am somewhat tired. You will have to excuse a short letter this time. Why yes make your dresses longer this winter of course but not to much. I was not atall well last night but am better today. Dr. B's run was changed & he will only be at home every other night but I will soon have a good woman with me. Write soon to your loving sister.

M. M. Brown

[October 6, 1887 Maggie gave birth to a son James Albert.]

Maggie to her sister and brothers

Rincon NM
Oct 21 1887

My dear Sister & Brothers

   I know you are anxious to hear from me so I will write although my eyes are not very strong yet. James Albert, or Albert as we will call him was two weeks old yesterday. He weighed 5¼ pounds when born   has not cried since he was four days old   has dark hair & eyes a very pretty little mouth but rather large nose   perfect hands & feet. Dr. B. thinks there is no one as smart as his "son" I am feeling very well but quite weak have good old Carmen the Mexican woman that lived with us before we came to Va. She is devoted to the babe & me. We had our first frost last night but it is so bright & warm now at 2 o'clock in the eve. Fall is lovely here indeed all the year is. Pa seems bent on keeping his Cumberland home & misconstrues my letter altogether so there is no use in me writting to him but if you were here I know all could be better but be patient he may think as we do some day & then all will be right. Dr. B. wrote to him of the birth of Albert. Tell Dan Albert is only 4 days younger than him his birth day being the 6 of Oct & D. A. the 12. Ask W. J. what he thinks of his name sake. He is named for pa & Dr. B. & Dr. B's brother & my brothers. I am nursing a puppy with the babe but he is awfull ugly. I must close for this time.
   Much love with a write soon your loving sister

Maggie Brown

Pa to newborn James Albert and then to Maggie and Charles

White Walnut
Cumberland Co
Va

Oct 23 1887
   Mr. James Albert Brown
My dear Son,
I heard of your arrival a week or two since. I avail myself of extending a <u>hearty welcome</u> to you as a citizen of our planet & hope you will ever be as you were in your arrival "a little ahead of time" in that case you will never be <u>left</u> by the train. Though I must say you must not judge all our planet by the locality in which you landed. Some may be worse & some better. You must

look around some before you make up your mind & listen at what
your good Ma & Pa tells you. Oh how I wish I had you in my
arms a while I would squeeze your little bones so much   Good
bye I must talk some to your Ma & Pa.

My Precious Daughter & Son

I congratulate you & certainly join in thanking God for his care
over you & the dear child I received the Drs letter in due time &
just got Maggie's card   sent to Amelia Jane I got a letter from
home a day or two since. All are well   I would have written
sooner but have been very busy first one thing & then another &
I felt so much like talking to the "baby" I thought I would write
some to him I have not lost my "fondness" for little children yet.
I am trying to get ready to go home got all the crop up in good
order & will try to sell some of it before I leave. I cannot write a
long letter this time for I must go back to the store as the young
man who keeps store is not here & I fill his place when he is gone
& they have run out of envelopes so I must fold this in the "old"
way like we used to do when I was young. Good bye & God
Almighty keep you in all his love & protection write often I am
ever so anxious to hear from you all   Your loving Pa

W. J. Keller

Maggie to her sister and brothers

Rincon NM
Nov 7th 87

My dear Brothers & Sister

   Your letters were received a few days since. I was sorry to
hear of your being so bad off but am very sorry I cannot help you
just now   but Dr. B. says Dannie you learn to shoe a horse real
well & there is a blacksmithing outfit he will buy & in the spring
if you come out here you can make money if you are bound to
leave home I want you to come to me & you can do as well here
as any where. We have been at such a heavy expence this fall
now there is four to board besides our own family   we have had
to have help   Dr. B. has a boy hired   he has to pay $15.00 per
month & board then the woman will have to be paid & last month
he had to get his meals in Silver City where he is running to now.
All together has taken all he has made. I will try to send D. A.
some shirts next month or the last of this. I do wish I could do

more for you all. I have only two dresses a searsuccer I got last spring & a calico   I wont need much this winter but we are trying to improve the place so you see it will need economizing but Dr. B. will always keep a good table & feed every one well that is around us. I must write to Pa he wrote a letter to Albert so I will have to answer it. I know pa will think I am persuading you to come out here but you let him know I am not. I wish all of you would come. Well Albert is doing finely   he has not cried for a month or since he was four days old. I almost forget I have a babe   he will be tall I think has a long head like his papa.

With best love to all I will close. Hope to hear from you again soon. Have just taken out about ²/₃ pounds of butter it looks so nice & yellow. My Jersey cow has a calf 2 weeks old. I am a long time closing. Write to your ever loving sister

Maggie Brown

Maggie to Pa

Rincon Dona Ana Co NM
Nov 11/87

My dear pa

I know you are thinking hard of us for not writting sooner. I wrote to the children & was going to write to you the same day but something happened to prevent & so I have commenced a letter & find I only have two small pieces of paper to write on but as I have so little to write I think it will do. James Albert or Albert as we call him received your letter in due time but it was open when it came [Pa had folded the stationery itself to act as envelope]   I suppose he appreciated it as I think he is one of the best children I ever saw never cried for a month. he cried this eve a little but has never had the colic or a exoice [canker] in his mouth yet. I have not been well since he was born have neuralgia nearly all the time but am able to do part of my work & attend to it all. Things went rather haphazard while I was sick & Dr. B. on the road. He is at home now only every other day. He only lost one day on my account. We have a big family now four besides ourselves. A boy working on the place, Will Brown & the old Mexican woman & boy that we used to talk about when there. We never had any frost until the 20 of Oct. [rest of letter missing]

Maggie to her Brothers and Sister

Rincon, NM

Nov 24/87

My dear Brothers & sister

This is Thanksgiving but we have had no big dinner although
we have much for which to give thanks & do. I would be so
happy if we could all be together once more & if God spares us &
blesses us for another year we will. I think you would do well to
gather chestnuts another year & ship out here. Dr. B. bought me
one pound the first of this week & paid 40 cts for the pound
making them worth $25.00 twenty five dollars per bushel. How
was the chestnut crop this year & are there any hickery nuts on
the hill & if so gather all you can & I will see if I cant sell them
for you for something.

I commenced this letter as you will see two days since I am very
anxious to hear from you all. Have received only one letter in the
last six weeks. I am so busy I have so little time to write. Dr. B.
is at home so little I have to attend to everything. He got a lay
off of 4 days will go back on the road Sunday. Is it very cold
there yet   the first fire we had in the house was the sixth of Oct.
Yesterday & today was the coldest days we have had. Pa dont
write anymore. I can't tell why. I would like to hear from him.
How are you all fixed for the winter. I do wish I could do
something for you but as soon as Dr. B. gets his salery   it has to
go out for something on the place. Never mind hold out this
winter & I hope if God spares me I may be able to do something
for those I love as if you were my own children.

Write soon & don't wait on me. I send stamps for you to write
often.

Your loving sister

M. M. Brown

Maggie to Pa

Rincon NM

Dec 19/87

My Dear Pa and family

I will write you a few lines today. I have so little time for
letter writing am very busy all the time. Mrs. Sangre [See
October 8, 1885 and June 21, 1886] has been visiting me for the

last 3 weeks & I felt like if I had time to sit down I ought to talk
to her. She left today. I have the care of the milking of 14
(fourteen) cows although they don't give much it takes a good
deal of time to attend to it. We don't expect much Xmas only
Dr. B. will take a day off & be at home a while. It will be so
lonesome for me after Xmas. . . . I will be very busy now until
after Xmas want to kill some pigs & sell them to help pay the
man that is herding & milking the cows. I don't want Dr. B. to
have to pay him. We have Will Brown's catch 14 cows 1 Bull & 12
calves we are to take care of them for half the profits of the milk
& half the increase   which will be about 10 head in the next year.
Albert has one calf I gave him my cows calf which is just 3 weeks
younger than he is. I would like to hear from home a little more
often.   Well much love to all your most aff daughter & Sister

M. M. Brown

Maggie to Pa

Rincon NM
Jan 20/88

My very dear Pa
   I wrote to D. A. & all of you & sent the letter off the same day
I received your letters. Not having much to write I concluded to
wait a while. No pa I would not think hard of you for making a
home for yourself but am so sorry it cannot be closer to us which
it might be but for your thinking different. I think every time I
write I will say nothing more about it but I will. Albert is
beginning to notice when I lean over the cradle. He jumps &
throws up his hands & laughs   he has blue eyes & they are
straight but I think if he looked more like Mattie I would think
more of him. He has a long head or rather face with a double
chin. He is just his papa over except the eyes. I am writting with
him on my lap. Now it is near bedtime. This is Dr. B's night in
Silver City. He is there one night and one at home. I get very
lonesome. . . . I have a sow in the pen fattening that they say
will weigh 300 when fat. I dont expect to cure any of her meat
just take the lard and sell the rest can get 10 cts per pound for all
I want to sell. I want to keep enough hogs after this year to
make my own bacon. It is from 16 cents to 20 cts per pond in the
stores. . . . Well Albert is asleep & I will have to go to bed or he
will wake up. Will write to W. J. & A. J. some other time I have

to send this letter off by the man that takes the milk to town. I
will not have time to write in the morning. You ought to see my
outfit   two cans each holding 2½ gallon flat on one side & one
swung accross the horse in front of the saddle all my own
invention. I run the ranch. Dr. B. is only a <u>visitor</u>   Good night
my dear pa

Your ever loving daughter
M. M. Brown

Maggie to Pa

Rincon NM
Jan 24/88

My dear Pa,

I have very little of anything to write & suppose you have
gotten my letter by this time. I really have so little time to think
of or do anything but my housework. I am very anxious to have
Dan come but Dr. B. said he could not send the money by the
first of this month but by the first of next   he has a chance to get
a good team & wagon which he thought he had better get & then
D. A. is not out of employment now. We want to get some
plowing done at once for an early garden. Yesterday I went up to
Rincon to straighten up my milk business. The Mexican that
milks takes the milk to town & one of us has to collect & fix up
the business. I had no idea they were such nice people up there.
The first time I have been up to visit since I came back from Va.
Well I will write to the rest of them. With much love   your aff
daughter

M. M. Brown

Maggie to Dannie

Rincon NM
Feb 7/88

My dear Brother,

I am almost counting the days when you will be here.
Telegraph at Raton New Mex[9] when you get there so I can go up
to meet you if I can leave Albert that day. Some days I can leave
him & some not. Now don't get confused at those big depots &
take the wrong train. Suppose you will be on the eve of starting

when you get this. Give love to one & all. Write the day or two before you start when you will start

Your loving Sister
M. M. Brown

Maggie to Pa

Rincon NM
Feb 24/88

My dear Pa

   I was very glad to receive your letters but some what disappointed thinking the next thing I heard after D. A. received the money for his ticket would be a letter telling us when he was coming. Every day he delays will be money for Dr. B. had calculated to get out an early crop of vegetables & then bought all he can raise and engaged the team for D. A. to work as soon as he got here. I have made a great many sacrifices to get him here. Well I will tell you what I have had in the way of clothing since last June 2 calico dresses 2 pair of $1.25 shoes & 2 pair of stockings & 2 skirts but fortunately we don't need much in this country if we stay at home. I think if D. A. comes & we raise the crop we hope we can altogether send A. J. to some school. I would like very much to have her go to school & think she will appreciate the opportunity & take better advantage of it than I did. I will close now & hope you will have a home. I will write to W. J. for Albert. You must write to me often. Your most affect daughter

M. M. Brown

Maggie for Albert to W. J.

My dear "little Unclie"

   I hope the wagon you are making will be big enough for mama to pull me in. she takes me out in her arms & I soon get tired & go to sleep & sleep for 2½ & 3 hours. It was very bad here for three or four days it rained & snowed too. The mountains are white with snow but it was so warm today here every thing looks nice. I thank you very much for the card. I am very well supplied with little bootees. Mama got me 2 pair & I have been given 4 pair. I put them on when I go out & will wear them when mama makes my dresses short. Mama could read your last letter very well & it was very interesting. You must write again soon.

Your aff nefew J. Albert Brown
Will write to A. J. soon
M. M. B.

Maggie to Amelia Jane, then to W. J. and to Dannie

Rincon NM
Mar 21/88

My dear Sister

I wrote to Pa a few days since. I suppose the strike is over
now. Dr. B. was caught in Silver City the other end of his run
did not get home for 2 days. I have some accounts of such hard
cold storms in the east & just 25 miles from here it snowed on
the 17 & 18th of this month but here it only rained a little & a
thin skim of ice on a tub out of doors. I do think we have the
finest climate in the world. Write me just how things stand
between you and Mr. C. I think there being only the two of us
we might confide in each other. I am past my day of secrets but
you might tell me yours. Don't say anything more than you have
to about Mr. C. in the Valley for those that seem to be your best
friend may make mischief. Albert is getting brighter every day.
He is such a comfort to me. Hope Pa is better. I feel so uneasy
about him. I have nothing of importance to write so will write a
few lines to W. J. & D. A.   Write soon to your loving Sister
M. M. Brown

My dear brother W. J.,

I could hardly realize that you had written that last letter it
was such an improvement on the others & in such a short time. If
you keep on that way you will soon be the penman of the family
no joking about it. I do think so much of you & do wish you &
Albert would be companions if he lives to be grown although you
are nearly 15 years older than him. You write often. I love to
read your letters you write things the others don't think of.
Your loving sister
M. M. Brown

My dear brother D. A.

People are beginning to think the big brother I spoke of coming
is a fraud   but I hope to see his big figure looming up soon. If
any thing should happen you miss trains or any thing be sure to
telegraph. I think you had better take the rout with least

changes. I think you had better to go Staunton & take one of those R.R.   Will Brown took the C&O got his ticket for $38.00 you can see which you can do best by. If you are where there are two don't get confused or frightened but just keep your wits about you. Hope to hear from you soon.

Your loving sister
M. M. Brown

Maggie to her family in Virginia

Rincon NM
April 14/88

My dear friends

I wrote a letter a few days since   have just received your letter of the 8th. I beg leave to inform Mr. Clay [the young man courting Amelia Jane in Virginia] we are not living among savages & the Mexicans are <u>much better</u> than the negros although they speak a different language from ours & the white people with whom I visit are more intelligent than it was my fortune to meet while in Virginia   of course we will be very much disappointed if D. A. does not come but if he has any scruples at all about coming I would rather he would not. There is one <u>great</u> difference in this country & that people have to comply with their promises or they are not thought well of. People are what you might call self-made   it is just according to how they act as to how they are received. If anyone is caught doing any little mean thing he is ever afterward looked on with suspicion. We killed a hog yesterday that weighed 230. She was not very fat. Dr. B. says if she had been fat she would have weighed over 300. We have 3 more up town but will not bring them down here yet. I only kept the middling & lard. Sold the rest for 9 cts and 10 cts per pound. Well as I am real tired I will close. With love to one & all from your loving daughter & Sister

M. M. Brown

By the way if D. A. should come if he gets to Rincon & not meet Dr. B. there or me he had better go to the Post Office & he can get any information he wants. I am very sorry for his sake he did not come in the early spring for it will seem very warm to him now.

Maggie to her father and siblings

Rincon, NM
May 14/88

Dear Pa & family

I have received letters twice from you & the family since I wrote. Thought from D. A.'s letter of the 27 of April I would hear the following week from him on how he was coming then I would write to you I had received such a letter. You know now why I have not written for so long   it is getting very warm now. Albert is getting very interesting   he will be quite a little romp I think. He squeels and laughs a great deal & is perfectly happy when can get hold of his papa's whiskers & pull   so is his papa who thinks there is no boy like his. Dr. B. is getting very domestic. He says he is always glad when the engine heads for home & sorry when the time comes for him to leave. I received a letter from Alma Jordan. She said you & A. J. are going to make them a visit. Where will W. J. stay? if I may ask   I am almost afraid to make any inquiry about your affairs for fear of being accused of presumption or scolded in the next letter. I am really sorry my solicitious feeling will be miss construed. I suppose from A. J.'s last letter we will get a letter from D. A. today or tomorrow telling when he will come. It was not necessary for you to go to so much expence to fit him out. Here on the place we just need enough to cover our selves decently. Will Brown just wears a pair of overalls & a blue shirt of the same kind. When Dr. B. comes home he puts on an old pair of cordurory pants all out at the seat & Will has an old pair of low quartered shoes of Dr. B's he wears without socks. I hope you& A. J. will have a nice time in the valley. I owe Ed Shuff a letter which I must answer soon but between sickness & work I have had very little time to write. With love to all

your aff daughter
M. M. Brown

Maggie to Pa

Rincon NM
May 27/88

My dear pa

Wednesday Bro Wm McCorkle came up from El Paso to spend a month or more with us & when he goes home I expect his wife.

The babe nor I either are well last week. The weather is very dry now I think is the cause of us feeling badly. We have heard nothing from D. A. for so long thought perhaps he was going to take us by surprise   so Friday I saw some one coming up the R.r. track   I thought it was him so ran to meet him & hollered for him to come on then saw it was a neighbor. They all laughed very much at me.

Albert looks just like W. J. did at his age is nearly 8 months old & has no teeth yet.

I have so little to write to interest you I hardly know what to write.

your loving daughter

M. M. Brown

Maggie to Pa

Rincon NM
May 31/88

My dear Pa

Why is it we don't hear from any of you. I am so anxious about you all. We have been looking for a letter for so long. Now just sit down & write to me. What is the matter? Don't keep any thing back. I think you might have enough confidence in me to tell me your plans & troubles. Bro Wm Mccorkle is with us & will be for the next 3 weeks. His wife is coming up next week to stay a while too. His health is bad & he came up to rest & hunt. We walked out in front of the house. Dr. B., Bro. McC., & Will Brown & me carrying Albert. Will & I were looking at some fine cactus he had trimmed up[10] & Dr. B. & Bro McC. had their guns to kill rabbits. I heard Dr. B. shoot and say I would rather kill that than a dozen Coyoties (or wolves) & we looked up & he had killed a large wild cat. It was about the size & color of Flora only it had black spots underneath. It has been quite cool here for the last few mornings.

Hope to hear from you all soon I am very busy trying to clean my house & have company too is all I can attend to well let alone write. Give much love to all. If I can I will write to the children in the morning.

Your loving daughter
M. M. Brown

Dannie and then Maggie to their father and siblings in Virginia

Rincon
N Mex
June 24th 1888

Dear Pa & family

I am here all safe & sound after traveling 2704 twenty seven hundred and four miles. I didn't count them all my self but this is correct in Mosouria and eastern Kann every thing is flooded from the train I could see corn that would take me at the chin that the top blades were just floting on the water I saw some cabbage in head in Kann   I saw Pikes peak 150 one hundred & fifty miles away that and other mountains I saw were white with snow. Ride on the train from Kann City & every nation in the world is represented there and hard costomers they are too.[11] You ought to just see these mud houses with a garden on top of them & a ladder to go up on to chase the chickens off. Things are not as shaby as you think they are I caught them [Maggie and Charles] by surprise so that I could find out what I would eat after they got used to me it was all right & dont you forget it. Dr. was at the Depot just starting on his run when I come in he saw me & knew me we had a talk of about 5 mins about the first thing he said was Dan you can have lots of fun here they catch fish that weigh from 75 to 100 lbs.[12] I saw some cats [catfish] puled out last night about two feet & half long that nice aint it. You think it is hot there but is the honest truth that there is a thermomiter here boiling over one in a cole [sic] place registers way up there I used to jest about thermomiter runing over but I never saw it be fore. Give my regards to who think enough about me to ask and tell them the indians have not got my scalp & dont think they ever will[13]   I will close with love to all

Your afft Son & Bro Dan

will write some more soon

Rincon NM
23d

My dear pa & Sister

D. A. arrived safely today about 1 o'clock he has gone down to the river with Mr. Armstrong who is stopping here now with his wife until their home is ready for them to move in. Mr. A. is a great fisherman sends off from $200 to $500 worth of fish every

other day. I want D. A. to go in with him & they can catch more.
Now I am delighted of course to have D. A.   will keep him if we
can until he gets better acquainted with the country then can get
a better place for him.

Your aff daughter
M. M. Brown

Dannie then Maggie to Pa in Virginia

Rincon N.Mx
July 11th/88

Dr Pa & Family

We received the letter you was to write a day or two after I
left a few days ago. You asked me how my money had held out
well I had about (3) three dollrs left when I got here. I had to
buy my grub from KC here it cost me 25 cts a meal I got about a
qt of coffee at Raton for five cents ($1) one dollar got away from
me in the clear I think it was stolen out of my pocket. The grub I
started with soured on my hands. The letter you wrote when I
left come on on the same train I did. I past Larned [town in
Kansas where Pa had lived for six months in 1879] just before
day & couldn't see it. That is answers to all your questions I
think. I have 16 hooks seting now will set 50 as soon as I get
them I can make about ($20) twenty dollars a week with them
with 15 hooks   I made $3.60 in two mornings I get from 10 to 15
cents a lb for them   we havent caught any that weighed over 25
lbs since I have been here but one got on a hook and some fellows
from town come along & puled it out & looked at it & put it back
& started to pull it out again & the fish he had pulled out & he
got back   they thought it would weigh 100 lbs. Tell Mr. & Mrs. B
much oblige & give them my regards

July 12

My dear friends

Dannie will write for me. He is most too sanguine about
catching fish it is true he could make all he says if he could catch
his fish but some one robs his hooks. Yes he has been practicing
with a rifle Dr. B. borrowed for him but with my little one I can
beat him & Dr. B. both they don't like to acknowledge it but facts
speak for themselves. The babe can sit alone & is very bright.
Bro McC went home last week but his wife is still with us. [rest
of letter missing]

Maggie to Pa

Rincon NM
Aug 12/88

My very dear Pa

I am sorry you have not received our letters as promptly as they were written. I did not know you were in Cumberland until I received your letter. D. A. is not doing any thing now fishing. He spent all the money he made on those he did catch for fishing tackle & lumber for a boat to go at it in earnest when the river went dry or so near it there is no use trying to fish.[14] He is carrying milk up to town for me. I am not making much on it. He only goes once a day. He can get a place on the R.R. to work but he has been feeling badly & I don't like for him to go away yet. After it gets cooler & there is no danger for him to go I think he will go. It is very warm now. Albert is growing nicely can sit a lone but has no teeth yet. How are A. J. & W. J. getting along? Don't you think you had better go to see Mr Wiseman. He might have a nice place for you this winter I think it would be much better for you to be at home. I am almost afraid to speak to you as a father. You are so apt in your next to give me a reprimand. Your aff Daughter

M. M. Brown

Dannie to Pa

Rincon N.Mex
Aug 12th 1888

My dear Pa

Well this is my time to write will write but there is nothing to write. We are getting along as well as usual. Doc has not lost his place yet he got orders to borrow a key from an office above here until one was sent him & he has been making his regular runs ever since. The Rio Grande is nearly dry when full it is about half the size of the James at H[writing illegible]. Now it has about half as much water as Rock Fish   places that were bout (6) six feet deep (2) weeks ago is dry land now.

How did you make it over the trents from the depot this time did you get lost or not.

if you would like to stomp after pole cats come out here Doc & me killed (5) five in less than five minutes not long ago. Well I

will have to close as the bugs are about to eat me up lots of em
here   write soon to your Afft

Son D. A. Keller

Dannie to Amelia Jane

Rincon N Mex
Aug 28th 1888

My very dear Sister
    We enclose (2) two dollars for you to get a dress with I send
you $1 & sister M the other   it is right warm here now but not
as warm as it was when I come out here. I have been killing
some ducks killed 4 day before yesterday well I will have to close
as I have to take Docs grub down & it is nearly time for the train

Love to all Your
Aff Bro D. A. Keller

Maggie, then Dannie, then Maggie to Pa

Rincon NM
Sept 9/88

My darling Pa
    Yours of 2d to hand I will hasten to write I was going to write
any way. I think I see the hand of providence in your comming
home at the time you did   God is kind to us in many ways we do
not see. Oh! I would rather see my dear little sister dead than
disgraced. I hope D. A. will soon get a place he can help you
both. Dr. B. lost $32.00 thirty two dollars for losing his key [See
August 12, 1888] I don't think D. A. is very well contented here
& will come back as soon as he can get the "where with." I am
very sorry he came he seems like an older child to me more than
a brother indeed, that is the way they all seem. My dear pa you
don't know how I feel for you. I know how you suffer. I think you
did the best there was to do & it is better I think to have W. J.
with you. He can help you so much & be company for you. Albert
has one tooth in   a little fretfull   think more are coming

Rincon N.Mex
Sept 9th 1888

My dear Pa
    We received yours today would say if Clark [the young man
courting Amelia Jane] loves his life haff so much he thinks he

loves A. J. he had better let their affairs dorp[sic] forever the trip can be made from here there in about (4) four days & it will be made if this is not droped here & now. I dont suppose he thinks when he writes them love letters that he has one foot over the grave & the earth is fairly crumbling under the other but never the less it is so.

Sr M seems to think I am not satisfied here. I like here first raite if I could get something to do I have an eye on several places now that if I get either it will pay from ($60) sixty to ($75) seventy five dollars then I will be contented.

I have a sore shoulder now from shooting ducks I kill lots of them. They had a wreck on the RR just below here last night nobody hurt. Well I will close you may burn this as it may pay in the end so it will never appear against me as I mean what I say.

Your Afft Son

D. A. K.

N.B. Since reading D. A. letter I think you had better watch that young mans movements. I am so surprized at A. J.

The place D. A. speaks of is night watch man at the Depot. If they make a change in the running of the mail trains from day to night they will need one & the Agent told Dr. B. he would give it to D. A. if he needed one. Well as Albert is in bed I will close for the present. Oh yes D. A. is going to take lessons in civel engeneering from a friend of Dr. B's got him a book yesterday. We have had no steady work for him now to pay wages. He just carries the milk in the morning 1 gal & 6 pints. Then the days Dr. B. don't come home he carries up Dr. B's dinner. We have gotten him some clothes & will get more as the winter comes. I feel so sorry for him. He is so hurt about A. J. What does C[lark] mean by both knowing how to "box" so well? I hope though as you have A. J. away it will all blow over. Well I think we have given you enough to read for a while.

Your loving daughter

M. M. B.

Maggie to Amelia Jane

Rincon NM

Sept 12/88

My own dear Sister

We received a letter from pa a few days ago saying you had

gone to Staunton. I am glad. Hope you will have a nice time but
don't you go & fall in love with some fellow over there for I
expect we will send for you the first of Nov to come out here. We
had the agent & a young telegraph opperator down to tea one
day last week. I like them so much. You can have nice company
out here. The agent looks like Ed Shuff something & the
opperator is small but a pure blond. We sent you $2.00 two
dollars to Howardsville the 27th of Aug hope you will get it all
right. Dr. B. says you get Uncle Will to see what is the best he
can do between the C&O & B&O RR for the first class tickets to
Deming. We want to know also how much you will need,
[end of letter missing]

Maggie to Pa

> Rincon NM
> Sept 12/88

My dear Pa
    D. A. & I wrote you quite a long letter Sunday & directed it to
Willis but since reading your letter over I think you may still be
in H-ville. We sent the letter of C[lark]'s [Amelia Jane's suitor] in
yours to Willis [a post office in Virginia]. I have talked to Dr. B.
& he thinks we had better try to get A. J. out here. That boy can
go to Staunton but cannot come out here very well. You will see
in our letter of Sunday what we think of it. Now what do you
think of us getting A. J. out here in Nov? I wrote to A. J. today
but did not intimate any about the affair only said you wrote us
she [had] gone to Staunton on a visit
    Dont know why she has not written I feel uneasy about her.
> With love in haste
> Your aff daughter
> M. M. Brown

Maggie to Pa

> Rincon NM
> Sept 17/88

My own dear Pa
    I received a letter from A. J. yesterday she does not intimate
that there is anything wrong. Seems to be quite contented but I
put about as much confidence in her as D. A. does. He seems to
know her better than we do. I spoke of sending the money for

her to come out but he said he would not trust her with the cash
to send it to Uncle Will. He also seems to think her letter is a
blind. She asks for money in it twice to get things. Now Pa I will
just tell you I have sent her more than I have gotten. D. A. has
no place yet. Of course what we get all comes out of Dr. B. Can
you furnish the money for her expences outside of her ticket. I
think with ($25) twenty five dollars besides she ought to be able
to get her a plain dress & hat & shoes. Let her have enough in
case of emergency should she need it on the road. If she has any
over we will send it back to you. You don't know how it hurts me
to know my _dear_ pa has so few comforts in his old age. If she
comes out here you need to have no more care of her   I can
watch her. I will have nice company to visit her or more I know
how this thing hurts your proud heart. I think I am my "dadie's
own girl" in that thing. It has always been my motto if I can't go
with my equals I _wont_ go with my inferiors. D. A. is toning down
some. I tell you he has a good heart if he could just control his
temper it would be alright but he is comparatively a boy yet. He
& Dr. B. are devoted to each other. Dr. B. likes him so much.
Well I hope my plan will meet with your approbation. Of course
these are only plans subject to your approval or not. I wrote to
A. J. as though they were established. D. A. and Dr. B. say they
dont think it would do for you to try to keep house with A. J.
alone again. There might be some very serious consequences from
it. With much love for my "_little_ man" brother

Your ever devoted daughter
M. M. Brown

P.S. Write just as _often_ as _you_ can we will do the same you have
some one to keep a sharp look out over in H-ville on C[lark].

Maggie to Pa

Rincon NM
Oct 22/88

My dear Pa,

   I have not heard a word from you for over 3 weeks. Where are
you & what are you doing? It is quite cold & rainy here now but
we have had no frost yet. Dannie killed a sand hill Crain last
week it netted 8 pounds measured 6 feet 9 in accross the wings
from tip to tip. You never saw anyone so proud of any thing as he
was of that. Indeed I believe he would be contented to spend his

whole of his life hunting. He & I have some little spats about it
he cant [letter blurred]   good for the horses but he has to take
his gun. Dr. B. has sold some ducks in Silver City for him but not
more than enough to pay for amunition &c. Albert is real sweet
when we call "Dan" he will say "Dan" too. Today I found out how
he gets over the floor just lies flat on his belly & pulls along with
his elbows. Have not heard from A. J. since we heard from you.
The rains have come too late to do the grass good this fall but the
Mexicans all say it will make good grass for early spring. Well all
but Albert & I have gone to Nestors to see the Mexicans dance
Will Dan & Dr. B.   he [Nestor] has built a house joining our
ranch. He has a dance up there about once in two months. The
Mexicans are very like the negroes about dancing [white
stereotype about blacks]. I dont know when D. A. will write.
Dr. B. goes away tomorrow so I want to send my letter by him.
Give lots of love to W. J. & your own dear self

your loving daughter
M. M. Brown

Maggie to Pa

Rincon NM
Nov 6/88

My Dear Pa

Your short little letter was received with A. J.'s a few days
since. We have not heard a word from A. J. but the letter you
sent us for over a month. I think she treats us real mean.

D. A. went to work today on a $60.00 sixty dollar job goes to
work early in the morning & then has from 7 to 10 oclock in the
fore noon then gets off to come down to his supper & spend the
night here. He will board here. The place is at the Depot   he
handles express freight sweeps out Depot keeps up fires &c   It is
a place that requires much vigilence to keep things in order. Now
it is good pay & sure I do hope D. A. will spur himself up & keep
things in order. You urge him. He is promised a place in the
carpenters gang just as soon as they put on more hands. It pays
$2.50 per day to the best. But he has to pay 75 cts per day board.
I doubt if they put on more hands before the first of Jan'   he has
to work two months before he gets any pay. He also has a
valosipede [velocipede: a lightweight, hand-propelled 3-wheeled
railway inspection car] to come & go on. Albert is 29 inches tall

but does not stand alone yet. Well they are all very much excited over the election.[15]

Dr. B. was up town until 11 o'clock last night recording bulitens. Well D. A. is going back has been to breakfast. I will close for the present. With much love

Your aff daughter
M. M. Brown

Maggie to Pa

Rincon NM
Nov 19/88

My dear Pa

D. A. quit work after having worked 10 days. The R.r. is cutting down all of the forces now as they do every year the last 2 months of the year. Also cut down the wages 10 percent of all employees so D. A. will only get $17.65 seventeen dollars & sixty five cents. He will send you $10.00 ten dollars as soon as he gets it & with the other buy him shoes & hat & gloves but he went to work this morning to do some carpentering for $1.75 per day & board if he suits the job may last until Xmas. We have gotten him shirts shoes & other things since he came. I am doing all of my own work now. I tell you it is awfull hard on me to be all alone as I am when Dr. B. is gone. If I had some one to watch Albert which is so much trouble now just beginning to crawl. We have fire places & he gets up to the hearth & eats dirt. I also milk 3 cows myself & have to go some distance to the cow pen. I some times bundle him up put him in his little 2 wheeled cart Dr. B. made him & pull it with two buckets to milk in & one [rest of letter lost]

Charles to Pa

Rincon NM
Nov 19th 1888

Dr Friend

Dan wishes to send you some money & has not time to write himself. Enclosed you will find $10.00 of the first money that he has made since he has been here. We are all well and are some what surprised that we have not heard from you for some time what is the matter? Albert has four teeth and is perfectly healthy is one of the brightest babes that I have seen for a long time.

Will write more some other time with much love for all, to you
and the family I remain very truly Yours &c

C. A. Brown

Dannie then Maggie to Pa

Rincon N Mex
Nov 25th 88

My very Dr Pa

I received your letter yesterday. There is no indications of us
ever having any more clear weather here & a person that never
saw any here would think we had never had any   it tried to rain
all day yesterday   & last night the bottom just droped out of the
clouds. I lost my place at the depot the Co cut the men off   just
lost it in time to get another   at a $1.75 one dollar & seventy five
cints a day & board lost one day   I get my $10.50 every
Saturday night. There is some mining fever here now it broke out
about a week ago but you bet I have escaped so far although I
wish them success. If they strick it rich I am willing to take
mines out in so much a day. This is Sunday but Sister M. has got
two tramps at the wood pile all the same. I sent you $10.00 last
monday hope it will reach you safe will try to send you more
about Xmas. Tell W. J. I havent forgoten him yet will write to
him soon thats all

Your Afft Son
D.A.K.

P.S. [in Maggie's handwriting] Yes had 2 tramps at the wood pile
because Will Brown & D.A. Keller could not cut wood & neither
could I. Every room in the house is wet & I suppose I will have
to carry dust on the roof to stop it or hire tramps to. I have not a
shoe to turn water and have more out door work than any one

8

New Mexico/Virginia:

1888–1929

I am a derelict in the Zaragossa of the sea of life—homeless, that is with no place that I can set foot where some one does not possess the right to say "move on."
[C. V. Mead, Las Cruces, New Mexico to Maggie, Clermont Plantation, Cumberland, Virginia, July 26, 1909]

The final section of the Browns' correspondence logs change, not rest. The search for "home" took on a chronic quality. Even after they had purchased a Virginia plantation, Maggie and Charles negotiated for property "elsewhere." Only death stilled the moving.[1]

In 1889 tentacles of harsh fate began choking off the Browns' survival options: a giant water crisis hit the Mesilla Valley, Charles was fired from the railroad, and the unirrigated ranch lands stretched scorched and barren. The water emergency that hit southern New Mexico in the late 1880s was caused not only by drought but by mines and other industries in Colorado and northern New Mexico that tapped the headwaters of the Rio Grande. The large concerns diverted such quantities of water that ranchers of the lower valley, like Maggie and Charles, sometimes lacked even drinking water. The only remedy for the Mesilla area was construction of a dam, but not until the late 1890s were entrepreneurs in Las Cruces able to interest outside investors in such a project.

The Browns could have eked out a livelihood from Charles's work and Maggie's dairy sales. But right in the crunch of the drought, Charles was fired. Despite dire warnings from Maggie, Charles had aligned himself with a shady scheme masterminded by Dannie. It was a "foolproof" system: Danny fished near Rincon, packaged his daily catch, addressed the bundle to C. A. Brown c/o Silver City, and sent it as baggage on Charles's railroad run. Arriving in Silver City, Charles claimed his freight (carried gratis, since he was an employee) and sold the fish to butchers there. Resentful of the covert operation, some of the butchers complained to railroad officials that ill-packaged and *illegal* fish were being marketed by Charles. Ignoring an initial warning from the railroad, Charles continued his traffic until company officials sent him a notice of dismissal.

Without salary, Charles was thrown back upon the ranch for income. And at that period, the arid lands were useless. In panic, he tried to dig a diversion canal to his property. And immediately he was pulled into a heated court battle (the usual litigation when a New Mexico rancher fought for an irrigation ditch) to establish water rights first to his source and then to the path across intervening property. He lost major decisions. Maggie complained that an over-weight of Hispanic jurors threw the outcome against him.

Frustrated there, Charles decided to mortgage the ranch and leave New Mexico for somewhere else, not Virginia, but further west, perhaps Washington State. Maggie, of course, pressed for a return to Virginia, an option Charles refused to allow himself. He *did* pacify her with a promise: if they ever returned to Virginia, the property bought there would be in her name, an unusual promise, which, to his credit, he eventually kept.

The promise did nothing to ease the current crisis. With no irrigation rights, the land could not be mortgaged and Charles had not even money for moving to a more promising land. Again Charles dabbled in odd jobs: medicine, real estate, mines, and construction work. And Maggie held on, only little Albert lightening her drudging days:

I wish you could see Albert he is a gay boy he is rolling around me now. He talks both Mexican & English says most anything. [April 9, 1890]

Albert hunts up the old boards takes the claws of the hammer pulls the nails out & then straightens them & does it right   then they are for use to him in chairs the floor or anywhere he happens to strike he seldom mashes his fingers if he does he don't cry. [March 14, 1890]

Because remuneration was so meager on the Rincon ranch, Charles and Maggie jumped at a suggestion from Dannie (working with a bridge building crew) that they rent a fruit farm and join him in La Mesa, a fertile valley some thirty miles southeast. With relief and optimism, Maggie and Charles moved, Maggie assuming responsibility for farming, Charles for setting up a medical practice. The fruit business promised to be lucrative, and Maggie tried to convince her brother W. J. to move from Virginia and become her partner growing grapes and melons.

W. J. was not receptive. Virginia life was too engaging. There were fresh romances. First Pa, in his sixty-sixth year, married a young woman in her twenties. This marriage was not a business alliance like the disastrous marriage with Mattie Spangler. Pa and his Alice dallied and flirted like a young couple. It was a surprised but delighted Maggie who wrote congratulations to this new "sister/mother." The second romance, Amelia Jane and a distant cousin, got a sour response from Maggie: "I want A. J. to come out here. . . . I know how anxious some girls in Va are to get married but I think A. J. ought to see some of the world first" [March 14, 1890].

The letters do not spell out Maggie's reasons for being angry at the engagement, but they do demonstrate her emotional fury. For years, there was bad humor between Maggie and this loved little sister. This tension, however, did not spoil the happiness Maggie felt about the new life in La Mesa.

The La Mesa community appreciated Charles and even paid bills; the fruit, in irrigated fields, ripened, promising a rich spring harvest. In general all was turning for the better and perhaps the best was that on December 22, 1890, Maggie was delivered of a second son whom she named John Daniel.[2] No letters remain sharing the exciting news. Still, the baby must have seemed a harbinger of blessings, a hope for good things to come.

But little John Daniel was the beginning of the end. The whole of 1891 is accounted for by one lone paragraph in Mary Gose's typescript:

In March of 1891, the entire family was stricken with La Grippe, Russian Influenza. there was no other doctor to be had and the only help they had was a Mexican woman. Maggie and Dr. Brown were both in bed, very sick with it when both children [Albert and Johnnie] took it. Albert caught it first, then Johnnie. Albert was terribly ill with it and my Mother realizing he had a very short time to live said, "Oh, Albert, do you have to leave us?" He looked up at her and said, "Yes, Mama, and Johnnie too." Johnnie was not yet sick at that time, yet in five days both children were gone.[3]

Gaping silence rather than letters marks the grief. Leaving the two small graves, Maggie and Charles, childless, moved back to Rincon, not to the waterless ranch but to the town. There Maggie rented a small hotel and lunchroom which she ran with the help of a black cook. Charles applied for position at the Mescalero Indian Reservation[4], made repeated muddled attempts to rent his ranch,[5] and tried to get appointed railroad physician. After months of trying, he got on with the railroad.

The sense of futility must have been profound for both Maggie and Charles. They seemed to have tried desperately to conceive a child. Between 1892 and 1893 Maggie had one stillbirth and one miscarriage. The losses of four children within three years must have made New Mexico seem an extended grave and Maggie could not have wanted to stay. But they literally had no money. Even Charles was ready to return to Virginia. A young man, a tubercular patient from Virginia, convalesced with Maggie and Charles and put them in touch with a new dream for going home. Some of his family's plantation property, property which bordered Pa's land, was for sale. His descriptions of it gave Maggie's nostalgic fantasy palpable shape: the pitched roof, the stately white columns, the sweep of porch, the full shading oaks, the rolling grassy meadows, the meandering streams. Negotiations began but stretched on for eight long years. Still the place, Clermont, offered Maggie a modicum of hope.

Though no letters suggested Maggie's being pregnant, on June 1, 1894, Maggie gave birth prematurely to a daughter, Mary Augusta Brown. She was Maggie and Charles's seventh child. Mary's own apocryphal-sounding vignettes tell about the event:

It was 114° in the shade on the day that I was born. I suspect that was one reason for my premature birth for mother herself was cooking over a hot stove in that heat. I weighed two-and a half pounds. I was so tiny that the wife of the manager of the Harvey House took me all over town and showed me to anybody who would look at this phenomenally small baby. A gambler slipped his ring over my wrist, they later told me. And another put a silver dollar on the end of my nose and it covered my eyes, nose and mouth—hardly sanitary! She even took me into the saloons to exhibit me.[6]

It sounds unbelievable that Maggie would have permitted such wholesale exhibition of the tiny precious life. But perhaps at that juncture, she did not care. No earlier concern of hers had saved the children she loved. She may have come to feel that fate marshalled infant destinies with its own inscrutable design, not to be gainsaid by mere parental devotion.

Only a handful of letters remain from 1895 to 1896, and most of those concern Charles's business. A rare one touches Maggie's worry about her frail baby daughter:

I am real uneasy about her [Mary]   I notice her throat is a little swollen. She is a little treasure. . . . I will send a little picture of her   she had had a spell of croup & we had this [photograph] taken by a traveling artist it is not very good. . . . she is so sick now I cant hardly do anything. [December 26, 1895]

The twentieth-century reader, accustomed to prolific snapping of baby pictures, may miss a poignant meaning in this message of the photograph. For the nineteenth century the taking of a baby's likeness was part of a ritual of death—something done before it died. It was a heartsick Maggie who sent the photograph to Pa.

Maggie wanted to go back to Virginia. The longing at this time sprang not from a dislike of New Mexico, for she had grown to love the territory, the wide expanse of cloudless, blue sky, the crisp dry winters, and the straight-forward, forthright people—both Anglo and Hispanic. And it was this New Mexico earth that held the bodies of her children, the graves holding both pain and presence.

But to return to Virginia and to set up housekeeping and business required capital. And the prospect for it jumped suddenly to them from an unexpected source: the rugged Sierra Madre Mountains around Ortiz, Sonora, in northern Mexico. Burt Ruple, another old Virginian who had mined in the Black Range, felt he owed his life to Charles's doctoring. So on the verge of a strike he pledged: "I owe my life to you and when I wear diamonds you must wear larger ones. My life down here is hell but things are coming my way" [October 8, 1898].

The grimy letters he wrote and sent out by vaquero gave the resourceful Maggie fresh possibility. The stained pencil written letters today are smudged and torn from folding, refolding, and fingering as if read and reread. Maggie more often than Charles answered them. Here at last from this "worn out, half dead" friend came the "lucky strike." Burt could see the gold "in every pound of sand on the Yaqui." Maggie could see it, too. And the gold would be her ticket back to Virginia.

When Burt's letters stopped abruptly, Maggie turned detective, tracking his whereabouts, plying mining concerns in Chicago that had financed Burt's venture for information. After a full year of tedious correspondence, Maggie discovered what had happened. Alone and poor, Burt had died there in the mining dump—a desolate end for himself and for Maggie.

With Burt lost as an option, Maggie, like Charles in the early years, propelled the family through a series of strange, nervous moves— *seven*, between 1900 and 1906. First, in mid-1900 they visited the Kellers in Virginia and looked over Clermont Plantation. Then by February 1901, they were back in New Mexico, renting their ranch to a Senor Gonzales, and themselves taking a small adobe house in Rincon. December 1902 found them again in Virginia beginning a year's lease on the Clermont Plantation,[7] expecting at the end of that time that the property would be up for sale. It was not. Therefore, Maggie and Charles arranged to rent the old Brown estate, Charles's family home. That "going home" was short-lived for two reasons: Charles couldn't make his medical practice pay because he waived fees for all his old friends, and rent on the elegant home became prohibitive. That avenue exhausted, Maggie uprooted the family and whisked everyone back to New Mexico.[8]

That was 1904. In April 1905, Charles opened negotiations by mail with attorneys in Virginia to buy the Clermont Plantation—to buy it in the name of Mrs. Martha M. Brown. When transactions dragged, Maggie stepped in, setting up an appointment herself with the Virginia realtor, which she and Mary went back to Virginia to keep. She succeeded in closing the transaction. In early 1906 Maggie, Charles, and Mary moved into their Virginia home: Clermont Plantation.

There are no records of the scene—how the three of them stood on the wide veranda or in the foyer of the old home at the foot of the spiral staircase with its hand carved balustrades. There are no letters that confess to homesickness for the little adobes blending into the desert earth, for the cottonwoods shimmering and whispering in the New Mexico wind. There is nothing to describe what memories came to Virginia of the little people left in early graves in New Mexico: Mattie, Albert, Johnnie, and the stillborns.

The Virginia community applauded the homecoming as a success. They knew Charles at the very last had cashed in on a magnesium mine. Though it was no windfall fortune, it carried the flash of a good story. Cloaked in the aura of the mythic West, Charles returned to his stable community, a symbol of the frontier. He embodied for the stationary segment of his family that deep part of the American character: the possibility of moving elsewhere.

Mary Gose's description of Clermont is heavy with romance. In part she saw the place through Maggie's eyes, eyes which probably always contrasted the lush Clermont with the arid desert. It stood for the values Maggie had struggled to find or to implant as she set up housekeeping in the "birdcage" cabins of the Colorado mining camps and in the sunbaked adobe dwellings of New Mexico. As Mary Gose wrote of it years later Clermont was not just a place, it was a way of life:

Clermont offers her benign sheltering great oaks, her twenty-foot high crepe myrtle, her white pillered portico with the slate floor, the massive slate roof, the panelled stairway with its hand-carved scroll-work and the graceful balconies, above all its atmosphere of peace and dignity to those who seek surcease from a troubled world. Beautiful, gracious Clermont dreaming in the benign warmth of a September afternoon with its hammocks under the great oaks where one lies and looks up and up, and the bobolinks in the woods and the whipporwill lashing out his lonely but brisk call, and the crickets whirr.[9]

On their green lawn beneath their spreading oaks, however, Maggie and Charles must have become aware of western changes in themselves. According to Mary, her parents became virtual bards of the West. The mountains, gorges, deserts and camps, the "boys," the "Mexicans," the wild cats, the cowboys, the Navajos—these memories were the fireside stories at Clermont. And Maggie and Charles wrote letters, urging friends in New Mexico to visit Virginia and begging for western news. After her parents died, Mary once went back to New Mexico and was welcomed as if she were a loved child returning home.

The nineteenth century did not indulge in self-analysis as does the twentieth century, so Charles and particularly Maggie were likely unconscious of the discrepancy between their image of themselves as people bent on "staying" rather than on "moving" and their real migrant selves. Fascination with the unknown had infected them. Settled on their plantation a scant seven years, they hankered to go elsewhere. First they wanted to travel to California to escape the gloomy Virginia spring. Then, they envisioned a complete move, not to another Virginia location, but back to the West. Charles claimed to Mary that "your mother and I" are negotiating to sell the place; yet it was Maggie who directed transactions. She advertised the property in northern publications; she answered ads offering "swaps": western for southern land. In the end, nothing came of the efforts. But it is striking that the efforts came at all, considering the years of dislocation in which Maggie's single-minded aim was to move back to Virginia to a place that had the symbols of home: family room, bay window, and fireplace.[10]

One of the reasons Charles cited for wanting to go back west was disenchantment with family there in Virginia, whom he accused of "unbearable jealousy and envy." Perhaps some relatives challenged property rights. More likely Charles, accustomed to the western readiness to accept the unconventional, felt oppressed by the clique of southern kin who would have assumed right to pass judgment on his daily behavior. After the openness of New Mexico the traditions of old Virginia cloyed.

One cannot credit the West with changing personalities. The different circumstances precipitated new behavior. In crises persons acted differently. When Charles failed to support the family, Maggie had to draw on her own resources to bring in money. When Rincon failed to supply a school for Mary, Maggie took responsibility for searching for teachers and procuring books. She was not a nineteenth-century feminist, forging new roles for herself as a woman; she was simply doing what she had to do to meet to the needs of the moment. The fact, however, that in the West she did not have to battle a culture that had a centuries' old restrictive code for women freed her behavior from defensiveness. The spontaneity with which new roles could be opened in the West made her forget the heavy limits of the southern code. When she returned to the South, Maggie continued to act with spontaneous disregard for traditional barriers—for her South, she was an unconventional woman.

One unusual document remains testifying to the unconventional "southern belle" Maggie had become. In 1920, Maggie wrote what must have been a fiesty letter to Virginia Senator Arthur Capper protesting what she had read about use of iron torture chambers on conscientious objectors imprisoned at Alcatraz. What remains is a copy of the indignant reply sent to Senator Capper from the Adjutant General, P. C. Davis, defending the practices assailed by Maggie. There is no way to discover Maggie's motivation. Was it concern for social justice? Was it personal contact with conscientious objectors or with prisoners who had been abused? Whatever sparked the impulse, the picture is noteworthy: Maggie, nearing sixty, undaunted at confronting a United States senator about a California prison practice.

That vigorous protest was one of Maggie's last actions. She died in April 1920. Another of her last recorded concerns was a polar swing to the domestic. She wrote Mary (teaching in a school for the deaf in the Staunton, Virginia area) a cheery letter filled with details about dresses, skirts, and hats she was making over "like new" for Mary. Little swatches of the materials were folded with the letter. Here was a delight in fashion, coupled with the practical discipline of frugality. The final word in the letter is "beautiful."

The only account of Maggie's death comes from Mary Gose's transcript. Though Maggie's ankles had been swelling and her breath coming short, she continued walking two miles a day to visit Amelia Jane. She stretched her last day to include an extra few miles to the edge of the property to see yoked oxen plowing a field—a new sight for Maggie. And that night she died, perhaps aware, perhaps unaware of her end—quietly in sleep.

Brief information about the ten years Charles lived after Maggie's death comes from Mary Gose. At the time of her mother's death, Mary was teaching near Staunton, some one hundred miles northwest of Clermont. She moved to Clermont to fill the space left by Maggie, to fish and hunt with him, to sit quietly in the evenings as he read. But Maggie had not left a vacuum. Her restraining hand was set to brake him even from her grave. She had been convinced that when she died he would get sucked into some quack scheme. To forestall his mortgaging the Clermont property, Maggie put a restraining clause in the deed, requiring either her or Mary's signature on any mortgage. Maggie's suspicions were founded, and Charles did convince Mary to join him in taking out two thousand dollars on the plantation. One of his last letters was a reply from a Colorado firm to his inquiry about gold mines near Denver.

Death for Charles, as for Maggie, was quiet. No extended illness, no sudden accident—only a slowing down. The day of his death Charles enjoyed a savory noon meal. He felt unwell that evening and in the night grew steadily worse. Into a cold, rainy evening, Mary sent John, son of the housekeeper, to summon a doctor, but Charles died before help came. Supposedly young John said to Mary at Charles's death,

"He was the best man that ever lived." He was buried next to Maggie near the small church they had built on the plantation.

In the typescript Mary reflected on her parents: her father, the good, kind physician with an insatiable hunger for the new; her mother, the woman whose beauty and zest had been beaten down over the years into a stern pragmatism.

Aesthetics, even the aesthetics of a human life, seek resolutions. And an editor feels a fierce urge to force personal documents into a satisfying conclusion. But to the end internal contradictions riddle the Browns' lives. Demographers Peter Morrison and Judith Wheeler hypothesize a "pioneer personality" as a United States type, a frontier mind captured by an "image of elsewhere." Such types live a perpetual odyssey, always lured by a frontier where the past can be let go and the future newly shaped. While the goal of such types seems to be finding a "home," a place of centering, the paradox is that in the end the essence of such lives has to lie in their process not in their final achievement. The treasure of lives such as Maggie's and Charles's, lay not in an end, but in a journey.

The body of the Brown correspondence translates from the nineteenth century the sound of life as it came to the Browns in Virginia, Colorado, and New Mexico. Through the throes of the daily events come their strategies for survival, the fevered gestures to bridge the gap between frontier and "home," their crises of values as tradition evolved into new behavior.

While Maggie and Charles penned their weekly letters to Virginia, stretching miles to encircle what they had left, to tell stories of strange earth and people, to couch in perspective the stress of unprecedented demands, to assess the reality of their dreams—they wrote with only their immediate family and friends in mind. Often the letters were the only solace in otherwise bleak days. In measure the letters afforded the only stable presence in Maggie and Charles's life of dislocation.

How would they respond to the making public of their private world a century later? Their energetic community orientation might make them glad that their lives became paradigms to support and enlighten a later century. The correspondence stands in a sense in place of the stone monument they, and the millions of other private persons like them, will never have. More fitting than stone, the letters continue in tribute to be a living presence.

Letter texts May 1889–July 1929

Maggie to Pa

Rincon NM

May 15/89

My own dear Pa

You don't know how anxiously we looked for your last letter just 6 weeks it was from the last time you wrote. We were beginning to think we were forgotten. It is now two months since we have heard from A. J. Dannie left this morning for Silver City. I hardly realized he was going until he was gone   we have been having so much trouble with the Widmers [Ralph Widmer, Charles's drugstore partner in Rincon, 1884] about our ditch so had to go to court Saturday it was tried but the jury hung & yesterday had it over   but they just recourse to such awfull <u>Lies</u> we were beaten. It will cost Dr. Brown a bout $30.000 or $40.000 any way. I dont know when D. A. will get through up there although he was so quarrelsome & said so many bad things to me when he got mad I miss him. Hope he will do well. If he will just hold his temper & let some one teach him something he would do so much better. Dr. B. will see him every day either morning or night the time is changed now. Dr. B. spends one night in Silver City & one night here but more time in Silver City than here 22 hours in Silver City & 14 at home. I do feel so blue about the state of affairs now. Dr. B. has advertized to prove up in June don't know how much this will cost. We were just beginning [to] see our way out when this thing comes up. Well I will close with much love to both. Tell J. W. [sic] he ought to hear Albert talk Mexican he says "What is this" in Mexican and "look," write more often.

Your aff Daughter

M. M. Brown

N.B. Will tell you a little more about Albert & his Mexican. I tell him to shut the door in English & they tell him in Mexican   he understands both & will do both.[11]

Yours &c

M.M.B.

Amelia Jane to Maggie and Dannie then an appendix by Maggie forwarding the letter to Dannie

Churchville, Va
May 16th 1889

My <u>very dear</u> Sister and "<u>big bro</u>"

It has been almost two months since I received a letter from either of you. I was writing to Pa the other day and I told him I had not heard from you for so long and Sister Maggies letters were never those long sweet anymore but I suppose one cause of that is her health was so bad. I feel like crying some times when I listen & look for a letter from my dear Sister and brother. I never thought you would neglect me, Dannie, but I have almost come to the conclusion you have almost forgotten you had a little sister in Va. I just tell you your little sister has not forgotten her big brother. I feel like he is something sure to look to. I would feel worse than I do I suppose if I did not have such good kind cousins and friends they all seem to think so much of me and try to make me happy. I expect to go to Staunton next week Aunt Mary wants me to stay some with her she is so lonesome. You can answer this and direct to Staunton care of Capt. Shuff.

I know you will think I am just writing for money but I assure you I am not, though I would like so much to have enough money to get me a nice summer hat and a few other things that I need. I hope you will try to send it and write immediately as I will need the things when I am in Staunton. I want to attend the commencements. The preacher is here this morning expects to spend the day   the girls are ironing   I will have to go and help. Write very soon to your loving Sister

Amelia J. Keller

[note appended by Maggie]

Dear Dannie

Why did you not send your shirt? The washing is done for this week but I will wash your draws. Now don't fail to send your shirt draws & all of your dirty clothes. I think we have gotten all of A. J.'s letters she does not say she had written any more. I wrote in Mar. after she wrote acknowledging the money. Of course you know when you can send her any money so you write to her. I will write to pa today. Albert & I both have been sick so I have not written yet. Your well wishing Sister

M. M. B.

I send you A. J.'s letter I sent it to Dr. yesterday he says I shall write to her he cannot draw any money until the 15th of June if he does he might lose his job. I can't help think hard of A. J. I did not write oftener because she said she was going from place to place to visit & I did not know where to write but none the less I wrote the last letter.

Maggie to Pa

Rincon NM

May 23d/89

My dear Pa

I wrote only a few days since to you but as D. A. sent a letter down to you I will write some more. We received a letter from A. J. last eve. Her last letter was to us acknowledging the receipt of the money D. A. sent her in Mar over two months since. Now she writes again asking for money. Well you see D. A. only got some $37.00 in Mar bought his tools paid express & sent her $5.00 so you see he had very little left over. Now he has only done $7.00 worth of work since   had to get himself shoes socks &c out of that. Dr. B. got him a hat 2 shirts at 90 cts each borrowed $4.00 to take him to Silver City bought him a matress for him to take around with him it is all wool cost $4.00 took D. A. to the clothing store & told them to let him have what he wanted & if D. A. did not pay he would   of course D. A. will pay this but I want you to understand how it is. I have paid $1.00 per month for his working ever since he has been here. When he comes home he comes to rest & he does it. I think from what Dr. B. says he has to walk a "chalk line" with his boss. I think it will be a good thing for him. The job will only last about six weeks. By that time he will want to rest. Dannie is nothing but an overgrown boy. Hope he will get to be a man some day.

We will prove up next month then I think I will go to Silver City for a while I have not spent 24 hours off this place since I cam down from Deming 2 years since. Have had little or nothing to wear but what Mrs. Byron gave me. Our little over & above our table expences go to hire Mexicans to do what no one else will do & I cannot such as shoveling out dirt of the ditch. Last month Dr. B. paid $27.00 for such work. Always such little dribs they count up   then the water has risen but once & while it was so   we could not use it   we had the suit with old Widmer which went against us   he having bought over the Mexican jury. So there will be a bill of costs. Dr. B. will have to pay off $22.00. Albert has not been at all well & I have had such a cold I could not speak above a whisper. Am all right now. Much love to you both   your affate daughter

M. M. Brown

Maggie to Pa

Rincon N M
July 8/89

My own dear pa

Your long looked for letter has come at last. I am so sorry you are too busy to write oftener   but why does not A. J. write more often   D. A. & I together have gotten two letters since the first of May one a few days since. . . . Now Dear Pa your word is out to me that you are coming out next Spring   I am counting the months now better than half are gone. D. A. was only in Silver City two weeks took all he made to pay his board & some other things he bought for himself & sent A. J. $5.00 he only got $3.00 per day. He is happy now he is catching some fish. Dr. B. takes them up and sells them for him. We are having some warm weather now. Looks like it may rain after awhile I must write to W. J.   I will say once more I am saving the calf to fatten for you all   now if you are sure you will come I think it would be well to have A. J. come this fall but I want you all to come because you can't eat the calf by yourself   on the 23d of this month we made final proof on our land will get the final receipt in a few days & the deed when the Gen'l. land office gets around to it but we can lean [lien] it when ever we please or as long as we please & we have one of the best titles there is to 80 acres of the best land the sun ever shone on. . . . Now I must write to W. J.

Your devoted daughter
M. M. Brown

N.B. I entertain W. J. with Albert so you must not think hard of me not writting to you of him. He is growing more like W. J. every day. Oh! Yes come out & we will change the order of things in stead of Taffy pulling frollick   let it be teeth pulling   my teeth are awful   front teeth gone   but Dr. B. says I am getting better looking to him every day   don't you pitty him he must be getting blind to think that

Yours lovingly
M. M. B.

Maggie to W. J.

Rincon NM

July 8/89

My dear Brother

I think you are improving in your writing. I do want you to improve so much. I am sorry D. A. dont care to improve if he can fish he don't aspire to anything higher. Yesterday 3 weeks ago Mrs Hoys little boy 3 months older than Albert fell in a tub not half full of water & was drown in 5 minutes. They had the tub to water horses. Now we have two tubs just like hers & I have to watch Albert very close to keep him out of them. He loves to play in water so I have been at D. A. to finish hewing out a log. He commenced 2 weeks ago today to use for the horse   but it seems like he can't get it done. Well W. J. I have a puzzel in the shape of a dog. First it would puzzel you to find a hair on it next to find its tail. Now dont you know it is a beauty. I got it for Albert. It is very playfull. Now W. J. you help pa save money to come out this winter.

With lots of love

your sister

M. M. Brown

Maggie to Pa and W. J.

Rincon NM

Aug 5/89

My own dear Pa & Bro'

Although you owe me a letter I will write not having much to write I will have to entertain you with Alberts little tricks & ways   he is all the company I have when Dr. B. is gone   D. A. fishing yet   is doing very well has bought a half interest in a net. He is laying up money to buy him a $37.00 gun expects to hunt a good deal this fall.

Aug 9

My darling pa yours of the 28 received last night. Now don't you see the necessity of being near some of your larger children. Oh! how I feel for you. Just think you are upwards 60 [September 24, 1889, Pa would have been sixty-six.] Do you think your arm will ever be strong again? Don't you think you had better come to us? We love you so much. You will not be able to do much this

winter. Dannie is not here now went down on the river to a bout
5 miles from here to fish took the wagon & team will be back this
morning. He is not getting as much for his fish as he did. I feel so
sad about your arm I don't feel like writing about any thing else.
Do write soon if only to say how you are. Consider what I have
said & let me know what you think.

Your most loving daughter
M. M. Brown

Maggie to Pa

Rincon NM
Aug 23d/89

My own dear Pa
   I have been <u>very anxiously</u> looking for a letter. I want to know
how you are getting along. Now I do want to have you come out
this winter if you can raise enough to pay W. J.'s fair out we can
get enough for you. Dr. B. is expecting to get notice to resign
any time as they are getting it on all sides of him   but he stands
high in the Department. We are going to make arrangements to
rent a fruit Ranch near Las Cruces (2 miles from the town). Now
if we do you just must come. There are 4 churches, a public & 2
private schools & the agricultural college will be there.[12] Now
W. J. will have the advantage of schools & us all of churches.
Just give up the mill & come out in the spring. Dr. B. has gotten
another job for D. A. at Fort Byard 8 miles the other side of
Silver City.[13] It will last a couple of months do hope he can hold it
until it is done. Now dear pa think over this & I hope you will
think favorably of it. We can all be together. We think if we go
down there for a year or so that we can get things started there
& by that time the water question will be settled. Don't you
begin to feel like you would like to see us. I just want you to
spend one winter here & see the difference then if you dont like
you can return to Va. Now Pa I dont know what to make of A. J.
She is surely not so busy she cant write   her last letter to us was
the 26 of June. I don't know where she is to answer it. She said
she was going to Middlebrook. Received a letter from Mattie
C[alhoun] the 28 of July. She did not seem to know where A. J.
was. we have just gotten 4 letters from her this year. I hope she
wont get married before she comes out for I think she can do so
much better here. There is more drinking in Va than here   &

there you don't know who does drink.[14] I will venture to say
there is not a young man in Dona Ana Co (that is doing any thing
at all) that is not getting over $50.00 per month. Now I want to
see A. J. married well & happily. Pa I have such a good husband.
My wishes are his. He agrees with me in nearly every thing. We
are getting to be what is called middle aged people but Dr. B.
don't look any older than he did in Va. Well I will close with a
hope for you to answer <u>soon</u>.

P.S.   I thought I was done but find I have said nothing about
Albert. He is getting to be a great boy. If he can get a hammer &
nail he is contented. He loves to handle such things is very
independent & so fearless   can climb most anywhere. The other
morning we were both busy & the cow was standing at the
kitchen door to be milked & when Dr. B. went out to milk her
Albert was under & had hold of two tits trying to milk. D. A.
thinks he is a great boy. He had on a pair of new pants & Albert
looked & then turned his [head] first to one side & then the other
& grunted his approval. He notices every thing. Now you come &
we'll kill the fatted "sow" & calf also. We have a two year old
steer we'll kill so you see you wont lack for meat. Well it is near
time for Dr. B.'s train to come by & I must close.
　　Your most loving daughter　　　　　M. M. Brown

Maggie to Pa

Rincon NM
Sept 23d/89

My dear Pa
　　Yours of the 12 was duly received I am glad you are in such
vigorous health   but am sorry you think if you were to accept my
invitation to spend a few months or a year with us it would be
considered spunging by us or any one. I think you would have
been hurt if Grandma would have spoken of a visit to you as
though you or any one else thought it spunging. It will now be 13
years (in Xmas) since we married & you have never visited us.
We thought we would make you this offer if you were inclined to
accept   it would be a great pleasure to us. Dr. B. has a 20 day
"lay off" expecting some cases of confinement [women ready to go
into labor] which wanted his attention. He has got things looking
nice around. Those grapes were of the most common kind in the

country they were off the place we expect to rent next year. The
finer grapes are too high to buy to dry.[15] How much corn has
W. J.? If he had one acre of corn here irrigated, it would bring
him $75.00 (seventy five dollars) if you had your mill here it
would pay you 30 cts per bushel (they pay money here for
grinding 75 (seventy five cents) for 140 (one hundred & forty
pounds) that is the weight of the Mexican measure "Fanega."[16]
then no one need lack for society here. No pa do not urge A. J. to
write. Day after tomorrow will be 3 months since we got the
scratch of a pen from her. D. A. thought she might lack for
stamps so he just sent some stamps with his compliments but she
never even took that hint so let her alone as far as I am
concerned. I have spent a great many wakefull nights thinking of
her but she is older & able to take care of herself now. Since she
left H'ville she has never written a nice kind letter. They have
been perfectly selfish. You can send her this & let her see what I
think of her. What is she doing now? She knows I am worked
almost to death doing two womens work besides my sewing.
D. A. is very hard on his clothes & they require a great deal of
patching. I know other women that have sisters who live at home
& have a great deal of work to do but they can manage to sew
some for a little nefew. Indeed I know a lady that never made a
stitch of clothing for her little girl. Now I would not of course
expect her to furnish anything for Albert but if she would offer it
would show such a kind spirit. She I know has a great deal of
time & no care. Tell W. J. I have a nice hat. It is a $5.00 hat but
Dr. B. got it below cost for me to wear horse back riding but I
will send it to him as another hat will do me also some flannel
shirts they are the kind Dr. B. wears on the R.r. in winter. Since
they were washed they have gotten too small for him   they will
do for you or him. One has a small hole in one sleave I will fix
that. We are thinking of going up the River about 14 miles where
there are some wild turkeys. D. A. is just crazy to go with his
new gun. It is a very fine gun. Now he has got his gun reloading
out fit & shells which all cost some $44.00 (forty four dollars &
something) he has no money to buy ammunition so Dr. B. buys
his ammunition & he is going all the time. We have had some fine
messes of quail & duck. Well I suppose you are tired of this so I
will close with much love to <u>all</u>   your afft daughter
M. M. Brown

Little Albert, via Maggie, to his grandfather

Rincon NM
Oct 6/89

My dear Grand pa

This being my second birthday I thought the best thing I could do to commence another year would be to write to my dear Grand pa. I am a big tall boy for 2 years & Mama made me a dress yesterday [Boys in the South wore dresses until they were around four years old.] with a pocket in it & papa gave me a pewter dollar to put in it. When I love my papa I call him "old many" I call Dannie "Nannie" I call candy "camey" & Water melon I call "Dia" it is San-dia in Mexican   "cio" is what I tell Dannie to do "Hush" when he talks cross to me. Mama is not well but I suppose it is because I wont let go of the "titie." There is a new man put on the run papa has but we don't know yet who is "let out" papa or the other man Ralph Widmer.

Well I believe this is all I have to say I will close. Love to "Uncly" and your self
your aff nefew [sic]

James Albert Brown

Maggie to Pa

Rincon NM
Nov 2d/89

My dear pa

Well we are afloat again. Dr. B. was removed the middle of last month. As there was another democrat in his place I think it was for other reasons & those reasons were for breaking a postal law forbidding the postal clerks "trafficking"   there was quite a fuss about Dr. B. selling those fish (not only by the department at the time) but by the butchers. They wanted Dr. B. to pay license but he did not have to. Never-the-less they got very mad (& so did I) I said there would be trouble come of it for I had read the law carefully   but D. A. said "Oh! you just want to keep me from making any thing" so it went on then the authorities threatened to seaze them saying they were not healthy then I just said Dannie you will have to stop or ship them in your own name. So he stopped. This is the way it was done. D. A. & pardners caught the fish & shipped them by the same train Dr. B. went on & to C. A. Brown then Brown sold them when he got there. All Dr. B.

got out of it was 10 cents each way for a lunch. The last lot shipped nearly all spoilt before they were sold. The department have given no reason for Dr. B's removal but just a day or so before it came a letter making inquiry about the fish did come. Well we will mortgage or rent the place and leave for some place perhaps Washington State. Will write you more fully as soon as we can find out. you see by the date of this letter it has lain some time unfinished. Well suppose D. A. has written you from his new location. We have heard nothing from him only he had gotten there all right. He wrote a letter for me to send with this so will. We are selling out as fast as we can want to leave the first of the year. D. A. got word from those men [a bridge construction crew] he could get work all winter. I hope he will keep the job. I don't want him to help us if he just helps himself is all I ask. We had quite a snow here the 5 of this month about 4 inches on the level the Mexicans say it has been 50 years since a snow as that. Well I will close & send this off. Hope it will find you well. Love to W. J. & self

Your aff. daughter M. M. Brown

Maggie to Pa

> Rincon NM
> Dec 9/89

My darling Pa

Yours of the 30th just received we cannot sell our things very well for cash so have to go somewhat slow. Now let us know what is the very least that Mill can be bought for cash. Please write by return mail for Dr. B. seems bound to go to Wash[ington] but I think if we could buy that place cheap he might come back there [Virginia]. We want to leave by the first of the year for some place.

Now don't delay. I will tell your our plans. If we can come back there we can trade our things all we have cattle & house hold goods for about $300.00 three hundred dollars worth of sheep then we can raise about $500.00 five hundred on the place but not sell. We can sell the sheep.

Will write more soon. Your loving daughter

> M. M. Brown

N.B. D. A. came up the day before thanksgiving & staid until the Monday after.

Maggie to Pa

Rincon N Mex
Dec 12/89

My dear Pa

I wrote you a few days since very hurriedly will write more fully now. Dr. B. talks as though he might change his mind & come to Va. This river going dry has been very discouraging. We can't tell how long it will run now although there has been quite a good deal of water for the last month now but up above here they are taking out another large ditch that is what is robbing the river here.   the large ditches in Colo & north New Mex. We can't raise any thing without water from the river here. Now tell me is that a good mill? How much land attached & if it over flows? Is there any high land there near it? Is it a good sheep country all about it? Dr. B. says he will rely on your judgment if you advise us to buy. Is there any timber to run the saw mill &c. How far to R.R.? Is there any prospect of our coming nearer? Now papa you take this letter and answer as you read. Yes have you had any chills yet?

You don't know how much pleasure it gives me to look forward to a home with a big family room where all can all gather together & enjoy each others society. D. A. does enjoy coming "home" so much he is a great home body. There I could have my dear sister with me & perhaps learn her to love me. I don't think she cares much for me   when she did write there was little love in her letters. Now I know you love me by your dear leters. If a hosts were to tell me you did not I would not believe them. You don't want to see me any more than I do you. You see we'll not have very much money but if you could get Mr. Wilson to buy out old B[ateman] & tell him not to let B[ateman] know we want the place. Now dear pa let us hear from you very soon. We have very little to live on & it is so expensive living. Dr. B. has a few days work over-seeing on the public road that will buy us a little sugar & coffee. He owes in all about $100.00 one hundred dollars. Our plans now to trade what we have for a car load of sheep & if we come east for him to go with them to Kan' City & sell out & then come on. the people have no money now. I have the scheeming & planning to do. I have a great many plans for getting along there. I will tell you Dr. B. says any property bought in Va is to be bought in my name. I want to have chickens hogs & sheep you look at the sheep market & see the money there is in sheep. The mill will keep the hogs & chickens with very little cost. The mill will be put in your control. I think I have written all. Give much love to my dear little brother & tell him to apply himself. I would like for there to be one real smart one in the family. I think he is to be that one. I do want to help make him so. D. A. don't care to be. He hoots at anything like polightness or good breeding. I think that is why he don't like that country where you are but at heart he is alright. Now I know you are tired so good bye for this time.

Your ever loving daughter

M. M. Brown

N.B. Oh! yes I must tell you about D. A. & Albert. They do love each other so much the other day when D. A. went a way Albert cried after him. A was asleep when D. A. came and we were all sitting around talking when he awoke he raised up about half asleep saw D. A. & cried "Nannie"   knew him [Dannie] in a moment. If he sees a cartridge or cap he say "Nannie ooten" leaves off "sh"   He talks a good deal now.

Your lovingly

M. M. B.

What do you think of having to put mosquito Bar over Albert in Dec. to keep the flies off

Maggie to Pa

Rincon

1/3/90

My dear pa

Your long looked for letter came to hand in due time. We were very glad to get it. Dr. B. is in favor of buying some land there as we get able. We are very unsettled yet but have given up the idea of leaving the territory yet. D. A. wrote the people down there want Dr. B. to come down he has made them a proposition & if they accept we may go there   poor Dan he can't lay up any thing. He said he was sick & could not come up Xmas   we went to meet him Xmas eve but the train he should have come on brought this letter so Dr. B. wrote to him to come on as he said he was coming Saturday or Sunday anyway. I was afraid he would get sick down there. He came Thursday & staid until Monday. Said it cost him $18.00 per month for board. It did not

cost all these & a good deal of company but $15.00   He just had
money enough to pay his fare up & enough to buy him some
amunition. I have been trying to get him to lay up enough for a
suit of clothes he is just in rags. When Dr. B was on the road &
D. A. got shabby he would buy some things for him but poor
fellow Dr. B. he has not but one vest & two old coats & old pants
to his name he has not gotten himself a suit since last September
a year & that was only $16.00. He never was so shabby as now &
nothing to get new with. I thought you would go over to see
A. J. Xmas. I would like to have sent her something but had not
the where with. Mrs. Byron sent Albert some little toys & the
merchants up town gave him a few little things & that is all he
got. It did not seem like Xmas to me. We have all been real sick
think the new disease "La Grippa" or Russian Influenza. Well I
must write to W. J. I could read all of his letter. Write again
soon. Much love

Your aff daughter
M. M. Brown

Dannie to Maggie

Earlham [about 30 miles
NW of El Paso]
New Mex
Feb 9th 1890

Dr Sister

Yours received as to me buying your stock I have not got the
money to pay for them with & if you can sell them to any one
else do so this work will be finished this week some time & I
want to follow them to the next as work in La Mesa wont amount
to any thing until July & I think I can get about 3 months work
with this Co on bridges in New Mex   then I will be able to help
you all some & you can keep your stock. Will Halton died last
Thursday after being confined to his room 4 days   as the
Mexicans say the corner stone of La Mesa is dead there was a
percession nearly half a mile long
Well I will come home as soon as this work is finished
Your Aft Bro

Dan

Albert, through Maggie, to his grandfather

Rincon NM

Feb 27/90

My dear Gand pa

The nice present of $3.00 big dollars were received this morning & are invested in stock so it will bring me some increase or interest don't you think that quick work. Last year Mama bought me 2 full blooded Angora Goats for $5.00 (or kids) this morning we bought 6 femails white kids for the $3.00 so you can see I have 5 nanies & 1 fine billie   1 nanie is a fine one too. Mama wants to keep them until I am 10 years old then I will have a good many as they nearly all have 2 kids & the full blooded ones have much nicer wool than sheep. Their meat is better too. Well Uncle Dan was here from Thursday to Monday he hunted every day but the day he went away we enjoyed his visit very much hated to see him go so far away. He has turned out whiskers looks better. Pa has a small pox case he is getting along nicely Papa has been busy vaccinating the little Mexicans. We were getting uneasy about you before we got the letter. Now let us hear from you soon. I say "Tankee" for the dollars.

Your affectionate Grandson

James Albert Brown

Maggie to Pa

Rincon NM

Mar 14/90

My dear Pa

I have received no letter since I wrote last but I will write any way. I want A. J. to come out here. D. A. says he will pay her way out & I say I will pay it back in /92 if she wants to return. I think she might pay me a visit. Then I know how anxious some girls in Va are to get married [A. J. would have been about twenty-two years old at this time.] but I think A. J. ought to see some of the world first then I can get her the school here this summer which will pay her $90.00 for 3 months & above all I will have her company. It would be a great pleasure to D. A. for her to be here when he comes homes. Then you come out next Spring. Then if you want to we will all go back in /92. Things look brighter than they have since we have been in NM. You are the one I look to to influence A. J. if I had been like she is when

young & had a sister I would soon take up the proposition. She
need not jump at the first one that proposes for fear she will be
an old maid. I married plenty young [age 22]   Let me know what
you think of this   write soon to your loving daughter

M. M. Brown

N.B. I must write you something about Albert he hunts up old
boards takes the claws of the hammer pulls the nails out & then
straightens them & does it right   then they are for use to him in
chairs the floor or any where he happens to strike he seldom
mashes his fingers if he does he don't cry.

Give much love to W. J.

Yours affly
M. M. B.

Maggie to Pa

[Across the head of this original letter is a note from Pa to his young
fiance Alice. Sharing with her letters from Maggie, he would acquaint
her with the western branch of family.]

Save this letter & send it back to me next time you write

WJK

Rincon NM
Apl 9/90

My dear Pa
   Yours of the 2d just received. Well the most important thing
mentioned in it is of course the hint you give us of getting
married again. [Pa would be sixty-seven October 23, 1890.] Well I
have thought often you would be some happy if you did have
some one to look after you & yours. Indeed I was just talking to
Dr. B. only the other night that if we went to La Mesa that there
was a widdow there   the mother of the Halton Bro's who D. A.
thought a goodeal of & if we could get you out here it would be
realy funny if you two would make a match now that you have let
me know so much tell me all   who is it? how old?   & all about
her. Tell her she can't have my pa unless she helps me to get him
out here to see us all. Tell her not to be afraid to come most of
the white people are civilized & some of the Mexicans & as to
Indians I have not seen any for 4 years & they were scouts that
went through Deming while we were there & this is all I have
seen in Southern New Mex.   we have about decided to go to La

Mesa   just as soon as Dr. B. can get off from a case he is waiting
on. They are going to commence a new Methodist church there
the first of May. They are very anxious for Dr. B. to come down
R. Halton wrote him a letter that there was no Dr. on that side
of the river now & there are 3 or 4 little towns.

I wish you could see Albert he is a gay boy he is rolling around
me now. He talks both Mexican & English says most any thing.
You will hardly have time to write to D. A.   he says he will be
through the first of May. Las [Los] Lunas, Valincia [Valencia] Co.
N.Mex, is his address. He sent Dr. B. a check for $30.00 to buy
him some books he needs. He is glad we are going down to La
Mesa as he is going back there to work. I send you his last letter.
This is about as long as any. Albert is crying to have his gown on
so I will close

Your loving daughter
M. M. Brown

Maggie to Pa

Rincon NM
April 21/90

My own darling pa
    I wrote last but I will write again any way. I received a letter
from A. J. telling me who her intended was. It just makes me
sick. Now you take a view of it & see how objectionable it is. You
& Uncle Henry are more alike than any of the rest of the family.
Why when I was there the last time I noticed it more than ever
before & Dan is more like Uncle H. than any child he had as I
wrote A. J. she had just as well marry her own brother. You said
the only objection you had to Dr. B. was his relationship [Maggie
and Charles were third cousins]   well we made comparisons
before we were married. Our grandmothers [the Fall sisters]
were so unlike. Grand ma Brown was black eyed & dark hair &
one of the dependent little women while Grand ma Keller had
blue eyes light hair & just independent & energetic as could be. I
think A. J.'s is older than Dan too if I am not mistaken. She still
talks as though she does not want to come out here   but if she is
so anxious to get married she had better do so. I looked forward
to having my young sister with me some & living over in a
measure my own young life. I never envy any young girl a better
life than I had in my girl hood. Whenever I think of it I thank

God for giving me such good parents   their conversation was always of the finest & if I do say it my self you never saw a more innocent girl than I was. If I got with girls that liked to talk about indecent things I would get disgusted & leave them. There was never anything that passed between Blair Turner & I that would not do for the ears of any one that is why I always like Blair so much. I am so sorry that W. J. does not help you more. I look for D. A. soon he says he is getting anxious to come home. Dr. B. saw his boss who has left the bridge & gone on the R.R. Pile drivers he said when D. A. got done on the bridge & he would let him know he would try to make a vacancy for him & give him $2.00 per day as carpenter. It did me a great deal of good to hear that. I sent your letter to him & he said he had written to you. His address is Las [Los] Lunas or in English The Moons. That reminds me when I wrote to you all from Colo that we were coming to New Mexico D. A. wrote back "yes there were great inducements held out to emigrants to the Moon." Now I have got a joke on him he was the first one to go to the moon or moons. Well our very best wishes for you & all of your undertakings

Give much love to W. J. & tell him to write soon

Your ever devoted daughter
M. M. Brown

Maggie to Pa

Rincon NM
May 30, '90

My very dear Pa

I received your letter in due time like to hear you speak so enthusiastically of your future pardner of course we were supprized to hear that she was younger than me but you know what is best for you so I have nothing to say. I hope you will both be very happy. Let us know when it is to be so we can make our calculations accordingly. Well Papa A. J. has made a breach between her & I that will be hard to mend if ever. The first was her letter to you. She was so "troubled" about coming out & at last "did not want to come" then her letter of last week came to me that she would come "maybe" if she had the money to take her back to Va in hand before she left there. Now I was the one that was to pay her way back if she was to come. Now pa I have

written to her for the last year off & on to come but if she were
to come now I do not think I could receive her with kindness to
think all of my offers have <u>troubled</u> her   then her lack of faith is
more than I can bear. I shall not <u>trouble</u> her any more with an
invitation let alone an offer of any kind. She wrote me she had
your <u>full</u> consent [to get married] but from her letter to you I
hardly think so. Now she wrote me some time ago that Dan
[Amelia's fiancé] was going to leave home & Aunt M was so
distressed about it I think Aunt M has influenced & encouraged
this thing to keep him at home. Well I must close.

With much love to <u>all</u>
your Devoted daughter
M. M. Brown

Maggie to Pa

Las Mesa Victoria PO N M
July 27/90

My dear pa
   Your kind letter was duly received & would have been
answered before this but I sent it to D. A. & was waiting to hear
from him before I wrote   then my eye got so sore I could not see
to do any thing. Now it is shut so you will have to take things in
to consideration. I want you to understand we had nothing to do
with sending that book. Dr. B. was very much opposed to it but I
thought let Dan have his fun. He is such a good boy we have to
let him have his fun if it is at our expense. He has not answered
your or my letter yet   but Dr. B. and I think there is nothing
better could be done for you   W. J. & all around than for him to
come out here when he is not at work for himself   Mr. Halton
will give him 75cts per day. Now our plan is this an early
vegetable garden   the land will have to be prepared this winter
but odd times he don't have to be idle. Now Pa tell Alice to write
to me   I think of her as a dear sister (<u>a younger sister of course</u>)
I never felt easy about your other marriage but this I do. I have
not answered A. J.'s last letter because she spoke of going over
the mountain & I did not know where to write. Will write to
W. J. our plans &c your most loving daughter

M. M. Brown

Maggie to W. J.

La Mesa Victoria NM
July 27/90

My dear brother

Now my dear I want to write to you a clear business letter. We have wanted you with us for a long time but would not say any thing until we got pa's consent now he says you can come   now there   is "big money" in an early vegetable garden but D. A. has no taste or liking for any thing of the kind & Dr. Brown has no time as his practice is growing now. I will get the ground Dr. B. says he will plow it & you & I will go in halves on all expenses & divide the profits if we manage things right we ought to clear from $200 hundred to $300 hundred dollars a piece next year can commence shipping things in March. This winter you can get work from Mr. Halton at 75 cts per day. If you could save some money to pay your fare out I think D. A. would lend you some. He likes to work on the carpenter gang or rather bridge building. You & I could have our own seperate business   we will see how much we could make. Grapes are getting ripe have had water melons for 2 weeks. Now this way you could make enough odd times to buy all of your seeds. We will try to get you out as soon as possible. Let me hear from you at once. You can get work the day after you get here if you want it at the price I spoke of. My eye is hurting will have to close your aff sister

M. M. Brown

I know you will come if A. J. dont oppose it

[There are no letters at all for the year 1891. Mary Gose's typescript and inscriptions in the family Bible yield the following information: December 22, 1890, Maggie gave birth to a son John Daniel. In March, 1891, the whole family was stricken with Russian Flu; within five days of each other Albert (age, $3^{1}/_{2}$ years) and Johnnie (age, $2^{1}/_{2}$ months) died. Before summer Maggie and Charles moved back to Rincon, not to the ranch but to the town itself where Maggie ran a small hotel and lunchroom while Charles applied for railroad positions and worked at odd jobs.]

Maggie to Amelia Jane

Rincon NM
Aug 1/92

My dear Sister

You are mistaken about me not writing to you for so long. I

have had nothing interesting to write. I am so sorry to hear of pa's failing so. We will send him some medicine to put in a bottle of wine and take as a tonic. If it does him good we will try and send him some [words smudged]   Dr. Brown says for him to get white wine if he can Angelico or sherry. Take a wine glass full three times a day before eating. I do hope he will get well. Dr. Brown will also send him some of his own pills from 1 to 4 is a dose. They are fine liver pills but never take them more than twice a week. I am looking for D. A. home Saturday. For the two Sundays he has been home & you ought to just see him eat. Mellons are getting ripe here now. Peaches have been ripe since the 20th of June. How are you & your beau making it we don't hear any thing more about him are you going to be married & take us by supprize? Ask Alice [Pa's new wife] why she does not write any more? I always enjoyed her letters. Give much love to W. J. Tell him I would like so much to get his picture. I have yours & D. A. since you have grown up but not his

Much love to pa & Alice and your self

Your aff Sister

M. M. Brown

[Between 1891 and 1893 Maggie had a still birth and a miscarriage.]

Maggie to Pa

Rincon NM   Nov 4   1892

My dear Pa & Family

Your letter has lain unanswered because I have been too sick to write & blue too. I don't suppose there is any one more unsettled just now than we are. The river the source of life of this whole Valley has been has been dry for 3 months but now it is raining & I suppose there will soon be water in it again   then we will let out the ranch for so many years for making the ditch on it or to it. Times are very dull but they say it is because of election times.[17]

Tell A. J. I think D. A. has a girl on his mind & I don't think she can count on getting very much from him. He bought him self a $5.00 hat & says he will get a suit to match. The girl is a very nice one & good. When D. A. takes a notion to buy any thing he generally does. He is getting real fine looking if not pretty. Just tell A. J. to keep me posted and I will try when the time comes

to help her out. Tell W. J. to get me 50 pounds of Hickery nuts &
ship them by freight to us either Dr. B. or D. A. Keller & we will
pay him for his trouble (we never see a nut of any kind out here)
to put them in sacks one sack in the other so they wont run
through & two or three tags. If there is any Chestnuts we would
like some of them. If he can do so get them right away. People
here get such things from their friends in Ohio or did last winter.
We can see some snow on the mountains but in front of the house
the leaves are green in the peach trees yet. Hope you are all
well. D. A. has been on the R.R. since the 25 of last month came
home Sunday at 11 o'clock & returned at 1:20 look for him to
morrow night.

With much love to all your
affectionate daughter
M. M. Brown

John McLeod to Dr. Brown

[This brief, urgent note for Charles to treat a gunshot wound suggests
the tenor of the times in Rincon.]

Nov the 14 1892

Doc Brown Please come to my Place as soon as you can get Here
Bring Instruments to take a Ball out of a mans arm   Come as
quick as you can   And Oblige

John McLeod

A friend in California to Charles and Maggie

[This letter documents the widening circle of the Browns' friends as
well as environmental tension in California between mining and ranching concerns. It also illustrates the dire complications of malaria fever.
Internal evidence suggests the writer of this unsigned fragment may
be Mr. Sangre whose wife supported Maggie in the grief of Mattie's
death.]

Auburn California 7/5.1893

Dear Friends in Rincon,
    Your letter is before me awaiting a reply. For the past two
weeks I have been suffering with maleria, and have more than
ever longed for the higher and purer atmosphere of the Caballs.[18]

Of what use is it to live where everything in the line of fruit and vegetables can be easily grown and be so litterally "stuffed" with malerious poison that one cannot eat and enjoy them. Far better a diet of bacon and beans with malaria and all its attendant discomforts left out.

It is just 3 years this month since I left San Francisco to come up into the foothills to "thaw out." Mrs. S. was in Nevada caring for her sister-in-law where she remained until November when she came here and I opened a shop and commenced work and commenced "shaking"[19] about the same time after an interval of 44 years. At present I haven't life enough to shake only to chill and ache. This is a town of about 1300 inhabitants and the county seat of Placer Co one of the old mining towns that has taken a new growth recently as the result of the fruit industry. But so far as I can learn no one is getting rich raising fruit in this locality for the Eastern market. With the rocky nature of the county and present irrigating facilities not more than 1/10th of the land can be tilled and put into condition to yield any return. And as the mines in this lower end of the county are nearly exhausted this must be a very ordinary county at best and it seems to be nearly at its best now. Of course if hydraulic mining in upper Placer should be resumed and create a house market for the supplies of this part of the county then would become a season of great prosperity and Auburn and vicinity would "boom." It is estimated that there are about $300,000,000 of gold still in the mountains above us that can be saved only by the hydraulic process. This work was stopped because of the damage to rivers and low lands along the streams filling the river channels and covering the valley farms with debris. But so anxious are the owners of the mining lands to resume work that they offer to build dams across the canyons and prevent the wash from filling the rivers and on this condition C[letterwriting illegible] has passed a bill permitting the work to be resumed under certain restrictions which a government commission will see enforced.

Your suggestion in regard to bees is a good one but I do not believe I would like it now. What I would do if I recover is mine work and that only—I never intended to do anything else when I came west and would not now engage in any other work if I could avoid it.

Pa to Dannie

[A Virginian, George Clark, victim of tuberculosis, moved west on

doctor's orders. Later, recuperating at the Browns', he described Clermont Plantation to Maggie. When the property opened for sale, Maggie
tried to purchase it.]

Trent Mills

Lucyville P.O.

Cumberland Co

Va

Dec 18/93

My Dear Son

D. A. Keller

Rincon, N. Mx

This is to let you know who Mr. Geo Clark the gentleman that
wrote you sometime since is that you may assist him in getting a
situation. Mrs. Wilson who we used to board with got a letter
from the young mans Father who is doing business in Richmond
& is a Brother in-law of Mrs. Wilson & Mr. J. R. Jones. Any way
you can help the young man will be very much appreciated by
them & also by Mr. Clark.

Your aff Fr

W. J. Keller

George Clark to Dannie

El Paso, Texas   Dec 21st   1893

Dan A. Keller Esq

Rincon NM

Dear Sir:

Your kind favor of the 20th to hand many thanks for your
prompt reply—I have made my arrangements to be in Rincon
between Xmas & New Years & should you not be there, I shall
go to Dr. Browns as per your letter. I will have a letter from
your father in a few days, & then I'll feel better satisfied as you
will then know who I am &c. Do you think there is any show to
get the place at Rincon now held by the Mexican you spoke of it,
although it will be work, I have never done before, yet I am
willing to do most anything to make ends meet. I hope you may
have a merry Xmas & I am truly sorry it is so, that I cannot be
with you on that day. If convenient, I would like to hear from you
again before coming up. Hoping to see you soon, Believe me

Yours Truly

Geo R. Clark

PS
I have written home, that I expected to locate at Rincon & I know Father will be glad to hear it, as he will feel contented about me, knowing I am with Virginians—

GRC

Charles to Pa

Rincon N.Mex   Feb 2d 1894

Mr. W. J. Keller
Dr. Friend

My wife wrote you in regards to the Jones place,[20] and I knew nothing of it and therefore you do not know what I wish to know. Mr. Clarke has told me what the place is, but what I wish to know is what is the least that it can be bought for, and if I should buy I want to know how much it would probably cost to buy every thing he has on it just as it lies   for instance teams furniture implements in fact such stock as would be necessary to run it don't come out with any proposition but just find out and if I should need any time how much I could get or what interest &c. And write me full particulars.

If they get in the big ditch that they contemplate taking out here, I can sell for from five to ten (5 to 10) thousand and I am coming back to old Va but that cannot be accomplished before next fall or spring. And I simply want to know what I can depend upon before I make any bargains for my place here and if I buy there I want this property to pay for everything which it ought to do. I do not intend to take less than five thousand for this place. Work him down to the very lowest notch for I do not wish to carry any dark horses in the latter part of my life—And if we can get this place you and I can make money out of it if I can succeeed in carrying out my plans they are simple to [carry out] the people in that country never think of doing what I propose to do—

We are all well except Mrs B. and she has the only cold on her lungs that I ever saw her have, altho, she is better, she is not well by a long way.

Write to me fully upon what I have written you—and other subjects—

With love and regard I remain as ever

Truly Yours &c
CABrown

Mr Clark wishes me to ask you what will be done with the Mill property, if it will have to be sold now that old Mr. Wilson[21] is dead? Please find out all that you can about it and write fully upon this also you may think that I am asking too much of you in regards to this, but I assure you if I succeed in what I am after it will be greatly at your benefit and then we will be all together—I love the climate of NM but am getting sorely tired of the people—and if they get this big ditch land will take a boom and I will get rid of what I have and come back   have been all over a great deal of country since I left Va but in my opinion "there is no place like home" and I say God bless the old state and if all of her people loved her as I did [sic] do she would [be] strong indeed.

Well I have written enough and hope that you will fully understand me.

Will write you in regards to my wifes health
so do not make your self uneasy—

With love from both—
Affect.
CAB

[June 1, 1894 Maggie gave birth to a daughter, Mary Augusta.]

Maggie to Pa

Rincon Sept 27th [1894]

My dear pa and family

Your ever welcome letter of the 18 came yesterday   you spoke of your pen going so fast it did not go fast or long enough. We do love to read your letters they can't be too long. Well, I am on our own ground once more & we have made the discovery that our house is not the true first house on this hill in excavating the Mexican found part of an old Astec [Aztec] mill you know the astecs were driven out of this country by the spanish about 300 years ago. I have not been well since I came down here but I suppose a goodeal of my bad health is caused by my teeth which are few and far between. Then every thing I eat goes to milk. Mary Augusta looks fine & is a splendid child. Tell Alice I do love her for I think she is a dear sweet little woman from what you & A. J. say of her   I have been very busy putting up fruits for a young batchalor friend of ours the country is over run with fruit

this year   principally peaches. Cornelous Jordan & wife are
living in Las Cruces over our county seat.[22] I only saw them as
they passed through but Dr. B & Danny have been to see them &
like his wife very much   I will have to close as Mary is wanting
to be washed and dressed. Give my love to A. J. & tell her to
write to me I love to get letters from home.

your loving daughter M. M. Brown

Maggie to her family in Virginia

Rincon NM
Dec 26/95

My dear ones at home
   Your nice presents came yesterday & your letters today. I got
the packages in the morning & had pies for our Xmas dinner out
of the berries. D. A. was here. Mary & I are not well but we
enjoyed our presents & return many thanks. I am real uneasy
about her. I notice her throat is a little swollen. She is a little
treasure. I would love to see her and Jimmie [Amelia Jane's son]
together also she talks only a little about like he does I should
think. She says Dan very plain & has for the last 5 or 6 months. I
will send a little picture of her. She had had a spell of croup & we
had this taken by a traveling artist it is not very good. We are
having some cold weather now but have had no snow or rain yet.
I wish I had one of your fine turkeys. They are 20 cts per pound
here too high for us so we just had a fat hen. The persimmons
came in better shape than ever before not one of them was
molded. I am eating them. I do love them so much. Dr. B. has
the wheat already to send   he told D. A. he would give the
wheat if D. A. would advance the freight but he seem to be short
of money now. I am going to fix up something for Jimmie as soon
as Mary gets better but she is so sick now I cant hardly do any
thing. I will close & write again soon. She has nearly spoilt my
pen I can hardly write. Thanks to one and all for the kind
remembrance. I wish I could return it but we are very close
pushed this winter. I send you pa the babes picture but it is not
good as the tent was cold & bad light.

With much love
your aff sister & daughter
M. M. Brown

Pa to Dannie

"White Walnut"
Hatcher P.O.
Cumberland Co
Va

May 1st/96
    Mr. D. A. Keller
    May 9th/96   W. J. had your letter & took it to A. J.s when I
started this letter & I wanted to hear what you said about going
to Chicago & I have been waiting to hear from you. I have not
heard from Maggie for a long time & she owes me two or three
letters. I understand that Dr & her have moved to Rincon again.
I moved to White Walnut on 20th Ap. & have been very busy
ever since   W. J. is working with me & works very well too. We
just finished planting 8 or 9 acres corn & I want to plant about 2
acres broom corn & about 1$^1/_2$ acres sorgum. I have a sore foot
which bothers me some but I am going to bathe it in Mullen &
pine tags   Mr. Bateman is home & says he had a foot affected in
the same way & it cured him. A. J. & all are well or was last
Monday. Mr. Bateman wants me to work for him & my foot holds
me back but I think I will get all right in a day or two. In moving
some body stole my pen the one Dr. Brown gave me & I am
writing with a turkey feather so you must make some allowance
for this letter. Wheat is looking tolerable well & I will have more
than enough to bread me & my land for corn is good & I think I
will have plenty of corn & I have some oats sowed it is looking
well. Everything is moving on in this country about as usual. I
have not seen Jinnie W.[23] since ever we moved you can send this
to Maggie & the Doc or hand it to them when you pass. Be sure
to write as soon as you can

Your afft Fr
W. J. Keller

P.S. Alice says I must send her love to you, Maggie, Doct Brown
& the babie. She is all right now as we are on our own land & in
our own house. She has turkeys & chickens & 3 pigs in pen
W. J. K.

Pa to Maggie and Charles

"White Walnut"
Hatcher P.O.
Cumberland Co
Va

Oct 28th/97

My dear Daughter & family
At Rincon
NM

Your letter of 21st just to hand & contents carefully noted. First
I am truly sorry you have been so sick & am just as much so to
think that you have such a bad opinion of me as to accuse me for
want of affection or want of interest in your welfare.

Now I spent some money & took great pains to have you
brought up in the right way & now to be charged with a want of
affection & a want of interest does look a little like my money &
pains were throwed away. I am not willing to think you meant
any such thing but you are still sick & feel badly   if you were
home & could see me & know my feeling toward you & Dr.
Brown you would not think of talking as you did in your letter.

Now I have said all I wish to say on that subject.

Answers to questions No 1 "who has the Jones place"   I do not
know nor does anybody else   No 2 "what do they ask for it"   I
don't know nor does anybody else   No 3 "what are their terms"
I don't know   No 4 "how much land is there"   600 or 700 acres
No 5 & "Have timber" lot of timber & a fine chance of young
pines coming on. No 6 "How much in fruit"   dont know but
commissioner who is closing J. R. Jones estate[24] has advertised 25
or 35 bushels apples for sale   No 7 "any grass or pasture land"
I think there is several hundred acres in broom grass.

Tell Dr. B. I brag on him & have been anxious to have you all
here & just now there is a fine opening for a Dr in this
neighborhood two of our Drs have died just around here. The Dr.
who attended me when I was sick has died. Mr. Jones place is
unsettled just now but when they straighten it out I will let you
know how it is. The commissioner has everything advertised
except the land to be sold on 9th Nov (97) cattle, hogs, horses, 70
barrils, (350 bushels) corn, 28 bushels wheat, hay fodder,
household furniture   I think the Wilson property would suit you
and Dr. much better   it has a very good orched & good house
but I believe D. A. has his eye on it.

You tell the Dr I am not in the habit of advising people what to
do & I just mention the vacancy there is here & would be glad if
he could arrange to take it but we are in a poor country most all
negroes & they are poor & no account & the old Dr who attended
me ran himself to death taking care of them & then got nothing

for it. [Of course, Charles as a doctor ran himself "to death" for patients of means and got nothing for it.]

Your letter found us all well except colds had a very dry fall but plenty of rain now. W. J. & us all are getting up crops W. J. has a good tobacco & good corn & wheat looks fine. With this goes my best wishes for your health & prosperity
Your aff Fr W. J. Keller   P.S. Alice gives her love to you all
W. J. K.

Pa to Dannie

Hatcher P.O.
Cumberland Co
Va

Dec 27th/97
Mr. D. A. Keller

Rincon N.M.

My dear <u>Big Boy</u>

I certainly was glad to get your letter of 19th   it just got here today. W. J. went to A. J.s on Xmas day and got home today & brought your letter up from P.O. I must tell you what we were doing on same day you wrote 19th   Mr. Bateman was here & ate his birthday dinner with us & as I did not have a birthday dinner on 24th day of Sept which is my birthday & Alice said I could eat my birthday dinner with Mr. Bateman I was 74 years old 24th Sept & Mr. B was 74 years old on 19th Dec but Alice did not kill a turkey but had a good fat chicken & a heap of good things & Mr B enjoyed every thing we had & so did I W. J. done his part too.

Now I got something to tell you sure enough. Your Uncle Henry [one of Pa's brothers] wrote me sometime last summer that he & May (his wife) thought of coming over to see us but would not come before Oct if at all so Oct passed & no Henry & I give them out & was not looking for them & on 6th Nov Alice & I were shucking corn over at stable busy as bees & Mr. Henry came poking around the shuck pile having come up the hill behind stable & I do not think I was ever surprised more than I was to see him & at first just for a moment I did not know him & I was so glad & I looked around shuck pile & saw May siting in the buggie I started for her & I forgot to introduce Bro to Alice but he & her got acquainted all the same. Well you bet we had a good time from then to the 18th when we had to give them up. They started home & we went with them to outside gate on James place. We all Alice, May Bro & I went to see A. J. & Tom Brown we called to see Mrs Wilson & Miss Jinnie. Miss Jennie was sick in bed but we went in to see her all the same. We went to see Jesse Perkins & Bro & I went to see Dr. Parker who lives on the place Mrs. Lancaster used to own. Bro H was very much taken with our country. I got a letter from him a few days ago & will say he is all right had a good crop corn & tobacco. The corn we will feed to our horses & hogs we have one hog which will weigh 300 lbs & some sheep which we may kill about first March. The tobacco a part of it has been sold & a part is still in barn ready to sell. The whole crop tobacco weighed about 1800 & will bring over $100.00 one hundred dollars clear of all expense. I think he can raise 400 lbs next year. Alice & I will clear up a good patch ourselves & try our hand. I am feeling tolerable well now   you know we have plenty land. Several parties who <u>know</u> say I have the best tobacco land in the country. W. J. is fixing to clean up some land too. I make a few brooms now as winter is here. I did not think Texas Coinage of Silver regulated the price of wheat & everything else. It is just now as it allways has been & will forever be   that <u>supply & demand will regulate prices & dont you forget it</u>[25]

Please write on receipt of this letter to your

Old & Aff Pa
W. J. Keller

Pa to Maggie

Hatcher P.O. Cumberland Co
Va
July 4th/98

Mrs M. M. Brown
Rincon NM

My Very dear Daughter

I suppose you are hoping for a letter from me this time & so I will drop you a few lines to let you know I am yet alive and tolerable well for an old man. I just heard of the death of Mrs Julia Shing   she died 24th of June was 85 years old Peter Shing her husband is still living & is 89 years old. Those old people are very dear to me have shown me great kindness ever since I married Mrs. Shings youngest sister [Mrs. Shing's youngest sister would be the Alice to whom Pa is currently married]. Peter the one above mentioned is the oldest one of the family & is 14 years older than I am. W. J. is trying away on his crop & it looks tolerable well but it needs rain very much now   A. J. was well a week or two since. I am working at the mill now getting it ready for new crop. I ride down & back. Alice is well & busy as a bee in a tar bucket attending to her chickens & a hog she pulls grass for hog gives chickens savings

all send love to you& all

Your aff Fr

W. J. Keller

[Following is first of series of letters to Charles from Burt Ruple, a fellow Virginian, who is mining in the Sierra Madres in northern Mexico.]

Burt Ruple to Charles

Camp July 21—1898

Friend Doc—

I guess that you think I am dead or thrown off on you or something only you know I am too mean to be dead and that I wouldn't throw off as long as I was alive. I have been working like hell and have felt tired worn out and half dead and beside have had no chance except once to write and then to tell you the truth felt so dont care a ——— that I didn't. I guess you have felt the same as I. I haven't heard from you so I guess it is a stand off. I am down about 40 ft and am now waiting for surveyer to come and survey. When I get the survey made I am going to quit work until rainy season is over unless I sell before. I expect a party about 20th of Aug. with stuff and expect to make a deal with him. Tell Mrs. B. that I received her letter and will do as she requests. I wish to God I could come up but I cannot as my business here has got to be watched. I expect by the first of the year to write a six figure check if everything goes right and our old agreement is as good as gold. Write to me whether you hear from me or not. The mails are not to be relied upon. I havent heard a word from you since the first of last month. I feel too mean to live. The climate is hotter than ———! I cannot stand up to hard work until it gets cool again. It is all right as long as you dont have to work hard. I sent this in by Vaquero so must close as he is waiting   as ever

Burt

Burt Ruple to Charles

Grande

Oct 8   98

Dear Doc

Your and the madam letters received after wandering around the country for few weeks. I have something definite in sight but when it is by guess and by God whether I am going to eat or not it takes the liver out of me. I spend every cent I can get hold of to push along the cause and actually go without sufficient clothes and grub and then what few dollars I can get, come like pulling teeth and with a grumble. I have placer proposition on foot it is a sure winner. Copper bonded for $6000000 a good gamble and money to denounce gold but the delay in getting it may do me up. Now if you have a party who wants to put up $200 to denounce a good ledge 3 ft silver and gold, trot him out. I am not going to denounce anymore for the other boys it takes too hard pulling. The 200 will denounce and survey and do 50 ft of work. The only thing is I will have the money in advance party to have $1/2$ interest and leave all dealings to be made by me. The claims the boys are interested in I will see through but will not get in on anything else. The ore in ledge runs 50 oz silver and from one to two ounces gold. If they want to get in they will not have time to stutter about it. From now on it is put up or shut up with everybody, old man, except you. I owe my life to you and when I wear diamonds you have got to wear larger ones. My life down here is hell and worry but things are coming my way. The people I have on placer will buy anything I can show up a little. I want to show up this ledge a little and it will be good for ten thou. in four months as good as the bank of England. They offered me $1.00 adobes a month to prospect and for this amount I expected to get the benefit of one years prospecting hire. I can make better money by selling out what I know of the ledges in chunks if I can get money to tie them up and put down small holes. I know of a dozen ledges that are way up on acct. of being hard up cannot make a move. Address S. G. or if important write to both Ortiz and S. G.

As ever

Pa and then Alice to Dannie

Hatcher P.O.

Cumberland

Va

Oct 18th/98

My <u>Dear</u> Son

San Marcial

N.Mx

Your letter to hand, will say I got one letter from you since you got home & wrote to Maggie the next day after I got it & told her to send it to you. I have been as well as could be expected but think I have no strength but I still get stronger   I had a <u>good shake</u> last Wednesday. I went to [words illegible] & I took the hardest chill I have had since I was first taken & had two since (one last Wednesday) I feel so well now & hope I will soon be all right I am going down to mill in the morning to fill a free mortice wheel for Mr. Bateman   I am building a stable got it up & the rafters on   it is 20 ft wide & 30 ft long & 14 ft high I will have [letter torn]   crib in it the upper story to put feed & broom corn. I am glad you have not lost your affection for your <u>old</u> <u>Father</u>   I saw the notice of your marriage [to a young woman from New Mexico named Georgie] in the "Christian Advocate" (W. J.'s fountain pen is no account & I am going to use a pencil) as you could not show your marriage certificate the notice will answer   shall I send you a copy? Now as I have never given you any expression of my opinion about your wife will say I think it is a great improvement on Miss Jinnie [a young woman in Virginia whom Dannie had courted half-heartedly.] & I think she—your wife—is a <u>good woman</u> & hope you & her will be happy but be sure you do your part & hope she will do hers. the storm blowed off part of our hen house roof & it fell on our turkey coop & broke it but I think I can fix it up again   I believe I am done writing you can send this to Maggie & tell her to write to her "old Pa,"

Your Aff Fr

W. J. Keller

P.S. And you be sure to write I am glad your Boss is so kind to you   Alice will write some   W. J. K.

Dear Dannie

As your Pa has written I thought I would write a little too as it

has been some time since I wrote to any of you   I miss you &
Gorgie so much just felt like I could not do with out you. I have
not seen Amelia since you left here but hope she is all rite your
Pa is getting a long all rite so far just once & a while a chill over
takes him   give my love to Maggie when [you] see her & kiss
Mary for me   will close write soon to your folks
You Aff A[lice] E. Keller
Give my love to Gorgie & tell her I would love to see her.

[The following was appended by Pa.]

P.S. I forgot to tell you to thank the Doc for the present he sent
me I brag on my son in law & have showed the spectacles to all
my friends but the glasses are too strong for me & I will get
them changed sometime
Your Aff Fr

                    W. J. K.

Burt Ruple to Charles

                    Suaqui G[rande] Nov 8 98
Friend Doc.
    I just got letter from Lee and take back all I have said. Poor
fellow he is in hard luck being all broken up in health the way he
is. I can feel for him as when you first met me you know I was in
the same fix. If your man S. will only pan out I will break it off in
some of these rascals down here yet. I cannot move ore from
dump until I pay stamps on titles and also taxes. I have three
months to do it in. Keep rustling and should S. go back on us get
some one else. I can show them something that is no gamble but
a sure thing. I prefer a mining man but get anybody that has
dough. I must have proof of their reliability before I show them
anything. I am sick of single blanket experts. Send me your old
Globe Democrats when you get through with them. I am liable to
have my grub shut off any time but must chance it. God knows
that with a few dollars I could make a stake and it makes me sick
when I think of the stuff I wasted in the past ten years. I am
getting so that I believe nothing that I hear and only half I see.
Write me all you know about Simpkins. How do you know he has
money. You know it is a vital point to know that he is all right as
I am here waiting for him. I wrote him a straight business letter
and should hear from him in about a week. If he is really what

you think he is he will not fail to come. If I dont make connection soon I am son—ed. Even now I am eating on my face and bumming stamp money. You write as often as you can it cheers me up to hear from you. I cannot write often. How are the NM camps. I am between the "devil and the deep blue sea" all the time. With regards to madam and baby I am

Yours as ever
B——

Burt Ruple to Charles

[Following are three fragments of a single letter from Burt. Though the date is missing, internal evidence places the correspondence sometime after November 8, 1898.]

. . . price, you to make your rake off over and above that price. Of course the ledge will not asay up where sampled as a hand picked assay but I think there are very rich stratas in it. Here the deeper you go the better the ore goes as a usual thing. There are several ledges that I have done a little work on that if developed would make good mines, but I go to the end of the rope every month and that is all I can do. Powder fuse and caps cost like the very deuce here and sometimes I go shy of grub to get what is necessary. The trouble is the distance from the R.R. but the ore could be worked here at an advantage. There is good wagon road to within one half mile of the ledge as wagon roads go in this country. The thing is doctor to get a little money to work on. Now listen not one cent of your stuff goes into mine.

. . . but we must get a sale on some property and work with this money. Lee and Jake are genuine stuff, but I would hate to even use much of their money but all of us must work to one end, that is sell something and get a working stake. I think this ledge gives us a chance and if you think you can sell it I will sink a hole on it. I am a little shy of stuff or would go to work at once. I will wait your reply and if it is encouraging I will put a ten or twenty foot hole on it and see what it looks like. I only wish we had a show to make a small sale so that I could make money to work on. If I cannot put myself on a paying basis before long Lee and Jake are liable to let me down. Even if they should I would go to Arizona and I can get grub staked there where I am known and people have confidence in me. I will not leave this country where I know there is way up mineral

. . . and perfectly undeveloped. There are only a few mines that have been developed in this country and they have paid big returns. At La Duro that little mine has paid seven million dollars in three years. If we could only develop a property like that we could buy a few acres back in Virginia and take things easy. Beans, beans, beans, how would some hot cakes go with a little butter made by Mrs B. If a man had a million he couldent get anything to eat in this country. I gave you my address in a previous letter but here goes again. Suaqui Grande, Sonora Mex. Tell Mrs. B. to write me every week. It cheers me up to hear from her. Her letters are full of news. Yours are short and full of business. I hope Mrs B's heart trouble is better. Tell Mary that "Uple" has the burro and saddle but it is hard work to find her a good gold mine but that . . .

Burt Ruple to Charles

[another undated fragment, placed by internal evidence, probably in early 1899.]

. . . to break out at any time. Sunday night two of them passed my camp and one of them said to the other that he was going to fire at my camp fire which was nearly out. My bed was about fifty feet from the fire and when he spoke I cocked my rifle. He heard the click and walked into camp with his hands above his head and asked me to take a drink out of a bottle. I told him it was bad medicine to monkey with a Gringo and that he came as near being a dead Yaqui as he ever could until he died. He said he thought it was a Mexican camp or he wouldent have said it. He said the Mexicans were coyotes. You see a man is none too safe here. There is gold in every pound of sand on the Yaqui. That is the truth but it takes time and work to find a pocket rich enough to work. I have sunk at least 25 holes to bedrock but havent found pay dirt except in one place and that was sluicing dirt and no water except in rainy season. It takes work, time, patience and a few dollars but if they stay with me I will pull out with a stake for all I dont get (cold leaded) and if I get that my only regret will be that luck would not allow me to repay the debt of gratitude I owe you. To Shallenberger I owe nothing   I am taking bigger chances than he   he risks 12.50 a month I am taking an even break with the devil to put it in French. There is a place in Canyon del Suaqua where I did some work without results but I dreamed the other night that I was taking out gold by the panful and I am going back there to do some work. You can get gold anywheres there but in small quantities but I am going back. I am not superstitious but I have a "hunch" and am going to follow it. With regards to Mrs. B. and the baby believe me

yours truly

B. R.

Pa to Maggie and Charles

Hatcher P.O.

Cumberland Co

Va

January 1st 1899

My Dear daughter & family

I received your letter dated 19th on Xmas eve was very glad to hear from you. The Xmas gift was received on 27th for which please accept our most hearty thanks. Alice & I went down to A. J.'s on 29th & delivered "Santa Claus" presents   we had a lot of things in our jersey such as 2 pie mellons 4 citrons 2 pumpkins 1.4 Burke navy beans ½ sour Bread ½ dozen good brooms 3 gallons "Sugar Amber" mellons (sorgum) 5 or 6 games besides our best wishes which was very much appreciated. A. J.'s last boy is just like the rest of her boys (very small) but as good as they can be. We staid over there until yesterday evening & came home in the rain & I have a bad cold now & it sleeted and snowed last night and it is on the ground now & pretty cold at that. W. J. took 3 days for Xmas & behaved very well & just finished shucking corn day before Xmas & is very anxious to go to striping them. You will please excuse this short letter for I have 4 or 5 more to write   D. A. Joseph Will Miss Mary Jane Bill Clark Bro Henry Bro Fritz as I owe all a letter & it will take me some time to write them. I hope you all have a merry Xmas & a happy new year

Give our love to all from

Your Affectionate Fr

W. J. Keller

Burt Ruple to Charles

Ortiz   Feb 23

Dear Doc—

I guess you think that I am dead or crazy or something and I
guess I am. You said in your last letter that perhaps the boys
would send me a bit or two this pay day to pay stamps on copper.
While I should like to save copper all right my belly comes first
and I will have to either pay up in Suaqui or quit the deal. I owe
sixty adobes for board and cannot stay with copper or anything
else without something to eat. I went to H. on borrowed money
to get money I sent Cochran to pay for denouncing and surveying
gold ledge. He wasent there and no one knew where he was. The
books showed he had drawn the money. I expected to get this
and pay what I borrowed and also [portion of letter missing]
I received papers and shall be glad to get more. Believe me
anytime and always yours   Burt
Best to madam and baby. I guess baby has forgotten me.
Address Suaqui

Burt Ruple to Charles

Ortiz June 1 1899

Dear Doc—

I gave a Mr Allyn a Chicago expert a letter of introduction to
you and told him to see you when he went through Rincon.

I dont know whether you saw him or not but on his report
hangs my hopes for the present although we have other parties
who will take hold if his people do not but I think that he is well
pleased with property. I trust the world is looking brighter to
you. Things are going to come right for me in course of time but
they come awful slow. If my meals came as slow I would starve. I
have promise of salary from June 1st but wont believe it until I
get the money in my pocket. If things do not come my way I will
be in a hell of a fix as I am way in the hole, but "nothing venture
nothing gain."
Write me Ortiz once and afterward S. G. If you saw Allyn let me
know what he had to say

Yours truly
B.

Best to madam and baby

Maggie to Danny

Rincon N M

Nov 12/99

Dear Danny

Your letter of the 29th just received directed to Mary. Why didnt you direct your letter to me   The R.R. men are all unsettled they dont know if the Division will be changed down here or not. Think they will   know by the first of the year.

The Road Master Fred Johns & Mrs. Ferry of Nutt were riding from Nutt to L[ake] Valley   on Ayres machine & it jumped the track. Mrs F. got pretty badly skinned up. [Fred Johns] is carrying the Harvey house girls[26] & most any one that asks him around. He is a gay widdower his wife was not dead 6 weeks before he was going with the girls. Mary is going to school I will send you some of her writing I would like for you to [section of letter missing]
where will you live? Answer my questions. I was looking for that deed every mail after you wrote me from Howardsville that you & your wife were going out the next day after you wrote to fix it up   therefore we thought we had given ourselves plenty of time when we sent for Passes & wrote out that option. Since then we have put on some improvements & when we sell will get more. I see by the papers there is snow in the northern end of Territory but we are just having fine weather very little wind. Had some last month. Send us some persimmons when they get good.

This is all I believe this time. Tell W. J. to write   with love & best wishes   Your aff sister

MMBrown

John A. Kruse to Charles

Chicago Gold Placer Mining Co.
    704 & 705 Gaff Bldg.

Chicago   June 1st 1901

Dr. C. A. Brown
    Rincon, N. M.
Dear Sir:—

I have your favor of April 24th which was forwarded to me from Suaqui Grande, and I regret exceedingly to have to inform you that Mr. Ruple died in Nogales, Ariz. about a year ago.

If you desire any further information, will be most happy to give you all that I have in relation to his death, or any other matter.

> Yours truly
> John A. Kruse

Maggie to W. J.

> Rincon NM
> Nov 9/1901

My dear brother

I send you my answer from Mr Fox so you see if this young man don't suit you will get the appointment. Now if you want it & there is a change I will send you a message to Cumberland & if you have not got the money you go to borrow it & so when you get your job you can soon return it. Now this is your best plan go over the road that will take you into the Dearborn Station Chicago. Dr. B. says if you get the appointment they will send you a pass from Chicago here. Tell them all to write. I get awfull lonesome & wish I could see you all. Kiss the little ones. It will not cost you over $10 or $15 per month and may be less if you room and board with me. It will be a good thing for you to get out & see how other people live. I do hope you will come. Love to all

> Your loving sister
> MM Brown

John A Kruse to Maggie

Chicago Gold Placer Mining Company
    704–705 Gaff Bldg.
  234 La Salle Street

> CHICAGO   March 13, 1903

Mrs. Dr. C. A. Brown
  Hatcher P.O., Virginia
Dear Madam:—

On my return from San Francisco I found your favor of Feb. 4th in relation to the Ruple estate. In reply would say that Mrs. Ruple's address is Nogales, Ariz. The amount of interest which the estate has in the Placer property is in the neighborhood of 450 shares, but that is subject to an agreement that the interest is not to be delivered under the agreement with Mr. Ruple until after the money put in to equip the property is paid back. Such was the agreement that Ruple and I made with the Company. His interest is also liable for an amount of several thousand dollars for which he was indebted to the Company. With these limitations it is in tact. He did sell 50 shares or $5,000 worth of stock before he died, and that at his personal request was delivered, but any of the interest of the entire estate outside of this cannot be delivered outside of the conditions named above.

I have no doubt that Mrs. Ruple desires to do what is right in this matter, and if you consult her she will probably write you to that effect.

Yours very truly
John A Kruse

Mrs. Burt Ruple to Maggie

Nogales Ariz. May 15 [1903]

My dear Mrs. Brown,—

I received your kind letter some weeks ago and pleased to hear from you but sorry that you were not well. I must thank you for your kind invitation to come and see you and I am only sorry I cannot accept it, I am so far away and my circumstances are not of the best at the present time. I am in hopes they will change before long. In Mexico everything is at a stand still the Co. has not done anything since the death of my best beloved husband so I cannot tell how I will come out but live in hopes that I will realize something out of the mines. It seems that I know you and the Dr. for I have heard Mr. Ruple speak so often and so kindly of you both. And always said when we sold our mines he would not forget you. I can tell you my heart is broken and I cannot see or understand why he should die and so many worthless men allowed to live.

My health is not very good and has not been since his death   I am going to the country on Saturday   I am in hopes that the change will benefit me. I hope you are all well by now and I would be pleased to hear from you soon again. I close with love to you and Dr.

I remain
Sincerely Your Friend
Wonda Ruple

Dr. J. P. Kaster to Charles and Maggie

J. P. Kaster, M. D.,
    chief surgeon   TOPEKA, KANSAS, November 2nd, 1903
Dr. C. A. Brown & Wife
    Hatcher, Cumberland Co., Va.
Dear Sir and Madam:—

I received your very kind invitation of October 27th to come
and pay you a visit and enjoy a hunt with you. Nothing in the
world would give me greater pleasure, than to visit your country
as I have never seen that part of the United States, but owing to
the press of business and cares, I cannot get away. Mr. Mudge
and Mr. Fox like myself, would be very pleased to enjoy your
hospitality, but it is impossible for them to get away. Mr. Fox has
been promoted and is now Sup't of a portion of the line in
Kansas. Wishing you all kinds of success, I beg to remain,

                            Yours very truly,
                            J. P. Kaster
                            Chief Surgeon

Ivah Shallenberger to Maggie

[This letter from Maggie's New Mexico friend, Ivah Shallenberger, is
the first typewritten letter in the collection.]

San Marcial, NM June 5th, 1904
My dear friend Mrs. Brown—

This is to the Doctor and little Mary as well, so all can read it.
I just finished reading the letter you wrote to Bertie and me
together and your last to me also the postal card. I was so glad to
get all your letters. You write just as you talk and It seems just
as if I had had a talk with you.

I am glad you are happy and doing well in your new home but
also glad that you do not forget your old friends so far away.

I am sorry to say Mrs. Brown that even if we can go to see you
that it will be impossible for us to be there in August, as we do
not intend even trying to go until September, and if it is as we
hear and the Company will not grant passes to employees after
July, we shall have to give up our trip altogether. I hope not, for
we planned to have a fine time and we have not taken a trip for
nearly a year, except for the little trip down to see Mamma. I
really think that even if we can get passes we shall not go before

Oct., for we went in Oct. and were gone all Oct., all Nov. and ten
days in Dec. on our wedding trip and the weather was so nice
that we shall always go at that time of the year when we go east.
It will be a hard disappointment to me if we can not go, for all
our relatives on both sides of the house live in St. Louis and I am
very anxious to see them. Bertie sent me your letter the last
time she wrote. She said she was coming up to see me in July,
but I shall not look for her until I see her coming. I have been
hopeing to have her visit me for such a long time.

Roy is home at last and is at present asleep on the lounge in
the room where I am writing and he is snoring pretty loud. He
seems quite tired out as there was so much going on during
Commencement week and of course he went to all that he could.
He is as hungry as he is tired. I guess they do not feed them up
very well at the College boarding house. He is very much
improved and we feel well pleased with his year there, and he
wants to go again next year, and of course if he wants to go, he
shall. He is a pretty spoilt kid, but he thinks he is terribly
abused. He is over six feet tall now and as straight as an arrow.
He will work in the drug store all summer and help Charley out.

Mr. Shallenberger has been at home for four days on his
regular lay over trip and just went out this morning at 7:30. It
seems so lonely without him for he is such a home man, and loves
only to be at home. I wish you could see him. He looks so young
and thoroughly happy and good natured that it does one good to
look at him. He is always smiling and as full of mischief as ever.
It seems to me sometimes that he is fairly bubbling over with
good feeling. He has been regular passenger man now for a year
in March and it is so nice to know just when he will be home and
just where he is at all times. We have a dear little home and are
as happy as mortals ever get to be in this world, I suppose.
Charley is doing very well in the drug store considering the hard
times on the road and the awful drouth in among the agricultural
and stock circles. He is a rustler and all business and a good
steady young man.

I have nearly a hundred young chicks and twenty old ones, so
you see with getting three meals a day and my house work and
sewing together with a little reading, writing, visiting and
receiving calls, church work, helping Charley in the bookkeeping
and getting out hundreds of letters for him and the little extras
that go to make up the time, I am a very busy woman. I am so

well all the time, but not strong like I used to be, still, I have not been sick since we were married except a little cold. I am so thin, I should be ashamed for you to see me. I have been thin for about four or five years, in fact ever since I commenced teaching.

Mrs. Harlan and Mrs. Brown were just here on a little visit. It always makes me think of old times and you folks when I see them both. Mrs. Brown had rooms at Mrs. Harlan's all year. Maughs was here working in the Supt. office until Dec. then when business got so dull and they had to reduce the force, they sent him up to work in the depot at Albuquerque, and from there to Deming, where he now is. Mrs. Brown had just closed a successful nine months term of school here and is very much liked by all who knew her. She is a lovely teacher and lady and wins friends wherever she goes, by her nice ways. She is going home this summer to Mississippi and St. Louis to spend the summer. I hope she will accept the school here next year, but she does not know yet.

Mrs. Harlan's little girl is a lovely child, but full of mischief and fun. She was three years old in Oct. but she appears to be five. Jock is home from school, the Roswell Military School, where he has been going all year. Lulu Mellick graduates this year in her home. I imagine she is a lovely girl.

I have not seen Bertie for nearly a year, but if she does not come up pretty soon I will go down to see her, think I shall anyway. I must stop and wake Roy up and make him go to bed. He seems worn out. He played ball to-day and I guess he is pretty tired.

This machine [the typewriter] is just the thing for the three boys. They think it is great fun to try to write on it, but if they had to write by the hour they would not think it such fun.

The weather is fine. It has not been warm at all yet. Mr. Shallenberger's parents stayed until the middle of February. They had intended staying until warm weather but the old gentleman's [health] grew so much worse we were afraid he would not live to get home. He failed very rapidly indeed. It was too high for him here, as he has heart trouble. Mr. S. was afraid of it, but they wanted to come so and we wanted them, and his doctor thought it would help him. You knew he has been an invalid for a great many years.

I will close now, with our best to both of you. Mr. S. seldom gets to write when I do for I always write when he is gone.

I hope you will show me that I am forgiven by a speedy reply, from your loving friend and one of your children,   Ivah

P.S. Mrs Stalker was over the other day, Friday, and she had her little dog that Mary gave her. She thinks the world of him and he is always with her. She wished to be remembered to all three of you and asked after you and wished she could see you again.

Attorney William M. Smith to Charles

[This is one of the numerous letters from the Virginian who represented Charles in the litigation involving the purchase of the Jones property, Clermont Plantation, in Virginia.]

UNITED STATES DEPOSITORY
5683

R. H. LYNN Vice President
A. G. Clapham, Cashier,
N. B. Davidson, President

The FIRST NATIONAL BANK
of Farmville

FARMVILLE, VA.   20 May   1905

Dr. C. A. Brown
New Mexico
Dear Sir:
   The Jones case was continued from the regular term of the Court in Cumberland to the Prince Edward Court which is now in session. The case has just been finally disposed of. The sale was confirmed to you at $2720 on the terms set out in the decree, the terms of job in the hand bill which I send you with the privilege to you to pay $2660 in cash in stead of $2720. In other words you will be given a discount of $60 if you will pay cash—I advise you to do this if convenient to you the $60—I thought best to advance $60 on your former bid rather than not get the property and had I not done so, you could not have gotten it—As the other party offered the amount I proposed to pay for you—I realized that I had gone $60 above the amount you authorized me to bid in your last letter but as $3000 was your level in your final letter to me before the sale, I was satisfied that you were willing to go $2720 in terms or $2660 cash rather than be out of the deal for ever as would have been the case. I congratulate you on

getting it at this price & hope you may see it as I do that you
have a bargain, but if you are not pleased with the price &c. let
me know at once—

Yours truly
WMMSmith

Elmo D. Carter to Maggie

[Elmo Carter, one of the Jones' family still living in the plantation home
on the property purchased by the Browns, blocked their moving in
until he left.]

July 4—1905

Dillwyn Va
F.F.D. #2

Mrs. C. A. Brown
    Rincon New Mexico
Dear Madam
I received your letter a few days ago asking about getting 3
rooms of the House in the course of 30 days. I am sory to say
that after being with Mrs. Wilson [previous owner] 18 months I
said when she left that I never would have any one in the house
with me any more. So I dont want any one in the House till I get
out & I think it will be more satisfactory with both of us in the
future. How are you all getting on? Well I hope. Give my regards
to Doc

Yours Respt
Elmo D. Carter

William M. Smith to Maggie

WM. M. SMITH
Commonwealth's Attorney

CUMBERLAND, VA 11 Sept   1905

Mrs. Martha A. Brown
    Hatcher, Va.
Dear Madam,
    I am in receipt of your letter stating that you wanted to make
an appointment with me for some day to meet me at my office.
Replying will say I will meet you the day you name this week.
    I do not think the Amt will allow you any rebate on your
purchase of the Jones land—The Commissioner announced on the

day of sale that the sale was made in group & not by the acre.
The question was asked if he [word blurred] the number of acres
& he said he did not—But sold the land subject to former sales of
the Jones land—

Yours truly

WmMSmith

C. V. Mead to Maggie

[C. V. Mead had been one of Maggie and Charles's friends in New
Mexico.]

Las Cruces N. M. July 26, 1909
Mrs. M. M. Brown
Clermont Plantation
My Dear Mrs Brown

Yours very welcome and high appreciated surprise of 22 is just
received. It is needless to say that it called up many pleasant as
well as some sad memories. There is little left me now but
remeninscences and your letter is another instance that
circumstances appear to combine in making them pleasant.

My domestic relations are in the unhappy condition they have
been for sixteen years. I fought everything from within and
without—for all those trying years to hold onto my landed estate
till it should, as I was sure it would, be worth something and
until I was dragged into the district court and clubbed into letting
it be disposed of for half or less of its true marketable value.
Even at the sacrifice price it realized enough to allow all of them
to live with a comfort as near as necessary to luxury if it is taken
care of. I am a derelict in the Zaragossa of the sea of life—
homeless, that is with no place that I can set foot where some
one does not possess the right to say "move on,"[27] That, however,
is more than offset by the warm welcome that I find securely
fastened to so many latch strings. I am now domiciling with Cad
Bruce and Eve who is one of the most adorable of women.

I am now in my 76th year and while nothing indicates that I
am any more, there is abundance to remind me that I am no less.

Mrs. M. and Doc and Anita are living in the old homestead
(from which I am debarred) in, as I learn, somewhat swell style,
Charlie is in Colton California and Ina is in Larned Kansas.

Cruces, indeed the whole valley, is wonderfully improved. You
would not recognize the place were you to revisit it.

Bob is in El Paso, has a very nice home and is on a veritable cyclone rush in the real estate business. He is doing a large business and I am persuaded with satisfactory results. Cad Bruce has the old McClure transfer business here and doing fairly well. The Hesson boys—Ed and Frank—made some lucky bits in real estate a part of which found farms in unencumbered El Paso inside property for which I expect they would refuse $50,000.00. I don't know whether you remember or, indeed, whether you knew the Goodman boys—Lewey and Joe. They are in El Paso. Joe has retired on a rent roll of $900.00 a month. Pearl Baley and Freddie Peacock were married on the 23 Oct. They are based primarily in El Paso till the fine house he is building on his ranch near La Arecion is finished. Oscar Snow is a bonanza rancher on a 1200 acre alfalfa farm below Mesilla. The old padre—Lasaign— was buried last Tuesday. Old Dr. Horatio Stevenson is very frail.

Yes I spent two weeks with my old friend Charlie K. very satisfactorily to myself. His conubial relations seem a little odd but they appear to be happy which, after all, is the main thing.

I certainly appreciate your invitation to make a visit to your old Varginny home and I would certainly enjoy it as one of the times of my life but in getting as much happiness out of my life as possible I am admonished that the so doing is circumscribed by limited resources. What was gained by my long struggle in holding onto my land was but little to my personal benefit.

It gives me great pleasure to learn of your recovered health. Long may it continue!

You must remember me to Dr. B. Tell him I can imagine how much pride he takes in the corn and "tobarker" and tell him to let mercy temper his wrath when he learns that an old grass widower is writin to his wif. If Dan is within reach remember me to him as well as our old friend William B.

With highest regards,
Sincerely Yours
C. V. Mead

Cousin Gussie Brown[28] *to Mary Augusta Brown*

[Internal evidence dates this letter between 1907–10. Though a fragment, it introduces feminist thinking of the early 1900s to the body of correspondence: Mary's questions surely sparked Cousin Gussie's following response.]

BRITISH INDIA STEAM VACATION CO. LTD.

. . . greatest difficulty lies in acquiring the necessary expensive education & getting started in a practice which in a woman's case must necessarily be a town practice. However, starting is probably easier for a woman than for a man as there is a considerable unsupplied demand in the larger towns for the services of women in connection with schools, children, etc. and the public seems to feel a natural confidence in the reliability of a young woman that a young man has to establish for himself. Still it is uphill work. In any case you have a long time before you for you cannot start to practice medicine very young. You should pay special attention at High School to the Natural Sciences, Botany, Zoology & Physiology as a starter. I think your desire to become a physician is a reasonable & proper one & I see no reason why you should not succeed, though the difficulties are not small.[29]

In a general way, however, it is better for a girl to marry if she has a proper opportunity, & I hope you will do so. An educated, efficient married woman is of great value in a community & is sure of a useful career. Do not be over shy or undervalue yourself; learn to talk readily & show your best & friendliest side at once; it will be of great use to you in helping yourself along in the world, both as a woman & as a physician to be able to place yourself at once on friendly terms with the people you meet, so study to please to make yourself agreeable and remember that others may like to hear you talk as much as you like to hear them.[30]

Now I realize that I have given you a great deal of advice for one sitting, but you can take what appeals to you & let the other go, which is what most people do anyway.

I do not know just what I shall do on my return to California but I am afraid I shall not be able to come to Virginia as I would love to do. I have been junketing about as long as I can afford. Perhaps you can come to California some time later.

It is good of your father & mother to take care of Uncle Will. Don't let them take life too hard.

Affectionately
Cousin Gussie

March 24th

Hubert Poole to Charles

[This fragment is a response to Charles's open inquiry to the Post Master in Bonanza, Colorado, on the whereabouts of the "boys" from the Bonanza camp of the 1800s.]

Bonanza, Colo Jan 27th, 1915
C. A. Brown M. D.
Dillwyn Va—
Sir—

Your letter of Jan 17th was handed to me by the P. M. Dr. B.
F. Cantwell—I suppose to me as I have been a resident of the
Kerber Creek Mining District for the past Thirty-Five years, and
remembered a Dr. Brown who was here in the early 80s. So will
in a terse manner mention a few of the old timers that are now
here, as well as the ups & downs of the camp. Being egotistical in
a small degree will state myself first—My name is Hubert
Poole—miner—resident of Exchequer in the 80s called by some
"Mayor of Exchequer" aged at that time 35 years—a close
neighbor to George and Mac Ritner, owners of the Exchequer
mine—both were ex confederate soldiers—from Texas—my next
neighbors were—Pete McCardel—A.S. Carpenter & Sara
Galloway (the colored laundress at that town—Saml F. Rathrow
and Henry McGraw—John Raymond and Tom Cooper—You may
remember them all—the Ritners returned to Texas—and have
passed the Great Divide—McCardel went to Arizona Carpenter to
Idaho—Mrs Galloway to Kansas—Saml F. Rathrow lives in
Denver with his family—and Henry Magraw is in Montana
Thomas Cooper is on the Police force at Cheyenne—John
Raymond resides 11 miles below Bonanza on a Ranch—I have
lost track of Dr. Ramsey and Sparrow—Norman P. White still
lives in California—I had a letter from him a month or two ago—
he was well—lives in a cottage at Sawtelle near Solder's home—
he no doubt would like to hear from old friends—Pomp Howard is
at the Soldier's Home in California—& Dan Howard resides at
Saguache—Q.T. the corpulent saloon keeper returned to Texas &
died some years ago—James Kerny died a short time back at
Leavenworth Kansas—he was entirely Blind, and lived at the
Soldier's home—his son aged 30 resides here and has some
property—Chas. Leavett has left & lives at San Diego
California—All the old timers that were here in 81, who live here
now—are Sol Harding James F. Buck & wife—LW Sharpe & wife
(late Mrs McMullen) Chas H. Eaton John Jaques Nellie Smeltzer
(the dress maker) C Widmayer   John G. Ashley—
Amos McDuffey is in Arizona—Dan McIntosh (owner of the
Superior Mine) died last spring. The few English that were with
me have all left some in Scotland one in South Africa—Alex

Harenc being the only one in Colorado, he has a ranch in the San
Luis Valley—During the past 30 years all the original settlers on
Kerber Creek between Villa Grove & Bonanza have died—you
may remember them by name

P. C. Stacy to Maggie

[This letter concerns Maggie's attempt to trade her Virginia property
for land in the West.]

P. C. STACY
                    REAL ESTATE, LOANS INVESTMENTS, INSURANCE
205 TYE BUILDING
    Phone 484
        CHICKASHA, OKLAHOMA
                                        June 25, 1917

Mrs. C. A. Brown
    Dilwyn, Virginia
Dear Madam:
    I received your letter several days ago and note what you say
in reference to the land. The party who owns this land would not
care to trade it for Virginia stuff. However, I believe if you would
desire to buy this land that you could buy it reasonable. Also, on
reasonable terms and then you could later on sell your land and
be in a position to pay for this. I am making this as a suggestion
to you.
                            Very truly yours,
                            P. C. Stacy

Maggie to Mary Augusta

                                Friday   [winter circa 1919]
My darling
    Your letter just read, you are no "stick" you hurt my feeling
when you speak of yourself that way. The young boys taking a
fancy to you shows they think you young also. Now just listen we
got a letter from Canada as I wrote you from a Mr. Kidder & he
said he had heard we would sell 600 acres for something less than
$12,000 for cash. Well I wrote to him land was advancing fast &
we wanted $15,000 but would take ½ down & full in 2 & 3 years
at 6½ interest in order to make a quick sale would put in some
house hold furnature   I said the piano but did not mention the

big pieces now darling we <u>must let go</u>. I thought he might be
back down but here comes a letter he will be here about the 13th
of Feb. to look over it. We also got a letter from Robersdale Pa.,
in this mail for a discription of farm which I will answer at once.
Should we live through this flu we may yet go to California to the
orange Exhibition & escape the wet gloomy Spring. You just go
on with your work & we will attend to this end of things. Am
going to find out who buys this old furniture & see what we can
do with it. Mr. Bodmer said if we sold he would give you $75.00
for the Silver tone that would put you in California nearly. You
get the dress & waist I marked & the Crep-de-chin for another.
John has gotten his shoes alright. Ruby was up last night. Pearl
is getting on fine has crocheted 2 scollops without the thumb.
Last Sunday a week ago Woodrow & Ruby were in the church
yard & Woodrow said "How is that little old Pearl? Not sucking
her thumb, is she?" he has never shown any feeling for his awful
act. Poor Lillian was so pleased when I told her what you said
about doing something for her feet tears came in her eyes. she
said her feet were better & thanked you. We will get them over
to Cousin Beck's it will be a help to all. Then John can go to
school right a long. He can be cousin Jake's boy as he is papa's.
Yesterday I thought I was taking Flu I took 3 tablets of Calomel
& last night it nearly killed me up to 9 o'clock   I went to bed &
woke up about 1 o'clock just thumping & could not get enough
water so got up & took 2 tablets of <u>assefetedy</u> [asafoedita, herb
used as an antispasmodic] (You know what I mean) & now I feel
alright. M.June [the cow] is not fresh   if we eat gravy we can
get along so so with out buying butter but we have to skimp. I
must close now & write that letter to Pa about the farm. Can
write better when no one is around just you take care of yourself
is all I ask

    Your loving mother   M. M. Brown
Did the wind blow you out of bed?

Charles to Mary Augusta

My dear Daughter

    Mama is writing so I think I will try it for I must have
something to occupy my mind, for things are gloomy outside,
began raining yesterday at 5 and has to let up yet, have plenty of
wind, and the [word smudged] are all down at last. The fall has

been so open that the grass is green yet, and the rabbits will not go into the traps. John has caught two and brags over Lizzie & Lillian for they have caught nothing. [John, Lizzie, and Lillian were live-in help on the plantation.] We had just a skin of snow yesterday morning but it is all gone. We have not heard from Mr Park yet, but I feel confident that we will, he seemed to be highly pleased. Then there was a man by the name of Bolinger that was with him that seemed just carried away with the place he had bought out Mr Park and was expecting a man to come and buy him out and he said that he wanted to locate a place before he sold this time.

Its just this Mary we must sell this place and get out for jealousy and envy are doing us untold damage and we must get away from your Mammas people   I feel that all of our trouble comes from them—

Of course land is going up fast but can we live though this eternal turmoil   sometimes I blame it on one some times on another but I some times think its all of them. But we stay at home and make our selves happy—we get along very nicely—we sit around a good fire untill nine oclock, go to bed and sleep all night, get up at 6:30 and get Alma off to school John seems to be doing well at school, Mrs Moseley is kind to him and he likes her comes home and gets his hogs fixed and gets his lessons at night goes to his traps in the morning & is ready for school. Latest Alma has just come down, says she took a bath, she looks like it. I expect I'd better stop now, don't you think I have run out?

good Bye
Affct.
Dad

Betty Smith, Stenographer, to Charles

J. D. McKee
2002 Commonwealth Building
Pittsburgh, Pennsylvania   May 15, 1919

Dr. C. A. Brown
Route 2, Box 52
Dillwyn, Va
Dear Dr. Brown:

Your letter of the 13th inst received this morning, also the enclosed letters from Stark Bros.

After having read your letter over, and thinking you may wonder why you did not hear from M.McKee and have your correspondence returned, I have decided to answer your letter myself, so as to let you know we received your letter, Mr. McKee has gone to California and will not return until the first part of June, so therefore I cannot say whether or not he knows of somebody who would like to buy your farm, but will give him your letter immediately upon his return.

I, myself think it must be an excellent farm you have, and judging from your letter you must be a very dear old couple and daughter. I just love farms and all the people who live on them if they are elderly, especially.

Now hoping you have much success in selling your farm, I hope to remain

Sincerely yours.
Betty Smith
Mr. McKee's Stenographer.

Please do not mention this letter in your's to Mr. McKee. Thank you. BMS

Maggie to Mary Augusta

Darling, do not go alone with a young man hunting, there may be some there to talk. I know you do not think of it but do be careful to keep down talk. Your own mind is so pure & sweet you do not think about other evil minds.

Is Stuart the brother of Mrs. F's   you saw on the train going to S.?   you with Mr. Proffitt. Set your cap that way for once. May be we had better take a trip to Florida & see the Rattons. May be we can get them to boom our apple land. They are such promoters.

My darling, whenever I read your sweet letters I just feel like sitting down and telling you how dear you are to me.

I feel like little Virginia may be taking the "Flu.' Now you write to us so much about being careful. Now, we are careful. I look after papa & when it is bad I don't go out at all. I am feeling much better & papa is better than he has been for 4 years this time of the year. You get yourself in good shape for "Flu." I hope you will not have it. I have heard that those that had it last year are not having it so bad.

How old is this widdower? Has he any children? If you don't like him, don't let him blow his breath on you. Good night, darling, a kiss would be a treat.

Mamma

P.S. The Idol of America or U.S.A. is about to fall in the dust. I am sending you some clippings from the Dispatch.

Adjutant General P. C. Davis to Virginia Senator Arthur Capper

[This letter rebuts a letter Maggie wrote to Senator Capper protesting alleged use of iron torture chambers at Alcatraz, California. The force of this defense suggests the impact of Maggie's letter.]

WAR DEPARTMENT

THE ADJUTANT GENERAL'S OFFICE

WASHINGTON

IN REPLY
REFER TO
AG330.14 (USDB.,P3)
  Pris. Sec. JAP/gm

February 4, 1920

Hon. Arthur Capper,
United States Senate,
Washington, D.C.
My dear Senator Capper:

The receipt is acknowledged of your memorandum dated February 2, 1920 in which you refer to the Secretary of War, a letter dated January 28, 1920 from Mrs. M. M. Brown of Dillwyn, Viriginia, Route 2, Box 52. With Mrs. Brown's letter was also a clipping alleging the use of iron torture chambers at Alcatraz, California. The Commandant of the Pacific Branch, United States Disciplinary Barracks, Alcatraz, California states: "No cruelty is or will be practiced on prisoners. The means now used to make them comply with their sentences or stand while others work are the most humane of any in the country."

The newspaper clipping undoubtedly refers to the use of what might be termed a vestibule door, a double door which is large enough to permit a man to stand between the doors without any pressure being exerted upon his body, but which is not large enough to permit him to sit down or lie down. A similar arrangement is used in many State institutions. It is intended for use with those prisoners who refuse to perform their daily tasks of labor. During the hours when the other prisoners are doing their duty the men who refuse to perform their daily tasks are placed in the vestibule door. Such an arrangement is absolutely necessary if the Commandant is to maintain control of the prison. Any man placed in the vestibule door can secure his release by informing the overseer that he is willing to do his daily task. The two prisoners referred to were placed in solitary confinement because they refused to answer the questions of the census taker. Those questions had nothing whatever to do with the fact that they may have had objections to war. The solitary cells at Alcatraz are well ventilated. The statement that men confined in solitary were ignored by the surgeon of the barracks is a lie. There has been no neglect of duty upon the part of the medical officers at the Disciplinary Barracks with reference to visiting the men in solitary confinement. It may be further stated for the information of Mrs. Brown that only six prisoners, so-called conscientious objectors, remain in confinement at the Pacific Branch.

General Prisoner Dart referred to was released on January 27, 1920. General Prisoner Rodolph also referred to in the clipping has of his own volition gone to work and performs his daily task the same as other prisoners. In the case of Robert Simmons. He is a colored man who was drafted in October 1917, and never stated that he was a conscientious objector until he was in France in September, 1918, when being asked to stand inspection he refused to do this, stating that he was a conscientious objector. His conduct since he has been in confinement has been bad.

In reference to the case of Philip Grosser. He states that he is in sympathy with the Bolshevistic movement in Russia and would carry arms in defense of that movement if opportunity afforded. This statement by him is not in keeping with the ideas of the conscientious objectors who refuse to do military duty on the ground that it is wrong to kill under any conditions or circumstances. He says he is a conscientious objector of the political and not the religious type and offers this as his reason for refusing to work.

The present Commandant at Alcatraz, Col. J. B. McDonald, has been most kind and considerate in his treatment of the prisoners committed to his care. Practically no use was made of the solitary cells at Alcatraz from September until January. It may be further stated for the information of Mrs. Brown that the so-called conscientious objectors confined in the Disciplinary Barracks are men who have been duly tried and convicted by General Court-Martial of military offences and their cases have been reviewed one or more times with a view to clemency, and clemency has been given in many cases.

Sincerely,
P. C. Davis
The Adjutant General

Maggie to Mary Augusta

[This is Maggie's last letter in the collection. She died in mid-April of 1920.]

Dillwyn R2 Box 52
Va
Mar 1/20

My darling

I have put more to this & ordered you a 2 piece dress of Rose linen something like the one Winnie got in Farmville once. It was only $4.59 & I thought it would be nice to wear with your little hat this spring   everyone spoke of how becoming Rose was to you   the scarf & hat   I am nearly done the voil. I can clean up your blue poplin skirt for an underskirt for your new dress but will have to have something for camesol make some of that dark blue thread into some tatting like Aunties & we will put it on the top. I will take the pocket off of the poplin & run a string in the top in place of the belt. Can't you use some of your white skirts. I will send that little grey skirt you may make use of it rainy days. It may be Dona can get you 2½ yards of some kind of goods to make you a skirt or 2¼ will be enough of yard wide goods. Now say some pretty week you go over to Staunton & have a good picture taken for your mother   just let all cares drop & look sweet like you can. Tell Mr F. I will come & dance that set. It will never do for you as you are there to <u>teach Sunday School not dancing</u> for him to just let me know when it is. It would not take any apple so great to come to bearing in <u>this soil</u>. Little Pearl is very ill with pneumonia just yesterday 104. Do you get the National   if so I will tell you how I am making your dress   on page 26 No 16 × 2 Price 9.98   dont send the apples

because it is costing so much now for plain food   but we do want
to know about the apple butter every time papa goes to the Mill
they ask him if we have heard any thing. It costs me $1.00 a
week for sugar alone. I sent Cousin Dona 2 pints of butter
yesterday & will send them some until onions get in it. I notice
the girl with the Rose dress has a blue hat with a Rose band on it
how would you like me to send your last summers hat & you get
it fixed up but it was not becoming   you send me your little blue
turban hat & I can fix it like Mattie H.' hat get some large
pansies & put a piece of Grogette over them as she had & no one
would ever know it as the same hat. Will write more Sunday
M. M. B.
This is not the voil I ordered but Alma thinks it beautiful.

W. F. Page to Charles

[This is the last piece of correspondence involving Charles. He died
January, 1930.]

Denver, Colo July 30, 1929

Dr. C. A. Brown.
Dillwyn, Va.
Dear Dr. Brown,

Was surprised and pleased to receive your letter and to learn
you were still on earth. Can not imagine any gold property
allowed to remain idly when so near the seats of industry but
your knowledged gained in the west should make you some what
of a judge of a possible mine. I am pretty well out of mining
myself but just now have a trip to Lordsburg, N.M. in view to
look over some properties, and shall remember my visit with you
when passing by Rincon. I have referred your letter to a Kansas
City friend asking him to write you, if he felt he would be .
interested.

With best regards I am,

Very truly yours,

W. F. Page

Notes

Chapter 1

1. Important works have come out recently by historians who use personal documents to introduce fresh outlooks on the nineteenth-century frontier experience. See, for example, Schlissel, *Women's Diaries of the Westward Journey;* Faragher, *Women and Men on the Overland Trail;* Myres, *Westering Women and the Frontier Experience 1800–1915;* Riley, *Frontierswomen, The Iowa Experience;* Stratton, *Pioneer Women: Voices from the Kansas Frontier;* Hampsten, *Read This Only to Yourself: The Private Writings of Midwestern Women, 1880–1910;* Rotter, "'Matilda for Gods Sake Write': Women and Families on the Argonaut Mind," *California History* 58 (Summer, 1979) 128.

2. "Bureau of Immigration of Virginia Registry and Descriptive List of Virginia Lands" (Richmond, Virginia, 1879), p. 1.

3. B. C. Keeler, *Where to Go to Become Rich,* pp. 99–100.

4. Gillam, *Virginia's People: A Study of the Growth and Distribution of the Population of Virginia from 1607 to 1943,* pp. 52–53, 116–18. For Charles Brown it was significant that Colorado in the 1880s was gaining a reputation as a place for doctors. Healthseekers were flocking to Colorado's supposed curative climate. Miners' money plus their hand-to-mouth life style augured wealth for physicians. See also Ingham, *Digging Gold Among the Rockies or Exciting Adventures of Wild Camp Life in Leadville, Black Hills and the Gunnison Country,* p. 431.

5. Smith, *Colorado Mining,* p. vii.

6. Wyatt-Brown, *Southern Honor,* pp. 174–75, 198.

7. Keeler, p. 63.

8. The phenomenon of "waiting wives" was a commonplace in frontier migration. A husband struck out to canvass the terrain, while his wife managed herself, the children, and often, too, a family business or farm. Sometimes the "waiting" stretched for years. Husbands evidenced varied degrees of sensi-

tivity to the hardship thus asked of wives. Bishop Daniel Tuttle, first Episcopal bishop of Montana, was one of the empathetic husbands:

My own deary, it is real <u>hard</u> for you—You are a <u>poor</u> deary, I am sure—I <u>know</u> it is hard for me to be so far & so long away from you—And [I] have all the dissipation of novelty, & the excitement of work in a new important field to take off from my loneliness & my longings. You have neither—it must be—it is, hard for you, poor deary—But, darling, can I do otherwise than make this cruel separation even longer—for a whole <u>year</u> or more? [September 3, 1867] *Letters of Bishop Tuttle*, microfilm from Montana Historical Society.

For additional information on wives awaiting frontier husbands, see Peavy and Smith, "Women in Waiting in the Westward Movement," pp. 2–17.

9. For exploration of the world of women in the nineteenth century, see Ryan, *Womanhood in America From Colonial Times to the Present;* see also Degler, *At Odds: Women and the Family in America from the Revolution to the Present.*

10. Frederick Jackson Turner, "The Significance of the Frontier in American History," American Historical Association, *Annual Report for the Year 1893* (Washington, 1894), pp. 199–227. Both critics and supporters consider Turner's words to have articulated the western myth of the American character, a character locked into masculinity and economics:

From the conditions of frontier life came intellectual traits of profound importance. The works of travelers along each frontier from colonial days onward describe certain common traits, and these traits have, while softening down, still persisted as survivals in the place of their origin, even when a higher social organization succeeded. The result is that to the frontier the American intellect owes its striking characteristics. That coarseness and strength combined with acuteness and inquisitiveness; that practical, inventive turn of mind, quick to find expedients; that masterful grasp of material things, lacking in the artistic but powerful to effect great ends; that restless nervous energy; that dominant individualism, working for good and for evil, and withal that bouyancy and exuberance which comes with freedom—these are traits of the frontier, or traits called out elsewhere because of the existence of the frontier.

Chapter 2 (Colorado–Virginia: 1880–1881)

1. Watkins, *Gold and Silver in the West*, p. 27.
2. Ibid., pp. 28, 34.
3. Paul, *Mining Frontiers of the Far West, 1848–1880*, p. 19.

4. King, *A Mine to Make a Mine: Financing the Colorado Mining Industry, 1859–1902*, pp. 56–57.

5. Ibid., pp. 60–61.

6. Ibid., pp. 58–61.

7. Paul, pp. 115–16.

8. See Wiebe, *The Search for Order 1877–1920*, pp. 1, 46.

9. Watkins, pp. 135–36.

10. Wolle, *Stampede to Timberline, The Ghost Towns and Mining Camps of Colorado*, p. 298.

11. Rotter, "'Matilda for Gods Sake Write,'" p. 130.

12. Faragher, *Women and Men on the Overland Trail*, pp. 103, 147–48.

13. Degler, "What Ought to Be and What Was: Women's Sexuality in the Nineteenth Century," pp. 420–21.

14. Degler, *At Odds*. In agreement with Degler's contention that nineteenth-century women enjoyed and discussed sex, Elizabeth Hampsten in *Read This Only to Yourself* provides interesting evidence that North Dakota working-class women in the nineteenth century wrote about sexual matters with comparative freedom. It was not the sexual act but birth control that restrained their sexuality. Especially see Chapter IV, "'Don't Read Aloud': Class and Sexuality, Disease and Death in Women's Writings," pp. 96 ff. Reed, *From Private Vice to Public Virtue: The Birth Control Movement and American Society Since 1830*, corroborates the findings of Degler and Hampsten that the terse warnings of Social Purity Movement leaders such as John Cowen and William A. Alcott did not describe the sexual behavior of nineteenth-century couples. Indeed, the wide interest in birth control methods suggests desire for sex as other than mere procreation.

15. Foote, *A Victorian Gentlewoman in the Far West, The Reminiscences of Mary Hallock Foote*, pp. 3, 22–23.

16. Peavy and Smith, "Women in Waiting in the Westward Movement," pp. 2–17.

17. The mining camps *were* lucrative markets for produce. See Smith, *Rocky Mountain Mining Camps*, pp. 125 ff. As with most of Charles's other money-making schemes, this one, too, touched base with reality. The invariable failure sprang from lack in Charles, rather than from unsoundness in the idea per se.

18. To his credit Charles avoided debt (except to his family "for whom" he lost several thousand dollars; in the parlance of the old South that would not have been "debt" but "family loss"). All his life he extended his services with a gentlemanly largesse that kept his personal coffers empty. In the early 1900s a first attempt to resettle in Virginia failed precisely because in Bridgewater Charles's patients were old family friends whom he refused to charge.

19. G. Thomas Ingham wrote in the 1880s of the futile stampeding of Leadville after its boom was over:

It is astonishing what a vast number of people are still rushing to
Leadville; yet we were told by reliable men from there that there were

perhaps ten thousand idle men in that city, many of them without money or means of subsistence, depending upon "luck" for a square meal, and on their blankets for lodging. . . . Leadville has had its "boom" is doomed. . . . Yet they are still striking new mines, and the daily reports that some poor prospector has "struck it rich," will still attract fools enough to keep up the "boom" a while longer.

See Ingham, *Digging Gold Among the Rockies*, p. 431.

20. Organized religion was one of those "methods of civilization . . . worked out east of the ninety-eighth meridian and well suited to conditions there," but that broke down and had to be modified when eastern institutions crossed the Great Plains. See Grimes, *The Puritan Ethic and Woman Suffrage*, pp. 17–18. For documentation of women's leadership in evangelizing the frontier see Jeffrey, *Frontier Women*, pp. 95–106.

21. Charles's mother, Mary Brown, and his sisters lived in New Hope, Virginia. It was a small town some ten miles northeast of Staunton and about twenty miles southeast of Bridgewater, site of the Brown family home. One reason for the cold relations between Maggie and the Browns was that Maggie believed they had wealth which, in truth, they had lost. In her Typescript, Mary Gose noted that the "terrible pride" of the Browns kept them from making public their misfortune (Typescript, p. 13).

22. Maggie could rely that Charles would have ready memory of her reference:

Who shall ascend the mountain of the Lord?
And who shall stand in his holy place?
He who has clean hands and a pure heart,
   who does not lift up his soul to what is false,
   and who does not swear deceitfully.
He will receive blessing from the Lord,
   and vindication from the God of his salvation.
   (Psalm 24: 3–5, AV)

23. Nineteenth-century connotation of "fatter" requires qualification for twentieth-century readers. While contemporary women eschew weight gain, women of the 1880s, particularly those of the middle-class whose weekly labors included washing clothes and sheets by hand, and who lived in a world often at the mercy of rampant disease, "thin" implied "sickly," "prone to illness"; whereas "fatter" implied "buoyant health."

24. Andrew Rotter, in a study of correspondence of men in mining camps without women, notes that the general incompetence of men as cooks "frequently reminded them of their sweethearts, wives, and mothers who had fed them in the past."

25. Colorado, by 1880, had an influx of health seekers. Frank Fossett in his classic guide to Colorado maintained:

There are thousands of invalids, suffering from a wide range of chronic disease, who come on a pilgrimage in search of health. In many cases the relief is surprisingly rapid.

See *Colorado: Its Gold and Silver Mines, Farms and Health and Pleasure Resorts*, pp. 46–53.

26. Rather than being unique, Charles's kind of continued indecision characterized many western men, for example, the esteemed Episcopal bishop, Daniel Tuttle, who wrote to his wife, waiting like Maggie, in Virginia with a young child:

Now deary, my own old deary, I do not want from inclination to do this winter in Montana—But from duty I may feel that I must do it—What do you think & say—Please write me—And if I should want to do so would Mrs. Grenshaw be willing to give you a home until Sept. 1868. I tell you these things, darling, because they are revolving in my mind—I may come to you this winter, but if I should not, I want to ask you what you think of it, & whether you can have a home with Mrs. G. for a longer time [July 19, 1867]. *Bishop Tuttle Letters*, Microfilm Division, Historical Society of Montana.

27. Frank Fosset, *Colorado: Its Gold and Silver Mines*, p. 566, writing in 1880 about the Gunnison mining fever, corroborated Charles:

The present destination of so many thousands of adventurers is generally termed the Gunnison Country—almost an empire in extent and natural resources. This until recently unknown land beyond the great mountains of the continental divide has been and still is the scene of a mining excitement such as the world has seldom witnessed. . . . Prospectors begin to flock in from Leadville, and the reports they brought back caused a stampede for the new mines. . . . But all previous accesions of population were trifling in numbers compared with the human "tidal wave" that came in the spring and summer of 1880.

28. Bishop Tuttle, *Letters*, 1868, noted a similar situation in the mining frontier of Montana: kind, generous people who had little regard for the amenities of formal religion. For similar assessment of miners in Bonanza, Colorado, as godfearing without the structures of a church see Brown, *Ghost Towns of the Colorado Rockies*, 46.

29. "Laundressing was a common job for women in the West. Women who were laundresses comprised one of the largest occupational groups for females on the nineteenth-century mining frontier. Despite competition from the Chinese, there were always enough dirty clothes for the common woman, who only had domestic skills, to find work." See Parker, "'I Brought with Me Many Eastern Ways': Non-Indigenous Income-Earning Women in New Mexico, 1850–1880." Ph.D. diss.

30. The newly discovered "empire of mineral wealth" in Gunnison County lay within the boundaries of the Ute Indian Reservation, and the Utes there did not resist the miners' encroachment as had the Sioux in the Black Hills of the Dakotas. Maggie may have heard about the Sioux raids of resistance. But

Charles was correct that there were no Indians within a hundred miles of Hayden Creek in 1880. See Fossett, p. 366. See also Lamar, *The Far Southwest, 1846–1912: A Territorial History*, pp. 243 ff. Duane A. Smith writes in *Colorado Mining*, p. 24: "The Brunot Treaty 1873 forced the Utes to cede the heart of the mining land to prevent hostilities and allow prospecting but nothing would satisfy the miners until the Indians were gone." In 1882 G. Thomas Ingham wrote of similar U.S. government breaking of a treaty because of miners' determination to prospect on the land of the Sioux. Pressure not policy prevailed.

> In 1876 the Federal government responded in a similar fashion to pressure from intractable miners in the Black Hills of the Dakotas. After Custer's discovery of gold and hostile Indians in 1874, the department of the Interior first proclaimed that persons must not trespass upon the Indians' domain. And the United States government made a new treaty with the Indians: the Sioux had to make surrender of territory so the miners could go there without restraint. Not only individual miners but large Eastern mining companies wrested such action from the federal government.

Ingham, *Digging Gold Among the Rockies*, pp. 34–36.

31. Roads were critical to the existence of a mining camp. Up the steep rocky slopes, teamsters had to transport food and building materials.

> To promote good roads, the miners' meetings paid for surveys, regulated widths, appointed supervisors to see that roadways were in good condition and, despite a reluctance to tax themselves, even went so far as to approve special maintenance taxes. Often, rather than paying money, a citizen could work off his taxes at a specified rate per day.

Smith, *Rocky Mountain Mining Camps*, pp. 53–54.

32. Being "sick" was a nineteenth-century euphemism for menstruation and/or pregnancy. For further discussion of woman's language for sex and bodily functions see Hampsten, *Read This Only to Yourself*, pp. 102–11.

33. This sounds as if Maggie had been pregnant before Charles left. And while she comes to have a history of miscarriages, there is no further evidence to support or preclude her having had one in the first two years of her marriage.

34. Fanny and Charles, according to Mary Gose in her Typescript, had been "very fond of each other." Supposedly her love for Charles was why Fanny never married. For whatever reason, Charles named his favorite greyhound "Fannie." And in 1886 he sent a message to Fanny by way of Maggie who was visiting in Virginia: "Tell Fanny if she will just come out with you I will show her what doubled and twisted love is, and also give her her share of it too" [April 1, 1886]. Most of Maggie's letters that Charles saved have some reference to Fanny. But because so few of Maggie's letters of the period are extant, it would be hasty to conclude that Charles saved those particular letters for their allusions to Fanny.

35. Maggie and Charles were decidedly southern in their approach to child-

rearing. Northern childrearing emphasized breaking of self-will and building of conscience to raise up God-fearing, hard-working, well-motivated children; it sanctioned corporal punishment and a withholding of affection. Southern parents, however, encouraged their babies' individuality, trying not to bruise young egos too soon, and rather than break a child's will, indulged the young in having his or her own way. "Whether rich or poor, [in southern families] there was no lack of fussing over small ones; babies were fondled by neighbors, kin & visiting strangers." Wyatt-Brown, *Southern Honor*, pp. 130–43.

36. This is the clearest reference in any of the letters to the actual birth control method used by Charles and Maggie. James Reed notes a rhythm method of birth control, advocated in the nineteenth century for the "strong-willed," that sounds as if it might have been the method Charles and Maggie were using: limiting intercourse to the period from the sixteenth day after the *end* of menstruation to the twenty-fifth day. See Reed, *From Private Vice to Public Virtue*, pp. 12–15. Such timing would, according to twentieth-century gynecology, be a time of relative safety from conception. But the uncertainty of the precise day of ovulation even in the most regular of menstrual cycles complicates the reliability of this method.

37. There is later mention of a black miner, partner of one of the Dinkles. This could possibly be he. There were some blacks in the Colorado mining areas. Discrimination existed, but until the number of blacks increased, there was little organized resistance to them socially. See Smith, *Rocky Moutain Mining Camps*, pp. 34–36. In 1861 when Colorado separated from Kansas as a territory, the census recorded that of 18,136 males in the area 89 were blacks. See Hollister, *The Mines of Colorado*, p. 116.

38. At many Colorado mines there was an influx of highly professional foreign born mining engineers. Most were from Ireland, Great Britain, and Germany. See Paul, *Mining Frontiers of the Far West*, pp. 122–28. See also Smith, *Rocky Mountain Mining Camps*, pp. 24–28.

39. The coming of the railroads and new booms in gold and silver brought rushes of speculators to the Arizona territory during the 1880s. See Paul, *Mining Frontiers of the Far West*, pp. 159 ff. See also Lamar, *The Far Southwest*, pp. 463 ff.

40. Bonanza City, founded early 1880, was located nearest of the four camps in the area to the best lodes of the vicinity and in time outgrew and assimilated neighboring camps. In the late summer of 1880, Bonanza City was "a fair type of a new Colorado mining camp, having one restaurant, two saloons, one saw mill and a dance hall." Griswold, *Colorado's Century of "Cities,"* pp. 226–27. See also Brown, *Ghost Towns of the Colorado Rockies*, pp. 44–52.

41. According to Mary Gose's notes, Mrs. Eskridge was a young wife in much the same position as Maggie. Her husband Brook Eskridge had set out for Pueblo, Colorado, around the same time Charles left for Hayden Creek. Mrs. Eskridge, who had a young son about Mattie's age, lived across the street from some of the relatives Maggie stayed with in West View, Virginia. These

two "waiting wives" exchanged news from the West and had planned to journey together to meet their husbands. Gose, *Typescript*, p. 10.

42. By the 1880s the Sioux, Utes, Apaches, Navajos, and Comanches were making fierce sporadic attempts to stave off the relentless advance of speculators and settlers onto their "official" reservations. See Smith, *Rocky Mountain Mining Camps*, p. 51. See also Lamar, *The Far Southwest*, pp. 227, 241–51.

43. 1880 began as a boom for Bonanza City, fell into a mid-year slump from which it was suddenly rescued by one Mark Beidell and his successful operation of the Michigan Mine and Mill. The year ended optimistically. See Griswold, pp. 226–27 and Brown, pp. 44–48.

44. Assaying and surveying were two of the simplest tasks of the novice mining engineer. There were plenty of self-appointed "experts." Observers of the 1880s describe some of these "pseudo-assayers" as men "who made cheek take the place of brains, trained by two weeks spent in sweeping out the laboratory of some alleged assayer." But as the function of the assayer was to test ores, usually by some simple chemical process, there were a number of instances of reputable physicians or druggists turning assayer. See Spence, *Mining Engineers and the American West*, pp. 65–66.

45. According to Wolle, the smelter built in Bonanza City in 1880–1881 was not equipped to handle the low grade ores of the area and so lay idle for years. Wolle, p. 299.

46. Colorado Springs, founded officially in 1871 by the colorful William Palmer, builder and president of the Denver & Rio Grande Railroad, was a settlement dramatically different from Hayden Creek and Bonanza City. Known, even before the 1870s, as the city of schools and churches, it had been founded to attract and hold people of means and social standing. Though the only springs were soda springs some five miles away, the town had been named Colorado Springs because the founders hoped the nice, rich, eastern spa sound would attract refined people. Mills, smelters, saloons, gambling houses, were confined to the neighboring Colorado City, and the railroad publicized Colorado Springs as a health resort and a "scenic wonderland." The city abounded in physicians to staff the Fountain Colony, a medical facility of questionable repute, for terminal cases of tuberculosis. See Sprague, *Newport in the Rockies*, pp. 34 ff.

47. Charles's sister, Millie (Mrs. A. B. Gillespie), was teaching at a school in Longtown, Mississippi, a rich farming region to which numerous Virginians migrated in the economic depressions following the Civil War. A part of the area was even called for a time "Little Virginia."

48. Charles was not atypical in his express determination to stay west until he made money. Duane Smith notes what he calls a common case, another Bonanza City miner, Clarence Mayo, whose resolve matches that of Charles:

Mayo who drifted into Bonanza in 1881, wrote his brother back East:
"The district is having a terrible boom and if the mines turn out to be

good it will be a second Leadville." The mines, however, as Clarence found out, did not turn out that way and within a month of the letter, Mayo went on to Gunnison. Despite pleas from home, Mayo wrote firmly: "I will never go a step till I have made some money."
Smith, *Colorado Mining*, p. 29.

49. Following fast on the first rush of miners to every mining camp were the prostitutes. As a camp song verse testified: "First came the miners to work in the mine / Then came the ladies who lived on the line." Smith, *Rocky Mountain Mining Camps*, p. 59.

50. During the rush and early boom periods, one of the most lucrative businesses was that of providing room and board. Smith, *Rocky Mountain Mining Camps*, p. 64. For more on women's success in this economic enterprise, see Jeffrey, *Frontier Women*, pp. 119, 126. A rollicking account of setting up a boarding house in California during the gold rush is given in Ballou, "'I Hear Hogs in My Kitchen': A Woman's View of the Gold Rush," pp. 42–47.

51. Reverend William McCorkle was the Methodist minister and friend of the Keller family who had assisted Maggie's mother on her deathbed. It seems that in 1881 he proposed to work a missionary circuit in Colorado; however, there is no evidence that he actually did that. Nevertheless, by 1886 he and his wife had moved as Methodist missionaries to El Paso, Texas. From there he corresponded with Maggie and Charles in Rincon, New Mexico. Several times he visited them there and preached to the Anglo and Hispanic residents. He looked upon the Browns as firm friends and when they returned to Virginia, he wrote to them from his own relocation in Alabama for support at a time when his spirits were flagging because of religious tensions.

52. Leadville became the yardstick against which other Colorado camps were measured. Opened in 1877, by 1880 it had grown from zero population to over fourteen thousand. In 1880, Leadville silver mines produced over eleven million dollars. Helen Hunt Jackson was convinced that there was no reason everyone in Leadville should not be a millionaire. Smith, *Colorado Mining*, pp. 27–28. Charles was not alone in viewing Bonanza as another Leadville. Mining historian Wolle writes: "As Bonanza City grew it became the center of the district and in time absorbed the populations of other towns. So promising was the outlook that by January, 1881, Bonanza was spoken of as the "New Leadville." Wolle, p. 298.

53. "The city marshal or chief of police supervised all police activities, had charge of the jail, and served in such other capacities as street supervisor and dog catcher. The salary varied, but was never very high: that of a marshal might range from $900 to $2000 per year." Smith, *Rocky Mountain Mining Camps*, pp. 122–23.

54. Mattie's eyes did not recover. Maggie later wrote Charles a description of the resulting deformity, "The lower lid seems like it is turned inside out" [April 3, 1881]. Four years later she wrote Pa from Rincon, New Mexico, "We think Mattie sweet but not pretty as her eyes are badly crossed from those

sore eyes she had before we left Va" [August 19, 1885]. There is also an extant daguerreotype of Mattie, age four, in which the eye problem is noticeable.

55. In her letter of March 23, 1881, Maggie responded to this sexy suggestion of Charles: "so you have not gotten out of the old way of 'wanting it' at night. Never you mind you wont have to suffer much longer, will you?"

56. In her typescript Mary Gose noted that a Number 8 pipe fitted a very large stove, the average size taking a Number 7. She felt that this purchase of the Number 8 was a sign of Charles's wish to shower Maggie with the best. *Typescript*, p. 56.

57. Although Charles here made light of Jim Dinkle's transplanting his extended family from Virginia to Colorado, such mass relocation was precisely what Charles's own mother and sisters badgered him to do for them. Later Maggie would try to convince her father to join them in the West with the three young children. For large scale moving of extended families, see Williams, "The Frontier Family: Demographic Fact and Historical Myth," pp. 40–65.

58. See footnote 36 and Charles's letter of September 20, 1880. Charles concluded that letter reminding Maggie to time her Colorado arrival so that she would be in the "safe" days of her ovulation cycle, so that they could have sexual intercourse with minimum risk of pregnancy.

59. Longtown was just that: a settlement stretching along the groove between two hills. Until the early 1900s the Longtown area was populated by well-to-do plantation owners and lumber merchants. The region was also the site of artesian well springs frequented for health purposes. There are records of two good schools having thrived in the area: Palmetto Academy, a boarding school, and a public or day school. This latter was founded by a Dr. Sam B. Agee from Appomatox County, Virginia. [I am indebted for this information to librarian Mrs. John A. Bryant, Crenshaw, Mississippi 38621, who talked with me by phone June, 1982.]

60. This is likely another reference to Maggie's and Charles's timing of intercourse to effect birth control.

61. This is another scarcely veiled allusion to sexual desire and the concern a woman of the nineteenth century would have had for carefully regulated sex if she wanted to avoid pregnancy. See section on nineteenth-century fertility in Grabill, Kiser and Whelption, *The Fertility of American Women*, pp. 12–24.

62. Maggie wrote her father after Mattie's death in June 1886 that Mattie had had premonitions of her death [Deming, New Mexico, July 3, 1886]. In her typescript Mary Gose recounts a similar story of Maggie recalling that her two young children Albert and Johnnie had foreknowledge of their deaths in 1891. Maggie said she had asked the very sick Albert: "Oh, Albert, do you have to leave us?" He answered her, "Yes, Mama, and Johnny too." In five days both children had died. *Typescript*, p. 186.

Chapter 3

1. Ingham, *Digging Gold Among the Rockies*, pp. 358–59.

2. Mrs. Rose was a character in her own right. Years before, waiting, as Maggie had been, for her husband's summons to meet him in the West, she grew so impatient that she packed up her children and belongings in a wagon and started trekking to Colorado. En route, so the story went, she spied, coming towards her, some unkempt, rough-looking men on horseback. Just as she was readying her defenses, she recognized the group's leader as her very own husband. According to him, he had seen, from afar, a woman with a nose so large that he was certain it could belong only to one woman—his wife.

After they had settled in Colorado, Mrs. Rose continued living like a legend. One tale involved her riding all night to a town where her husband was serving as judge to relay to him a warning that some men planned to shoot him as he presided the next day on the bench. Mary Gose, *Typescript*, pp. 108–109.

3. Helen Hunt Jackson, quoted in T. H. Watkins, *Gold and Silver in the West*, pp. 96–97.

4. Foote, *A Victorian Gentlewoman in the Far West*, pp. 3, 11–14, 25–26.

5. Grimes, *The Puritan Ethic and Woman Suffrage*, pp. ix–26. Grimes pursues the thesis that woman's suffrage in the West was motivated by political pragmatics rather than egalitarian ideology.

6. Ibid., p. 9.

7. See Stoeltje, "A Helpmate for Man Indeed, pp. 26–41.

8. Hampsten, "This Is Christmas Eve and I am in Tintah," p. 678.

9. For theoretical argument for literary analysis of writings of nineteenth-century women see the seminal work of Hampsten, *Read This Only to Yourself*, Chapter 3, "'Not to Use Correct and Elegant English Is to Plod': Class and Language in Women's Writings," pp. 48–95. See also Schlissel, "Diaries of Frontier Women: On Learning to Read the Obscure Patterns." For additional approaches to analysis of personal correspondence, see also Allport, *Letters from Jenny;* Idem, *The Use of Personal Documents;* and Macfarlane, *The Family Life of Ralph Josselin, A Seventeenth-Century Clergyman.* See also Fothergill, *Private Chronicles: A Study of English Diaries.*

10. At times these burros were called "pack jacks" and their drivers, "packers." For another genteel lady's view of burros, see Bird, *A Lady's Life in the Rocky Mountains*, pp. 180–81; Smith, *Rocky Mountain Mining Camps*, pp. 68–71. Idem, *Colorado Mining: A Photographic History*, p. 85. Burros carried loads of 250 pounds when trails were poor. The jacks could also haul supplies in and ore out of the same mines. Thomas Ingham, in his chapter of suggestions to those who would venture into Colorado or mining in the west stressed the importance of having a burro:

Buy one. It costs but a trifle to keep a burro; he will live chiefly upon the pasture along the way and they are of great assistance in moving from place to place; and are remarkably sure-footed and will climb the most rugged mountains where other animals could fail. There are thousands of them in use in the Rockies, as pack animals (p. 435).

11. In 1880 Frank Fossett wrote concerning Indian resistance to the encroachment of miners in the Gunnison area which was then the Ute Reservation: "There is some prospect of their being expelled by the invading army of prospectors, should they [the Ute Indians] conclude to oppose manifest destiny." *Colorado, Its Gold and Silver Mines*, p. 566.

A contrasting view of the Indian population comes from a contemporary of Frank Fossett, Sidney Jocknick, who had served as an Indian agent:

The Indians as a rule were patient and forbearing with parties of gold settlers whom they considered trespassers in their country. They would sometimes escort them to a mountain pass, significantly point eastward, and say, "Go." A party thus conducted out generally took the hint and stayed out.

Jocknick, *1870–1883, Early Days on the Western Slopes of Colorado*, pp. 321–22.

From the 1860s the Colorado Indian tribes were pushed into confines too small for their hunting existence needs; hence these tribes desperately increased their raids upon the white settlements. In 1864 a frenzied showdown occurred between an ill-trained volunteer army of whites and bands of Arapahoe and Cheyenne at Sand Creek. The result of the bloody white victory was to further inflame the Indians. The final solution of the Colorado territorial government was to break all standing government treaties protecting Indian land in Colorado and force the Indians from Colorado into Utah. See Lamar, *The Far Southwest*, pp. 240–51, p. 359 ff.

12. Once the railroad began to push down to El Paso, Texas, from Santa Fe with some connections between New Mexico and Arizona, 1873–1883, New Mexico began to advance in mining. Gold strikes in the 1880s were giving rise to famous mining towns in Socorro county. See Myrick, *New Mexico's Railroads—An Historical Survey*, pp. 66, 144–48. See also Jones, *Old Mining Camps of New Mexico 1854–1904*.

13. With the advent of the railroad into New Mexico heavy machinery for use in mining and smelting was shipped from eastern manufacturers to revolutionize the mining industry there. Michael Inglis, "Mineral Mining," p. 122.

14. The Black Range Mountains in southwestern New Mexico became famous for silver production as early as 1840. Interest in the mines of this area, however, flagged until the 1880s when the Apache Indians had been bled by the U.S. Army and when railroad connections had been constructed. See Myrick, pp. 9, 20.

Fairview, New Mexico, from which Haynes writes, is at the foothills of the Black Range. It was the second mining camp (Chloride being the first) formed by prospectors and miners swarming over the Black Range in the 1880s. In 1882 Fairview was renamed Winston in honor of Frank H. Winston, who set up a mercantile business there in 1882. See Pearce, *New Mexico Place Names:*

A Geographical Dictionary, pp. 180–81, and Looney, *Haunted Highways: The Ghost Towns of New Mexico*, pp. 147–48.

15. See Ryan, "Family, Community, and the Frontier Generation, 1770–1820," pp. 18–59. Ryan concludes that the frontier created a sense of private interest and psychological independence from the corporate family and community. This argument of hers about the New York frontier does not seem to hold true for the Colorado/New Mexico frontier of the Virginia Browns. Perhaps the Browns' pattern of family configuration from the South, particularly in the aftermath of the Civil War, bound Charles and Maggie to their extended families with links of responsibility and affection more pronounced than those of the frontier generation just removed from Puritan ancestry.

16. A more usual pattern, one that Maggie herself later emphasized, was that women on the frontier felt themselves to *age prematurely*. Julie Roy Jeffrey mentions a twenty-year-old Kansas pioneer who wrote home, "I am a very old woman . . . my face is thin and sunken and wrinkled, my hands bony withered and hard," unpublished paper, "Form on the Frontier: A Comparison of Frontier Journals and Reminiscences," p. 10.

17. This was Fanny, a dog Charles grew fond and proud of. Upon the family's return to Virginia in the early 1900s Charles had numerous tales to recount about the expertise with which this particular dog tracked jackrabbits in Colorado. Gose, *Typescript*, p. 110.

18. Mary Gose's typescript refers to two Aunt Bets. One was a black servant who had helped raise Maggie. The other was Aunt Bet Jordan, unmarried sister of Maggie's mother Amelia Jane Jordan Keller. Aunt Bet Jordan came to live with Washington Keller to care for the children until he married the widow Mattie Spangler around 1878. The reference here seems to be to Aunt Bet, the black servant, who, though aging and unwell herself, sought out Washington Keller to assist with the children as he went into the throes of his divorce.

19. See Barker-Benfield, "The Spermatic Economy," p. 389 ff. Barker-Benfield gives historical background on late 1880s ovarian surgery that punctured, burned, resected, and otherwise tampered, to ill effect, with uterus and ovaries.

20. Amelia Jane would have been twelve or thirteen years old, beginning her first periods of menstruation. It is obvious that to Maggie and Pa instruction in such matters was properly given only by females. For further discussion of such ritual duties performed by older women for younger women see Smith-Rosenberg, "The Female World of Love and Ritual," pp. 4–5. See also Cott, *The Bonds of Womanhood*, p. 182.

21. Mary Gose gives the following account of Pa's wife's departure:
finally she hired a drayman, packed everything in the house while he [Pa] was away on business into the wagon, and pulled out for parts unknown leaving no word of explanation. All she left in the house were some old, worn-out quilts. The children gathered some straw, piled it in

a corner of the kitchen and were sleeping there when their father came home.
Gose, *Typescript*, p. 81.

Chapter 4

1. Ingham, *Digging Gold Among the Rockies*, p. 352.
2. See Copp, *American Mining Code*, pp. 197–200.
3. Reeve, *New Mexico, A Short, Illustrated History*, p. 65.
4. Scott, *The Southern Lady: Fron Pedestal to Politics, 1830–1930*, pp. 19 ff. Bertram Wyatt-Brown emphasizes the southern propensity for giving repeated advice about conduct. See *Southern Honor*, p. 132.
5. In 1882 Thomas Ingham counseled his readers who would venture into Colorado:

People should get acclimated to such high elevations gradually, and not rush into the mountains to a great elevation too suddenly from a lower atmosphere as the sudden change often produces disease (p. 278).

6. The bizarre behavior of the second Mrs. Keller is illustrated in an incident recorded by Mary Gose:

Uncle Dan [then an adolescent of perhaps fifteen] was often the target of her [Pa's wife's] temper. One day she chased him around and around a big oak tree in their yard with a horse pistol, terrifying him and the other children.

Gose, *Typescript*, p. 80.

7. Duane Smith in *Rocky Mountain Mining Camps* details how vulnerable mining camps were to fires, suggesting the fierce character Maggie may have seen in the approaching flames:

A fire in a mining camp almost defies description. Once started, it burned furiously and rapidly with intense heat and dense smoke. Jumping from building to building, scattering burning brands throughout the whole community, the flames relentlessly advanced. The fire burned until it consumed all available fuel in its path. (pp. 93–97)

8. A certain amount of work had to be done on a mine annually, and usually within a specified period of time, for the mine-owner to avoid forfeiture. See Paul, *Mining Frontiers of the Far West 1848–1880*, pp. 168–72.

9. For other examples of frontier men's extended absences from home and their women, see Myres, *Westering Women and the Frontier Experience 1800–1915*, pp. 170–73. In her reminiscences about life in central New Mexico in the late 1800s, Agnes Morley Cleaveland commiserates with the lonely plight of women left at home while their men went about the business of the larger world:

Not many of our women neighbors got about. Not many had reason to with their menfolks to carry the responsibility of looking after their cattle. It was this deadly staying at home month in and month out, keeping a place of refuge ready for their men when they returned from their farings forth, that called for the greater courage, I think. Men walked in a sort of perpetual adventure, but women waited—until perhaps the lightning struck. The terrible isolation and loneliness in which most ranch women lived called for the last reserve of moral stamina.

No Life for a Lady, pp. 156–57.

10. Salida was a mining town at the junction of the South and Middle forks of the South Arkansas and also the junction of several wagon road passes. It was a new mining town that had sprung up in the early 1880s. Smallpox in such a junction of traffic would have, indeed, been disturbing to occupants of nearby camps and towns. See Wolle, *Stampede to Timberline*, p. 295.

11. New railroads built in 1882–83 opened new developments in Idaho. Gold discoveries in 1882 became known to the public nearly a year later. Then railroad publicity advertised the new gold region generating a flurry of interest in the area. Almost by default eastern Oregon and Washington were labeled with the same possibility, though without the same grounds. Charles had very likely caught rumors of the northwestern excitement. See Paul, pp. 148–49.

12. In an era in which women were counselled to think of their household duties as almost religious obligations, Maggie's behavior, "just leaving every thing unwashed" to go off for a morning of extended visiting, becomes noteworthy. For more on consignment of women to strict domestic perfection, see Reed, *From Public Vice to Private Virtue*, pp. 19–35. See also Strasser, *Never Done: A History of American Housework*.

13. There was a Corona College for women said to be the first of its kind in the United States founded in 1854 in Corinth, Mississippi. The founder, Reverend L. B. Gaston, was from Gastonia, North Carolina; his wife, from Clarkesville, Virginia. The school had two departments, preparatory and collegiate, ten pianos, and an extensive classical library. Young women from surrounding states, Texas, Tennessee, Alabama, were enrolled. During the Civil War the school facility was used as a hospital. Corona College could easily have been the school with which Millie Brown Gillespie was affiliated.

I am indebted for this information to Mrs. Fred E. Rogers, 118 5th Street, Corinth, Mississippi 38834, longtime resident of Corinth, who spoke with me at length by phone about the history of Corinth.

14. During the Civil War Colorado had remained loyal to the North, primarily because the first territorial governor Wiliam Gilpin was determined to keep Colorado in the Union at all costs. After the war Colorado retained its Republican Party allegiance. See Lamar, *The Far Southwest*, pp. 118–22, 241.

15. Nineteenth-century "ladies" were expected to have ornamental accomplishments like foreign languages, playing musical instruments, singing, and decorative sewing. Maggie's enthusiasm for Amelia Jane's learning to play the piano did not mean that she espoused the concept of "useless" education for

women. Her own life showed her to be a "free and useful" woman. The southern woman was different from the northern woman in that refinement did not rule out for the southerner a powerful drive in the practical world. Maggie's behavior would not support many of the arguments resurrected by twentieth-century feminists concerning the nineteenth century. See Delamont and Duffin, eds., *The Nineteenth-Century Woman: Her Cultural and Physical World*, pp. 134–63.

16. From the early 1870s Grant County in New Mexico, which included places like Silver City, Lordsburg, and Carlisle, was being touted as the Comstock of New Mexico. Silver City was about sixty miles west of Rincon where Charles intended to move. An exciting first hand account of the boomtown atmosphere of the area is contained in the recollections of H. B. Ailman, *Pioneering in Territorial Silver City.*

Chapter 5

1. By 1880 Silver City was the supply center for the southwestern corner of New Mexico. Local merchants received over four million pounds of goods annually from the East and carried on a thriving wholesale and retail trade. They purchased gold and silver bullion from the surrounding mining camps and sent it to the East. See Lundwall, ed., *Pioneering in Territorial Silver City*, p. 166. Rincon, meaning "corner, box canyon" was so named because it is built in a corner formed by two nearby mountains. It marked the south end of the dreaded Jornada del Muerto along which early-day travelers, immigrants, and animals died of thirst while trying to cross the desert. Pearce, ed., *New Mexico Place Names*, p. 133.

2. Keleher, *The Fabulous Frontier*, documents the fierceness of the New Mexican frontier. In his Introduction Keleher sums up the territorial condition in a citation from a report made by W. G. Ritch, Secretary of the Territory, in 1874:

It is well to bear in mind the entirely anomalous condition of the people and Territory in the Union, and that the power in all cases has not been vouchsafed to human wisdom to eradicate the abuse of years in a day. Before its Acquisition by the United States the first law of nature, became the chief thought in the family circle, and the main business of life with each family. There was no time, opportunity or impulse for social or intellectual improvement. They had been beset on all sides by hostile and nomadic Indian tribes, and also with not a few of the outlaws, a hair brained and graceless set, ever present on the frontier of an advancing American civilization.

Keleher, pp. 16–17.

Later in the same work (p. 25) Keleher sketches the frontier population of central New Mexico in the late 1800s:

Camp followers, saloon-keepers, gamblers, horse thieves, gunmen, inevitable in every new country, made for color and adventure. For twenty years, from 1870 to 1890, there was no like area in the entire west which offered so much sure fire action, in such a short time, as the southwestern part of New Mexico. In addition to riffraff and drifters, there came many men who were honest, able and fearless, who could think quickly, and shoot straight from the hip. . . . When the State of Texas officially issued a book naming 4,402 fugitives from Texas justice, it contended that the State of Texas was finally rid of nearly every prominent desperado and that New Mexico had been the place of refuge for most of the criminals.

3. The Apaches had a word for the white men who were messing up their hunting grounds. They called them "god-dammies." Looney, *Haunted Highways: The Ghost Towns of New Mexico*, p. 178.

4. Lamar, *The Far Southwest 1846–1912*, pp. 146–50. See also Lamar, *New Mexico's Rise to Statehood*.

5. Gonzalez, *The Spanish-Americans of New Mexico*, p. 6.

6. See Zeleny, *Relations Between the Spanish-Americans and Anglo-Americans in New Mexico*, Ph.D. diss., p. 122. See also Gonzalez, pp. 117–18. See also Myrick, *New Mexico's Railroads—An Historical Survey*, p. 59.

7. New Mexico advertised itself with the hyperbole typical of the way every part of the United States was wont to tout itself during the late nineteenth century. For example, the Mesilla Valley in New Mexico called itself "the greatest garden spot in all the Southwest." This statement was meant to include Rincon. It was said to have the richest alluvial soil "in America, if not in the world." See *New Mexico the Land of Opportunity*, pp. 223–24.

8. Walter Prescott Webb attributes the eastern lack of sympathy with the arid southwest to the fact that common-law principles controlling water derived from humid England. He contrasts the system the Spanish developed in the Southwest for land acquisition and water rights with the unsuitable plans legislated by the nineteenth-century U.S. Congress. Webb, *The Great Plains*, pp. 385–452.

9. The Southern Pacific Railroad, building east from California, and the Santa Fe line, building from the north, met in the cluster of tents and wooden shanties that formed the new railroad town of Deming. In 1869 a group of miners from Pinos Altos discovered silver in a hill nine miles southwest of Pinos Altos. Their new mining camp was christened Silver City. Lundwall, pp. 148, 166.

10. The western local color writer Eugene Manlove Rhodes, a resident of the Rincon area in the late 1800s, peopled his short stories with the "villains and varmints" of the newly exploding boom towns. See, for example, "The Numismatist," set in Silver City, Deming, and Rincon of 1884. Rhodes, *Stories of Virgins, Villains and Varmints*, pp. 26–37.

11. Gose, *Typescript*, pp. 129, 145–46.

12. *New Mexico, Its Resources, Climate, Geography and Geological Condition, Official Publication of the Bureau of Immigration*, ed. Max Frost, p. 116.

13. The description of adobe construction in the Albuquerque of the 1880s would also have fitted the houses in Rincon:

Virtually all of the building materials had to be obtained from the local environment. Adobe bricks were painstakingly formed by hand, and adobe walls had to be continually replastered to prevent erosion. Windows were covered with leather or cloth draperty selenite (crystalline gypsum) slabs, or wooden grates. The lack of elaborate carpentry tools made complex furniture design an impossibility. Floors were either finished in hard-packed adobe dirt or, if the family were wealthy enough, with brush mats or jergas (woven floor coverings).

Johnson, *Old Town, Albuquerque, New Mexico*, p. 57.

14. Myrick, *New Mexico's Railroads*, p. 40.

15. See Elder, "Approaches to Social Change and the Family," pp. 185–229.

16. Geertz, *Interpretation of Culture*, p. 218.

17. Migration analyses indicate that "chain migration" is the usual pattern: people moving to places where family and friends have already settled. Blain T. Williams studies this phenomenon in "The Frontier Family: Demographic Fact and Historical Myth," pp. 40–65.

18. Norwood, *The Story of American Methodism*, pp. 50–51.

19. Gose, *Typescript*, p. 129.

20. Ibid., pp. 145–46.

21. Flora was the mare with colt that Charles, in Bonanza, Colorado, had bought from Jim Dinkle in June of 1880 [June 8, 1880; June 28, 1880]. By October 1880, the horse was lost and Charles was hoping that the snows of winter would force her back to him [October 3, 1880]. Nothing else was said of the horse until January 10, 1884, when Maggie wrote Pa:

Dr. Brown heard of his mare he bought a few weeks after he came to the state. She had a colt that spring & when it was six weeks old lost her & colt & never could hear of them again until about two months ago he heard of her & finds out she has now a colt & is with fold [solecism of foal] with a blooded colt   the one that was with her when lost was also a blooded horse he will be 4 years old in July if we can get her that will be a great lift but will cost about $15.00 to do so.

22. Mr. Towser Appleton was Maggie and Charles's prized dog. In her typescript Mary Gose extends the anecdote of Towser's missing of the train:

Now, the next day after my father left for New Mexico, who should come limping up to my mother's door but Towser Appleton. His feet were sore and bleeding and he was very glad to find his family. Towser was a huge dog and when he put his feet on my father's shoulders his head was above my father's head. Father's height was five feet and eleven and a half inches. Towser was half bloodhound and half greyhound. His devotion to the family was absolute. When my father sent for my mother, she of course took Towser. She took him in the coach with her and when she changed trains at Poncha, she did not know where to put him, but a drummer, a fellow passenger, told her, "That's easy, have him lie down between these two seats that I am occupying and I'll put my feet across the seats that I am in." So she told Towser to get in and lie down and be very quiet and he did and he was. She said that when the conductor came through that the dog looked just like a big, black suitcase there and no questions were asked. When she got to the Junction she took him to the baggage car where he rode the rest of the way. They could never after leave him behind when they moved. I think they would almost as soon have left little Mattie, the apple of their eyes, as Towser.

Gose, *Typescript*, p. 60.

23. The church of San Antonio in the Pecos Village, with its proximity to the pueblo ruins from which the Pecos Indians had departed by 1850 became associated with the legend of Montezuma's return. Actually the legend seems to have "leaped" (as folk legends are wont to do) from northern Mexico to the Pecos area of northern New Mexico. Historian John Kessell conjectures that the sixteenth-century Spanish chroniclers in time sympathetically associated the origin of the Aztecs and Montezuma in the ruins north of Mexico with similar ruins in New Mexico.

When in the romantic atmosphere of the nineteenth century, Pecos became a bona fide and easily accessible ruin, it is no wonder that such specters took up residence here.

Kessell further theorizes that the folk belief that Montezuma would return may have become a convenient ruse employed by the Pueblos to ward off inquisitive whites.

Charles's tale of the "beacon fire" was another aspect of the legend of Montezuma's return. The story may have originally involved one of the Pueblo's sacred snakes used in kiva ceremonies. The sacred snake metamorphosed into fires also linked to kiva ritual. By 1880 the legend was embellished to hold that Montezuma had chosen the Pecos as his people and had commanded them to keep a sacred fire burning in a cave until his coming again. Adolph F. Bandelier thought he had found the room where the sacred fire was kept. See Kessell, *Kiva, Cross, and Crown*, pp. 470–73, 554.

The Atchison, Topeka, and Santa Fe R.R. in February 1884 used the legend of Montezuma's return as a promotional gimmick to advertise the rebuilding of the old Montezuma Hotel in Las Vegas, New Mexico. The hotel had been destroyed by fire in January 1884. The newspaper release about the reconstruction concluded: "The 'Pueblo prophecy' shall be fulfilled. 'Montezuma' shall return." Kansas City *Daily Journal*, February 24, 1884.

24. Rincon is situated in Doña Ana County, one of the oldest counties in New Mexico; bordering Mexico, much of its area was acquired from Mexico

only in the Gadsden Treaty of 1853. In the 1880s the county was more noted for mining strikes in the area's Organ Mountains than for agriculture. The plains around Rincon are treeless and waterless, a bleak terrain. Nevertheless, the strip of land bordering the Rio Grande, which runs but a few miles from Rincon, was reputed to be the "garden spot" of the Southwest. But the river in the late 1800s was capricious—flooding during the wet season, going dry for long periods in times of drought. An 1890 report from the Bureau of Immigration stated that irrigation remained a problem in the area even then. Rincon was at the junction of the southern branch and main line of the Atchison Topeka & Santa Fe Railroad. See *New Mexico, Its Resources, Climate, Geography and Geological Condition*, pp. 163–67. *New Mexico the Land of Opportunity* (1914), pp. 221–26.

25. It was the railroad lines that had literally created the towns of Rincon, Deming, and Silver City. In addition to the sections of land adjacent to the railroad routes awarded to them by Congress, and which they sold at prices low enough to induce homesteaders to buy readily, the railroads by their very presence stimulated the economy. The average price of grazing land was $1.25 per acre, timber land $5 to $20 per acre, agricultural land along the water ways $2.50 to $10 per acre. *New Mexico, Its Resources*, p. 199.

26. In her typescript, Mary Gose writes about her father working through the parish priest to persuade his Hispanic parishioners to be vaccinated:

When my father first started practicing in New Mexico, smallpox raged among the Mexicans. They felt it was a scourge sent from God and they were not supposed to do anything about it. When my father learned why they would not be vaccinated, he went to the priest and explained to him what he wanted. "And you'll do it for twenty-five cents a patient?" asked the priest astounded. Father answered, "Yes." "*Well*, come back Monday morning and you will have all you can take care of." Father started out Monday morning and they stood in line. He vaccinated all day long, the next day, and the next day.

Gose, *Typescript*, Clermont section, p. 13.

27. Not only Rincon but the whole of New Mexico was a little-known, little-understood portion of the United States in the 1880s. Entrepreneur W. C. Hazledine, in his speech celebrating the coming of the AT&SF railroad to Albuquerque in 1879, made the laconic statement:

New Mexico will no longer be known as *Terra Incognita*. Writers in leading New York papers will no longer say, as they did a few years ago, that New Mexico ought to be annexed to the United States nor will old world lawyers, in drafting legal instruments, locate New Mexico in South America.

Reeve, *New Mexico*, p. 89.

28. Southern New Mexico had remained in the hands of the Confederates until May 1862. Confederate sympathy continued to affect the Mesilla Valley area well into the 1870s when there were still political shoot-outs between

rival "southern" and "yankee" political factions. Baldwin, "A Short History of the Mesilla Valley," p. 321.

Mary Gose in her typescript commented on Maggie's antipathy for Yankees even in New Mexico:

Maggie's feeling about the Yankees was a natural aftermath of the "War Between the States" as she, with other Virginians who underwent that tragic time and its more tragic aftermath, from which she and the doctor still suffered through the dragged-out Panic of '73, termed what the Yankees called the "Civil War."

Gose, *Typescript*, pp. 116–17.

29. New Mexico historian Marc Simmons explains that the appellation "Mexican" was used in the 1800s for New Mexico's Hispanic population by Anglos of strong liking and natural sympathy for the Hispanic residents, even though the term was technically an error. See Marian Russell, *Land of Enchantment: Memoirs of Marian Russell along the Santa Fe Trail*, afterword by Marc Simmons, p. 163. The point is also made by historian Terrence Lehman: "In New Mexico of the late 1800s, Anglos commonly referred to Hispanos as 'Mexicans,' a nonderogatory term used solely for convenience of identification when proper names were not known." Lehman, *Santa Fe and Albuquerque 1870–1900: Contrast and Conflict in the Development of Two Southwestern Towns*, Ph.D. diss., p. 11.

30. Walter Prescott Webb noted the grim humor rising from the arid land:

"This," said the newcomer to the Plains, "would be a fine country if we just had water."

"Yes," answered the man whose wagon tongue pointed east, "so would hell."

Webb, *The Great Plains*, p. 320.

31. New Mexico was known by Anglos as the land of "poco tiempo," the land of "slow time." See Lummis, *The Land of Poco Tiempo;* see also Gonzalez, *The Spanish-Americans of New Mexico*, p. xi.

32. John Upton Terrell deplores the Apache "myth" that likely ran undercurrent to Dannie's question:

Apache is an American Indian name better known around the world than any other. It has been taken into speech, fiction and history to indicate fierce and barbaric individuals as well as criminals. . . . The oft-repeated and widely believed accusation that all Apache were by nature obsessive murderers is absurd as the postulation that all early white invaders and residents of the Southwest were motivated by laudable ideals. The reputation as incorrigible malefactors was fastened on them by the circumstances that they were more cunning, more capable, more determined and more dangerous as fighters than most Indians.

Terrell, *Apache Chronicle*, p. xi.

33. The railroad juncture at Deming had been completed "with only handguided mule-drawn scoops, dump cars and the back-breaking labor of hundreds

of Chinese coolies imported from China." Most of the Chinese remained in the area after the completion of the railroad section. Ream, *Out of New Mexico's Past*, pp. 92–94.

34. In her typescript Mary Gose reflected on Maggie's idyllic recollections of childhood:

My mother's early life, up until she was married was happy and carefree. Everything was beautiful, everybody petted her and she was the beautiful Maggie Keller. The happy, carefree girlhood of Maggie's haunted her for the rest of her life. In this respect she was more of a dreamer than was my father.

Gose, *Typescript*, p. 122.

35. Maggie and Charles were distant witnesses to one of the last major Apache outbreaks led by Geronimo, which began around May 18, 1885. Forty-two men, including Geronimo, Nachee, Mangus, Nana, and Chichuahua, accompanied by ninety-two women and children, were in the group that, in alarm that an ever more punitive U.S. government was going to further restrict their perimeters, fled from Fort Apache in Arizona to the Mogollon Mountains of southwestern New Mexico and thence down into Mexico. The Apaches, pursued by a strong command of U.S. troops, traveled nearly 120 miles before stopping for food and rest. Historian Ralph Hedrick Ogle interprets the incident with typical Anglo bias: "Bringing death and destruction to nearly every ranch within striking distance of their route through southwestern New Mexico, they crossed into Mexico about June 10, 1885." See Ogle, *Federal Control of the Apaches: 1848–1886*, pp. 231–32. See also Worcester, *The Apache Eagles of the Southwest*, pp. 288–95.

Chapter 6

1. Wheeler, *The Railroaders*, p. 176

2. Ibid., p. 172.

3. Kelly, *Mother Was a Lady*, pp. 152–53.

4. Schlissel, *Women's Diaries of the Westward Journey*, p. 326. Habenstein and Lamers, *The History of American Funeral Directing*, p. 392. Vinovskis, "Angels' Heads and Weeping Willows: Death in Early America," p. 557.

5. Gorer, *Death, Grief and Mourning*, p. 143.

6. In the 1880s under the leadership of Frances Willard the Woman's Christian Temperance Union became one of the most significant women's organizations in the country, especially in the South. The strategy of the members was to work for pledges of total abstinence and statewide prohibition laws. See Scott, *The Southern Lady: From Pedestal to Politics 1830–1930*, pp. 144–51. On the other hand, consumption of hard liquor was a cultural function of virility in the South. In certain circles "temperance and moderation" were considered two to four glasses of mint julep and toddy and sometimes straight

liquor and wine at the evening meal. Numerous deaths and illnesses were alcohol-related. Still, drinking was a hallmark of male solidarity. See Wyatt-Brown, *Southern Honor*, pp. 278–80.

7. In Virginia there had been an increasing interest in education since the end of the Civil War. Schoolteaching was a respectable occupation for women; thus it was one way that women who needed to support themselves could do so. See Dabney, *Universal Education in the South*.

8. Carroll Smith-Rosenberg points out how readily women rallied to each other's support in times of distress in the nineteenth century. See "The Female World of Love and Ritual," pp. 334–58.

9. "On the frontier the usual solution to the problem of the children's education was not to send the children East or move to town but to establish a local school." See Myres, *Westering Women and the Frontier Experience 1800–1915*, p. 182. It is noteworthy that Mary Ella Brown, who in this letter writes of preparing for "new situations," was forty-two years old.

10. Lillian Schlissel points out that death in the mid and late 1800s was part of the fabric of life in a way that it is not in the 1900s. People then had pictures taken of the dead in caskets and kept such memoirs along with their other family photographs. Details of death were exchanged and dwelt upon. See Schlissel, *Women's Diaries*, pp. 131–34.

Chapter 7

1. Success in the West meant success in business. Women, as well as men, shouldered financial ventures. See Myers, *Westering Women;* Glenda Riley, *Frontierswomen, The Iowa Experience*. New Mexico historian Joan Jensen documents patterns of women like Maggie Brown assuming charge of ranching while their husbands were absent for long stretches. "New Mexico Farm Women," pp. 65–68.

2. Bertram Wyatt-Brown points out that in the old South naming was a means of preserving the family, establishing a sense of loyalty among generation. See *Southern Honor*, pp. 120–21, 125.

3. New Mexico was promoted as one of the healthiest areas in the world. Particularly, it was advertised as the hope for consumptives. A typical flyer from the 1890s read: "The Rio Grande Valley is the best resort for consumptives in the world. The atmosphere is rare and dry, and the sun shines every day." (Albuquerque, New Mexico, 1893). The New Mexico Bureau of Immigration in 1890 argued for its climate being a natural for the healing of lung diseases: "The requisites of a climate curative of consumption, are, according to the best medical testimony, *altitude, dryness, equability of temperature, light and sunshine*, and a *porous soil*." Frost, ed., *New Mexico, Its Resources, Climate, Geography and Geological Condition*, p. 93.

4. A small town some twelve miles northeast of Howardsville, Virginia,

Scottsville was the county seat of Albermarle County until Charlottesville was established in 1762. It was the crossroads for north/south, east/west travel and served as a shopping center for the many "gentleman estates" in the surrounding area.

5. Will Brown, Charles's older brother, was a heavy drinker. Mary Gose noted in her typescript:

On his [Will's] return from the Civil War, he drank like a fish. Finally, his mother became so desperate that she packed him up and sent him out west to his younger brother Dr. Charles Brown, charging him with his further care. Dr. Brown found himself loaded with his brother's bills, including those for his liquor which often amounted to Dr. Brown's entire pay check. Will Brown was really a war casualty, but he proved a great trial to Maggie as well as to his own brother, the doctor. Will formed, for some reason, a violent distaste for Maggie which did not relieve the situation at all. Maggie was apparently kind to him. At times, as in the gift of the colt, she was a great more than kind. When he was sick she waited on him and fed him, but he gave her small thanks for this.

Gose, *Typescript*, p. 152.

6. The nineteenth century was the great century of Methodist missions. Women, particularly, supported mission activities by being ministers themselves or, as Maggie did here, by raising money to help mission causes. See Bucke et al., *The History of American Methodism*, pp. 59–128.

7. The letters document that Maggie was near death in labor, November, 1883. Charles's letters to Maggie from Colorado suggest several times that Maggie had had problems with pregnancy. Whether she had almost died during delivering in Virginia is hard to determine.

8. Maggie's estimate here that she could negotiate Amelia Jane a salary of $65 a month was optimistic. Even in 1914, the average New Mexico teacher's salary was only $61 a month. See *New Mexico The Land of Opportunity* (Santa Fe: 1914), p. 63. In her typescript Mary Gose pointed out Maggie's energetic attempts to foster education in Rincon. Maggie not only advertised for teachers but boarded them at her house. However, teachers were hard to employ for the isolated Rincon. The ones that did come married quickly and soon left.

9. Through the Raton Pass, a formidable mountain barrier, the first railroad entered New Mexico in 1878. Raton remained one of the chief junctions of the AT&SF Railroad and the principal town in the northeast corner of New Mexico. Myrick, *New Mexico's Railroads*, p. 9.

10. Part of Will Brown's eccentricity included performing certain tasks in meticulous ways. Mary Gose illustrates Will's behavior at the Clermont plantation in Virginia in the 1900s.

There was a bad mudhole and Will gathered rocks and laid them painstakingly, row after neat row until he built up the bank and then filled it carefully with small stones. At another part of the plantation,

Will built a flawless dam of small cobblestones across and filled it in with other small stones.

His great joy was raising watermellons, cantalopes and cucumbers. All of the work possible he did lying down on the ground, resting on an elbow. With his free hand he would crumble the soil very fine for his watermellon seed, pick out every little weed, or place every stone or pebble meticulously in its exact place.

Gose, *Typescript*, pp. 152–54.

11. Dannie was correct that the Kansas City depot was a veritable mix of all nations. Oscar Winther in his study of railroads on the frontier notes that the intriguing mysteries of the West attracted a world of tourists. "A group of westbound passengers not infrequently consisted of a mixture of Europeans and Americans, some wealthy travelers, immigrants, adventurers, and seasoned westerners." See *The Transportation Frontier Trans-Mississippi West 1865–1890*, p. 121.

12. Reports about the American frontier assumed a tall tale, folk style that embellished fabulous rewards and pushed to the extreme fiendish hardships. Exaggeration characterized the humor of the American West. See Blair and Hill, *America's Humor*, pp. 115, 555.

13. Danny assumes the posture of the formula western hero who reduces the tragic Indian/white tension to a stereotypic game and ignores righteous Indian resentment at being restricted to ever smaller and less desirable land areas. See Winther, p. 140 and also Hagan, *American Indians*, pp. 92–121.

14. The Rio Grande was, especially during the late 1800s, a river of extremes:

Following the advent of the miners among the mountains along the upper reaches of the river, and the sawmills that gnawed away the timber, the Rio Grande assumed a more sullen and capricious character. It came roaring down in sudden floods during the wet season, and sometimes went quite dry in its bed for weeks together when the weather had long been dry. It introduced two new elements of danger to crops and ditches by flood, and danger to crops by drought.

New Mexico Land of Opportunity, p. 224.

15. The presidential election of 1888 sparked tension with Republican Benjamin Harrison losing the popular vote but winning the electoral college vote over Democratic incumbent Grover Cleveland. In the popular vote Harrison mustered only 5,477,129 (47.9%) to Cleveland's 5,537,857 (48.6%); while in the electoral vote Harrison, with his win in populous states, bested Cleveland a respectable 233 to 168.

Chapter 8

1. The letters from those last years (1888–1929) are proportionately few.

Thus the difficulty of piecing together a chronology from this untidy finale was substantial. In the single year 1881–82, for example, there were thirty-four letters; and in the next year and a half there were forty-nine; but during this last forty-one year stretch, there remain only some sixty-five letters. For certain critical years of the period there remain none. There is not a single letter in the collection, for instance, from 1891, the year in which Maggie and Charles lost, within five days, their two sons. And only two letters are left from 1894, the year in which Maggie and Charles's daughter Mary Augusta was born. To further complicate a reconstruction of the Browns' experience, many of the extant letters are unsigned, undated or only partially dated. Supplementing to a small degree the dearth of letters are other kinds of documents: bills, receipts, contracts, records of court proceedings, wills, railway passes, and business correspondence. At times helpful, they require taxing detective work to fit into proper context. Mary Gose's typescript bridges important spaces; she is the source of information on the deaths of James Albert and John Daniel. A page in the family Bible left the only record of John Daniel's birth.

2. Maggie and Charles said they named their first son James Albert after Maggie's father and brother and a deceased brother of Charles—all Jameses— and after Charles himself whose middle name was Albert. There is no available explanation of John Daniel's name; however, again the names link generations of both families. There were three John Browns: Johannes, Charles's grandfather; John George, Charles's father; and John S., another deceased brother of Charles. There was at least one Daniel each in the Brown and Keller lines: Herman Daniel Braun, Charles's great-grandfather (Germany); Daniel (Dannie), Maggie's brother.

3. Gose, *Typescript*, pp. 185–86.

4. The application for position of doctor on the Reservation involved taking a Civil Service examination and being cleared and appointed through the New Mexico territorial representative to the House in Washington, D.C. Honorable Antonio Joseph held the position. There are two letters from him to Charles in the collection. Joseph was an interesting personage. In 1884 after a split in the Republican Party, Antonio Joseph was elected delegate from New Mexico territory to Congress: a smiling, urbane merchant and land speculator from Taos, New Mexico. Sleek and apparently unobtrusive, he campaigned with nice, neat, and slick talks. New Mexico Governor Edmond Gilbert Ross distrusted Joseph. Ross was probably uncertain as to how much Joseph genuinely supported the Anglo causes in New Mexico. See Keleher, *The Fabulous Frontier*, p. 165.

5. Charles's interminable problems with getting water to his ranch dramatize what was an ordinary frustration with land boundaries and water rights in New Mexico. In early 1893 Charles began a long attempt to have an irrigation ditch on his property connected with the AT&SF right-of-way ditch that had been recently constructed between Rincon and the newly established town of

Hatch some five miles due west. Among the many problems complicating the matter were the ill-defined boundaries of the ranch. Supposed official surveys in 1881 and 1885 had not been clearly filed with the Department of the Interior in Washington, D.C. The AT&SF Railroad representative, C. F. Esley in Kansas City, admitted that their original survey of the property they had sold to Charles had been imprecise. Certain stretches, now critical in determining connections with the irrigation ditch, would have to be resurveyed before rights could be established.

6. Gose, *Typescript*, p. 186.

7. According to Mary Gose's typescript, Maggie threw one grand open house during that year at Clermont:

hosting a big riding tournament during the day full of games and competitions, then ending with a huge buffet banquet in the evening—a grand spread of foods on the dining room table—roast pork, fried chicken, roast beef, fried rabbit, fried squirrel, all kinds of breads, cakes, pies and gallons of hot coffee and punch.

Gose, *Typescript*, Clermont Section, pp. 5–7.

8. By late 1904, Charles (56) and Maggie (50) were back in Rincon where they rented a small house, and Charles received reappointment as surgeon on the AT&SF Railroad for the year 1905. Problems about determining boundaries of the ranch continued. Now the issue was not so much connection with a major water ditch as with simply clearing the title so the property could be sold.

9. Gose, *Typescript*, p. 189.

10. Peter A. Morrison and Judith P. Wheeler in their research on the American tradition of migration found certain people prone to a pattern of mobility.

Migration is frequently a repetitive episode, and observed mobility rates tend to reflect repeated and frequent moves by the same people rather than single moves by others. People with a history of past moves show a disposition to move again—possibly because some of the characteristics that make people likely to move are persistent characteristics; because successful moves may lead to attempts to achieve further success by moving again; or because not all moves are made with the expectation of a permanent stay at destination. . . .

What it seems to come down to is that migration may be purely self-selective, chosen perhaps by "pioneer individuals"—persons with a wider vision of the possibilities offered by unknown areas and a perspective toward the future wholly different from that of their nonmigrating counterparts.

See "The Image of 'Elsewhere' in the American Tradition of Migration," pp. 8–9.

11. The Rincon area, even after the Gadsden Purchase, remained richly Hispanic. U.S. courts in the area issued documents in both Spanish and English

well into the 1900s. See Zelany, *Relations Between the Spanish-Americans and Anglo-Americans in New Mexico.*

12. In 1889 the New Mexico territorial legislature passed a bill providing for location of a university at Albuquerque, a school of mines at Socorro, and an agricultural college at Las Cruces.

13. Fort Bayard was established August 21, 1866, to control the Apaches and protect miners and prospectors coming into the area to relocate mines abandoned during the Civil War and search for new claims. The fort was an active army post until 1899 when it became an Army hospital for tuberculars. Pearce, *New Mexico Place Names*, p. 58; Lundwall, *Pioneering in Territorial Silver City*, p. 144.

14. Mary Gose includes a memory of Maggie's in the typescript that further emphasizes her championing of the western frontiersman over the Virginia gentleman:

Maggie always felt great respect for gamblers and saloon keepers too and always said that she never knew one of them to treat her other than with the greatest respect and gentleness.

Many years later, on arriving back in good old Virginia from the "wild and wooley west," she saw, as she descended from the train, a group of well-dressed gentlemen, evidently from the Court House. One of them was cursing, being far gone in his cups [euphemism for being intoxicated]. On being warned by one of his companions that there was a lady present, he said, "Why? What of it? I see those things every day." She said it was quite a reception in her genteel Virginia. She frequently mentioned after that she thought she must have been spoiled in the West for there she was always Something Special and she had never heard a man curse before a lady (and they were always considered ladies out there until they had proved themselves otherwise) in the entire time she had been away—proving they knew there was a lady present.

Gose, *Typescript*, p. 65.

15. The Mesilla Valley was called the garden spot of New Mexico. To the already fertile region, the Spanish introduced a variety of fruit and vegetable crops. Among the most successful of these was the grape. And in the late 1800s Juarez, Mexico, maintained a large wine industry from grapes produced in the Mesilla Valley.

16. Marian Russel in her memoirs of New Mexico life in the 1800s explained the *fanega:*

We used the old Mexican measures for everything. Our corn measure we called a "fanega." It was made from a buffalo hide. The purchaser held the hide and was permitted to shake it down three times. The amount of shelled corn the old hide measure would hold was about two and one-half bushels.

See *Land of Enchantment*, p. 118.

17. By "dull" Maggie usually meant the economy was sluggish. Indeed, the

times followng 1892 were hard, with an economic depression spreading across the whole United States. New Mexico was especially stricken because the period had been preceded by years of severe drought. See Wiebe, *The Search for Order, 1877–1920*, p. 91 and Myrick, *New Mexico's Railroads*, pp. 10, 70.

18. In the years after the Spanish introduction of horses into New Mexico in 1540 herds of wild horses were concealed in mountains and canyons, contributing place names to such localities. The reference in this letter is to the Caballo Mountains, east of the Rio Grande in central New Mexico. Pearce, p. 23.

19. Malaria victims who had had inadequate treatment for the disease often had periods of freedom from all symptoms, only to have chronic relapses to the chills and fevers. In the nineteenth century, "shaking with the ague" was a common affliction. Gilbert, "The Cry Was: Go West, Young Man, and Stay Healthy," p. 140.

20. Mary Gose includes background on the Clermont Plantation estate in Virginia in her typescript:

Originally, Clermont was mostly a part of the Archibald Cary grant. It consisted of some fourteen hundred acres, nine hundred acres were of the Cary Grant. Joe Irvin purchased the property some time in the late seventeen hundreds with the intention of building a home in order to be near his friend, Col. Carter Page. The dwelling was built by Col. Page for him. According to Mrs. Jennie Scott Wilson, daughter of Powhattan Jones, an older son of Powhattan won the estate from Charles Irvin, Joe Irvin's son, in a gambling debt in 1815. The entire place became intensely cultivated numerous tobacco barns, slave quarters, feed houses, and stables. The entire place was fenced with rail fencing.

Gose, *Typescript*, Clermont section, p. 1.

21. Old Mr. Wilson's widow remained for some ten more years at Clermont Plantation until about a year before the final sale of the property was completed in 1906. When Maggie and Charles went to Virginia in 1903, they rented a number of rooms in the Clermont plantation house from Mrs. Wilson.

22. Cornelius Jordan was president and director of the experimental station at the New Mexico College of Agriculture and Mechanic Arts in Mesilla Park, New Mexico. The college had been funded by a legislative charter in 1889. Among other things it was experimenting with production of sugar beet seeds. Until the 1890s American sugar beet seeds were bought from Germany and those seeds were reproduced only every other year. The New Mexico College successfully bred a plant that seeded every year. In April 1897 Cornelius Jordan sent Charles samples of sugar beet seeds and also a shipment of chrysanthemum plants. See *New Mexico*, pp. 82–83.

23. For several years Dannie courted two young women, one in New Mexico and one in Virginia. Jennie Wilson was the young woman in Virginia. Dannie finally married his New Mexico love, Georgie.

24. The two commissioners were Col. W. J. Hubard, who in 1905 vigorously

opposed confirming the Jones land sale to Charles, and W. Lancaster, special commissioner of the Circuit Court of Cumberland County in Virginia, who supported the land sale to the Browns.

25. The reference would be to the Populist movement and the Silver coinage issue. Farmers, particularly southern farmers, had been subject to worsening economic and social conditions as the nineteenth century came to a close. Though various forces caused the decline in agricultural well-being, farm discontent focused on the currency issue, magnifying this grievance out of proportion to all others. See Wiebe, pp. 84–87, 104.

26. Frederick Harvey, concessionaire for all the meals served along the Santa Fe railroad system, had added in the late 1800s the innovation of special waitresses: young women of good character, attractive, and intelligent, eighteen to thirty years old. "The crisply aproned Harvey Girls dazzled lonely Westerners, who married an estimated 5,000 of them." See Wheeler, *The Railroaders*, p. 144, and Myrick, p. 41.

27. The euphonious sound of Zaragossa fits stylistically with Mead's pompous diction. Reference is to the Sea of Saragossa, an area of gulf weed in the North Atlantic. Into this floating mass all drift matter was reputed to find its way. The metaphor works poignantly for Mead's sense of himself as loose in the currents of life.

28. This is probably Augusta (Gussie) Braun, Charles's cousin who studied at Coe College in Iowa in the 1880s. Her part of the family retained the German spelling of the last name, *Braun*. According to Mrs. Lolita Cox Smith, who donated the letters in this collection to the University of New Mexico Archives, Cousin Gussie was fond of Mary and left her a small inheritance. It is probable that Mary, whose middle name was Augusta, was named after this Cousin Gussie.

29. Cousin Gussie was in advance of her time. The medical profession was not easy for a woman to gain acceptance in. "As late as the 1920s, a third of all medical schools still barred women." Carl N. Degler discusses the problems of professional women in the early twentieth century in *At Odds*, Chapter 15, "Women's Work: The First Transformation," pp. 362–94.

30. This advice for Mary to set her sights for marriage as well as for medicine was in line with the general trend of the period for women. In the early twentieth century American women's social training counseled them to cultivate their appeal to men. See Ryan, *Womanhood in America*, pp. 169 ff. See also DeLamont and Duffin, eds., *The Nineteenth-Century Woman*.

Bibliography

Primary Sources

Albuquerque, New Mexico. University of New Mexico. Charles Albert Brown Collection of Letters.

Albuquerque, New Mexico. University of New Mexico. Mary Augusta Gose, "Whistling in the Wind." (Typescript)

Secondary Sources

Ailman, H. B. *Pioneering in Territorial Silver City. H. B. Ailman's Recollections of Silver City and the Southwest, 1871–1892*, ed. Helen J. Lunwall. Albuquerque: University of New Mexico Press, 1983.

Allport, Gordon, *Letters from Jenny.* New York: Harcourt, Brace & World, Inc., 1965.

Allport, Gordon. *The Use of Personal Documents in Psychological Science.* New York: Social Science Research Council, 1942.

Baldwin, P. M. "A Short History of the Mesilla Valley." *New Mexico Historical Review* 13 (July 1938): 321–29.

Ballou, Mary. "'I Hear Hogs in My Kitchen': A Woman's View of the Gold Rush." In Christiane Fischer, ed., *Let Them Speak for Themselves: Women in the American West.* New York: E. P. Dutton, 1977.

Barker-Benfield, G. J. "The Spermatic Economy: A Nineteenth-Century View of Sexuality." *Feminist Studies* 1 (1972): 45–74.

Berkhofer, Robert F., Jr. *A Behavioral Approach to Historical Analysis.* London: Collier-Macmillan Limited, 1969.

Billington, Ray Allen. *America's Frontier Heritage.* Albuquerque: University of New Mexico Press, 1960.

Bird, Isabella L. *A Lady's Life in the Rocky Mountains*. Norman: University of Oklahoma Press, 1960.

Blair, Walter, and Hill, Hamlin. *America's Humor: From Poor Richard to Doonesbury*. New York: Oxford University Press, 1978.

Brown, Robert L. *Ghost Towns of the Colorado Rockies*. Caldwell, Idaho: The Caxton Printers, Ltd., 1973.

Bowen, Ralph H., ed. *A Frontier Family in Minnesota: Letters of Theodore and Sophie Bost 1851–1920*. Minneapolis: University of Minnesota Press, 1981.

Bucke, Emory Stevens, ed. *The History of American Methodism*. New York: Abingdon Press, 1964.

"Bureau of Immigration of Virginia Registry and Descriptive List of Richmond, Virginia." 1879, p. 1.

Cawelti, John G. *Apostles of the Self-Made Man*. Chicago: The University of Chicago Press, 1965.

Cawelti, John G. *The Six-Gun Mystique*. Bowling Green, Ohio: Bowling Green University Popular Press, 1971.

Cleaveland, Agnes Morley. *No Life for a Lady*. Boston: Houghton Mifflin Company, 1941.

Copp, Henry N. *American Mining Code: Embracing the United States, State, and Territorial Mining Laws, The Land Office Regulations, and a Digest of Federal and State Court and Land Decisions with Forms, Dr. Raymond's Glossary, and a List of Patented Claims*. Lancaster, Pa.: By the Author, Inquirer P. & P. Co., Stereotypers and Printers, 1882.

Coquoz, Rene L. *Tales of Early Leadville*, Parts 2 and 3. Boulder, Colorado: Johnson Publishing Company: 1964.

Cott, Nancy F. *The Bonds of Womanhood: "Women's Sphere" in New England, 1780–1835*. New Haven: Yale University Press, 1977.

Dabney, Charles W. *Universal Education in the South*. Chapel Hill: University of North Carolina Press, 1936.

Dabney, Virginius. *Virginia: The New Dominion*. Garden City, New York: Doubleday & Company, Inc., 1971.

Degler, Carl N. *At Odds: Women and the Family in America from the Revolution to the Present*. New York: Oxford University Press, 1980.

Degler, Carl N. "What Ought to Be and What Was: Women's Sexuality in the Nineteenth Century." *American Historical Review* 79 (December 1974): 1467–90.

Delamont, Sara and Duffin, Lorna, eds. *The Nineteenth-Century Woman: Her Cultural and Physical World*. New York: Harper & Row Publishers, Inc., 1978.

Elder, Glen H., Jr. "Approaches to Social Change and the Family." In *Turning Points: Historical and Sociological Essays on the Family*, pp. 1–38. Edited by John Demos and Sarane Spence Boocock. Chicago: University of Chicago Press, 1978.

Faragher, John Mack. *Women and Men on the Overland Trail.* New Haven: Yale University Press, 1979.

Foote, Mary Hallock. *A Victorian Gentlewoman in the Far West: Reminiscences of Mary Hallock Foote.* Edited by Rodman W. Paul. San Marino, California: Huntington Library, 1972.

Fossett, Frank. *Colorado: Its Gold and Silver Mines, Farms and Health and Pleasure Resorts.* New York. C. G. Crawford, Printer and Stationer, 49 and 51 Park Place, 1880.

Fothergill, Robert A. *Private Chronicles, A Study of English Diaries.* London: Oxford University Press, 1974.

Frost, Max, ed. *New Mexico, Its Resources, Climate, Geography and Geological Condition.* Santa Fe, N.M.: New Mexican Printing Company, 1890.

Geertz, Clifford. *Interpretation of Culture.* New York: Basic Books, Inc., Publishers, 1973.

Gilbert, Bill. "The Cry Was: 'Go West, Young Man, and Stay Healthy.'" *Smithsonian.* March 1983, pp. 138–49.

Gilliam, Sara K. *Virginia's People: A Study of the Growth and Distribution of the Population of Virginia from 1607 to 1943.* Richmond, Virginia: Population Study Virginia State Planning Board, 1944.

Gonzalez, Nancie L. *The Spanish-Americans of New Mexico, A Heritage of Pride.* Albuquerque: University of New Mexico Press, 1967.

Gorer, Geoffrey. *Death, Grief, and Mourning.* Garden City, New York: Doubleday & Company, Inc., 1965.

Gose, Mary Augusta Brown. *Typescript to Brown Collection.*

Grabill, Wilson H.; Kiser, Clyde V.; and Whelpton, Pascal K. *The Fertility of American Women.* New York: John Wiley & Sons, Inc., 1958.

Greever, William S. *Arid Domain: The Santa Fe Railway and Its Western Land Grant.* Stanford, California: Stanford University Press, 1954.

Grimes, Alan P. *The Puritan Ethic and Woman Suffrage.* Westport, Connecticut: Greenwood Press, 1980.

Griswold, Don, and Griswold, Jean. *Colorado's Century of "Cities."* United States of America: Don and Jean Griswold and Fred M. and Jo Mazzulla, 1958.

Habenstein, Robert W., and Lamers, William M. *The History of American Funeral Directing.* Milwaukee, Wisconsin: Bulfin Printers, Inc., 1962.

Hagan, William T. *American Indians.* Chicago: The University of Chicago Press, 1979.

Hampsten, Elizabeth. *Read This Only to Yourself: The Private Writings of Midwestern Women, 1880–1910.* Bloomington: Indiana University Press, 1982.

Hampsten, Elizabeth. "This Is Christmas Eve and I Am in Tintah." *College English* 39 (February 1978): 678–84.

Hareven, Tamara K. "Family Time and Historical Time." *Daedalus* 106 (Spring 1977): 57–70.

Hollister, Ovando J. *The Mines of Colorado*. Springfield, Massachusetts: Samuel Bowlers & Company, 1867.

Ingham, G. Thomas, Esq. *Digging Gold Among the Rockies or Exciting Adventures of Wild Camp Life in Leadville, Black Hills and the Gunnison Country.* Philadelphia: Hubbard Brothers, Publishers, 1882.

Inglis, Michael. "Mineral Mining," in *New Mexico Maps*, ed. Jerry L. Williams. Albuquerque: University of New Mexico Press, 1979.

Jeffrey, Julie Roy. *Frontier Women, The Trans-Mississippi West 1840–1910.* New York: Hill and Wang, 1979.

Jeffrey, Julie Roy. "Form on the Frontier: A Comparison of Frontier Journals and Reminiscences." Paper presented at the Berkshire Conference on Women's History, June 1981.

Jensen, Joan. "New Mexico Farm Women," in *Labor in New Mexico: Unions, Strikes and Social History*, ed. Robert Kern. Albuquerque: University of New Mexico Press, 1983.

Jocknick, Sidney. *1870–1883, Early Days on the Western Slope of Colorado,* unnamed publisher, 1913; reprint ed., Glorieta, New Mexico: The Rio Grande Press, Inc., 1968.

Keeler, B. C. *Where to Go to Become Rich: Farmers', Miners' and Tourists' Guide to Kansas, New Mexico, Arizona and Colorado.* Chicago, Illinois: Belford, Clark & Co., 1880.

Keleher, William A. *The Fabulous Frontier.* Santa Fe, New Mexico: The Rydal Press, 1945.

Kelly, Gordon R. *Mother Was a Lady: Self and Society in Selected American Children's Periodicals 1865–1890.* Westport, Connecticut: Greenwood Press, 1974.

Kempner, Helen Ashley. *Nelson Abner Cole: Colorado Pioneer.* Villa Grove, Colorado: Helen Kempner, 1987.

Kessell, John. *Kiva, Cross, and Crown: The Pecos Indians and New Mexico 1540–1840.* Washington, D.C.: National Park Service, U.S. Department of the Interior, 1979.

King, Joseph E. *A Mine to Make a Mine: Financing the Colorado Mining Industry, 1859–1902.* College Station: Texas A & M University Press, 1977.

Kolodny, Annette. *The Land Before Her: Fantasy and Experience of the American Frontiers, 1630–1860.* Chapel Hill: The University of North Carolina Press, 1984.

Lamar, Howard Roberts. *The Far Southwest, 1846–1912: A Territorial History.* New York: W. W. Norton & Company, Inc., 1970.

Lamar, Howard Roberts. *New Mexico's Rise to Statehood.* Albuquerque: University of New Mexico Press, 1978.

Lehman, Terrence. "Santa Fe and Albuquerque 1870–1900: Contrast and Conflict in the Development of Two Southwestern Towns." Ph.D. diss. Indiana University, 1974.

Looney, Ralph. *Haunted Highways: The Ghost Towns of New Mexico*. Albuquerque: University of New Mexico Press, 1968.

Lummis, Charles F. *The Land of Poco Tiempo*. New York: Charles Scribner's Sons, 1893.

Macfarlane, Alan. *The Family Life of Ralph Josselin, A Seventeenth-Century Clergyman: An Essay in Historical Anthropology*. Cambridge: Harvard University Press, 1970.

Morrison, Peter A. and Wheeler, Judith P. "The Image of 'Elsewhere' in the American Tradition of Migration." Paper presented at symposium on "Human Migration: Patterns, Implications and Policies," organized by American Academy of Arts and Sciences, New Harmony, Indiana, April 14–16, 1976.

Myres, Sandra L. *Westering Women and the Frontier Experience 1800–1915*. Albuquerque: University of New Mexico Press, 1982.

Myrick, David F. *New Mexico's Railroads—An Historical Survey*. Golden, Colorado: Colorado Railroad Museum, 1970.

New Mexico the Land of Opportunity. New Mexico, 1914.

Norwood, Frederick A. *The Story of American Methodism*. New York: Abingdon Press, 1974.

Ogle, Ralph Hedrick. *Federal Control of the Apaches: 1848–1886*. Albuquerque: University of New Mexico Press, 1970.

Parker, Kate Horsley. "'I Brought with Me Many Eastern Ways': Non-Indigenous Income-Earning Women in New Mexico, 1850–1880." Ph.D. diss., University of New Mexico, 1983.

Paul, Rodman Wilson. *Mining Frontiers of the Far West, 1848–1880*. San Francisco: Holt, Rinehart and Winston, 1963.

Pearce, T. M. ed. *New Mexico Place Names: A Geographical Dictionary*. Albuquerque: University of New Mexico Press, 1965.

Peavy, Linda and Smith, Ursula. "Women in Waiting in the Westward Movement." *Montana The Magazine of Western History*. (Spring 1985).

Potter, David M. "American Women and the American Character." In *History and American Society: Essays of David M. Potter*, pp. 278–303. Edited by Don E. Ferenbacher. New York: Oxford University Press, 1973.

Potter, David M., ed. *Train to California: The Overland Journal of Vincent Geiger and Wakeman Bryarly*. New Haven: Yale University Press, 1945.

Rasch, Philip J. "The Tularosa Ditch War." *New Mexico Historical Review* 43 (July 1968), 229–35.

Ream, Glen O. *Out of New Mexico's Past*. Santa Fe, New Mexico: Sundial Books, 1980.

Reed, James. *From Private Vice to Public Virtue: The Birth Control Movement and American Society Since 1830*. New York: Basic Books, Inc., Publishers, 1978.

Reeve, Frank D. *New Mexico, A Short, Illustrated History*. Denver: Sage Books, 1964.

Rhodes, Eugene Manlove. *Stories of Virgins Villains and Varmints*. Edited by W. H. Hutchinson. Norman: University of Oklahoma Press, 1975.

Riley, Glenda. *Frontierswomen, The Iowa Experience*. Ames: The Iowa State University Press, 1981.

Rotter, Andrew J. "'Matilda for Gods Sake Write': Women and Families on the Argonaut Mind." *California History* 58 (Summer 1979), 128–41.

Russell, Marian. *Land of Enchantment: Memoirs of Marian Russell Along the Santa Fe Trail*. Albuquerque: University of New Mexico Press, 1981.

Ryan, Mary P. *Cradle of Middle Class*. Cambridge: Cambridge University Press, 1981.

Ryan, Mary P. *Womanhood in America From Colonial Times to the Present*. New York: New Viewpoints, 1979.

Schlissel, Lillian. "Diaries of Frontier Women: On Learning to Read the Obscured Patterns." In *Woman's Being, Woman's Place: Female Identity and Vocation*, pp. 54–57. Edited by Mary Kelly. Boston: G. K. & Hall, 1979.

Schlissel, Lillian. *Women's Diaries of the Westward Journey*. New York: Schocken Books, 1982.

Scott, Anne Firor. *The Southern Lady: From Pedestal to Politics, 1830–1930*. Chicago: University of Chicago Press, 1970.

Slotkin, Richard. *Regeneration Through Violence: The Myth of the American Frontier 1600–1860*. Middleton, Connecticut: Wesleyan University Press, 1973.

Smith, Duane A. *Colorado Mining: A Photographic History*. Albuquerque: University of New Mexico Press, 1977.

Smith, Duane A. *Rocky Mountain Mining Camps: The Urban Frontier*. Lincoln: University of Nebraska Press, 1967.

Smith, Henry Nash. *Virgin Land, The American West as Symbol and Myth*. New York: Random House, Inc., 1950.

Smith-Rosenberg, Carroll. "The Female World of Love and Ritual: Relations Between Women in Nineteenth-Century America," *Signs* 1 (Autumn 1975): 1–29.

Spence, Clark C. *Mining Engineers and the American West: The Lace-Boot Brigade, 1849–1933*. New Haven: Yale University Press, 1970.

Sprague, Marshall. *Newport in the Rockies: The Life and Good Times of Colorado Springs*. Denver: Sage Books, 1961.

Stegner, Wallace. *Angle of Repose*. Greenwich, Connecticut: Fawcett Publications, Inc., 1971.

Stoeltje, Beverly J. "A Helpmate for Man Indeed: The Image of the Frontier Woman." *Journal of American Folklore* 88 (January–March, 1975): 26–41.

Strasser, Susan. *Never Done: A History of American Housework*. New York: Pantheon Books, 1982.

Stratton, Joanna L. *Pioneer Women: Voices from the Kansas Frontier*. New York: Simon and Schuster, 1981.

Terrell, John Upton. *Apache Chronicle*. New York: World Publishing, 1972.

Turner, Frederick Jackson. "The Significance of the Frontier in American History." Washington, D.C. American Historical Association, Annual Report for the Year 1894.

Tuttle, Bishop Daniel S. *Bishop Tuttle Letters.* Historical Society of Montana: Microfilm Division.

Tyler, Stephen A. *The Said and the Unsaid: Mind, Meaning and Culture.* New York: Harcourt Brace Jovanovich, Publishers, 1978.

Vinovskis, Maria A. "Angels' Heads and Weeping Willows: Death in Early America." In *The American Family in Social-Historical Perspective,* pp. 546–63. Edited by Michael Gordon. New York: St. Martin's Press, 1978.

Watkins, T. H. *Gold and Silver in the West: The Illustrated History of an American Dream.* Palo Alto, California: American West Publishing Company, 1971.

Webb, Walter Prescott. *The Great Plains.* New York: Houghton Mifflin Company, 1936.

Weigle, Marta. "Women as Verbal Artists: Reclaiming the Sisters of Enheduanna." *Frontiers* 3 (Spring 1978): 1–9.

Wheeler, Keith. *The Railroaders.* New York: Time-Life Books, 1973.

Wiebe, Robert H. *The Search for Order 1877–1920.* New York: Hill and Wang, 1967.

Williams, Blaine T. "The Frontier Family: Demographic Fact and Historical Myth." In *Essays on the American West,* pp. 40–65. Edited by Harold M. Hollingsworth and Sandra L. Myres. Arlington: University of Texas Press, 1969.

Winther, Osburn. *The Transportation Frontier Trans-Mississippi West 1865–1890.* New York: Holt, Rinehart and Winston, 1964.

Wolle, Muriel Sibell. *Stampede to Timberline, The Ghost Towns and Mining Camps of Colorado.* Boulder, Colorado: By the author, 763 Sixteenth Street, 1949.

Worcester, Donald E. *The Apaches: Eagles of the Southwest.* Norman: University of Oklahoma Press, 1979.

Wyatt-Brown, Bertram. *Southern Honor: Ethics and Behavior in the Old South.* New York: Oxford University Press, 1982.

Wyman, Leland C. *The Mountainway of the Navajo.* Tucson, Arizona: The University of Arizona Press, 1975.

Zeleny, Carolyn. "Relations Between the Spanish-American and Anglo-Americans in New Mexico: A Study of Conflict and Accommodation in a Dual-Ethnic Situation." Ph.D. dissertation, Yale University, 1944. (Microfilm.)

Index

431